W9-AFP-125

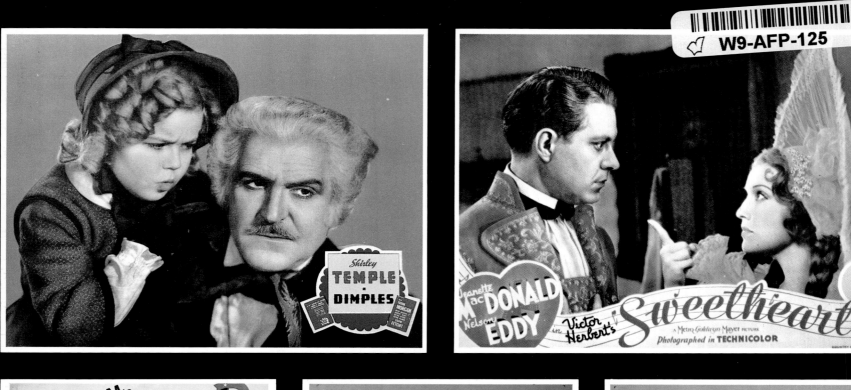

HOLLYWOOD MUSICALS

HOLLY

MUSIC

HARRY N. ABRAMS, INC.

WOOD

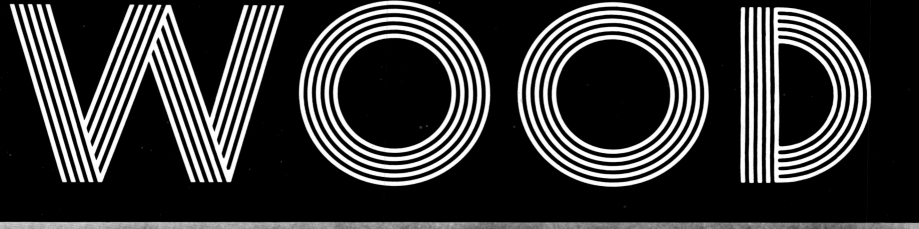

ALS

TED SENNETT

PUBLISHERS, NEW YORK

In loving memory of my mother

Project Director
MARGARET KAPLAN

Designer
JOHN S. LYNCH

Editor
LORY FRANKEL

Rights & Reproductions
BARBARA LYONS

Library of Congress Cataloging in Publication Data

Sennett, Ted.
    Hollywood musicals.

    Bibliography: p. 368
    "Filmography": p. 368
    Includes index.
    1. Moving pictures, Musical—United States—
History and criticism.   I. Title.
PN1995.9.M86S4   782.81'0973   80-25896
ISBN 0-8109-1075-6

Illustrations ©1981 Harry N. Abrams, Inc.

Published in 1981 by Harry N. Abrams, Incorporated,
New York. All rights reserved. No part of the contents
of this book may be reproduced without the written
permission of the publishers

Printed and bound in Japan

ACKNOWLEDGMENTS

To carry off a project of this size requires the help and support of many people. I have been extremely fortunate in this respect. I should first like to thank those who made it possible for me to screen a large number of Hollywood musicals: Emily Sieger, Patrick Sheehan, and Joe Balian of the Library of Congress Motion Picture Section; Irwin Danels, Lynne Vetrano, and Isadore Koblick of Columbia Pictures; Joseph Seechack and Wence Torres of Metromedia Television; Wally Dauler of Audio-Brandon Films; Pat Moore of UA-Sixteen; and Batch Reese of WCBS-TV. I also want to thank the staff of the Billy Rose Theatre Collection of the New York Public Library at Lincoln Center for their help in using the treasure trove of research material.

I am very grateful to the good people at Abrams: Margaret Kaplan for her unfailing kindness and support; my editor, Lory Frankel, for asking the right questions and for making me reach deeper into my feelings about and opinions on the musical film; John Lynch for bringing his enthusiasm, taste, and style to the book's design; Barbara Lyons for her valuable help with the photographs; and James Murch for obtaining permissions to reprint lyrics. Thanks also to my agent, Peter Miller.

A very special note of appreciation goes to Curtis F. Brown, who read and commented on the manuscript with his usual zeal and perceptiveness. His help was indispensable. Thanks also to Max Liebman, who gave me the benefit of his thinking on stage vs. film musicals, and who inspired me by being his own wise and inimitable self.

For the visual materials in the book, I should like to thank Bill O'Connell, Michael Mentone, Lester Glassner, Lou Valentino, and Jerry Vermilye for permitting me to use photographs from their marvelous collections. Jerry deserves a particular note of gratitude for his help in many other film book projects over the years. He has been more than an invaluable source of material; he has been a good friend. For their help with photographs, I should also like to thank Gene Andrewski, Doug McClelland, Mary Corliss of the Museum of Modern Art Film Stills Archive, Al Press of Columbia Pictures, Cinemabilia, Life Picture Service, The Memory Shop, Memory Shop West, and Movie Star News. My appreciation goes to Michael King, who allowed me to enhance the book with the beautiful poster and lobby cards from his private collection.

Thanks also to the studios that produced and distributed the musical films of more than five decades: Columbia Pictures Corporation, EMI Films, Inc., Lorimar, Magna, Metro-Goldwyn-Mayer Film Co., New World Pictures Corporation, RKO General Pictures, Samuel Goldwyn Productions, Sascha Film Gesellschaft M. B. H., Twentieth Century-Fox Film Corporation, United Artists Corporation, Universal Pictures, Walt Disney Productions, and Warner Bros. Inc.

As usual, my deepest gratitude goes to my family: to my wife, Roxane, whose love and support helped me through the rocky periods, and to my children, Bob, David, and Karen, who make it all worthwhile.

CONTENTS

INTRODUCTION

My love affair with the Hollywood musical began many years ago in a darkened neighborhood theater with the first kaleidoscopic images from one of Busby Berkeley's opulent extravaganzas. Or did it start with the first enchanting view of Ginger Rogers and Fred Astaire, dancing with romantic ardor in a dreamlike Venetian setting? It has continued through every decade, leaving indelible memories: a merry ride on a turn-of-the-century trolley as it clangs its way to the fairgrounds; a gleeful song and dance in the pouring rain; teenage gang members leaping with arrogance and pride down a New York City street; a coarse flower girl turned ravishing lady, glowing with happiness after attending her first ball. In recent years, the Hollywood musical may have altered its form, may move to a different beat, may even have nearly vanished from the scene, but the love affair persists, sustained by memory and nourished by the hope that the days of glory are not lost forever.

This book, then, is more than a history of the Hollywood musical: it is also a personal journey through more than five decades of a film genre that has afforded me lifelong pleasure and satisfaction.

Uniquely American in its exuberance and optimism, the Hollywood musical took root in the film colony during the first years of sound, when the very idea of actors singing and dancing on film made moviegoers giddy with delight. Although it drew much of its sustenance from other sources, mainly from the Broadway musical stage (it still does), it thrived in California soil, which gives the foliage its own form and coloration. Soon the musical film took on a style tuned to the special demands of motion pictures. Busby Berkeley liberated the stationary camera to conjure purely cinematic musical hallucinations. Fred Astaire demonstrated that dance on film was not only feasible but could be blissfully romantic and stylish. During the thirties and forties, the Hollywood musical blossomed into a flower unlike any other, cultivated on both sides of the camera by men and women who created visions of beauty out of the most gossamer of materials. By the early fifties, it was fully in bloom, although by the end of the decade, the petals were beginning to wilt.

In every decade, the musical film, whether waning or at its peak, has drawn upon a remarkable array of talents, working together as a tightly knit unit. All film is a collaborative art, but perhaps no genre requires such intense day-to-day collaboration as the musical film. The steps by which a musical is conceived, organized, hammered out, and pieced together into the film an audience sees are not only extraordinarily complex but also require an unusually close and continual interaction among the people involved. Speaking many years after codirecting (with Gene Kelly) *Singin' in the Rain,* arguably the greatest Hollywood musical, Stanley Donen said:

> Anyone who says that every picture is not a collaboration is an idiot. It's a question of how much you collaborate and who you collaborate with . . . nothing is more fun than finding someone who stimulates you, and who can be stimulated by you. The result, rather than adding up to two and two, multiplies itself, and you find yourself doing much better things—you are carried away on the crest of excitement. The more you collaborate with everyone—the actors, the cutters, the cameraman, the sound man—the better it's going to be. That is all a director is really, a collaborator with all of these people. (Kobal, *Gotta Sing, Gotta Dance*)

Those who participate in the making of a musical are locked into a process made up of many factors, including artistic inspiration, business acumen (or folly), clashing temperaments, and reluctant compromises. The process can be exasperating, or it can be exhilarating, as in the filming of *An American in Paris,* which was apparently sparked by the dedication of cast and crew, and by the unwavering belief of those at the helm, particularly Arthur Freed and Gene Kelly, in the possibilities of the movie musical. For those who would like to learn how a musical is created for the screen, there is no better source than Donald Knox's *The Magic Factory,* an "oral history" of the making of *An American in Paris.*

At its best, when all the collaborative elements have fused harmoniously, the Hollywood musical is a glittering amalgam of music, story, settings, costumes, and performances. The components may not always be of equal value—often the plot is merely a peg on which to hang the musical score—but each works toward a common goal: the creation of a fanciful world in which feelings run so deeply that they cannot be contained by words; only song and dance will do to express the emotion.

The physical components of a musical film are, of course, an integral part of its appeal. We respond with pleasure to color that bathes the screen with the richest of hues and tones (*Gigi,* for example), to settings that are sumptuous almost beyond belief (*The King and I*) or that simply enhance the mood of a song (the snow-laden woods in *Swing Time* in which Astaire and Rogers sing "A Fine Romance"). Our eyes are dazzled by costumes that beautifully evoke a vanished era (*My Fair Lady*) or that comment wittily on the musical's background (the amusingly exaggerated twenties apparel in *Singin' in the Rain*).

The musical score and the performances, however, remain the most important components of the musical film. Many a film

has been salvaged by its lilting songs, or made more than tolerable by the superior quality of the singing and dancing performances. On both counts, the Hollywood musical has been splendidly served over the years. The strains of the tunes by the great film composers echo throughout this book. It is simply not possible to recall the most durable musical films of the past without hearing, in memory that never fades, the melodies of Irving Berlin, Richard Rodgers, Jerome Kern, George Gershwin, Cole Porter, Frank Loesser, and Harry Warren, or the lyrics of Lorenz Hart, Ira Gershwin, Oscar Hammerstein II, Dorothy Fields, Johnny Mercer, and many others. The boundless charm, wit, or unabashed romanticism of their songs are imperishable.

And the performances! The formidable gifts of the leading musical players pervade every page of this book. Not only the giant figures, such as that personification of grace and elegance, Fred Astaire, or the irrepressibly happy, inexpressibly sad Judy Garland, or the ebullient Gene Kelly, but also the performers whose gifts may not be the stuff of legend but who truly warrant remembering: Alice Faye, Donald O'Connor, Doris Day, Howard Keel, Cyd Charisse, and so many others. They are part of the very texture of this book.

Behind the camera, the musical film has been well served by men and women of prodigious ability and imagination. Without subscribing to the auteur theory, one could attribute some of Hollywood's finest musicals to directors whose taste and professionalism are evident in every frame of their films. The most notable directors in this regard are Vincente Minnelli and Bob Fosse, whose musical films, for better or for worse, are informed by their personal vision. Occasionally, a musical producer has also played a decisive role in the films made under his aegis: certainly the most significant musical producer has been Arthur Freed, whose unit at MGM turned out a remarkable body of musical films in the late forties and early fifties. There is, as well, an army of talented people—set and costume designers, cameramen and carpenters, script girls and musicians—without whom these films could never be made.

I have tried to cover all important and many less important Hollywood musicals in the book. Readers who cannot find a favorite musical film will have to forgive me. I have deliberately omitted the Walt Disney animated features, since I consider them to be basically animated films with incidental music rather than musical films in themselves. I have also deleted fundamentally dramatic films in which only one or two songs appear as incidental adjuncts to the action. I do deal with several British-made musicals which I feel are essential to the book and which, despite their country of origin, reveal a Hollywood sensibility.

Among film genres, the musical has the most vocal detractors and the most ardent defenders. Those who cannot imagine why anyone should be singing or dancing on the Western plains, or on a Paris street, or in the court of a Siamese king will probably not be reading these pages. But for those who love the musical film as I do, this book is intended as a celebration of its many wonders and delights. Among the few pleasures in an increasingly dreary world, the Hollywood musical can still reward anyone who responds to its beauty, its joyousness, its melodic riches.

The music is beginning. The credits are starting to roll. Come celebrate with me.

page 1: The Hollywood Revue of 1929 *(MGM, 1929). Chorus girls pose in a publicity shot for this early all-star musical revue.*

pages 2–3: Gold Diggers of 1935 *(Warners, 1935). At top right, Wini Shaw and Dick Powell, the only patrons in a lavish nightclub, watch one hundred dancers tap their hearts out. The number, "The Lullaby of Broadway," was Busby Berkeley's personal favorite and probably his greatest single achievement.*

pages 4–5: Top Hat *(RKO, 1935). In one of their most romantic numbers, Ginger Rogers and Fred Astaire dance to Irving Berlin's "Cheek to Cheek."*

page 7: Rebecca of Sunnybrook Farm *(Fox, 1938). Shirley Temple dances with her favorite partner, Bill Robinson.*

page 8: Naughty Marietta *(MGM, 1935). Jeanette MacDonald as Princess Marie (Marietta) poses in an aviary. The budget for this film was not huge, and much of the money seemed to have been spent on MacDonald's costumes.*

page 10: The Wizard of Oz *(MGM, 1939). Filming the fabled walk on the road to the Emerald City. In the background: the Tin Man (Jack Haley), Dorothy (Judy Garland), the Scarecrow (Ray Bolger), and Toto.*

page 12: The Harvey Girls *(MGM, 1946). On her way West to an unknown future, Susan Bradley (Judy Garland) sings the plaintive "In the Valley When the Evening Sun Goes Down."*

page 14: Holiday Inn *(Paramount, 1942). Fred Astaire, midair, in his dance to "Say It with Firecrackers."*

page 15: Singin' in the Rain *(MGM, 1952). Gene Kelly and Cyd Charisse dance in the "Broadway Ballet."*

opposite: On the set of Easter Parade *(MGM, 1948), Judy Garland and Fred Astaire relax in their tramp costumes for the musical number "A Couple of Swells."*

pages 18–19: The King and I *(Fox, 1956). Teacher Anna Leonowens (Deborah Kerr) stands with the King of Siam (Yul Brynner) in the royal Siamese court of the 1860s.*

pages 20–21: Carousel *(Fox, 1956). The chorus demonstrates that "June Is Bustin' Out All Over" on a dock in Boothbay Harbor, Maine.*

pages 22–23: Mary Poppins *(Disney, 1964). That remarkable governess Mary Poppins (Julie Andrews) floats in on her umbrella, headed for the Banks household. An idealized Edwardian London was exquisitely reproduced in the film.*

pages 24–25: Hello, Dolly! *(Fox, 1969). Barbra Streisand joins Louis Armstrong in singing the title tune.*

pages 26–27: Cabaret *(Allied Artists, 1972). In his Academy Award–winning role of the leering, androgynous Master of Ceremonies at the Kit Kat Club, Joel Grey was the very image of decadence in the Berlin of the early thirties.*

© Walt Disney Productions

PART I
THE FIRST
SOUNDS OF MUSIC
1927~1932

October 6, 1927. A glittering audience of notables assembled at the Warner Theatre in New York City for a performance of *The Jazz Singer,* a film version of Samson Raphaelson's Broadway play—reputed to be the most innovative, even revolutionary film since flickering images had first appeared on a screen. They watched attentively as the silent images and florid titles told the lachrymose story of Jakie Rabinowitz, a young singer who abandons his Jewish faith and his cantor father's sacred calling for the fame and glory of being (gasp!) a "jazz singer." On the eve of the Day of Atonement, while his father lies dying, Jakie (now called Jack Robin) is expected to open on Broadway in his newest show. Torn by indecision but unable to dismiss "the cry of his race," Jakie rushes to his father's synagogue to chant the traditional Kol Nidre prayer. His father expires happily, and Jakie goes on to his greatest triumph on the stage.

Everyone wept dutifully, but what sent an electric current surging through the theater was not the film's tear-streaked tale of sin and redemption. At one point early in the movie, Jolson as Jack Robin was singing in a nightclub. After a full-throated rendition of "Dirty Hands, Dirty Face," Jolson sputtered with ad-lib enthusiasm, "Wait a minute, wait a minute, you ain't heard nothin' yet! Wait a minute, I tell ya, ya ain't heard nothin'! You wanna hear 'Toot, Toot, Tootsie'? All right, hold on, hold on. *(To the band leader)* Lou, listen. Play 'Toot, Toot, Tootsie.' Three choruses, you understand. In the third chorus, I whistle. Now give it to 'em hard and heavy! Go right ahead!"

Jolson's speaking voice, the first ever heard in a full-length movie, provoked a wave of astonished shouts and applause. Later in the film, when he launched into a lengthy emotional speech to his doting mother, the spectators burst into an uproar at hearing such natural and spontaneous dialogue. By the end of the movie, as Jolson went down on one knee, flung out his arms to embrace the world, and cried, "Mammy!" the audience turned into what Richard Watts, Jr., described as "a milling, battling mob." Tears streamed down Jolson's face. (He was in New York for the premiere.) Irving Berlin sobbed. Actor William Demarest, who had a small role in the movie, said years later that he felt a shiver run along his spine. Financier Otto Kahn turned to his wife and said, "You and I will never see a moment like this again."

It was, indeed, an extraordinary moment in film history—the first time that speech and song were incorporated into a feature film—but how had it come about? Specifically, how did that first fragment of dialogue—"Wait a minute, wait a minute, you ain't heard nothin' yet!"—appear on the soundtrack? As expected, there are contrasting versions. The most likely story, put forward by Jack Warner in his autobiography, is the simplest: Al Jolson, irrepressible as always and accustomed to improvising on the stage, began to ad-lib into the open microphone. It is not known whether anyone on the set responded with anything more than mild surprise. Suffice to say that when the scene was played back, the Warner brothers decided to keep it intact. They were so pleased, in fact, that scenarist Al Cohn wrote a second and longer passage of spoken dialogue for Jakie's moist homecoming scene with his mother.

However, Darryl Zanuck, then head of production at Warners, claimed that Jolson's scene with his mother was *not* written after hearing his ad libs in the nightclub but was improvised by Jolson in the spirit of the scene. He held that Jolson became so caught up in the moment that the words spilled forth into the open microphone. Again, when the Warner brothers heard the playback, they decided to retain Jolson's emotional speech. Zanuck added that the improvised dialogue was *his* idea, not Jolson's.

Whether it is Jolson, Zanuck, or Jack Warner who gets the credit for introducing "audible" dialogue in a feature film, the result was unequivocal: the spoken word had come to films, and the medium would never be the same. *The Jazz Singer* had risen above its primitive style and bathetic screenplay to show that even a soundtrack with only incidental songs or dialogue could vastly enhance the dramatic impact of a story. It had brought a normally composed New York first-night audience to its feet. It had received enthusiastic notices from critics, who were especially impressed with Jolson's voice. And within days after its release, it had startled and shaken the complacent leaders of the film world.

Time, however, has given *The Jazz Singer* a distinction it does not fully deserve. Contrary to popular belief, it was neither the first sound feature film (it was mostly silent) nor the first

page 28: The Hollywood Revue of 1929 *(MGM, 1929)*. *The chorus girls form a tableau in the ornate "jewel box" setting from this early all-star musical revue.*

page 30: The Jazz Singer *(Warners, 1927)*. *In a backstage scene from this landmark film, two chorus girls observe Jack Robin—born Jakie Rabinowitz (Al Jolson)—and his devoted Mary (May McAvoy).*

page 31: The Jazz Singer *(Warners, 1927)*. *Doting son Jakie Rabinowitz (Al Jolson) fervently embraces his mother (Eugenie Besserer). In their emotional reunion, Jolson had a long passage of audible dialogue, while mama was consigned to such titled dialogue as "That I should live to see my baby again!"*

Hollywood musical. (That distinction would go to *The Broadway Melody,* made over a year later.) It was also far from being the first evidence of sound on film. Performers had actually sung and spoken on screen for many years before 1927. Edison had experimented with sound most of his life, and another inventor, Lee De Forest, had developed a sound-on-film technique that was used in theaters as early as 1923.

For Warner Brothers, *The Jazz Singer* represented the culmination of several years of expensive and often ridiculed experimentation with sound. In 1925, spurred by the competition of radio, the studio had gambled on a sound-on-disk process called Vitaphone, developed by the Bell Telephone Laboratories. By early 1926, the Vitaphone unit was producing brief talking films in the form of one- and two-reel comedies and vaudeville acts, which were booked into a limited number of theaters with their feature films. With *The Jazz Singer,* Warners's original gamble was finally paying off.

Although the audiences flocking into the theaters were obviously enchanted by the novelty of sound, the reaction in the film industry was not always sanguine. Some studio moguls (including Samuel Goldwyn) adopted a wait-and-see attitude. Many writers on the film scene deplored the approaching end of the golden era of silent movies and questioned the artistic value of sound. Typically, critic Ernest Betts wrote, "I am convinced that films should be seen and not heard. The business of the film is to depict action, not to reproduce sound." Even Thomas Edison, when questioned about the future of talking pictures, replied, "Without great improvements people will tire of them. Talking is no substitute for [the] good acting that we have had in the silent pictures" (Geduld, *The Birth of the Talkies*).

Nevertheless, by the summer of 1928, it was already evident that sound was not a passing fad, and that there was no turning back to the silent film. Even in its crudest form, "audible" dialogue in a feature film was much more than a novelty. At first the studios reacted by adding sound effects, songs, or synchronized musical scores to recently completed silent films. Joan Crawford's *Our Dancing Daughters,* for example, had, according to the *New York Times,* "a musical accompaniment, several love songs, stentorian cheering, and, at the end, a chorus of shrieks." Stilted dialogue sequences, acted in the more stylized, more emphatic manner of silent films by performers ill-adjusted to sound, were often added to new features. (A more "realistic" acting style and more "natural" dialogue were already prevalent by the end of the twenties.)

As expected, there were many difficulties in converting to sound, including the need to muffle even the slightest noise that could be picked up on the soundtrack; the discomfort of the large, thickly quilted sound booths, containing cameramen sometimes prostrate with the heat; and the inappropriate voices of some silent-film stars. Even trained voices often sounded shrill or scratchy. Many of these difficulties, which were disappearing by 1930, would be satirized more than two decades later in *Singin' in the Rain.*

Amid the clamor over sound, Warners still held the upper hand and was not about to relinquish it to others. In July, 1928, the studio released the first all-talking film, *Lights of New York,* a crude gangster melodrama that grossed over a million dollars on

Mammy (Warners, 1930). Al Jolson performs with Meadows' Merry Minstrels. The film featured Technicolor sequences and a score by Irving Berlin.

opposite: The Singing Fool *(Warners, 1928). Unaware that his wife (Josephine Dunn) is unfaithful to him, nightclub owner Al Stone (Al Jolson) proudly holds her hand. Jolson's first film after* The Jazz Singer, The Singing Fool *was an even greater success. When Jolson urgently requested a heart-tugging number for the movie, composers DeSylva, Brown, and Henderson wrote "Sonny Boy" in four hours and sang it to him over the telephone.*

My Man *(Warners, 1928)*. *Ziegfeld star Fanny Brice brought her Yiddish-flavored inflections and comic pathos to her sound debut, playing a plain Jane in love with a shiftless fellow. She sang some of her best-known songs, including "I'd Rather Be Blue" and the title tune. Although endearing and funny, she somehow never caught on as a film personality.*

an investment of less than $75,000. Inevitably, there had to be a follow-up to *The Jazz Singer* for Al Jolson, but even Warners was astonished by the enormous success of *The Singing Fool,* which opened in September, 1928. The film became one of the largest-grossing of all time, earning more money than any movie until *Gone with the Wind.* Audiences were apparently enthralled by the sentimental story and by Jolson's repeated singing of "Sonny Boy."

Under Lloyd Bacon's direction, Jolson played a singing waiter who becomes a vaudeville star, then falls apart when his wife and small son ("Sonny Boy") leave him. Just when his fortune is rising again, "Sonny Boy" dies. A heartbroken Jolson goes onstage to sing his child's favorite song. (Guess which one.) Ultimately, he begins a new life with the cigarette girl who loves him. In between his tears of grief and remorse, Jolson performed seven songs, most of which became perennial favorites in his repertoire. "Sonny Boy" was a surefire crowd-pleaser for every singer who could manage a sob in his voice, but other songs, including "There's a Rainbow 'Round My Shoulder" and "It All Depends on You," remained safely in Jolson's corner. His films immediately following *The Singing Fool*—*Say It with Songs* (1929), *Mammy* (1930), and *Big Boy* (1930)—failed to duplicate that success, although they were popular with audiences who relished his florid, hyperemotional style.

Inevitably, success breeds imitation, and *The Jazz Singer* spawned a number of part-talkies in which emotional conflict between parents and children played an integral part. George Jessel, who had lost the *Jazz Singer* role to Al Jolson for reasons that have been disputed over the years, appeared in *Lucky Boy* (1929), a film so blatantly derived from the earlier movie that it even concluded with a "mother" song and Jessel's mother beaming in the audience. In *Mother's Boy* (1929), Irish tenor Morton Downey starred as a singer rising to stardom who gives up his big chance on opening night to sing at the bedside of his critically ill mother. Stage entertainer Sophie Tucker made her film debut in *Honky Tonk* (1929), playing a nightclub hostess whose snobbish daughter objects to the "tawdry" source of her expensive clothes and education.

By 1929 it was abundantly clear that the "talkies" and music were made for each other, and soon songwriters, vocal coaches, conductors, arrangers, dance instructors—in fact, anyone who had ever been associated with the musical theater—made their way to the film capital, hoping to find a comfortable niche. Throughout the year the screen was virtually flooded with musical films of every type and variety (many of them either partly or entirely in primitive Technicolor): all-star musical revues, stagebound operettas, frisky backstage musicals, dramatic stories with interpolated songs, and romantic or sophisticated comedies with song interludes. It was the year of the "all-talking, all-singing, all-dancing" movie.

Entranced by the possibilities of sound, the major studios lost their heads and tossed virtually all of their stars into musical revues, regardless of their vocal or terpsichorean talents. It was apparently not enough to demonstrate that the stars could talk—they also had to show their all-around "versatility." Metro-Goldwyn-Mayer set the pace with *The Hollywood Revue of 1929.* Like the others that would follow, it had color sequences, extravagant sets, and a roll call of star performers trying gamely but, on the whole, vainly to behave like musical comedy "mavens." With Jack Benny and Conrad Nagel as masters of ceremonies, the revue took them through their mostly awkward turns: Joan Crawford singing and dancing with more energy than talent to "Gotta Feeling for You"; Marion Davies performing "Tommy Atkins on Parade" as a member of the Grenadier Guards, then tap-dancing on a huge drum; Norma Shearer and John Gilbert enacting (in color) the balcony scene from *Romeo and Juliet,* then later repeating the scene in a "modern" spoof; and many others. The comedy sequences with Laurel and Hardy, Buster Keaton, and Marie Dressler, among others, were more tolerable, with Dressler especially funny as a raucous monarch singing "For I'm the Queen." The movie's most popular song was "Singin' in the Rain," performed by Cliff ("Ukelele Ike") Edwards in a downpour.

In 1930, *Paramount on Parade* trotted out its star list for a round of songs and sketches that were somewhat more polished and sophisticated than those offered by *The Hollywood Revue.* (Several sequences were in color.) Maurice Chevalier, who had made his American screen debut only a year earlier in *Innocents of Paris,* was seen most prominently, performing a musical *apache* number with Evelyn Brent, singing "All I Want Is Just One Girl" as a Paris gendarme, and joining with the chorus girls in a lavish Technicolor finale to "Sweeping the Clouds Away." Other segments had Ruth Chatterton as a French prostitute mourning the loss of "My Marine" (with Fredric March and Stuart Erwin in support), and Clara Bow, aided by Jack Oakie and a chorus of sailors, performing a vivacious rendition of "I'm True to the Navy Now."

With these musical revues, the studios were merely flexing their muscles, demonstrating to audiences the sheer novelty of hearing their favorite performers sing and speak. But one early talkie was a landmark that not only explored some of the possibilities of sound but catapulted the musical into prominence as the genre most in demand by the moviegoing public. At MGM, production head Irving Thalberg (a mere stripling of twenty-nine) commissioned songwriters Arthur Freed and Nacio Herb Brown to write a batch of songs for the studio's first all-talking film. The songs were designed to bolster Edmund Goulding's simple, sentimental story of two sisters who come to the Great White Way seeking fame on the musical stage. Since they both love the same jaunty song-and-dance man, there are the usual quarrels, misunderstandings, and moments of heartbreak before the bittersweet ending. The film was *The Broadway Melody* (1929), the first true musical out of any studio.

Considering the impressive number of stars that the studio drew on for *The Hollywood Revue,* it is surprising that the leading roles in *The Broadway Melody* were cast not with superluminaries but with actors who were suitable for their roles. To play Hank, the older, more sensible sister, MGM chose Bessie Love, a major silent-film star—she had appeared in *Intolerance*—whose roles had become so infrequent and mediocre that she had launched a tour in vaudeville. Anita Page, a seventeen-year-old blonde under contract to MGM for several years, was signed to play Queenie, Hank's frivolous sister. Charles King, a Broadway stage star who had played in the *Ziegfeld Follies, Hit the Deck,* and other musical

Sally (Warners, 1929). Florenz Ziegfeld's radiant blonde star Marilyn Miller made her screen debut in this film version of her 1920 stage show. Filmed in two-color Technicolor, Sally *concerned a waitress who pretends to be a Russian entertainer and finds both love and success. Her best song in Jerome Kern's score was "Look for the Silver Lining."*

The Hollywood Revue of 1929
(MGM, 1929). At the movie's close, the
stars, in yellow slickers, gather to reprise
"Singin' in the Rain." Most prominent
(front row, center) are Buster Keaton,
Marion Davies, and Joan Crawford. The
chorus girl second from the right in the
top row is Ann Dvorak.

Hollywood Revue of 1929 (MGM,
1929). Marie Dressler was raucously
funny singing "For I'm the Qeen" with
Polly Moran and Cliff Edwards. A
vaudeville and musical comedy star, she
made her film debut in 1914 opposite
Charlie Chaplin in Tillie's Punctured
Romance. Later, she gave a memorable
performance in Dinner at Eight
(1933).

Happy Days *(Fox, 1930)*. Ann Pennington heads the girls of the chorus in a bizarre musical number called "Snake Hips." Many of the stars, including Janet Gaynor, Charles Farrell, and Victor McLaglen, appeared in the lavish minstrel show finale, which ranged from the imaginative to the abysmal.

Show of Shows *(Warners, 1929)*. Winnie Lightner, a lively comedienne with a short career in films, mocked The Hollywood Revue's "Singin' in the Rain" with this number, "Singin' in the Bathtub." She danced with a group of beefy male "chorines" wearing shower caps and striped bathing suits.

Show of Shows *(Warners, 1929)*. *"Lady Luck," the final number in Warners's contribution to the cycle of all-star revues, carried lavishness to the point of absurdity. Filmed in color, the movie brought together seventy-seven contract players in a cluster of songs, sketches, specialty acts, and production numbers. Among the cast members were Beatrice Lillie, Myrna Loy, John Barrymore, Loretta Young, Douglas Fairbanks, Jr., Chester Morris, and Ann Sothern, still known here as Harriette Lake.*

Paramount on Parade *(Paramount, 1930). This antebellum musical sequence featured current and upcoming stars, including (from left) Fay Wray, Richard Arlen, James Hall, Jean Arthur, Gary Cooper, Mary Brian, Phillips Holmes, Joan Peers, David Newell, and Virginia Bruce.*

King of Jazz *(Universal, 1930). Cast and crew assemble to film the extravagant "Bridal Veil" number. According to the studio's publicity department, the veil was the largest and most lavish ever made. The movie featured the Paul Whiteman Orchestra and many leading performers. Somewhere in the cast, as a member of a group called the Rhythm Boys, was an unknown young singer named Bing Crosby.*

Paramount on Parade *(Paramount, 1930). Two moments from "Rainbow Revels," the movie's Technicolor finale, with Maurice Chevalier (as a chimney sweep) and the chorus singing "Sweeping the Clouds Away."*

shows, was cast as Eddie, the trouper who would sing the title tune at the drop of a hat.

Under the direction of Harry Beaumont, the cast and crew of *The Broadway Melody* began production with a mixture of excitement and trepidation. The problems of sound recording had not yet been worked out, and as the shooting progressed, there were unhappy surprises. It was discovered, for example, that the swish of beads embroidered on silver costumes reverberated through the recording machine. (Costume designer David Fox found the costumes more pliable when the beads were strung on rubber bands.) For another musical number, dresses with metallic fringes had to be discarded since their rustle recorded noisily. As one dilemma ended, another arose, demanding solution. At one point a persistent echo was removed by hanging heavy curtains on the set. Also, since the director wanted a more mobile camera than usual, a method had to be devised to keep the loud whirring of the camera off the soundtrack. Beaumont had the camera cabin placed on wheels, with shoeless sound men, holding out microphones, tiptoeing along with the actors as they moved. Because sound techniques were being improved almost weekly, the second half of the film sounds better than the first.

Although the movie now seems rather static after half a century of improved techniques, part of the excitement that it generated in its day can be attributed to this flexible camera. The backstage milieu was far from novel in 1929, yet few films to that date had moved so intimately into the dressing rooms, the seedy hotel rooms, or onto the stage itself, ablaze with light and bustling with activity. The characters who would later become clichés in the backstage musical, from the hopeful kids in the chorus to the overbearing impresario who controls their lives, are shown here in their purest form. Of course, there was also the impact of the spoken dialogue, which, with its brash patois of backstage life, bristles with colorful phrases: "coffee-and-cake jack" for a meager amount of money; "cracked ice" for Tiffany diamonds; "the lingerie" for women; and "inhaling poison" for drinking bad liquor. The dance director exhorts the chorus to work hard by saying, "Cut 'em deep and let 'em bleed." There is no pretense of refinement or culture in this environment.

In addition to a more mobile camera and the slangy dialogue, *The Broadway Melody* claimed another strong virtue: the performance of Bessie Love as Hank. While Anita Page's voice is abrasive (made more so by the primitive recording techniques), and Charles King's Eddie is tuned more to the stage than to film, Bessie Love comes through with acting of a surprisingly high order. Touching and credible as a not-so-young girl who gives up her dream of show business glory out of devotion to her sister, Love is given scenes that sometimes rise above the routine level of the rest of the film. Her most famous moment comes in her dressing room when she finally realizes that Eddie loves not her but Queenie. After pretending that she no longer loves Eddie, and sending him off to find Queenie, she collapses before her mirror, weeping as she removes her makeup with cold cream. As her sobs mount in intensity, she seems overwhelmed by a despair she cannot handle. The actress offers a genuine portrait of a girl whose tough exterior conceals a vulnerable heart.

Seen today, *The Broadway Melody*'s musical numbers may

The Broadway Melody *(MGM, 1929). Bessie Love and Charles King converse backstage. As Hank, the older, more sensible half of a sister act in vaudeville, Love gave an assured and affecting performance that was nominated for an Academy Award. She lost to Mary Pickford in* Coquette.

opposite: The Broadway Melody *(MGM, 1929). Anita Page and Charles King perform the title number. Page, a mere nineteen at the time of filming, retired from the screen at twenty-six. King appeared in six more films, but never made it to stardom.*

The Gold Diggers of Broadway *(Warners, 1929). Nick Lucas and Winnie Lightner lead the party festivities in this "talking and singing natural color picture." The movie's frantic shooting shedule sometimes called for eighteen hours of continuous filming, in heat so intense from the lights used for color filming that the players' hair smoked.*

evoke laughter rather than admiration, but they impressed 1929 audiences. The color sequence built around "The Wedding of the Painted Doll," with its storybook characters come to life and its elaborately costumed chorus girls, was especially admired as an example of the screen's new dimension. "You Were Meant for Me," sung by Charles King to Anita Page in a hotel room, was the movie's biggest hit song, while the songs performed by Bessie Love and Anita Page—"Harmony Babies from Melody Lane" and "The Boy Friend"—only convinced viewers that this sister act was *not* destined for stardom. *The Broadway Melody* was an enormous success, garnering wildly enthusiastic reviews. It became the first sound film to win the Academy Award as best picture.

Even as MGM was happily counting its huge box-office receipts for *The Broadway Melody,* imitations were being rushed into production. Backstage musicals, partially or, in a few instances, entirely in color, were being churned out at a hectic pace to meet the public demand. MGM itself produced *Lord Byron of Broadway* (1929), the tale of a composer's ups and downs, and reunited Bessie Love and Charles King in *Chasing Rainbows* (originally called *The Road Show*), about a vaudeville performer and her fickle partner. Other studios followed suit with *Broadway Babies, Broadway Scandals,* and *The Gold Diggers of Broadway,* all released in 1929. The last film, Warners's most ambitious contribution to the cycle, followed the exploits of several down-on-their-luck, money-mad chorines as they scheme to find rich husbands. Nancy Welford, Nick Lucas, and Ann Pennington were on hand to sing and dance to such tunes as "Painting the Clouds with Sunshine" and "Tip-Toe Thru' the Tulips."

At the same time that the success of *The Broadway Melody* was spawning many backstage musical films, producers with a desperate need for musical material turned to the stage for properties. Throughout 1929 and 1930, moviegoers could listen to the lilting strains of Sigmund Romberg, Rudolf Friml, Victor Herbert, and Jerome Kern, or the romantic lyrics of Oscar Hammerstein II. They could also enjoy the prismatic effects of the two-color Technicolor in which many of the operettas were filmed, either entirely or in part. It hardly mattered that the films were often stagebound and heavy-handed, devoid of any trace of cinematic imagination.

The 1926 operetta *The Desert Song,* with a score by Sigmund Romberg and Oscar Hammerstein II, was the basis for the first all-talking, all-singing operetta (1929). Filmed with Technicolor sequences, the movie starred John Boles as a general's effete son who doubles as the Red Shadow, intrepid masked leader of the insurgent Riffs in French Morocco. Carlotta King was totally wooden as the French girl who loves the Red Shadow despite herself, and Myrna Loy, still in the early, exotic phase of her career, played the spurned native girl, Azuri. Released six months after filming, the movie was criticized for its already primitive sound.

Sigmund Romberg was not the only composer feeding operetta music to the insatiable film industry. Early in 1930, MGM released *The Rogue Song,* a Technicolor musical adapted from Franz Lehár's 1912 operetta *Gypsy Love.* In his first screen role, opera star Lawrence Tibbett played a dashing bandit chief

Show Boat *(Universal, 1929). The ill-fated Julie (Alma Rubens, at right) embraces Magnolia (Laura La Plante), her friend from their happier showboat days, in this version of the celebrated Oscar Hammerstein II–Jerome Kern musical play. Filmed first as a silent, the movie was hurriedly turned into a part-talkie when it was evident that sound had arrived. Several of the original songs were retained, but the score was embellished with spirituals and other familiar songs such as "Deep River."*

The Desert Song *(Warners, 1929). In this scene from the first all-talking, all-singing operetta, John Boles (center), as the dashing bandit leader, the Red Shadow, confers with one of his followers. Crouched at the side of the bed is Myrna Loy as the native girl, Azuri.*

On with the Show *(Warners, 1929)*. *Two scenes from the musical that was advertised as "the first 100% Natural Color, All-Singing Production." The film's plot, concerning a wide-eyed former hatcheck girl who takes the place of a rebellious star, was similar in many ways to that of* 42nd Street, *released four years later. The only professional note was provided by Ethel Waters, singing two solos in her inimitable style.*

whose vigorous voice finally thaws an icy Russian princess. (Tibbett was seen to better advantage the following year in a lushly photographed MGM musical called *The Cuban Love Song.*) About the same time, Paramount presented its newest singing star, Jeanette MacDonald, in a dreary film version of Rudolf Friml's operetta *The Vagabond King.* Stage star Dennis King costarred in the Technicolor film about the French rogue-poet François Villon.

Not every musical film adapted from a stage hit of the period was a costume operetta fragrant with the romance of bygone years. Some were derived from shows with a contemporary setting and musical beat. Warners's *No, No, Nanette* (1930) transformed the 1925 musical comedy into a lively movie that retained the show's two biggest song hits, "I Want to Be Happy" and "Tea for Two." RKO's nautical musical *Hit the Deck* (1930), with Jack Oakie and Polly Walker in central roles, kept some of the Vincent Youmans music from the 1927 stage show. MGM's *Good News,* that perennially popular collegiate musical produced on stage in the fall of 1927, was given its first screen treatment in 1930, with Mary Lawlor, Stanley Smith, and Bessie Love as the principal cutups at Tait College. Other 1930 screen versions of contemporary Broadway musicals included *Follow Thru, Hold Everything,* and *Heads Up.*

One of the most popular stage adaptations of the period was RKO's *Rio Rita* (1929), adapted from Florenz Ziegfeld's 1927 success. Virtually a filmed transcription of the play, the movie, set in Mexico, had a melodramatic plot involving a stalwart Texas Ranger (John Boles), the ever-lovely Rio Rita (Bebe Daniels), two gag-laden clowns (Bert Wheeler and Robert Woolsey), and a mysterious villain known only as the Kinkajou. The plot was often ignored to permit songs by the leads or lavish musical numbers, staged at a Mexican fiesta or aboard a pirate barge. (The film was partly in black-and-white and partly in color, due to the limited availability of the studio's Technicolor camera.) Although it was locked into proscenium staging, the musical did attempt, however feebly, to give a sense of being filmed in natural surroundings rather than in a nightclub or theater.

Although the theater was a major source of performers and material, many early musicals used original songs and stories, featuring winsome or flirtatious heroines who enjoyed singing and dancing on any provocation, and stalwart or bumptious heroes with either money or "prospects." Such stars as Colleen Moore, Corinne Griffith, and Nancy Carroll, who had fared well in silent films with their good looks and ability to pantomime emotion, were suddenly called upon to sing, dance—and talk. Nancy Carroll in particular revealed a sweet if thin musical voice and a piquant personality in three early sound musicals, *Close Harmony* (1929), *Sweetie* (1929), and *Honey* (1930).

Janet Gaynor, an actress adept at portraying innocence and vulnerability, starred in *Sunny Side Up* (1929), her first all-talking film and one of the most popular original musical films of the period. Written by B. G. DeSylva, Lew Brown, and Ray Henderson, and directed by David Butler, *Sunny Side Up* cast Gaynor as Molly, a winsome New York waif who finally meets Jack Cromwell (Charles Farrell), the eligible young millionaire of her dreams. Enchanted by Molly, Cromwell invites her to

Rio Rita *(RKO, 1929). Bebe Daniels as the bewitching heroine of
the title. Speaking about the film many years later, Daniels recalled
that it was completed in twenty-four days, and that its improved
recording quality was due to the frequent presence on the set of her
second cousin, Lee De Forest, a pioneer in the use of sound.*

right: Rio Rita *(RKO, 1929). Don Alvarado, Bebe Daniels,
and John Boles in a scene from the part-color film version of Florenz
Ziegfeld's stage success.*

opposite: The Vagabond King *(Paramount, 1930). Dennis King as
the roguish poet François Villon and Jeanette MacDonald as the heroine
Katherine in Rudolf Friml's perennial operetta. MacDonald's problems
with the egotistical King peaked when he insisted on having his face,
especially his handsome profile, included in virtually every frame while
she sang a solo, "Only a Rose." Thereafter, MacDonald referred to the
number as "Only a Nose."*

opposite, above: Just Imagine *(Fox, 1930). Maureen O'Sullivan and John Garrick in a scene from one of the musical oddities of the period—a futuristic fantasy, both imaginative and absurd, set in the New York City of 1980. In this society, people are known only by serial numbers. The plot involved a trip to Mars, which turns out to be inhabited by sets of twins who wear shiny metal costumes and apparently are not opposed to dancing. The movie had a score by DeSylva, Brown, and Henderson.*

Delicious *(Fox, 1931). The popular team of Janet Gaynor and Charles Farrell starred in several musicals after* Sunny Side Up, *but none was as well-received or as popular. This film had a whimsical story concerning the romance between a Scottish immigrant (Gaynor) and a rich polo player (Farrell), but the best feature was a score by George and Ira Gershwin.*

Sweetie *(Paramount, 1929). Jack Oakie and Helen Kane, back-to-back in this typical collegiate musical of the period. Kane played a madcap coed who uses an air rifle to spur the football team on to victory, but the film's star was pert Nancy Carroll, who appeared in several other early sound musicals.*

Honey *(Paramount, 1930). Nancy Carroll, as a rich Southern girl posing as a cook in her own home, wins the affections of Stanley Smith. The musical's highlight was Lillian Roth's rousing rendition of "Sing, You Sinners."*

opposite, below: Good News *(MGM, 1930). Dorothy McNulty (better known in later years as Penny Singleton) leads the Tait College coeds in "The Varsity Drag." The second coed from the left, in the first row, is Ann Dvorak, who became a star in the thirties.*

Sunny Side Up *(Fox, 1929). A moment from "Turn On the Heat,"
one of the most outlandish musical numbers in early sound films. To cope
with the rising temperature, the girls have removed their Eskimo
costumes and are dancing in their 1929-style bathing suits. Their
orgasmic gyrations soon generate so much heat that a fire starts in the
background. The girls leap into the pool to escape the flames, as a
fountain spouts a watery curtain!*

right: Sunny Side Up *(Fox, 1929). Janet Gaynor, as the demure
heroine Molly, sings the title song for her tenement friends during their
block party.*

opposite, above: *A lobby card for* The Desert Song *(Warners,
1929). At center: Myrna Loy and John Boles.*

opposite, center: *A lobby card for* Sunny Side Up *(Fox, 1929).*

opposite, below: *A lobby card for* The Love Parade *(Paramount,
1929). Note that the film's sole star was Maurice Chevalier. Jeanette
MacDonald was merely featured, but she received top billing by her
third film, Monte Carlo.*

appear in the Southampton Charity Show and promises to rent the house next door to his for Molly and her neighborhood friends. Molly will pretend to be a rich girl, with maid and chauffeur. Many complications and songs and dances later, Molly wins Jack for her very own.

One of the first musicals created directly for the screen, *Sunny Side Up* is a charming, sometimes appealing, and sometimes appalling antique. Without stage material to fall back on, it avoids, to some extent, the rigid, inflexible look of many early musicals. (Original movie musicals often worked better, and continued to do so for many years afterward.) The early scenes in New York City have a surprising flavor and even pungency as the camera roams about the streets, picking up a woman washing her hair, men furtively reading the *Police Gazette,* and a battling Italian couple. The brash antics of Molly's friends, Bea (Marjorie White) and Eddie (Frank Albertson), as they exchange little quips or sing ''Pickin' Petals off a Daisy,'' give an amusing indication of musical comedy behavior in the late twenties.

Although the primitive sound equipment makes her voice resemble a chipmunk's, Janet Gaynor is pretty and engaging as Molly, and she is given the movie's best (and best-remembered) songs. Early in the film, she sings ''I'm a Dreamer (Aren't We All?)'' as she moons about Jack Cromwell, and later, when the two are in love, she joins him in a duet of ''If I Had a Talking Picture of You.'' (Unfortunately, the song is reprised by two simpering children.) At a block party in the city, Gaynor also enlivens the proceedings with the title song, does a little dance, and then invites all her neighbors to join in another chorus. Jack watches from the sidelines, entranced as she gets a dour man to smile and even makes the local undertaker dance. (At the party a small boy starts to recite, then decides he must go to the bathroom. The embarrassed tot is tiny Jackie Cooper.) On the debit side, *Sunny Side Up* has a simply awful performance by Charles Farrell as Jack Cromwell. An awkward sound actor and an even worse singer, he makes the hero something of a dimwit whose appeal to not one but two women is inexplicable.

In the deluge of musicals in 1929 and (to a lesser extent) 1930, there was a handful of films that were able to avoid the static, heavy-handed style that characterized most of the others. These films demonstrated that sound, far from being a deterrent to effective filmmaking, could actually work in league with the camera to enrich, enhance, or simply comment upon a moment of film, a sequence, or even an entire movie. With screenplays that were either entirely original or adapted from sources so old and obscure that they were practically original, the films combined voices, sound effects, and mobile camerawork in ways that impressed and influenced discerning moviemakers for years to come. Several of them were the creations of director Ernst Lubitsch.

By 1929, Lubitsch was already renowned as a director of ironic, sophisticated, and perfectly timed sexual comedies. Although he was dubious at first about sound, he finally conceded that it offered him the opportunity to add witty dialogue and sparkling songs to his tales of indiscretions, secret liaisons, and misalliances. He also decided that the traditional conventions and attitudes of operetta were being taken too seriously on the

The Love Parade *(Paramount, 1929). As the frustrated Queen Louise of Sylvania, Jeanette MacDonald awakens to sing of her "Dream Lover." She is wearing the revealing negligee that turned up in some form in almost all of her early films. MacDonald commented years later on the film's director, Ernst Lubitsch: "He could suggest more with a closed door than all the hay-rolling you see openly on the screen nowadays, and yet he never offended"* (Parish, The Jeanette MacDonald Story).

screen, and that it would be enjoyable to mock them in his own style. For his first talking film at Paramount, he selected *The Love Parade* (1929), adapted from a little-known Hungarian play called *The Prince Consort,* adding songs by Victor Schertzinger and Clifford Grey. His stars were Jeanette MacDonald, a vivacious redheaded singer who had starred in several Broadway musicals for the Shubert brothers, and Maurice Chevalier, the internationally famous French entertainer with the straw hat, protruding lower lip, and saucy, infectious musical style. It was MacDonald's first film and Chevalier's second sound feature, and from all reports, their professional rivalry was apparent to everyone. Both tended to overplay their roles, possibly in competition for the camera's attention.

MacDonald plays Queen Louise of Sylvania, who is not only frustrated at being unmarried but also annoyed with the court's obsession with finding her a husband. She finally settles on Alfred Renard (Chevalier), a military attaché in Paris who is supposed to be representing Sylvania but whose main activity is the pursuit of women, preferably married ones. The marriage of Louise and Alfred is a disaster, with Alfred's role as prince consort relegated to obeying his wife's every wish and command. Demoralized, emasculated, and simply bored, he decides to leave her. Louise, desolate at the thought of losing him, becomes his contrite and obedient slave. Of course Alfred consents to stay. On the sidelines, commenting on the action and sometimes serving as a lower-class contrast, are Lupino Lane as Alfred's valet and Lillian Roth as a flirtatious maid.

Lubitsch had not yet achieved the dexterity in blending all elements of a musical film that he later demonstrated in *One Hour with You* and *The Merry Widow*. Yet *The Love Parade* still benefits from the director's sophisticated "touch." From the beginning of the film, as chorus girls extol the virtues of "Champagne," and Lupino Lane reprises the song while preparing for another of his employer's intimate midnight sessions, the tone is like the champagne, dry and bubbly. Sexual innuendo is never far from the surface as Chevalier, a shameless roué, engages in a funny altercation with a woman and her irate husband, and then sings the praises of the city he has to leave in "Paris, Stay the Same," or as MacDonald is roused from an obviously erotic dream to face another morning without a man.

The movie has its share of sly Lubitschean moments: a busload of bored American tourists in Sylvania suddenly becomes interested when told that a castle cost $110 million to build; at Louise and Alfred's opulent wedding ceremony, the priest intones, "I pronounce you wife and man." Lubitsch uses sound in new and unexpected ways, mostly to achieve comic emphasis. Each time that Alfred tells a risqué joke, the punchline is rendered inaudible by a slamming door. To mock the use of a chorus in operetta, Lubitsch has a dog bark out a chorus of "Paris, Stay the Same."

The songs have the expected lilt and bounce of operetta, and one, "Dream Lover," was enormously popular. In addition to their duet of the title song, MacDonald and Chevalier are given other solos: she sings "March of the Grenadiers" as she reviews her troops, wearing a gleaming uniform, and he sings "Anything to Please the Queen" and "Nobody's Using It Now," the latter song an exasperated lament for his lost prowess as a lover. Lupino

Lane and Lillian Roth have two duets, "Let's Be Common" and "The Queen Is Always Right," but both songs now seem more arch than amusing.

After her promising debut in *The Love Parade*, MacDonald appeared in mediocre films for the next few years. Only one of her 1930 films has genuine merit. Ernst Lubitsch's *Monte Carlo*, based on an old play by Hans Müller and episodes from Booth Tarkington's *Monsieur Beaucaire*, was a sprightly musical in which MacDonald played a countess fleeing to the Riviera from an unwanted marriage to a duke. Down to her last ten thousand francs, she hopes to make a fortune at the gaming tables but instead finds romance with a count who poses as her hairdresser. This frivolous plot was handled deftly by Lubitsch, and the songs were pleasant though unexceptional. The film's central problem was the casting of British actor Jack Buchanan as the count. A popular performer on the British musical stage, he was much too brittle and arch to be convincing as the countess's ardent pursuer. (More than two decades later, he would give a brilliant performance as the flamboyant director in MGM's musical *The Band Wagon*.)

Monte Carlo does have one deservedly famous sequence in which MacDonald, on the train to the Riviera, sings "Beyond the Blue Horizon." As she leans out the window with her scarf billowing in the wind, the sounds of the train's engine whistle and spinning wheels form the background for the opening bars of the song. The train and the music accelerate as she sings joyously of her bid for romantic adventure. Peasants in the fields join in a reprise of the chorus as they watch the passing train. The stars also share a charming scene over the telephone in which he attempts to woo her in song. Afterward, she falls asleep with the melody running through her head.

Lubitsch was only moderately successful with *Monte Carlo*, but he did better with *The Smiling Lieutenant* (1931), derived from a novel by Hans Müller and Oscar Straus's 1907 operetta *A Waltz Dream*. This movie was unavailable for many years, until an English-language print was found in an East European archive in the late sixties. Its original reputation as one of Lubitsch's most felicitous and wickedly amusing musical confections has now been restored, and some critics number it among the best musicals of the early sound period.

Maurice Chevalier plays Niki, a girl-chasing lieutenant in the Imperial Guard of Austria, whose latest conquest is Franzi (Claudette Colbert), the leader of an all-girls' band. When the king (George Barbier) of the tiny country of Flausenthurm arrives in Austria with his daughter, Princess Anna (Miriam Hopkins), Niki is soon in deep trouble. During the parade for the royal guests, he winks and smiles at Franzi in the crowd, but Anna thinks that he is flirting with *her*. She is soon convinced that she and Niki are meant for each other, and to avoid international complications, the two are married. A very reluctant bridegroom, Niki drives Anna to distraction, until Franzi, after an initial bout of jealousy, teaches Anna how to lure Niki into her marriage bed. With Franzi's instruction, Anna and Niki are soon enjoying marital bliss.

The Smiling Lieutenant falters at times, but it is so replete with Lubitsch's artful and risqué touches that its lapses are forgivable. Niki and Franzi fall in love on sight, and Franzi shows

One Hour with You *(Paramount, 1932). In this musical remake of* The Marriage Circle, *Ernst Lubitsch put Jeanette MacDonald and Maurice Chevalier through their paces as a married couple whose flirtations with others cause not-too-serious complications. The team was charming, as always, but much of the amusement came from the artful supporting players, headed by Roland Young, Genevieve Tobin, and Charles Ruggles.*

Monte Carlo *(Paramount, 1930). On a train headed for romantic adventure on the Riviera, Jeanette MacDonald sings "Beyond the Blue Horizon." This scene is a splendid Lubitschean combination of sight and sound.*

opposite: The Smiling Lieutenant *(Paramount, 1931). Princess Anna (Miriam Hopkins) of Flausenthurm finally snares Niki (Maurice Chevalier) as her very reluctant bridegroom. Despite elaborate preparations, their wedding night turns into a disaster when Niki refuses to make love to her, insisting instead that they play checkers.*

not an instant's hesitation in agreeing to spend the night with him. (In the morning, they jubilantly sing "Breakfast Time—It Must Be Love.") While Anna sings to her maid about her feeling for Niki, Niki and Franzi are happily expressing their own love in counterpoint, with the song "Madness in the Moonlight." There is also a rueful moment of truth for Franzi when she realizes that she will never be able to maintain her hold on Niki. "Girls who start with breakfasts," she remarks, "usually don't end up with supper."

If the songs by Oscar Straus and Clifford Grey are not up to the best in the operetta cycle, they still provide delightful moments. His usual buoyant self, Chevalier sings "To Arms" at the start of the movie, and he doesn't have military matters in mind. "Live for Today" is the motto proclaimed in song by Franzi, an early liberated woman played with charm by Claudette Colbert. Her best scene comes with Miriam Hopkins, that mannered but often delectable comedienne. When Franzi visits Anna in the palace, they begin by slapping each other, then fall sobbing on a bed. They agree that they both love Niki and start to behave with girlish glee at the prospect of employing womanly wiles. Together at the piano, they sing "Jazz Up Your Lingerie." Anna proceeds to burn her old underthings and changes her wardrobe completely.

After *The Smiling Lieutenant,* Lubitsch was asked to direct *One Hour with You* (1932), a musical remake of his 1924 comedy *The Marriage Circle.* (George Cukor, who took over the director's chair for a few weeks when Lubitsch had to leave the filming, is listed as codirector.) *One Hour with You* may have been less awkward than *The Love Parade,* but it lacks the playful, inventive use of sound that characterized the earlier film. By 1932, sound was no longer a novelty, and Lubitsch apparently did not feel the need to experiment. Nor is the film as lavishly mounted as *The Love Parade.* Lubitsch merely deleted much of the irony and sexual innuendo from *The Marriage Circle* and added a number of Oscar Straus–Leo Robin–Richard Whiting songs. The result is charming but somewhat musty, like a pressed flower that has been allowed to lie in a drawer too long.

The plot is merely a fragile conceit concerning Dr. Andre Bertier (Maurice Chevalier) and his wife Colette (Jeanette MacDonald), whose marriage is temporarily threatened by Mitzi (Genevieve Tobin), Colette's flirtatious friend from her school days. Also involved are Mitzi's droll husband, Professor Olivier (Roland Young), who is amiably seeking grounds for divorce, and Adolph (Charles Ruggles), a befuddled family friend who adores Colette and makes no secret of his ardor. There are the usual misunderstandings, near-seductions, and threats of scandal, but everything is quickly settled. Some clever, lightly mocking touches in Samson Raphaelson's screenplay keep this slender story from vanishing without a trace. It is of so little interest to Lubitsch that he never really ends it—he merely has the Bertiers decide that they love each other, after all.

The movie's songs, amusing and often witty, include a MacDonald-Chevalier duet called "What a Little Thing like a Marriage Ring Can Do" ("It's lawful—and awful nice, too!"), MacDonald's solo of "Day After Day," and Andre's two songs about Mitzi: his admiring "Oh, That Mitzi!" and his perplexed "What Would *You* Do with a Girl like That?" Best of all is the cast's singing of the title tune. At the Bertiers' dinner party, the

Hallelujah! (MGM, 1929). Preacher Zeke (Daniel Haynes), converted from his sinful ways, leads his people in a powerful prayer meeting. King Vidor's film—the first all-black sound feature film—won praise from most critics but there were some important dissenting comments, notably from Robert E. Sherwood of the New York Evening Post, who wrote that the movie "bears regrettable evidence of the Hollywood taint." He also objected to "the long 'stage waits' between sequences during which the screen is empty and the audience hears nothing but the protesting roar of the sound apparatus in the agonies of readjustment."

Hallelujah! (MGM, 1929). Riddled with the sins of her brief lifetime, Chick (Nina Mae McKinney) expires in the arms of Zeke (Daniel Haynes). Unable to control his jealous passion, Zeke had shot her as she ran off with Hot Shot, the lover from her wicked past. All this melodrama was expressed in exclamatory dialogue, but the film had a crude power that persists to this day.

principal players take turns in singing a chorus as they glide about the dance floor, plotting stratagems for the evening. As a novel touch, the characters occasionally speak in rhymed couplets. Mitzi tells Colette, "Unless you're well-mated, this business of marriage is much over-rated." The stars play with vivacity, getting firm support from Charles Ruggles and Roland Young, those two past masters at portraying bumbling charm, and from Genevieve Tobin, who, in her numerous portrayals of the "other woman," often showed more skill and style than the heroine.

Lubitsch's early sound musicals—*The Merry Widow* was the glorious culmination in 1934—were soon to be replaced by brasher, much less elegant song-and-dance movies, but for a few years he brought his inimitable style to the musical genre. The Lubitsch characteristics—sophistication mixed with a certain skepticism, worldly continental charm, mocking irony, delight in sexual games—would be present in his later films, but they would no longer be set to the strains of a waltz or the witty lyrics of a comic patter song.

Another director who contributed a major original musical film to the early sound era was King Vidor. On the Hollywood scene since 1915, Vidor had directed such impressive feature films as *The Big Parade* (1925) and *The Crowd* (1928). After the arrival of talking films, he was particularly eager to explore the possibilities of using sound in dramatic juxtaposition with the images on the screen.

His concept for a first sound film was nothing less than daring for its time. He repeated a proposal made some years back to do a film with an all-black cast. To avoid another studio rejection, he added that he would work without salary. He also offered to invest the money he would ordinarily receive in the production if the studio would match that investment, dollar for dollar. MGM head Nicholas Schenck was reputed to have answered, "If that's the way you feel about it, I'll let you make a picture about whores" (Kobal, *Gotta Sing, Gotta Dance*).

With the studio's reluctant blessing, Vidor began his production of *Hallelujah!* (1929), the first all-black sound feature film. The cast was recruited mostly from the black districts of New York and Chicago. When the heavy sound equipment did not arrive on time at the location site in Memphis, Vidor filmed a number of silent sequences and added sound later at the studio in Hollywood. Coordinating the voices and the sound effects with the screen images was a tedious and maddening process that drove one editor berserk—Vidor recalled that in a rage he threw a reel of film at a wall and broke into helpless sobs.

Vidor's intentions in making *Hallelujah!* were entirely sincere: he wanted to evoke the religious fervor and unabashed sexual feelings of the Negro people he had known in his childhood and youth. But although his homage is well-meant, the film has distinctly racist overtones, assuming that the Southern black man is sexually obsessed, childlike, and riddled with primitive fears. Yet there is no denying the impact of its simple story of murder and redemption in the Deep South. The film centers on Zeke (Daniel Haynes), whose life is nearly destroyed by his passion for the seductive, promiscuous Chick (Nina Mae McKinney). When he accidentally kills his young brother in a brawl involving Chick's lover Hot Shot, Zeke is overwhelmed with remorse and becomes a preacher. But, despite the force of

his religious belief, he is lured back by the temporarily "converted" Chick. Tragedy ensues when Chick runs off with Hot Shot, and Zeke, firing his rifle at them, shoots Chick dead. He goes to prison but later returns home to his jubilant family. (The movie seems to suggest that a black man who commits a crime is merely surrendering to the innate criminality of his basic "black nature," and that his redemption is more important than retribution by the law.)

This tale is primitively told, with overwrought acting and dialogue that appears to have been punctuated entirely with exclamation points ("I'm hangin' on the edge of hell!" "I've been a wicked woman! Don't let me sin no more!"). But there are sequences that succeed in gripping the emotions, and moments that attest to Vidor's extraordinary feeling for the possibilities of sound. At the funeral of Zeke's brother, the intensity of the grief is overpowering as Zeke weeps with anguish and Missy Rose, the girl who loves him faithfully, clings to his leg. Later, at a vividly staged prayer meeting, new preacher Zeke ferociously scorns Chick and Hot Shot for their sinning. In the baptism ceremony that follows, Chick's convulsive conversion is startling to behold as she writhes and shrieks in a mixture of religious frenzy and sexual abandonment.

The film's most famous scene is Zeke's climactic pursuit of Hot Shot through the swamp. Vidor deliberately exaggerated the sounds of the swamp as Hot Shot flees from a vengeful Zeke. The cries of the birds and the lapping of the water intermingle with the lights and shadows that play on the figures of the men. Many years later, Vidor said, "Never one to treat a dramatic effect literally, the thought struck me—why not free the imagination and record this sequence impressionistically? When someone stepped on a broken branch, we made it sound as if bones were breaking. As the pursued victim withdrew his foot from the stickiness of the mud, we made the vacuum sound strong enough to pull him into hell" (Kobal, *Gotta Sing, Gotta Dance*).

The film gains strength through the spirituals, work songs, and traditional songs that are heard on the soundtrack at various points, including "Swing Low, Sweet Chariot," "Going Home," and "Swanee River." Unfortunately, against Vidor's wishes, the studio insisted on adding several songs by Irving Berlin to the finished film: "At the End of the Road," sung by the workers at the cotton mill, and "The Swanee Shuffle," sung and danced by Chick in her effort to seduce Zeke. Although they are not overly jarring, they seem an unnecessary intrusion on the overall mood and style of the film.

Rouben Mamoulian, the third important director of musicals in the early sound period, came to motion pictures with a growing reputation as an innovative stage director. His Theatre Guild production of *Porgy,* the play that would provide the basis for George Gershwin's 1935 folk opera, *Porgy and Bess,* had been tremendously successful in the fall of 1927. Approached by Paramount's Jesse Lasky and Walter Wanger to direct *Applause,* a musical drama of an aging burlesque queen, he agreed, provided that he be allowed to experiment with a more flexible camera than the new sound films ordinarily used. He was interested in unchaining the camera and moving it not only into the flashy façade of the burlesque world but also into its shabby corners and byways.

Applause *(Paramount, 1929). Kitty Darling (Helen Morgan), browbeaten and no longer young, gamely dances on the burlesque runway with her none-too-appealing colleagues. The film depicted the backstage milieu as harsh and joyless.*

opposite: Applause *(Paramount, 1929). In Rouben Mamoulian's landmark film, Kitty Darling (Helen Morgan) sings a plaintive rendition of "What Wouldn't I Do for That Man" to the photograph of her unscrupulous lover, Hitch.*

From its famous opening—burlesque star Kitty Darling giving birth in her dressing room—which swiftly establishes the main character and her milieu, to a final ironic shot after her death, showing her young smiling face on an old poster, *Applause* proved to be a landmark film with important implications for the development of sound. Its story is basically trite: Kitty (Helen Morgan, the legendary torch singer in her first film) is a worn, browbeaten singer-stripper under the thumb of her brutish lover, Hitch (Fuller Mellish, Jr.). Her life finally collapses when her convent-bred daughter (Joan Peers) joins her and discovers the sordid truth about her mother's life. The daughter ultimately finds true love with a young sailor, but Kitty commits suicide.

Applause does not have a pretty tale to tell, and, to Mamoulian's credit, he insisted on keeping it harsh and uncompromising, without studio gloss. Paramount wanted to glamorize Helen Morgan, but Mamoulian refused to allow it, and she is photographed as blowsy and unattractive from first frame to last. Nor are the other chorines in Morgan's burlesque show any more appealing; Mamoulian never softens their coarse appearance as they sing, "Come on—get a load of lovin' from a red-hot mama." Toward the end of the film, Kitty's daughter lifts a glass of water in a restaurant, and the picture dissolves to Kitty making an identical movement as she lifts a glass of poison to her lips.

Throughout the film, Mamoulian works to give his first sound film the virtue of motion, not only in the movement of the camera within a scene, but also in the swift way he segues from period to period, without cumbersome transitions. Kitty considers sending her daughter to a convent school, and we cut quickly to a close-up of the hands of a nun, who is talking to the child in a convent garden. A lapse of seventeen years is covered by a cut from Kitty's reading of an old love letter from Hitch to her reading of a letter from her daughter, now an innocent teenager.

Mamoulian also helped to move sound forward when he insisted on filming in one shot a scene in which Kitty sings a lullaby while her daughter simultaneously whispers a prayer. He was told that it couldn't be done—"you can't record the song and the prayer on one mike and one channel." Mamoulian replied, "Why not use *two* mikes and *two* channels and combine the two tracks in printing?" (Milne, *Mamoulian*). Despite opposition by the cameraman, the scene was recorded as Mamoulian wanted it, and the technique became common practice.

Several years later, Mamoulian was approached by Paramount head Adolph Zukor, who pleaded with him to direct a new musical film which would be diametrically opposite to the bleak burlesque world of *Applause*. The studio needed to keep its biggest musical stars, Jeanette MacDonald and Maurice Chevalier, constantly before the cameras in popular romantic musicals to prevent Paramount from toppling over the brink of bankruptcy on which it was precariously perched. At first Mamoulian was reluctant to work on a frivolous MacDonald-Chevalier vehicle, but he finally agreed. He asked Richard Rodgers and Lorenz Hart to write songs for the film. It was Mamoulian's firm belief that the place of the songs in the

Love Me Tonight *(Paramount, 1932)*. Pining Princess Jeanette *(Jeanette MacDonald)* is told by her doctor *(Joseph Cawthorn)*: "You're not wasted away. You're just wasted!"

Love Me Tonight *(Paramount, 1932)*. Mistaken for a baron, tailor Maurice Courtelin *(Maurice Chevalier)* enjoys the attentions of Countess Valentine *(Myrna Loy)*, while Princess Jeanette *(Jeanette MacDonald)* looks on apprehensively. Loy makes the man-hungry Valentine a genuinely funny character. Someone asks her, "Do you ever think of anything but men?" "Certainly," she answers. "Schoolboys."

story should be determined even before the screenplay was written, and that the lyrics should advance the plot. "This is the way an original musical film should be developed," he said much later, adding that "it so seldom happens like this" (Parish, *The Jeanette MacDonald Story*). Despite some studio rumblings at his maverick attitude, Mamoulian proceeded to follow his own dictum to create *Love Me Tonight* (1932), one of the true masterpieces in the musical genre, and a film of durable wit, beauty, and sophistication.

The story is slender: the romance of a bored and frustrated princess and a tailor who is mistaken for a baron. But from first moment to last, *Love Me Tonight* sparkles in every facet. The film begins with shots of Paris early in the morning, as the sounds of the people, including the washerwomen, the street workers, and the shoemaker, take on a musical beat that intensifies as the city begins a new day. (A symphony of sound had also introduced Mamoulian's stage production of *Porgy*.) The camera moves to the apartment of Maurice Courtelin (Maurice Chevalier) and pauses with almost a wink at the straw hat hanging on the wall. Maurice comes on the scene to sing an exuberant "Song of Paree" ("You'll sell your wife and daughter/ For just one Latin Quarter!"). Several moments later, and we are enveloped in one of the most imaginative numbers in musical films. Maurice and a customer, enthusiastic about a suit, begin to talk in rhyme, then Maurice sings a chorus of "Isn't It Romantic?" which is taken up—in succession—by the customer, a taxi driver, a musician, a troop of marching soldiers, a violinist in a gypsy camp, and finally by Princess Jeanette in her castle. A song carried across space and time has established a link between hero and heroine in a way that is both cinematic and enchanting.

Jeanette's life in the castle is clearly unexciting since the only other inhabitants are her elderly uncle, the duke (C. Aubrey Smith); his nephew, the improvident Vicomte de Vareze (Charles Ruggles); three twittering aunts; and the Countess Valentine (Myrna Loy), who acts as a kind of chaperone to Jeanette but whose mind is occupied exclusively with one subject: men. Jeanette's only suitor is the woebegone Count de Savignac (Charles Butterworth in a hilarious performance), who falls on his flute after climbing a ladder to her balcony. ("I'll never be able to use it again," he mourns.) Also in the castle are some elderly dullards, cleverly filmed in slow motion, who play a seemingly endless game of bridge. Small wonder that, despite her protestations, Jeanette is attracted to the impertinent but romantic Maurice.

Love Me Tonight loses no time in bringing the lovers together. On his way to the castle to collect money from the vicomte for himself and his fellow merchants, Maurice spies Jeanette, driving her carriage as she sings Rodgers and Hart's lilting "Lover." He rushes to her aid when the carriage tips over, leaving her with a sprained ankle. Immediately smitten, he insists on calling her "Mimi" and sings the tune of that title, while her face registers shock, then amusement. Returning to the castle, she has one of her frequent fainting spells. (Someone asks Countess Valentine, "Can you go for a doctor?" "Certainly," she replies. "Bring him right in.") The doctor is convinced that her fainting spells are due to romantic deprivation. "You're not wasted away," he tells her. "You're just *wasted!*" (She has been a widow for three

years, and her late husband was seventy-two.)

Maurice arrives at the castle, and his presence is so exhilarating that nobody is suspicious when the vicomte, anxious to keep his debts a secret, introduces him as a baron. In a matter of minutes, the old duke, the vicomte, and even the aunts are joyfully reprising "Mimi." Jeanette pretends to be annoyed with Maurice, and when they go on a magnificently photographed deer hunt, she deliberately gives him the wildest horse. Later, he joins Jeanette in a moonlit garden, where she has another convenient fainting spell but then finally confesses that she really loves him. Their duet of the title song has a romantic ardor that is almost palpable.

However, Maurice makes the mistake of criticizing the work of a seamstress, and he is forced to confess that he is actually a tailor. Consternation spreads throughout the castle as everyone sings "The Son of a Gun Is Nothing but a Tailor!" (In her amazement, one aunt drops a vase, which sounds like exploding dynamite when it crashes to the floor, another example of Mamoulian's use of sound for comic effect.) Maurice leaves the castle and boards the train for Paris. Jeanette races on horseback to catch the train as we see a montage of horse's hoofs and whirring train wheels. In an audacious scene, she stands on the track boldly, with her hands on her hips, defying the train to hit her. (She is also defying social convention.) Of course the lovers are reunited.

Whereas Lubitsch's sophistication occasionally takes on a sourish flavor, Mamoulian mocks the conventions of operetta with affection and the lightest of hearts. The viewer's spirits are lifted at hearing C. Aubrey Smith sing a chorus of "Mimi," or Jeanette's aunts clucking like demented hens at every dilemma, and there is authentic film magic in the sequence of the deer hunt as the music captures the movement of both the pursued and the pursuer as they race against the landscape. Mamoulian also extracted first-rate performances from every member of the cast; he drew from MacDonald and Chevalier the charm and sparkle they would match two years later in Ernst Lubitsch's *The Merry Widow*.

Orchids in a field of common daisies, the musical films of Ernst Lubitsch and Rouben Mamoulian were exquisite creations that brought wit and style to the genre. Most moviegoers, however, were unaware of the orchids and getting increasingly tired of picking daisies. The seemingly nonstop din of musical numbers in 1929 and 1930 was already more of a low hum by 1931. Only a fraction of the number of musical movies produced during the first years of sound could be seen that year, and many of them played to half-empty houses. In those bleak days of the Depression, audiences preferred the Western spectacle of *Cimarron,* the folksy comedy of *Min and Bill,* and the hard-bitten melodrama of *Little Caesar* and *The Public Enemy*.

Just ahead was another revolution in the Hollywood musical. It would be triggered by a man called "Buzz," and the rat-tat-tat of the soundtrack would be caused not by machine guns but by the dancing feet of his "little nifties from the fifties" and those "shady ladies from the eighties." The avenue he was taking us to was a mythical place called "naughty, gaudy, bawdy" Forty-second Street.

PART II
GETTING
AWAY FROM IT ALL
1933~1939

Busby Berkeley and the Warner Brothers
The Peerless Pair: Astaire and Rogers
On the Good Ship 20th Century-Fox
MGM Grandiose and Glittering Goldwyn
Their Voices Raised in Song
Bing and Paramount

BUSBY BERKELEY
AND THE
WARNER BROTHERS

In 1932, the musical film was virtually moribund. Exhibitors were marking their theater displays with signs announcing that their latest attraction was *not* a musical. "All-singing, all-dancing" generally meant poor business, and most producers were either dismissing their musical stars or putting them into nonmusical films. (They were even deleting musical numbers from completed films.) During the year, only three musicals of any consequence were released: two champagne cocktails with Jeanette MacDonald and Maurice Chevalier (*Love Me Tonight* and *One Hour with You*), and *The Big Broadcast,* the first of Paramount's helter-skelter all-star revues.

But at Warner Bros., executive production head Darryl F. Zanuck sensed that it might be time to revive the musical genre. With the country at the deepest point of the Depression, he felt that the public was ready for escape into a fantasy world where breadlines were replaced by chorus lines and money was made not by selling apples but by selling songs and dances on a mammoth theater stage. A lavish musical film could hardly make hunger and desperation vanish, but for ninety minutes or so, it could mute the pain in a burst of laughter and music.

Of course Zanuck knew that he would meet stiff resistance from the Warner brothers. When Zanuck asked, "Don't you believe we're ready to go into a musical cycle again?" he was not surprised by the emphatic "No!" The Warners had invested heavily in musical films during the first years of sound, even adding expensive color to many of the movies, but now, one of the brothers told him, "We can't even *give* them away!" (Gussow, *Don't Say Yes Until I Finish Talking*). However, Zanuck was not about to give up. He moved to make a new musical film—without the knowledge and consent of the embattled brothers. The title was *42nd Street.*

Three years earlier, among the rash of early musicals about the tribulations of "putting on a show," Zanuck had produced *On with the Show*. It featured a starstruck hatcheck girl (Sally O'Neil) who is sent onstage for her crucial opening night with the line "Go on and give them everything you've got!" With Zanuck's aid, writers-in-residence Rian James and James Seymour fashioned a screenplay that used some of the *On with the Show*

elements but added a tartness and cynicism born of the Depression. Harry Warren and Al Dubin supplied the bracing tunes—they also appeared in the film briefly—and Zanuck assembled a cast of veterans and newcomers. It included Dick Powell, a former band vocalist who had made two films for Warners; Bebe Daniels, adept at playing independent-minded or hardened women, and nearing the end of a long Hollywood career; George Brent, a dependable though stolid leading man; and Ginger Rogers, a vivacious redhead who had already appeared in twelve movies in only three years. To play the leading ingenue opposite Dick Powell, Zanuck signed Ruby Keeler, a singer and dancer from the New York stage, and the wife of Al Jolson since 1928. For the central role of the ailing, driven director of the show, he chose Warner Baxter, a popular actor who had worked in films since 1918.

When Mervyn LeRoy became ill, the film's direction was assigned to Lloyd Bacon, a prolific member of the Warners team who had directed Al Jolson in *The Singing Fool*. Although Bacon moved the cast through its paces with professional ease, he has become the "forgotten man" of the film. To direct the musical numbers, Zanuck hired a well-known dance director named Busby Berkeley. Highly regarded for his work in Broadway musicals of the twenties, including several by Richard Rodgers and Lorenz Hart, Berkeley had come to Hollywood in 1930 to work for Samuel Goldwyn on the film version of Florenz Ziegfeld's musical comedy *Whoopee,* starring Eddie Cantor. With the decline of the film musical, he was preparing to return to New York City, when he was summoned to stage the musical numbers for *42nd Street.*

Feisty and often abrasive, Berkeley was obsessed with his camera art. From the beginning, he was convinced that there were "unlimited things" one could do with a camera. With his very first movie, *Whoopee,* he had realized that the camera had only one eye: "That came to me wonderfully and naturally. I felt the camera intuitively" (Pike and Martin, *The Genius of Busby Berkeley*). From that point on, he used a single camera to film his spectacular musical sequences, rather than the traditional four cameras, which shot film from various angles, to be

page 64: *A Busby Berkeley formation from the water ballet in* Footlight Parade *(Warners, 1933).*

page 66: *42nd Street (Warners, 1933). In the title number, Ruby Keeler poses before the moving skyline of New York City.*

opposite, above: 42nd Street *(Warners, 1933). Hard-driving director Julian Marsh (Warner Baxter) watches attentively as the company juvenile Billy Lawler (Dick Powell) and star Dorothy Brock (Bebe Daniels), backed by the chorus, rehearse a number from his show* Pretty Lady.

opposite, center: 42nd Street *(Warners, 1933). Temperamental star Dorothy Brock (Bebe Daniels) is comforted by boyfriend Pat Denning (George Brent) and admonished by director Julian Marsh (Warner Baxter) for spraining her ankle on the eve of opening night. She is about to give up her starring role to young Peggy Sawyer (Ruby Keeler). The situation became part of musical film lore.*

opposite, below: 42nd Street *(Warners, 1933). Under Busby Berkeley's direction, "those dancing feet" tap out the title tune. With its cinematic imagination and its audacious combination of music and melodrama, this number was a precursor to the many others that Berkeley would create in the next few years.*

assembled afterward by the cutter. Berkeley concentrated on shooting each sequence in the actual way it appeared on the screen. He would visualize an entire number ahead of time, arranging it on yellow sheets of paper covered with pencil marks and notations—his personal "blueprints"—and then edit the number in the camera. Suddenly the proscenium arch vanished, to be replaced by Berkeley's purely cinematic world of kaleidoscopic patterns, smiling chorines in startling close-up, and visual effects both beautiful and bizarre. To this musical mix he frequently added the kind of hearty vulgarity and unabashed eroticism that was a trademark of Warners films in the early thirties.

Completed at a cost of $379,000, *42nd Street* was finally ready to be screened for Jack Warner. Zanuck recalls Warner's reaction: "He went out of his mind. He never knew until it was screened that it was a musical. Only one thing, he loved it" (Gussow, *Don't Say Yes Until I Finish Talking*). But brother Harry was in charge of finances, and he was the ultimate hurdle. After viewing the film in New York, Harry wired, "This is the greatest picture you've sent me in five years." Zanuck was vindicated, and *42nd Street* was released to acclaim and vast popularity.

For a movie that launched a new era in musical films, *42nd Street* wears its mantle of fame with an agreeable absence of pretension. One of its principal virtues is the screenplay, usually overlooked in the emphasis on Berkeley's production numbers. The script, laced with sardonic lines, is often funny, and it is forthright in its unglamorized look at life behind the footlights. The film also has in Julian Marsh, "the greatest musical comedy director in America," a central character of surprising depth for a lighthearted musical. (Marsh was modeled after Julian Mitchell, a well-known director for Florenz Ziegfeld.) Ill and weary, bitter at his fair-weather friends and the women who took his money, Marsh is still driven to put on one more musical extravaganza. And his swan song, *Pretty Lady,* is a success, despite his having to replace the temperamental leading lady (Bebe Daniels) with a raw kid out of the chorus (Ruby Keeler). Warner Baxter plays the role with a brooding intensity that, in the film's closing shot, ends in his exhausted satisfaction as he listens to the accolades for the last musical he will ever stage.

Throughout the movie, Marsh rehearses the chorus with a ferocity that conveys some of the desperation theater people must feel in the face of countless obstacles. "You're gonna work days, nights," he bellows. "You're gonna work until your feet fall off!" And when he recruits Peggy Sawyer (Ruby Keeler) to play the leading role, he pushes her to the edge of collapse in order to turn her into a star—a herculean task considering the very modest singing and dancing talents of Ruby Keeler. (More than three decades later, Keeler disarmed an audience at a retrospective showing of a Berkeley musical by declaring, "I couldn't act. I had that terrible singing voice, and now I see I wasn't the greatest tap dancer in the world either.") He tells her, "I'm gonna have a live leading lady or a dead chorus girl." His last words to her are part of movie lore: "You're going out a youngster but you've got to come back a star!"

The idea that life in the theater, especially the Broadway theater, was a bed of hard nails had filtered down through the years: success on the stage was elusive, heartbreak and disappointment were always waiting in the wings. (*Fame* and *A Chorus Line* are contemporary expressions of this idea.) Nevertheless, audiences continued to believe in the theater's glamour and romance, and, at least in the movies, a standing ovation was the performer's ultimate reward for all the pain and sorrow. Yet, although Peggy Sawyer triumphs and *Pretty Lady* is a smash hit, *42nd Street* was somehow different—different from its direct source, *On with the Show,* and its most important predecessor, *The Broadway Melody.*

Despite all the ebullient singing and dancing, the year was 1933, and the specter of the Depression still loomed large throughout the country. Its continued presence can be seen and felt in many of the nonmusical portions of *42nd Street*. The air in the theater rehearsing *Pretty Lady* is faintly acrid, not only with smoke and perspiration, but with fear. (Will the show fold before it opens?) The wisecracks are funny, but they are often harsh and blunt—"She makes forty-five dollars a week and sends her mother a hundred of it." Marsh's badgering of the cast hides a man at the end of his tether. (At the close of a grueling day, he tells his assistant Andy, "I'm not a machine. Come on home with me. I'm lonesome.") However glancingly, *42nd Street* acknowledged the world beyond the footlights, becoming not only a turning point in the musical film but a beacon for the immediate future.

Musically, the movie marks time until the last reel, although early in the film Bebe Daniels gets to sing and dance to "You're Getting to Be a Habit with Me," a tune that might have raised a few eyebrows—and hackles—a few decades later with its references to drug addiction. Berkeley reserves his elaborate effects for the production numbers that are part of Julian Marsh's show. The first is "Shuffle Off to Buffalo," which has newlyweds Ruby Keeler and Clarence Nordstrom all atwitter on their honeymoon express—the Niagara Limited—as they sing the slightly ribald lyrics, only to be separated when the train jackknifes into many berths. Occupying these berths are Berkeley chorines who offer up cynical comments on the newlyweds. In the next number, Dick Powell informs us that he's "Young and Healthy," whereupon scores of chorus boys and girls on revolving turntables—the first ever used in films—form kaleidoscopic patterns, some of them photographed from above in Berkeley's well-known "top shots." In an astonishing closing shot, the camera moves between the straddled legs of the chorus girls to pick up Dick Powell and the number's most prominent blonde, chubby Toby Wing.

It was the title number, closing the film, that attracted the most attention and established Berkeley as the master of a new type of musical. Like the celebrated "Lullaby of Broadway" that was to follow in a few years, "42nd Street" is a mini-drama that moves to the beat of New York City's raffish but seductive night life (or night life as the paying customer imagines it to be). It begins with Ruby Keeler in close-up, singing of "naughty, gaudy, bawdy 42nd Street," then taking off her long skirt to do a tap dance atop a taxi. The camera pulls back to reveal the entire street and its residents: a doorman, a nursemaid, a newsboy, and many others. In an upstairs room, a man suddenly attacks a girl, and in terror she leaps from the window, not only landing on her feet but also picking up the dance beat with a passerby. Her

Gold Diggers of 1933 *(Warners, 1933). For the opening number, "We're in the Money," Ginger Rogers led the Berkeley girls, wearing coin-covered costumes, in a dance with oversized coins. The number was a giddy pretense that the Depression was over at last. (It wasn't.) Rogers claims that her reprise in pig Latin was suggested by Darryl Zanuck, who heard her having fun with it on the set.*

opposite: Gold Diggers of 1933 *(Warners, 1933). Two formations from Busby Berkeley's "Shadow Waltz" number. While it was being filmed, there was an earthquake in Los Angeles that shook the set and almost injured some of the chorines. The entire soundstage was plunged into darkness.*

lover comes hurtling from the house and stabs her to death. Without pausing to linger on the crime, Berkeley brings out a bevy of chorus girls who tap-dance down the street in one of those close-order military formations he dearly loved. Joined by dancing boys, they form the Manhattan skyline out of painted boards. Perched atop a skyscraper are Ruby and Dick, smiling and waving to the audience. Public response to the number and the film was enthusiastic.

Inevitably, many of the people who had helped make *42nd Street* a success were reunited for the next musical film, *Gold Diggers of 1933*. The leads were again played by Ruby Keeler and Dick Powell, the new darlings of romantic moviegoers who found Keeler's pert Irish charm more relevant than her thin, nasal voice, heavy-footed dancing, and flat line readings, and were not put off by Powell's fruity tenor voice. (Fruity tenor voices were in season.) Ginger Rogers was back, this time playing an ambitious chorine appropriately named Fay Fortune. Mervyn LeRoy was assigned to direct, and Harry Warren and Al Dubin, clutching a new seven-year contract with Warners, were asked to write another musical score. Busby Berkeley was given free rein to create even more elaborate musical numbers.

As before, Warners reached into its past for the story line of *Gold Diggers of 1933*. The plot was derived from Avery Hopwood's play *The Gold Diggers,* which had been filmed by the studio in 1923 and again in 1929 as *The Gold Diggers of Broadway.* The latest variation centered on three down-on-their-luck actresses who become involved with a haughty Bostonian and his young song-writing brother. Not surprisingly, the story included the birth pangs of a new Broadway musical.

To carry out this narrative, other members of the hardworking Warners stock company were called into service. As the brother who gets bamboozled by the girls, the studio cast Warren William of the vulpine features and natty mustache. Expert comedienne Joan Blondell, who had already appeared in more than twenty movies in only three years, played the tough-minded but warmhearted Carol. And Aline MacMahon, later to be revered as a leading character actress, was Trixie, the gold digger with the sharpest tongue. Also on hand were Ned Sparks of the sour visage and monotone voice, and Guy Kibbee, this time as a soft-headed associate of Warren William.

The film begins with one of the most famous images of the time: Ginger Rogers, wearing a skimpy coin-covered costume, regales an audience that probably knew better with the joyous news that "We're in the Money." It was not uncommon for films of the period to insist that things were improving, and in the following year, the musical *Stand Up and Cheer* actually proclaimed the end of the Depression. Here, Rogers is delightfully oblivious to reality as she tells everyone that "the long-lost dollar has come back to the fold!" She is joined by chorus girls, similarly dressed, and they dance about the stage, forming patterns with oversized coins, including Berkeley's familiar "writhing snake" effect.

In "Pettin' in the Park," the first number in the projected show, Berkeley engages Powell and Keeler—and a crowd of park-goers—in a song-and-dance routine that is not likely to win a Good Taste Award with its amorous chimpanzees, a leering midget dressed as an infant, and chorus girls in metallic bathing

Gold Diggers of 1933 *(Warners, 1933). In the closing moment of the number "Remember My Forgotten Man," Joan Blondell raises her arms imploringly, surrounded by the silhouettes of marching soldiers and the pleading figures of the "forgotten" men. The New York Times was not impressed by the number, castigating its "shabby theme of bogus sentimentality."*

suits. Fortunately, things improve with the two numbers that close the film. In "The Shadow Waltz" Berkeley created an extravaganza that literally turned chorus girls into instruments of his imagination. It begins with a blonde Ruby Keeler dancing around Dick Powell as he croons the song to her, a violin in his hands. Blonde chorus girls wearing wide three-tiered skirts suddenly emerge to "play" their violins in a lavish white setting. The violins, illuminated by neon tubing, form glowing patterns in the darkness, after which the girls, like the violins, are arranged in their own kaleidoscopic patterns. At the close they join to form one giant violin, mechanistic elements no more human than the violins they are carrying. In a sense, this was the first true evidence of Berkeley's penchant for occasionally turning people into objects without individuality, with no other purpose than fitting them into his grand design. Because of this, critics often accused him of dehumanizing the musical film, although they tended to ignore the sardonic chorines or despairing war veterans of his other numbers.

The movie's final number, one of the best-remembered of all Berkeley creations, is "Remember My Forgotten Man," a bold plea on behalf of the many desperate, poverty-stricken war veterans on the country's breadlines. Paradoxically, the movie began by denying the Depression ("We've got a lot of what it takes to get along") and ended by deploring its devastating effect. Before the number begins, Berkeley himself makes an appearance, shouting, "Everybody on stage for the 'Forgotten Man' number!" When the curtain rises, Joan Blondell, dressed in the traditional tight slit skirt of the prostitute, is seen leaning against a lamppost. Talk-singing the lyrics, she bitterly condemns the viewers for sending her man to war, then deserting him in his hour of need. Black singer Etta Moten reprises the song beautifully, and we see the desolate faces of other suffering women. A policeman pulls in a staggering drunkard, but recoils in shame when Blondell points out the man's service medal. In a startling image, uniformed men marching in a ticker-tape parade suddenly change to men in a breadline. Soldiers march in silhouette on a half-wheel, and then men with haggard faces stride accusingly toward the audience as the song is reprised.

Footlight Parade, the third of Warners's backstage musical spectacles for 1933, repeated the successful formula: a "let's-put-on-a-show" story line, several opulent Berkeley production numbers, and a by-now familiar cast headed by Dick Powell, Ruby Keeler, and Joan Blondell. The most important newcomer was the star: James Cagney. As Chester Kent, the scrappy producer of "prologues" (short stage presentations between film showings), Cagney was playing his fourteenth film role and the first that gave him a chance to sing and dance. (He had appeared in the chorus of Broadway musicals and had danced in vaudeville with his wife.) Endlessly in motion, his light, distinctive voice threatening, exhorting, or cajoling others, he brought vitality to a film that sorely needed it in its narrative portions.

The plot was simple: After musical shows go out of fashion because of talking films, Kent turns to producing prologues, but the obstacles are formidable, personally and professionally. When he finally manages to put together three prologues, they are clearly not designed for any existing stage but for

Footlight Parade *(Warners, 1933). The "human fountain" that closes the astonishing number "By a Waterfall." Twenty thousand gallons of water were pumped into the pool every minute, and plate-glass corridors were built underneath the pool so that Berkeley could light and shoot it from the bottom.*

opposite, below: Footlight Parade *(Warners, 1933). Looking for his beloved "Shanghai Lil," James Cagney gets into a brawl in a sleazy bar. The musical number had its absurdities, but it was brilliant in its bold evocation of a corrupt milieu and in its audacious use of the camera. Berkeley plunges headlong into the action, panning across the smirking faces at the bar and tracking through the brawl with relish for every blow or broken piece of furniture.*

Fashions of 1934 *(Warners, 1934). A hallucinatory moment from the musical number "Spin a Little Web of Dreams." In "The Hall of Human Harps," one of several tableaux arranged by Busby Berkeley, befeathered girls became live adornments on a group of enormous harps. The number prompted one outraged mother to write an article entitled "I Don't Want My Daughter Growing Up to Be a Human Harp."*

Warners's massive facilities and Berkeley's camera wizardry. The first, "Honeymoon Hotel," echoes "Shuffle Off to Buffalo" in its leering approach to a pair of hapless newlyweds—Ruby Keeler and Dick Powell—who arrive at the emporium where "Cupid is the night clerk," and everyone, including the hotel employees and the usual contingent of saucy blondes, has a sardonic comment to offer.

The second prologue is quintessential Berkeley. In a sylvan setting, Dick Powell croons the song "By a Waterfall" to a rapt Ruby, then dozes off. Presumably to douse the flame sparked by his ardent singing, Ruby changes into a bathing suit and leaps into a huge pool. Behind her are one hundred chorines gamboling in a giant waterfall, swimming, splashing, and waving to the camera. There are frequent close-ups of their smiling faces. In the style that Berkeley would later use for several Esther Williams aquacades, they form various patterns, including a flower, a wheel, and the ubiquitous snake. The number ends with a view of an incredible revolving human fountain, as the camera pulls back to reveal the entire opulent setting.

The final number is a heady mixture of the exotic, the erotic, and the bizarre. In "Shanghai Lil," James Cagney plays a sailor looking for his lost love, the elusive Lil. He comes into a sleazy bar, choked with sailors and prostitutes, where everyone takes turns singing about Lil. One of the girls remarks, "That Oriental is detrimental to our industry," and it is clear that she doesn't mean canning mandarin oranges. A brawl ensues in which John Garfield, in his first appearance on film, is clearly visible. When Shanghai Lil turns up, she is Ruby Keeler, looking about as Oriental as Maureen O'Hara. "I miss you velly much a long time," she tells her sailor, and they dance together on top of a table. There is a call to arms, and Cagney joins the sailors in a march to their boat. In succession, the sailors form the images of the American flag, President Franklin D. Roosevelt, and the NRA eagle. Lil, now in sailor's uniform, turns to wink at the camera. She and Cagney flip a deck of cards to show an animated boat going out to sea.

The year 1933 had seen three popular musical films in a row, and with audiences continuing to express their approval at the box office, Warners was encouraged to continue. The following year, under Ray Enright's direction, the studio produced *Dames,* which contains some of Berkeley's best work. The plot was something of a nuisance, involving an eccentric millionaire (Hugh Herbert), his fawning relatives (Guy Kibbee and ZaSu Pitts), their daughter (Ruby Keeler), and an incorrigible song-writing nephew (Dick Powell). Joan Blondell was present again as a gold-digging chorus girl. But once more the story was merely a peg on which to hang the musical numbers, which are cleverly conceived, though not immune from Berkeley's usual lapses in taste. In "The Girl at the Ironing Board," Joan Blondell leads a group of blonde laundresses in a song and dance that has them using men's long underwear and pajamas as movable props. (Joan Blondell was seven months pregnant at the time and had to wear a large apron to hide her bulging stomach.) The staging of "I Only Have Eyes for You" is both preposterous and enchanting. Dick and Ruby fall asleep on a subway train, and Dick dreams of seeing Ruby's image repeated to infinity (actually chorus girls wearing masks). At the end, the girls, each with a board strapped to her back, come together to form a huge jigsaw puzzle of Ruby's face.

In the most effective production number, staged to Dick Powell's rendition of the title song, Berkeley has the audience play voyeur: he moves his chorines through a single day, showing them waking up, exercising, bathing, and putting on their makeup. Finally, after dancing with their stage-door Johnnies and engaging in some playful business with perfume, the girls get their reward: close-ups of each of their smiling faces. The number ends with a display of Berkeley's abstract patterns, including one striking sequence in which he used reverse action, a trick effect achieved by running film backward in the camera, to give the effect that the girls were flying straight up from the floor into the camera lens!

Berkeley staged the production numbers for two other 1934 musicals from Warners. In *Wonder Bar,* Al Jolson returned after a three-year absence from the studio to star as the proprietor of a popular Montmartre nightclub called the Wonder Bar. A kind of musical *Grand Hotel,* the movie concerned the romantic and melodramatic encounters that take place at the club. At several points the churning plot pauses to permit Berkeley to indulge in several lavish fantasies. In "Goin' to Heaven on a Mule," Jolson plays a black Southern field hand who dreams of going to a heaven that embodies every cliché concerning the simple-minded, illiterate, happy-go-lucky "darkie" who adores pork chops, watermelon, and possum pie. It is a well-mounted number, but one without a shred of sensitivity.

The film's *pièce de résistance* is Berkeley's staging of the Dubin-Warren song "Don't Say Goodnight," which is first sung by Dick Powell, then danced by Dolores Del Rio and Ricardo Cortez. The number features some of Berkeley's most imaginative effects: dancers whirling about the stage with a number of tall, white, movable columns, or waltzing through a forest in a shower of falling leaves, or (most striking of all) caught up in a series of mirrors that create the illusion of a vast number of dancers.

The following year marked a turning point for Berkeley. For a long time, he had wanted to direct an entire film rather than merely the musical numbers, and he was given the chance with *Gold Diggers of 1935.* For this film, he not only attended to story matters but also created his greatest number, "The Lullaby of Broadway."

In this edition, the "gold diggers" include not only the usual mercenary dames but virtually every member of the cast. Among the schemers who swarm about a posh summer hotel are a stingy millionairess (Alice Brady) and her children (Gloria Stuart, Frank McHugh), an eccentric, impoverished Russian impresario (Adolphe Menjou), and practically the entire hotel staff, which proclaims its easy corruptibility in an amusing opening number. Dick Powell plays an amiable desk clerk in love with Stuart.

The story tends to sag, but it is only partly due to Berkeley's inability to give it the pace and vigor that Lloyd Bacon managed in *42nd Street* or even *Footlight Parade.* The days of unlimited extravagance at Warners were coming to an end. Less money was available for elaborate musical numbers, and so more footage had to be given to the narrative portions. In fact, there are only three numbers in the movie, as compared to five in most of the other

Dames *(Warners, 1934). Four of the Berkeley beauties* (top) *who appeared in the famous title sequence, in which the director formed some of his most striking kaleidoscopic patterns* (above).

Dames *(Warners, 1934). In the musical number built around the song "I Only Have Eyes for You," lovers Ruby Keeler and Dick Powell fall asleep on a subway train* (top), *and chorus girls wearing masks of Ruby appear in Dick's dream* (above). *At the close of the number, the girls, each with a board strapped to her back, come together to form a huge jigsaw puzzle of Ruby's face. In between, the Berkeley girls formed various symmetrical patterns* (left).

following pages: Wonder Bar *(Warners, 1934). For this extraordinary musical number, "Don't Say Goodnight," Berkeley built an octagon of mirrors—each twenty-eight feet high and sixteen feet wide—that reflected the dancers and appeared to carry them into infinity. To keep the camera from being reflected in the mirrors, a hole was dug in the stage floor, and the cameraman lay flat on his stomach underneath the stage, crawling and moving around slowly with the turning of the camera.*

Berkeley films. In one, a number ostensibly produced for Alice Brady's annual charity show, Dick Powell croons "The Words Are in My Heart" as he takes Gloria Stuart for a moonlight ride in a motorboat. This is followed by another of Berkeley's intricately planned extravaganzas. The number features fifty-six blondes in evening gowns, pretending to play the white baby grand pianos that are moved about a shiny black floor to form various geometric arrangements. At one point they all come together to form one giant piano.

Fortunately, Berkeley returned to the human factor for "The Lullaby of Broadway." It is the one Berkeley number that never fails to astonish and delight audiences. Like the title number in *42nd Street,* it offers a mordant view of life and death in New York City's nighttime world. The number begins with singer Wini Shaw's face as a small white dot on a black screen. As her face moves into a close-up, she sings the melody of "The Lullaby of Broadway," foreshadowing the tale of a "Broadway baby" who "won't sleep tight/ until the dawn." Her upturned face dissolves into an aerial view of Manhattan, and then into Wini's story as she arrives at her tenement home after a night on the town. A quick feeding of her kitten, a day of sleep, and then another night of revelry, this time with top-hatted Dick Powell. In a massive nightclub, where Wini and Dick appear to be the only guests, two Latin dancers whirl to a softer version of the song, then each leads an army of boys and girls in a display of precision tap dancing. The scene becomes abandoned, and Dick and Wini are drawn into the turbulent action. When Wini runs onto a balcony to escape the crowd, she stumbles and falls screaming to her death. As the chorus sings in hushed tones, we move back to the New York scene, stopping at the girl's now vacant room, where her kitten mews helplessly for milk. The aerial view of Manhattan reverts to an overhead shot of Wini's face as she finishes the song. Her face dissolves into the same small white dot in the darkness.

As a cautionary tale of the dangers of life in a big city, "The Lullaby of Broadway" is not to be taken seriously. But as a self-contained segment of cinematic brilliance, it is without peer in the sound period. Here, Berkeley's photographic dexterity works not to design geometric patterns with no more feeling than an equation but to convey a hedonistic life-style that ends in tragedy. The sequence in the nightclub is especially remarkable, as the relentless precision tapping of the dancers takes on a sinister tone, and the crowd rushing to sweep Wini and Dick with them becomes a frightening mob, forcing Wini to seek shelter on the balcony.

Since limitless funds for Berkeley's effulgences were no longer available, only one musical—*Gold Diggers of 1937* (1936) —could claim a production number that approached his usual scope. This was the finale, constructed around the song "All's Fair in Love and War," in which men and women coyly conduct a mock war. Naturally, "No Man's Land" is separated from "No Woman's Land," and the women's principal weapon is perfume. The film had a few other bright songs, especially "With Plenty of Money and You," but the plot was a dull and rather nasty business concerning an insurance agent (Dick Powell) who has to protect the million-dollar policy drawn on the life of a wealthy theatrical producer (Victor Moore).

Until Berkeley left Warners for MGM in 1939, none of his

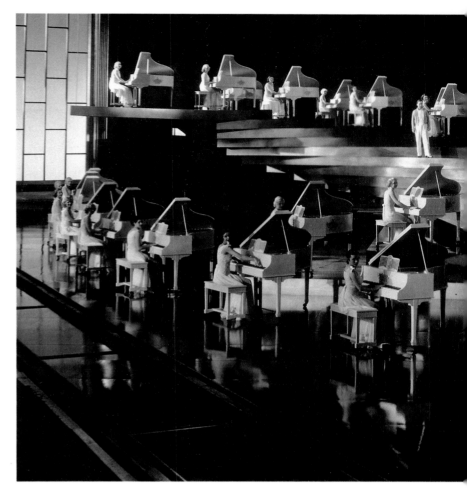

above: Gold Diggers of 1935 *(Warners, 1935). Nicoleff (Adolphe Menjou), a self-styled Russian "impresario," attempts to teach the girls his own eccentric version of classical ballet. A futile endeavor, since the final show becomes a "modern" Berkeley extravaganza.*

above, center: Gold Diggers of 1935 *(Warners, 1935). Director Busby Berkeley, standing at stage center, rehearses the musical number "The Words Are in My Heart," in which the girls "play" white baby grand pianos that move to form geometric arrangements. To shift the instruments, Berkeley placed a small man dressed in black under each piano and had him carefully follow the black tape markings on the black floor.*

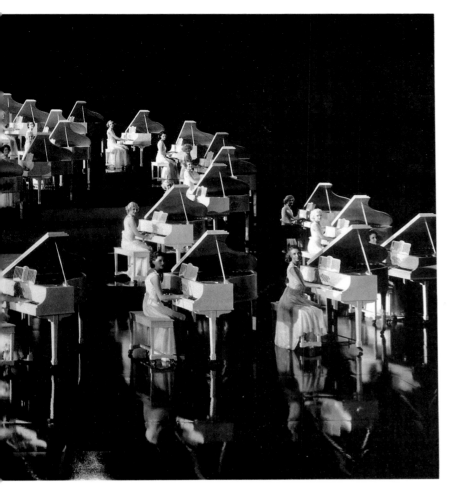

above: Flirtation Walk *(Warners, 1934). West Point cadet Dick Powell embraces general's daughter Ruby Keeler. This was the fifth teaming of America's "singing sweethearts."*

left: Gold Diggers of 1937 *(Warners, 1936). In the number "All's Fair in Love and War," Joan Blondell leads seventy helmeted, drum-playing, flag-waving girls through military drill formations, photographed from many angles.*

subsequent efforts matched his earlier work in size or ingenuity. He came closest in Ray Enright's *The Singing Marine* (1937), for which he staged an exotic musical sequence to the song "Night over Shanghai." Reminiscent of the "Shanghai Lil" number in *Footlight Parade,* it had Dick Powell observing the steamy night life in Shanghai, including a brawl and a killing. The number opened with a dramatic effect: the hands of harmonica virtuoso Larry Adler (appearing as a sinister Oriental all in black) were spotlighted as he played, giving them the appearance of startled butterflies.

In his six years at Warners, Berkeley had revitalized the musical genre, wrenching it almost single-handedly from the monotony and rigidity with which it had become afflicted. With his brash insistence on "trying anything that will work," he freed the camera to explore a new dimension in film and to become a collaborator in the action it photographed. With imagination and daring, he created cinematic effects that dazzle the senses. He could easily be accused of lapses in taste, and of dehumanizing performers, turning them into ciphers or geometric figures. It could also be said that the stars in the Berkeley stock company of the thirties never approached the skill or talent of their contemporaries in musical entertainment—such as Fred Astaire and Bing Crosby—or of the later musical figures—such as Judy Garland and Gene Kelly. Yet Berkeley remains a giant of the musical film whose finest numbers are rewarding to audiences who are willing to travel back to his vanished world of the thirties.

Berkeley himself offered this comment on his films: "You'll notice that I've always had terrific pace in my pictures. I never let them drag unless a slower pace or slowing down was called for in order to get something over to the audience dramatically. All of my pictures have to move. After all, it's motion pictures, and that means m-o-t-i-o-n." He added, "I wanted to do something new and different . . . something that had never been done before" (Pike and Martin, *The Genius of Busby Berkeley*).

He succeeded in his goal, and although his influence faded, the musical film was never quite the same.

Busby Berkeley's mammoth creations loomed largest among the Warners musicals of the thirties, but the studio produced many musical films without benefit of his services. A number of them, starring Dick Powell or Ruby Keeler or both, were agreeable efforts of more modest dimensions than the Berkeley spectaculars. Two of them, *Flirtation Walk* (1934) and *Shipmates Forever* (1935), reunited the singing sweethearts in military settings, under Frank Borzage's relaxed direction. *Flirtation Walk,* the better of the two, began in a Hawaiian setting, observed by Borzage in his characteristically romantic fashion, then moved to West Point for more military matters. The movie included some unusually extensive location work in both places. The highlights were an elaborate Hawaiian dance and a charming production of the title tune, staged at the academy's annual show. *Shipmates Forever,* filmed in part at the Naval Academy in Annapolis, offered Dick Powell as a crooner reluctant to follow in his admiral father's footsteps. Of course he is converted to patriotic fervor and wins the heart of dancing teacher Ruby Keeler, who resides at the academy. Aside from his return to Berkeley's fantasy world in *Gold Diggers of 1937,* Dick Powell was engaged in small-scale musical films at Warners for the rest of the decade, including

Broadway Gondolier (1935), Hearts Divided (1936), and Going Places (1938).

Away from Powell, Ruby Keeler was less active, but she managed to make a few more musicals before retiring from the screen. In *Go into Your Dance* (1935), she appeared as a nightclub dancer who helps an irresponsible Broadway star (husband Al Jolson) put on that inevitable show against heavy odds. The film featured Jolson's vigorous renditions of "She's a Latin from Manhattan" and "About a Quarter to Nine." Helen Morgan, shattered by years of alcoholism and beginning the final descent that would end in her death six years later, sang a poignant "The Little Things You Used to Do." *Ready, Willing and Able* (1937) had one delightful musical number in which Ruby Keeler and Lee Dixon dance across the keys of a giant typewriter to the tune of "Too Marvelous for Words."

Like much of the studio's nonmusical product, the Warners musical at its best had a brisk pace and a refreshing tendency not to take itself seriously, an attitude that MGM, for example, never seemed to grasp. But there is little doubt that its chief glory—and singular contribution to the genre of the musical film—lay in the dazzling, imaginative, and sometimes hallucinatory musical numbers of Busby Berkeley. Out of cinematic fantasies of geometrically arranged chorus girls, kinetic musical instruments, and settings of outlandish splendor, he fashioned a unique vision that continues to stun, amuse, enchant, and occasionally dismay audiences nearly half a century later.

Ready, Willing and Able *(Warners, 1937). Ruby Keeler and Lee Dixon dance across the giant keys of a typewriter to the song "Too Marvelous for Words." Dixon, a featured player at Warners for several years, reached the apex of his career six years later playing cowboy Will Parker in the original stage production of* Oklahoma!

opposite, above: Broadway Gondolier *(Warners, 1935). Joan Blondell and Dick Powell in one of the more modest Warners musicals of the period. Powell played a singing cab driver who achieves fame on radio by pretending to be an authentic Venetian gondolier.*

opposite, center: Hearts Divided *(Warners, 1936). Baltimore girl Betsy Patterson (Marion Davies) confronts Napoleon Bonaparte (Claude Rains) in Frank Borzage's musical romance. Betsy has her heart set not on Napoleon but on his brother Jerome (Dick Powell).*

opposite, below: Go into Your Dance *(Warners, 1935). Ruby Keeler and Al Jolson, then husband and wife, in their only film together. Keeler was still one of the studio's major stars, but Jolson's popularity was waning, and this was his next-to-last film for Warner Bros.*

The Peerless Pair:
ASTAIRE and ROGERS

About the same time that *42nd Street* was creating a sensation, film history was being made at RKO Studios. It all began casually, almost by accident—as history often is made. In the bleak Depression year of 1933, most Hollywood studios were in serious financial trouble. At RKO the situation was especially desperate; severe economy measures caused mass firings, and studio executives grappled over the choice of a replacement for David Selznick, who had resigned as production head to join MGM. Hoping to cash in on the success of *42nd Street,* RKO was planning its own lavish musical film, *Flying Down to Rio.*

RKO producer Lou Brock was determined to make Busby Berkeley's kaleidoscopic musicals for Warners seem shabby by comparison. He had sold studio head Merian C. Cooper on the idea of a musical that would bring together two of Cooper's favorite themes: South America and aviation. (Cooper was on the board of directors of Pan American Airways.) The story would be set in Rio de Janeiro and the climax would be an awesome aerial circus over the city. Dark-eyed Dolores Del Rio was cast as an impetuous South American heiress pursued by flying bandleader Gene Raymond. Other roles were to be filled with rising young musical performers.

Rising young musical performers? Surprisingly, one of Brock's earliest selections for the movie was a dancer who was neither rising nor young. At age thirty-four, Fred Astaire was already established as half of one of the theater's most popular musical comedy teams. With sister Adele, he had starred in a series of stage musicals that boasted scores by leading American composers, most notably George Gershwin. One durable song after another had been introduced in the insouciant, tongue-in-cheek style of the Astaires. But in 1932, Adele had retired to marry an English lord, leaving Fred's career in a precarious state. Neither handsome nor romantic-looking, he had always been considered the less gifted member of the team. While Adele sang the romantic ballads with the other male lead, he had usually played the callow juvenile charmer with irrepressible dancing feet. His first stage venture without Adele, Cole Porter's *Gay Divorce,* managed a moderate run despite mostly adverse reviews, but Astaire knew that his career was at a critical juncture.

He turned to the movies, somehow hoping that, against all

odds, he could become a star; not only that, he also wanted to control the filming and editing of his own musical numbers. He asked agent (later producer) Leland Hayward to get him a job in pictures. Hayward spoke to David Selznick, still at RKO, who told him about *Flying Down to Rio.* Presumably hoping to get a leading role in that film, Astaire signed with RKO. When he arrived in Hollywood, he found that it was still in the planning stages. Rather than have him languish, the studio agreed to lend him to MGM for a guest appearance in the Joan Crawford musical *Dancing Lady.* When he returned to RKO to make *Flying Down to Rio,* he found himself with fifth billing, directly after a cheeky redhead named Ginger Rogers.

By the time Rogers came to this film—her twentieth movie —she was familiar to movie audiences, mostly as a pert ingenue with a wisecrack for every occasion. A vaudeville performer at an early age, she began appearing in films around 1930, at the same time that she was playing in her first Broadway show. She had attracted most attention in two Busby Berkeley musicals, *42nd Street* and *Gold Diggers of 1933.* While none of her roles had given her much scope, she was already starting to develop the combination of knowing toughness and girl-next-door vulnerability that became her trademark.

As Erik Rhodes would later say (or try to say) in *The Gay Divorcee,* "Chance is the fool's name for fate." Whether it was chance or fate that brought Rogers to *Flying Down to Rio,* it was certainly the most important moment in her career. To play the supporting role of Honey Hale, a singer with Gene Raymond's band, the studio had cast an actress named Dorothy Jordan. When she chose instead to marry Merian Cooper and go off on her honeymoon, she was replaced by Rogers, who had made a few minor films for the studio. Rogers was told that her partner would be Fred Astaire, the stage star she had known briefly and even dated in New York a few years earlier. Now they would be acting and dancing together in RKO's elaborate effort to capture its share of the musical market.

Today, *Flying Down to Rio* contains little more than historical value as the film that first brought Astaire and Rogers together as a dance team. But in 1933, it was a popular example of the advances in movie-making. Producers were giddy with excitement

Flying Down to Rio (RKO, 1933). In a famous sequence, apparently intrepid chorus girls perform on the wing of a plane in flight. This number was filmed in an airplane hangar, using wind machines and a few planes suspended from the ceiling. Authentic background footage of Rio was mixed with aerial views of a more accessible Malibu Beach.

page 84: Ginger Rogers and Fred Astaire, dancing forehead to forehead in Flying Down to Rio (RKO, 1933).

Flying Down to Rio (RKO, 1933). A pause in the filming of the "Carioca" musical number. It introduced a dance in which the partners touched forehead to forehead and pelvis to pelvis, with hands clasped over their heads. Each partner had to carry out a complete turn without breaking head contact.

at the apparently limitless possibilities of sound cameras no longer confined to a few fixed places. Special effects could turn cameramen into wizards. Improvements in film stock and lighting made it possible to achieve a new richness of texture in black-and-white film. They also permitted the use of white sets in sound films for the first time. The dazzling effect that made white the worst possible color was gone, and designers could freely indulge their fantasies by creating immense, blindingly white Art Deco sets. From the costumes in the ''Carioca'' number to the famous airplane wing-walking finale, *Flying Down to Rio* reflects these changes in movie-making.

However, it is by no means a good movie, not even in the context of its own time. Hastily made in only four weeks and directed perfunctorily by Thornton Freeland, it gives too much footage to the tedious plot concerning Gene Raymond's pursuit of sultry Dolores Del Rio, with opposition from Latin rival Raoul Roulien. Fortunately, there is some compensation in the musical numbers. Wearing a gauzy black gown, Ginger Rogers sings ''Music Makes Me'' in her nasal but appealing style. (Later, Astaire does a rousing tap solo to this song—his first in films.) Raoul Roulien sings the insinuating tango ''Orchids in the Moonlight'' to a pliant Del Rio, who then does a few tentative steps with Astaire. The movie closes with its best-remembered number, in which Astaire sings the title song while airplanes soar overhead with chorus girls strapped to their wings. No matter how often this sequence is viewed the effect is equally astonishing and preposterous, and although we know that the girls are only a few feet off the ground, it is also a bit frightening.

At one point in the film, in a deluxe Brazilian nightclub, entranced patrons listen to the orchestra's rendition of a tune called ''The Carioca'' (''It's not a fox trot or a polka''). In a flash, a gaudily dressed chorus demonstrates the basic step: couples dance forehead to forehead with their hands clasped over their heads. Each partner must then execute a complete turn without breaking head contact. The ''Carioca'' refrain is repeated insistently.

And then, to the amazement of the audience (in both the nightclub and the movie theater), two people sprint onto the stage to show the other dancers ''a thing or three.'' The man says, ''I'd like to try this once.'' It's Fred Ayres and Honey Hale, otherwise known as Fred Astaire and Ginger Rogers, and although they do only two brief dance turns before the stage is overrun with extras, their place in film history is assured the moment they take the floor. It is not so much the breathtaking ease with which they perform the ''Carioca,'' it is more the look that passes between them as they dance: the amused, knowing look of complicity between two people who may or may not become lovers but who share a pride and pleasure in the way they move together. Later, in their romantic numbers, the looks they exchange will be tender, infinitely caring, even erotic. Here, in *Flying Down to Rio,* there is a sense of discovery, ours as well as theirs, plus a hint of the skill, radiance, and beauty that turned two dancers into a legend. It comes as no surprise when the movie fades out not on its nominal stars but on Ginger Rogers and Fred Astaire.

Although Astaire was convinced that he looked awful in the movie, the powers at RKO were not unaware of the magic that had been wrought by the new dance team. Still, it was a year

Flying Down to Rio (RKO, 1933). As singing and dancing members of Gene Raymond's traveling band, Ginger Rogers and Fred Astaire rehearse with the chorus, unaware that this first appearance together on screen would launch a celebrated partnership.

The Gay Divorcee *(RKO, 1934). Edward Everett Horton and Betty Grable sing and dance to the song "Let's K-nock K-nees." (This was already Grable's fourteenth movie since her debut in 1930.)*

before the two were reunited for a second film. Studio production head Pandro S. Berman decided that their vehicle would be *The Gay Divorcee*. (It was renamed because the original title was thought to be too risqué for the silver screen.)

Oddly enough, Astaire didn't want Rogers to appear in the film. He didn't think she could play the English heroine and didn't want to become part of another dancing team. Happily, his objection was overruled, and the film went into production. The unit that followed Astaire and Rogers through most of their films was assembled. Director Mark Sandrich, a specialist in comedy at RKO, was enthusiastic about the possibility of musicals and had asked Lou Brock to sign Astaire. (He went on to direct four more of the team's movies.) Choreographer Hermes Pan (born Hermes Panagiotopulos in Tennessee), who had worked on the "Carioca" number in *Flying Down to Rio,* was assigned to assist Astaire and to direct the group dances. Eventually he edged out the movie's official dance director, Dave Gould, to become Astaire's permanent assistant.

Although *The Gay Divorcee* triumphed as the film that fully established the Astaire-Rogers team, it retained one heavy burden from the stage version: its dated, rather empty-headed book. A throwback to the old Princess Theater musicals of the twenties, the plot was gossamer nonsense concerning a young woman (Rogers) who mistakes an amorous dancer (Astaire) for the corespondent she has hired in order to win a divorce from her long-absent husband. The dialogue was made tolerable not so much by the leading players who, after all, were principally hired to sing and dance, but by the supporting cast: Edward Everett Horton as a fumbling, asinine lawyer, Eric Blore as an eccentric waiter, Alice Brady as the divorcee's scatterbrained aunt, and Erik Rhodes as the ludicrous *true* corespondent, an improbably accented, flamboyant Italian ("Your wife eeza safe weeth Tonetti —he prefersa spaghetti!"). Blore and Rhodes had appeared with Astaire in the stage version.

Luckily, the musical numbers are outstanding. Astaire's solo song and dance to "A Needle in a Haystack" appears early in the movie and blithely defines the Astaire character for the rest of the series. No longer the callow, slangy youth of *Flying Down to Rio,* he is Guy Holden, an elegant and assured man about town whose airy sophistication conceals a romantic heart. He has seen the girl of his dreams, and now his feet refuse to remain still until he finds her. In that thin but marvelously expressive voice, he sings about his frustrating search for Rogers, then dances about the room. His shoes seem to have wings as he soars over a sofa, taps his heels in midair, and lands in a chair without missing a beat. All the while he is changing from a dressing gown into street clothes!

When Astaire finally finds his true love at a lavish Brighton resort hotel, she is not too pleased, thinking of him as a nuisance who persists in following her everywhere. But then they find themselves alone at night in a ballroom. An unseen orchestra begins to play Cole Porter's sensuous melody of "Night and Day." Annoyed, she tries to walk away from him but he blocks her several times and finally catches her wrist. They sway together in dance, and when she moves away again, he pulls her by the hand. Now she coils against him in surrender, and the melody becomes more insistent. Together they move into a dance that is

The Gay Divorcee *(RKO, 1934). This film's lavish production number, "The Continental," was a huge success with audiences (dance studios were kept busy teaching the step). It could also claim two firsts: at seventeen and a half minutes, it was the longest musical number in films to that date, and it was the first song to win an Academy Award.*

The Gay Divorcee *(RKO, 1934). At the end of their marvelous dance to "Night and Day," Ginger Rogers leans back and gazes at Astaire with wordless adoration. At this moment, the screen glowed with a moment of discovery they shared with every member of the audience.*

both lyrical and erotic. It is the first of their many resist-and-surrender dances of seduction, and it is incomparable.

What was the movie miracle that had taken place in that deserted ballroom? It was certainly more than the fact that two people, happily alone in a romantic setting, were expressing their feelings for each other, he with ardent longing, she with melting reluctance. Earlier musicals had thrived on the obligatory love duet between hero and heroine—Maurice Chevalier and Jeanette MacDonald had declared their eternal devotion on more than one occasion.

What made this number distinctive, even unique, was that the couple had chosen to express their emotions in *dance*. At a time when dance numbers in films were usually choral tapping sessions inserted into the movie at intervals, or eye-popping Berkeley extravaganzas with no relation to the story line, this first romantic duet by Astaire and Rogers both advanced and commented on the story line. As Astaire lured her into the dance, it was seduction without words. As Rogers was swept up in the spell of this sublimely graceful dancing man, it was surrender beyond words. No kiss was necessary (and in all their films seldom occurred) as this incomparable duo gave wings to romance.

The only song retained from the stage musical, "Night and Day" was performed peerlessly, but much of the film's budget went to its big production number, "The Continental." Until Astaire and Rogers proved that two gifted people in a simple setting could generate musical excitement, most musicals relied on elaborate, densely populated numbers for their big effects. "The Continental" is certainly elaborate; nearly one hundred dancers garbed in various combinations of black and white join with several solo singers (including Erik Rhodes and Lillian Miles) for seemingly interminable reprises of the Con Conrad–Herb Magidson song in a vast white set representing the esplanade of the Brighton hotel. Not unexpectedly, however, the highlight is provided by Astaire and Rogers, who burst through swinging doors and dance merrily about the set, their delight in each other evident in every movement.

From the posh playground of *The Gay Divorcee*, Astaire and Rogers went to the *haute couture* world of *Roberta* (1935), based on the Otto Harbach–Jerome Kern stage musical. *Roberta* is the least familiar film in the Astaire-Rogers series. (It has been available to television only in the last few years.) Surprisingly, it returned Astaire and Rogers to the supporting role status they had in *Flying Down to Rio*, although the characters they play are hardly the sappy nonentities of the earlier film. Astaire is Huck Haines, leader of a band called the Wabash Indianians. He accompanies his friend John Kent (Randolph Scott) to Paris when John inherits his aunt's dress salon. Rogers is the Countess Scharwenka, née Lizzie Gatz, who sings for a living at the Café Russe. ("At the café, you have to have a title to croon.")

It appears that these two are old friends who used to romp together in an Indiana barnyard, but they are not the movie's main concern. Most of the footage goes to Irene Dunne as an exiled Russian princess who works at Roberta's dress emporium and suffers unrequited love for John Kent. Her lugubrious pining and John's petulant, prudish behavior do not exactly make for a spirited plot under William A. Seiter's direction, and Astaire and Rogers, who are often relegated to the sidelines, have to work

Roberta (RKO, 1935). *Irene Dunne as Stephanie, head designer in Mme. Roberta's Paris dress emporium. Dunne sang in several thirties musicals, but she fared better as a delectable light comedienne in such comedies as* The Awful Truth *and* Theodora Goes Wild.

opposite, above: Roberta (RKO, 1935). *Weaving a magical spell that is almost palpable, Rogers and Astaire dance memorably, but all too briefly, to Jerome Kern's exquisite song "Smoke Gets in Your Eyes." Their dancing looked effortless, but all of Astaire's musical numbers, whether in tandem with Rogers or solo, involved long and difficult rehearsals. Few people were allowed in the rehearsal area, so that Astaire could control every phase of the number. He had a horror of repeating himself and would constantly seek new steps or new ideas for routines. Sometimes they would be suggested by a song or a lyric, or by an incident in the script. Other times they would be worked out in abstract, intricate combinations of rhythm and movement. But nobody objected to his working methods, least of all the composers, who were delighted to have Astaire's renditions of their music.*

opposite, below: *A lobby card for* Roberta (RKO, 1935).

doubly hard to keep the enterprise from drowning in Dunne's tears. Still, Dunne, who has a trained soprano voice, is given three of Jerome Kern's loveliest melodies—"Yesterdays," "Smoke Gets in Your Eyes," and "Lovely to Look At." (The last song was written especially for the film, with lyrics by Dorothy Fields and Jimmy McHugh.)

Although their role in the story is largely incidental, Astaire and Rogers cannot be suppressed. By this time they knew what the rest of the world was discovering: on any dance floor, they were a matchless pair. Astaire, with unhandsome features, diffident manner, and minimal sex appeal, was beauty in motion when he danced, and a leading man of the first rank. Rogers complemented him with her straightforward sexiness, tongue-in-cheek humor, and lithe dancing style. Astaire's later partners, for all their dancing skill, lacked the delicious air of conspiracy, the sense of amused wonder, that she brought to her films with him.

This is particularly evident in "I Won't Dance" (also written especially for the movie), in which the usual procedure is reversed as Rogers coaxes Astaire into dancing with *her*. In her lamé gown, she is naturally irresistible, and soon they are spinning about the room. Astaire also performs a dazzling solo to the same tune. Later, the two dance to a reprise of "Smoke Gets in Your Eyes," which had been rendered tearfully by Dunne in the café after Scott has left her. It is much too brief a duet, but somehow they make it unforgettable as they glide across the floor without quite touching, their faces conveying the longing and poignancy of Kern's melody.

By now Astaire and Rogers had become Astaire-Rogers, a smoothly functioning dance team deserving of the best the studio could muster, and for their next film, *Top Hat* (1935), the studio gave them just that. Though Mark Sandrich could not remove the dull patches in every Astaire-Rogers plot, he could make the film move smoothly, and he was assigned to direct *Top Hat*. The screenplay was coauthored by Allan Scott, who would collaborate on six of the Astaire-Rogers films. The extravagant sets depicting an ersatz Venice came from the unfettered imagination of RKO's Art Department, headed by Van Nest Polglase and his associate Carroll Clark. The musical score provided the icing on the cake: a batch of tunes by the masterly Irving Berlin.

The result was the most popular—and possibly the best—musical in the series, and an Academy Award nominee for best picture. Like *The Gay Divorcee*, *Top Hat* looks back to an earlier era when only the trivial and the frivolous were important. In fact, *Top Hat* resembles *The Gay Divorcee* in many ways: the "wrong identity" plot, the pursuit-and-retreat aspects of the romance, and the supporting presence of Edward Everett Horton, Eric Blore, and Erik Rhodes. *Top Hat* is also a paean to the Depression era's idea of wealth and elegance. It is set in a world that probably never existed, not even in the giddy and hedonistic twenties: a world where every room is a cavernous display of Art Deco furniture and artifacts, and everyone is dressed to the nines or possibly tens. The men seem to spend their lives in evening dress, and the women are wrapped in clinging satin and swathed in expensive furs.

Once again Fred Astaire plays a carefree, romantically inclined dancer. His best friend is Edward Everett Horton, a

Top Hat *(RKO, 1935). The incomparable supporting players (left to right): Erik Rhodes as the flamboyant dress designer Beddini; Edward Everett Horton as the perpetually flustered Horace Hardwick, and Eric Blore as his manservant Bates, constantly in a snit. Horton and Blore were regular performers in the Astaire-Rogers musicals.*

preceding page: Top Hat *(RKO, 1935). In an Art Deco setting, Astaire and Rogers dance romantically to "Cheek to Cheek." One of the team's most memorable, most lyrical numbers, it crystallized a relationship that had matured through the dance, belying the frivolous attitude they were forced to adopt in the gossamer plots of their movies.*

opposite, above: Top Hat *(RKO, 1935). Fred Astaire leads a line of dapper dancers in "Top Hat, White Tie and Tails." He had performed this routine in the 1930 stage musical called* Smiles, *and he decided to use it for this number.*

opposite, below: A poster for Follow the Fleet *(RKO, 1936).*

foolish sort married to the acerbic Helen Broderick. When Astaire's tap dancing annoys the occupant of the room below, it is no surprise that the complainant turns out to be Ginger Rogers. In the usual progression, they meet, he falls head over heels in love, and he pursues her, to an improbably gaudy Venice. The catch is that she mistakes Astaire for Horton, husband of her best friend, Helen Broderick. (Nobody thinks to ask why she has never met her friend's husband. It's too sensible a question.) Of course, Astaire and Rogers dance their way to love and understanding.

The *Top Hat* book is a fraction more tolerable than that of *The Gay Divorcee,* but only a fraction. More than ever, it's the musical numbers that matter, and they are all splendid. Astaire's first solo (the one that disturbs Rogers's sleep) is "No Strings," and it's an aptly named tribute to the dancer's effortless art. There appears to be nothing pinning him to earth as he soars through a series of steps that capture his happy-go-lucky nature. After Rogers has interrupted him—"Every once in a while I suddenly find myself dancing," he tells her—and captured his fancy, he sprinkles sand on the floor and dances on it gently as Rogers goes back to sleep.

Naturally, Astaire pursues his light-o'-love to the most convenient spot for dancing, where they can execute one of their most famous numbers. It's Berlin's "Isn't This a Lovely Day (To Be Caught in the Rain)?" and a thoroughgoing delight. Taking shelter from the rain in a deserted park pavilion, they confront each other with the familiar attitudes: he is ardent and hopeful; she is wry and faintly annoyed. What better way to change her mood than by engaging her in dance? It begins as a challenge dance, with Rogers copying his steps but trying to top them with her own, but it progresses to a stunning demonstration of their rapport as they spin about the pavilion stage. The most unforgettable moment comes when a clap of thunder sends them into double time, two whirling dervishes who are never—but never—out of control.

Top Hat spills over with musical riches. In a Venetian nightclub of staggering grandeur, Astaire is courting a reluctant Rogers, and with plaintive sincerity, he sings "Cheek to Cheek" into her ear. Soon, in a romantic adagio of matchless beauty, they are dancing alone in a dreamlike setting. Toward the end of the song, the orchestra's beat accelerates and they dance across a bridge, onto a balcony, and into a breathtaking climax. In these few minutes, the transformation is complete: Astaire is no longer a gauche band musician but an elegant, seductive man about Venice. Rogers is no longer the cheeky, flapper-like ingenue but an alluring woman responding to the night, the music, and her dancing lover.

The quintessential Astaire solo is "Top Hat, White Tie and Tails." In his dressing room, he gets a letter informing him that the girl he loves is winging her way to Venice. Overjoyed, he sprints onto the stage to announce that he "just got an invitation through the mails." He's going out to celebrate—"to breathe an atmosphere that simply reeks with class." But of course the "class" is already evident as he executes a spirited tap with only his walking stick as a prop. Behind him is a row of nattily dressed chorus boys. When the chorus disappears and the stage darkens, Astaire crouches into a lonely figure trying to ward off some

invisible terror. The lights come on and the chorus boys return, only to be "shot" down, one by one, by Astaire, using his cane as a machine gun. When the last chorus boy insists on dodging the bullets, Astaire snares him with an invisible bow and arrow. The entire dance is brilliantly, imaginatively done.

Top Hat was welcomed rapturously by the critics and the public. But then, in its mysterious and inexplicable way, the studio decided to shift the accelerating Astaire-Rogers bandwagon into reverse. Both The Gay Divorcee and Top Hat had taken place in the privileged world of the elegant rich where Astaire hardly ever removed his top hat and tails. It may have been an absurdly ritzy world, but it was Astaire's natural habitat. Afraid that movie audiences were no longer amused by the idle rich, RKO lifted Astaire and Rogers out of the late twenties and placed them in the mid-thirties. In their next film, Follow the Fleet (1936), they were cast as a self-confident sailor named "Bake" Baker and a slangy dance-hall hostess called Sherry Martin.

The plot was rather frayed around the edges. Derived from the 1922 play Shore Leave, which also went through several stage and screen versions as the musical Hit the Deck, it revolved about Astaire and Rogers as former dancing partners ("Baker and Martin, High-Class Patter and Genteel Dancing") who are reunited when the fleet comes to town. Their reunion is subject to the usual quarrels and misunderstandings, many of them involving the romance between Bake's buddy "Bilge" Smith (Randolph Scott) and Sherry's mousy sister Connie (Harriet Hilliard, later of television's "Ozzie and Harriet").

Unflappable as always, Astaire tries hard to cope with his new environment, but he never seems completely at ease aboard ship or in dance halls, and he works his jaws strenuously to make his gum-chewing gob seem authentic. Rogers is clearly more relaxed than he is, and she also shows improved skill as a comedienne. The dry, cynical attitude she assumes toward all the romantic folderol is a refreshing contrast to Harriet Hilliard's lovelorn demeanor.

Fortunately for everyone involved in Follow the Fleet, Irving Berlin was on hand to write the music, and he poured forth melodies that make us forget the tiresome plot. The score may be a notch or two below Top Hat's, but no matter: the songs have Berlin's irresistible lilt and emotional directness. They also give Astaire and Rogers the chance to display a comic dexterity that surfaced only occasionally in their earlier movies.

This comedy-in-dance emerges best in their routine for "I'm Putting All My Eggs in One Basket." Rehearsing for their nightclub engagement, Astaire runs the song through, barrelhouse style, on the piano. He sings it with Rogers, and then they break into a dance that uses slapstick without sacrificing gracefulness. They trip, slide, spill, and generally cavort to Berlin's bracing melody. At one point Rogers swings her arms so vigorously that she slaps Astaire and sends him reeling. It even ends with Astaire dumping Rogers on the floor unceremoniously.

Comedy is emphasized in other musical numbers. At a dance contest in the Paradise Ballroom, Astaire and Rogers win the competition (surprise!) and take over the floor to the tune of "Let Yourself Go." The choreography devised by Astaire is his homage to the popular dance steps of the period, but it is unlikely that either the Lindy or the Big Apple was ever

Follow the Fleet (RKO, 1936). Astaire and Rogers performing "Let's Face the Music and Dance," a miniature drama in which Astaire, a gambler who has lost all his money and is about to commit suicide, stops a distraught Rogers from doing the same. He sings to her, and then they dance on the moonlit terrace with melancholy elegance. At the end, their backs arched against an uncertain future, they sweep off the terrace in an audacious gesture of defiance.

opposite: Follow the Fleet (RKO, 1936). Ginger Rogers sings "Let Yourself Go," backed by a trio consisting of (from left) Jeanne Gray, Betty Grable, and Joy Hodges.

performed with such humorous aplomb. Midway in the movie, Astaire also sings and dances to "I'd Rather Lead a Band," launching a nautical tap dance that threatens to set his ship on fire.

Follow the Fleet does manage to pause for the obligatory "serious" numbers, including one romantic duet for Astaire and Rogers. Since the plot did not call for any ardent byplay between them (they spend most of their time either lightly bickering or making up), an encounter was invented. At a benefit performance, they dance in a self-contained miniature drama to Berlin's lovely song "Let's Face the Music and Dance." It is one of the most lyrical numbers they ever performed: a dazzling series of lifts and swirls that, as always, seem totally without effort.

The team was in top form in their next musical, Swing Time (1936). Not only is it one of their best (some say it is their best), but the film's handling of the tuneful score Jerome Kern wrote with Dorothy Fields is deft and smoothly professional. With Astaire and Rogers firmly established as the screen's foremost dancers, the movie could express exuberance and self-assurance without undue strain. Under George Stevens's direction, it moves from situation to situation, from musical number to musical number, happy and secure in the knowledge that the audience is aware of—and revels in—the myth of Fred and Ginger as dancing deities.

Like Follow the Fleet, Swing Time takes Astaire and Rogers out of the ritzy grandeur of Top Hat, but not as far. Astaire may have to hop a freight train, but when he does, he's wearing a top hat and tails. Rogers may have to work as a dance instructor, but she gives her lessons in an Art Deco ballroom about the size of Rhode Island. Swing Time may show the first evidence of the Depression in the Astaire-Rogers series, but it still cherishes the romantic world where lovers can sing and dance in a snow-laden wonderland.

This time Astaire is John ("Lucky") Garnett, a dancer with an uncontrollable yen for gambling but not much luck. When he misses his wedding to a haughty rich girl (Betty Furness), he is given an alternative by the girl's father: return home with five thousand dollars, or give up all claims to his daughter. Still in his wedding finery, Lucky hops a freight train to New York, where he meets and falls in love with a dance instructor named Penny (Rogers). They become a sensational dance team in nightclubs, and his luck even improves at the gambling tables. When Penny learns about Lucky's fiancée, she decides to marry an amorous bandleader, but that wedding is also disrupted. Inevitably, Lucky and Penny get together for a happy ending.

The screenplay, fashioned by Howard Lindsay and revised by the reliable Allan Scott, has a mite more substance than usual. The team's fluctuating romance is even amusingly handled. Yet the film soars only when the music begins. Most important, for the first time, virtually all of the musical numbers are tightly interwoven with the script. Whereas earlier films were obliged to accommodate the craze for new dances ("The Carioca," "The Continental") or to invent occasions for musical numbers ("Let's Face the Music and Dance"), the Swing Time numbers advance the story or deepen the relationship of the characters. It was the first time that dance was used in this fashion in films, but the influence of the Astaire-Rogers numbers was probably stronger

Swing Time (RKO, 1936). Astaire, in blackface for the first and last time, dances with the chorus in the amazing "Bojangles of Harlem." The number begins with Astaire reclining atop Harlem, with two oversized false legs stretching toward the camera, and it ends with Astaire tapping his way toward the camera, clapping his hands. The entire number is not only movie magic, it is the special magic created by the genius of Astaire.

opposite: Swing Time (RKO, 1936). In a lovely, snow-covered stretch of woods, Astaire and Rogers take turns singing Jerome Kern's "A Fine Romance." The setting, the song, and the mood of rueful romance combined to create one of the most memorable of all their numbers, even without a dance.

on the dance community than on the producers of musical films. Many dancers were excited by the moods and emotions expressed in Astaire's dancing and extended them into their own work, whereas most subsequent dance numbers in musical films returned to large-scale opulence.

The first dance in *Swing Time,* "Pick Yourself Up," is one of the best: trailing Rogers to the dance studio where she works, Astaire insists on receiving his first lesson. Exasperated, she tries to teach a basic step to her klutzy student (a clumsy Astaire is more graceful than most dancers at the peak of their form), but he keeps falling down. When the studio owner fires Rogers for calling a student hopeless, Astaire demonstrates his newly found prowess by performing a wingding of a number with his astonished teacher. It concludes with the dancers leaping joyfully back and forth over the low railing that rings the dance floor.

Except for Astaire's tour-de-force tribute to dancer Bill Robinson in "Bojangles of Harlem," other Kern songs are staged with maximum attention to their plot value. In Rogers's apartment, Astaire sings "The Way You Look Tonight" to her while she shampoos her hair, the white lather forming a sculptured effect that makes her look enchanting. Later, in one of the most beautiful settings in all their films, a snow-covered section of woods, they take turns singing Kern's "sarcastic love song," "A Fine Romance." The rueful lyrics of frustrated love combine with the romantic *mise-en-scène* to create a balance of resistance-and-surrender that was the hallmark of their work together.

The film's most remarkable musical number comes at the end. Convinced that he has lost Rogers forever, Astaire tells her in song that he is "Never Gonna Dance" (the film's original title). If he can't have her, his feet will never be used to express in dance the love and the longing he has felt for her. She listens, trying to retain her composure. Alone in one of those glistening white sets, they dance out the story of the film. Sometimes they dance pensively, side by side, without touching. Other times they whirl together in exuberant abandon. As the emotions change, so do the rhythms, and soon they are separated in space as they are in life, walking away from each other on opposite staircases.

The other great duet in the film, "Waltz in Swing Time," lacks the dramatic resonance of "Never Gonna Dance," but it remains one of the most celebrated of their dances. In a moonlit setting, to music arranged by Robert Russell Bennett, they express all the nuances of the professional, if not the personal, relationship they had developed over a few years. A glowing rapport, a mutual generosity and pride shine through every lift, turn, and glide of this romantic number.

Astaire's brilliant solo in the film is "Bojangles of Harlem," and it is the only blackface number he has ever done. Despite Astaire's sincerely meant homage to Bill "Bojangles" Robinson, a dancer he admired greatly, our heightened awareness today gives this number an uneasy overtone. Astaire, however, is as marvelous as he has ever been, constantly surprising us with imaginative variations. The highlight occurs when Astaire dances with three back-projected shadows of himself, silhouetted against a large screen. It is the first time he used trick

Shall We Dance (RKO, 1937). In the film's final (and title) number,
Astaire—having decided that if he can't dance with Rogers, he'll dance with images
of her—surrounds himself with a line of chorus girls, all wearing masks of Ginger Rogers.
He unmasks one girl after another until he finds the real Ginger, who is clearly at the left.

A Damsel in Distress *(RKO, 1937)*. *Fred Astaire, Gracie Allen, and George Burns romp through a fun house in the marvelous sequence that won an Oscar for dance director Hermes Pan.*

photography in a number, and it works beautifully as he moves in intricate counterpoint to the shadows.

Their next film, *Shall We Dance* (1937), moved them back up the social ladder, restored Mark Sandrich as director, and added one marvelous ingredient: a score by George and Ira Gershwin. It was Astaire who brought them to the movie—they had written memorable songs for two of his and sister Adele's greatest successes. New to the series, the Gershwin brothers went at their task enthusiastically, and came forth with a batch of their wittiest, most sophisticated songs. Everything seemed in order for another Astaire-Rogers triumph.

Unfortunately, the result was a falling-off for the series. The film's plot was just as foolish as the others, but it was hardly to blame. Astaire was back playing a dancer, this time a ballet star named Petrov (born Pete Peters in Pittsburgh), who sees a photograph of musical comedy queen Linda Keene (Rogers) and promptly falls in love with her. He pursues her aboard an ocean liner, and for reasons too silly to discuss, everyone comes to assume they are married. With the sort of convoluted logic only movies could muster, they decide that the only solution to their dilemma is to get married so that they can get divorced to prove that they're *not* married. After the obligatory quarrels, Linda dances into Petrov's arms, where she takes up permanent residence.

The dialogue by Allan Scott and Ernest Pagano is nicely scatterbrained, and Mark Sandrich keeps things moving at a reasonable pace. But there is a slightly dispirited air about the movie, a faintly mechanical quality about the stars' performances that keeps the champagne from fizzing as merrily as before. The most serious problem is that, although the film has its share of musical numbers, too few of them take advantage of the intimate, romantic, and infinitely graceful style the team had perfected in their films together. Only one, "They All Laughed," has a full quota of the Astaire-Rogers artistry; others are either perfunctory or ill-considered. "Beginner's Luck" lasts barely a minute, while "They Can't Take That Away from Me" makes the ghastly mistake of following Astaire's superb rendition of the song with a dance featuring a new partner, the "high-toned" ballerina Harriet Hoctor. The idea of removing Rogers from a romantic duet and substituting a dancer whose specialty was a backward bend that made it appear as if she were kicking herself in the head was not only misguided, it was positively criminal. It seemed almost as if the studio, out of some need to change a successful pattern, was also bending over backward, with similar results.

Still, there are some musical pleasures in *Shall We Dance*. In the engine room of a transatlantic ocean liner, Astaire diverts a group of black stokers by singing "Slap That Bass" and using the ship's machinery in a clever and intricate tap routine. And in a Central Park rink, he joins with Rogers for an engaging song and dance on roller skates to "Let's Call the Whole Thing Off." The song itself is a wry commentary on the stars' attitudes *off* the screen: he modest, unassuming, and inclined to wear his elegance lightly; she increasingly conscious of her "queenly" position in the movie firmament.

Their best number takes place at a rooftop restaurant. Rogers sings "They All Laughed," then, not too reluctantly, moves onto the dance floor with Astaire. He does a few serious ballet turns, which she mocks insolently with a furious burst of taps. He imitates the taps, then leads her in a dance which not only uses an astonishing variety of styles but also comments on and enhances each of the styles at the same time. At one point, they even leap atop two white pianos to execute their taps. In its humor, audacity, and assurance, the number is almost an anthology of Astaire-Rogers creations.

During 1936, there had been persistent rumors of an Astaire-Rogers breakup, and by the end of 1937, it was clear that the partnership was nearing its end. Astaire had finally proven that he could be a viable romantic leading man in films and didn't have to remain in sister Adele's shadow. Rogers had developed into a glamorous figure and an expert dancer under Astaire's tutelage, and her improved acting made her anxious to test her mettle as a comedienne. Although there was no personal enmity between them (the fickle public wanted to believe otherwise), there was a certain feeling that each was handicapped by being so closely identified with the other. It was basically a matter of professional pride.

And so they changed directions—and partners. RKO put Astaire into *A Damsel in Distress* (1937), giving him a P. G. Wodehouse story, another superior Gershwin score, and a first-rate supporting cast headed by the marvelous comedy team of George Burns and Gracie Allen. Astaire played his usual footloose American dancer, who this time comes to the rescue of a wealthy English girl forced by an imperious aunt to remain sequestered in their castle.

Unfortunately, when British dancing star Jessie Matthews turned down the role of the heroine, the studio, at a loss, turned to one of its contract players, twenty-year-old Joan Fontaine. Still awkward as an actress—she had made only four films—she was even worse as a dancer, and nothing that director George Stevens or a skilled cameraman attempted could conceal this fact. In her one duet with Astaire, "Things Are Looking Up," she scampers with him through a park setting, looking more like a starlet in desperate trouble than a light-footed gazelle.

To compensate for the lack of an adequate dancing partner, *A Damsel in Distress* gives Astaire three good solos and two exceptionally fine musical numbers with Burns and Allen. He wanders through a fog-heavy glade near the castle and sings, appropriately, "A Foggy Day." He dances and plays a variety of percussion instruments to "Nice Work if You Can Get It," and on a busy London street, he taps out a few choruses of "I Can't Be Bothered Now." With Burns and Allen, he dances in an English cottage, using whisk brooms and suits of armor as props.

The number that Astaire performs with Burns and Allen in an amusement park is easily the best in the movie (it won an Academy Award for dance director Hermes Pan). To the tune of "Stiff Upper Lip," the trio cavorts through a playland, sliding down chutes, giggling in front of trick mirrors, and high-stepping across moving boardwalks. Gracie Allen contributes one delightful moment: she jogs endlessly in circles on a turning disk, repeating the "Oompah Trot" that Fred and Adele Astaire had made their trademark in five of their shows.

At the same time, Ginger Rogers had gotten her wish, starring in films, especially *Vivacious Lady* (1937), that helped to forge a new image as an engaging comedienne. In fact, when it was decided to reunite the dance team, RKO paid more attention to Rogers than it did to Astaire, hoping to use her status as a solo star to bolster his slipping popularity. Their next film, *Carefree* (1938), clearly belongs to Rogers. As a girl whose romantic problems are complicated by psychiatry, she was playing the sort of role that became typical of her: the winsome, sometimes childlike girl who can't make up her mind, a proletarian princess with no powers of concentration. The same role might have been played with ease by Claudette Colbert, Irene Dunne, or any of the familiar heroines of lightheaded comedies in the mid- and late thirties. With its slapstick situations and romantic byplay, *Carefree* is actually more of a screwball comedy than a musical. (What else could account for the presence of Ralph Bellamy, the perennial sap of many a screwball comedy?)

For *Carefree,* Astaire put aside his professional dancing shoes for the first time to play a psychiatrist who tries to cure Rogers of her indecision about marrying Bellamy. When his treatment causes her to fall in love with him, he frantically tries to rid her of the feeling through hypnosis, then has to undo his work when *he* finds himself in love with *her.* It was hardly a conventional role for Astaire. He tackled it gamely, but one senses that his shoes were tapping impatiently, waiting for him to be released from all the sexual tomfoolery and be permitted to soar in dance.

Unfortunately, since most of the movie is concerned with Rogers's daffy changeability, there is not enough time for Astaire to spread his musical wings, or to do full justice to Irving Berlin's score. In "Since They Turned Loch Lomond into Swing," he dances, Scottish-style, on a golf course, using clubs, golf balls, and even a harmonica as props. Early in the film, he dances with Rogers in a dream sequence to the song "I Used to Be Color-Blind" (the number was originally scheduled to be filmed in color). A sleeping Rogers imagines herself in a garden setting with oversized flowers, as she and Astaire dance in slow motion. Later in the film, they join in one of their most beautiful duets. Realizing that he loves her after all, he confronts her on the dance floor and, in one of Berlin's prettiest songs, pleads with her to "Change Partners" and dance with him. After getting rid of the ubiquitous Bellamy, he lures Rogers onto the patio and into a trance. His hands move toward her and her body responds to his bidding, all in choreographed movements. In one striking moment, she glides backward in his direction although she hasn't seen his gestures at all. It's as if the invisible magnetic force that always drew them together was suddenly made palpable.

Although *Carefree* won mostly admiring reviews, the dwindling box-office returns, Rogers's eagerness to pursue a dramatic career, and RKO's financial problems made it evident that the team would soon separate. Their last film for a decade, *The Story of Vernon and Irene Castle* (1939), had a twilight feeling about it. The gaiety, insouciance, and general wackiness of their earlier films were replaced by a sentimental plot, mixed with tinkly tunes and decorous dances. Any movie that ended with Astaire dying in a plane crash and performing one last ghostly dance with his beloved wife could hardly send the spirits soaring in the usual fashion.

Vernon and Irene Castle had been international dancing sensations in the years before World War I. They not only made

slightly "wicked" American social dances like the Bunny Hug and the Turkey Trot look respectable, enjoyable, and spontaneous, but they also added a few new steps of their own (such as the Castle Walk). Their behavior and styles of dress became new standards of chic. It was inevitable that their story would be filmed eventually with their latter-day equivalents, Fred Astaire and Ginger Rogers.

The resulting film moves smoothly and pleasantly under H. C. Potter's relaxed direction. The screenplay traces the meeting and courtship of the Castles, their futile early attempts to establish themselves as a dance team in New York and Paris, their sudden rise to fame, and Vernon's accidental death in 1918. The movie is ostensibly a biography, but with its vapid, sugarcoated story, medley of old songs, and period setting, it seems more like a foreshadowing of the musical nosegays 20th Century-Fox was already beginning to cultivate and would carry into the forties (*Alexander's Ragtime Band, Coney Island, Mother Wore Tights*).

For the Astaire-Rogers fan expecting the usual quota of romantic duets or sleekly staged musical numbers, *The Story of Vernon and Irene Castle* comes as something of a disappointment. And yet it must be remembered that the dancing team is emulating or at least suggesting the style of another team, and instead of playing another variation of the-pursuer-and-the-pursued, they are established early in the film as a devoted couple. Their dances are therefore charming, cozy, but unexciting, like the performances of talented married friends we can easily enjoy—for ninety minutes, at any rate.

There are a few highlights. One is their rendition of the famous "Castle Walk," to the tune of "Too Much Mustard." The number, which features a kind of brisk skipping step, is brief but diverting. As an audition for entrepreneur Lew Fields, they do a dance called the "Texas Tommy," in which they whip around the dance floor with their hands clasped at the back of each other's necks. Best of all is the Montage Medley, which shows their zooming popularity. They dance the tango, the polka, and the maxixe, and in a stunning final shot, they whirl across a huge map of the United States as hundreds of dancing couples follow in their wake. For this shot, a map was painted on a floor mat and photographed from a forty-foot tower. None of these numbers can be faulted, and yet they somehow lack the exuberance and the romantic élan that made the dances in *Top Hat* and *Swing Time* so thrilling. They are adroit re-creations of an earlier style—they are Vernon and Irene, but not Fred and Ginger.

Watching their last dance together in *The Story of Vernon and Irene Castle,* we know with the hindsight of four decades that they were really spinning away into legend. Despite *The Barkleys of Broadway* a decade later, we remember them in the thirties as the peerless performers who tapped, whirled, and leaped their way into film history with the charm, grace, and inventiveness of their dancing. So many years after the peak of their time together, we can still watch their films with a joy that never diminishes. A familiar axiom about them, attributed to Katharine Hepburn, has been: "She gave him sex. He gave her class." All that is of little moment to what they both gave us: the boundless pleasure of their inimitable presence.

The Story of Vernon and Irene Castle *(RKO, 1939). The famed dance team introduces their own "Castle Walk" to the tune of "Too Much Mustard." Irene Castle objected to having Rogers play her in the movie, insisting that she was the wrong type. The studio persisted, however, and Ms. Castle, sidetracked by an antivivisection campaign, did not pursue the matter.*

opposite: Carefree *(RKO, 1938). In Ginger Rogers's dream, she and Fred Astaire dance in slow-motion to Irving Berlin's "I Used to Be Color-Blind." The number ended with one of the few kisses in the Astaire-Rogers musicals. (Who needed kisses? Their ardor was expressed in the dance.)*

ON THE GOOD SHIP 20TH CENTURY-FOX

Darryl Zanuck had been largely responsible for the note of gritty realism in many of the films made at Warner Bros. He had brought stage actors James Cagney and Edward G. Robinson to Hollywood, and in *The Public Enemy* and *Little Caesar,* he had made a movie legend of the ruthless gangster who ends his ignominious career in a hail of bullets.

However, his approach to filmmaking changed after he resigned as Warners's production head, because of a dispute over a company-wide salary cut, in April, 1933. In association with producer Joseph M. Schenck, he formed a new company, Twentieth Century Pictures. When Twentieth Century merged with the financially troubled Fox Corporation in 1935 to create 20th Century-Fox Pictures, gritty realism was replaced by family-oriented sentiment and spectacle. As vice-president in charge of production, Zanuck developed a group of carefully groomed and nonthreatening stars who appeared in homespun comedies, fictionalized historical dramas, and lighthearted musicals, bolstered by occasional ''prestige'' productions. Perched at the very top of Zanuck's star-laden tree was that extraordinary curly-headed moppet, Shirley Temple.

Before Shirley became a world phenomenon and 20th Century-Fox's greatest asset, the Fox studios (sans Zanuck) produced a few musicals that were light-years away from those they would make only a few years later. Obviously impressed by Warners's box-office receipts for their Busby Berkeley musicals, Fox took a turn at combining elaborate production numbers, a serviceable backstage plot, and a ''so-what'' attitude toward the Depression. The studio had the right ingredients for a tasty confection: attractive players, a reasonably large budget, and a desire to entertain. What it lacked was a master chef who could mix the ingredients skillfully, and the kind of sharp, funny performer—Joan Blondell, for example—who could spice the mix. When attempts were made to imitate Berkeley, his vulgarity was turned into mere salaciousness, with entendres more single than double.

Early in 1934, the studio released *Stand Up and Cheer,* which, like *42nd Street,* is a quintessential musical of the Depression years, as well as one of the oddest musical films ever to come out of Hollywood. A delirious attempt to exorcise the Depression with a mixture of song, dance, and wishful thinking, *Stand Up and Cheer* has as its central premise the creation of a new cabinet post in the government: a Secretary of Amusement who will banish fear and hopelessness in a gale of laughter. Assigned to this post is Warner Baxter, only a year after browbeating chorus girls in *42nd Street.* After a few setbacks, he triumphs by the simple expedient of announcing that ''the Depression's over!''

Gold Diggers of 1933 had taken on the Depression by having Ginger Rogers declare that ''we're in the money,'' and by Joan Blondell's heartfelt plea for ''the forgotten man.'' By contrast with the numbers in *Stand Up and Cheer,* these are models of subtlety. Early in the film, Nick (later Dick) Foran bursts through a wall of newspapers, exhorting Americans to face their tribulations with courage and determination. If those with real troubles can do it, ''Brother, So Can You!'' he sings. In succession, the theme is taken up by a worn mother with a dozen children, a sweatshop girl, two policemen in a storm, construction workers, and garbage collectors. The number is a vivid segment of musical propaganda.

Even more aggressive in its approach is the film's concluding number, in which Foran reappears as a Depression Paul Revere, riding through the clouds on his horse and urging everybody to be happy. ''We're Out of the Red!'' he sings. ''Put that twinkle back in your eye! The Big Bad Wolf is gone!'' In a scene that has a disturbing suggestion of Hitler's legions, we see scores of ordinary Americans marching to the song—sailors, nurses, firemen, farmers, policemen, soldiers, and many others— relentlessly calling for total belief in a lie: the end of a grim and terrifying national collapse.

There are several musical numbers that are clearly influenced by the Berkeley style. One number, however, stands apart, if only for its historic value. Vaudevillian Jimmy Dugan (James Dunn) sings a chorus of ''Baby, Take a Bow!'' to a group of chorus girls, who parade toward the camera in single file, smiling winsomely. Their performance fades, however, as soon as Dunn's daughter—tiny Shirley Temple—toddles onstage, puckers to the camera, and sings a variation of her father's song,

called "Daddy, Take a Bow!" She then performs a marvelous tap dance with Dunn. Her performance is assured and delectable, and represents the first feature-film appearance of the most adored film star of the decade.

Another Fox musical of that year was even more obvious in its borrowings from Berkeley. *George White's Scandals* (1934), the first of two productions derived from the stage spectacles of George White, had a standard backstage plot even flimsier than most, an assortment of gaudy production numbers, and performers who, if not conspicuously talented, were at least cheerful and willing. The stars were Rudy Vallee, Jimmy Durante, and Alice Faye in her film debut.

This time, the ingredient George White added to the mix was his own brand of salaciousness. Although the Berkeley musicals, with their leering midgets and bawdy chorines, were not exactly the apex of good taste, they seem almost innocent in comparison with White's creations for his *Scandals*. Wearing an abbreviated costume with a long white feather in her platinum hair, Alice Faye makes her first screen appearance singing "Oh, You Nasty Man!" She is joined by rows of dancing chorines, called the White "Scan-Dolls," who are photographed at odd angles à la Berkeley. In the audience, the men ogle and shout orgiastically. Another production number, to the song "Hold My Hand," offers a bit of voyeurism as girls in white gowns lift and wave their skirts as their images are reflected in a huge pool. In the most bizarre musical sequence, "Scan-Dolls" in polka-dotted "pickaninny" costumes dance with figures of black males strapped to their midriffs. A second edition of *George White's Scandals,* released the following year, offered more of the same.

Before taking over as head of production for the new 20th Century-Fox, Darryl Zanuck had wanted his own company to create a musical even more extravagant than *42nd Street* or *Gold Diggers of 1933.* He acquired the world rights to use the name of the Folies Bergère, Paris's long-running opulent revue, as a film title. The resulting film, *Folies Bergère* (1935), starred Maurice Chevalier in a dual role.

Derived from a 1934 play called *The Red Cat,* the musical had a mildly risqué plot line concerning a baron and his double, a popular entertainer, along with the women in their lives. Their interlocked dalliances are interrupted for songs by Chevalier or for lavish musical numbers. Staged by Dave Gould, who had choreographed "The Carioca" and "The Continental," these numbers are unabashed imitations of the Berkeley style, but had touches of their own inventiveness. In "Rhythm of the Rain," Chevalier and Ann Sothern splash cheerfully through the song on a rain-drenched set, while chorus girls form patterns with their umbrellas. Later, in a cleverly designed finale, they join the chorus in singing and dancing around replicas of Chevalier's famous straw hat.

Films such as *George White's Scandals* and *Folies Bergère* acknowledged the public taste for musical extravaganzas, but the musical style at 20th Century-Fox in the mid-thirties was generally more intimate, more lightly satirical, and even topical. *Thanks a Million* (1935), for example, took several well-aimed jabs at politics, an uncommon subject for musicals. Fred Allen, the dry-witted comedian in his film debut, played the manager of a singer (Dick Powell) who inadvertently becomes a political

George White's Scandals *(Fox, 1934). Rudy Vallee and Alice Faye, in her film debut. According to legend, the original leading lady walked off the movie, and Vallee had asked the studio to replace her with Faye, a chorus girl and radio vocalist. Faye claims, however, that she had already filmed her first number and was the logical choice for the role. (That same year, Faye was named by Vallee's wife in an explosive divorce case.)*

page 106: *Shirley Temple takes a bow in a publicity pose.*

opposite: Stand Up and Cheer *(Fox, 1934). This production number was clearly inspired by Busby Berkeley and his cohorts over at Warner Bros. The requisite patterns formed by the chorus were there, but the Berkeley spark was missing.*

Folies Bergère *(Twentieth Century, 1935). Ann Sothern, Maurice Chevalier, and the chorus splash their way merrily through the musical number "Rhythm of the Rain."*

George White's 1935 Scandals *(Fox, 1935). A year after* George White's Scandals, *a second edition appeared, again starring Alice Faye. Here, looking very much like the then-popular Jean Harlow, she sings "Oh, I Didn't Know" in front of a "wall" of chorus girls. (The movie marked the first screen appearance of dancer Eleanor Powell, who would shortly move to MGM.)*

You Can't Have Everything *(Fox, 1937). Alice Faye sings "Afraid to Dream" with Tony Martin. (They were married soon afterward.) Faye played an aspiring playwright—a granddaughter of Edgar Allan Poe—whose serious drama is turned into a musical hit by writer-director Don Ameche. The cast included ecdysiast Gypsy Rose Lee, making her screen debut under her true name, Louise Hovick.*

opposite, above: On the Avenue *(Fox, 1937). In the number "Slumming on Park Avenue," Alice Faye, wearing a tight, slit skirt and absurd hat, leads her raffish friends to the "swanky" part of town for a round of singing and dancing.*

opposite, below: One in a Million *(Fox, 1936). Sonja Henie takes to the ice in her movie debut. All of her films called for her to leap, spin, or glide about a mammoth rink, either alone or with a skating chorus. Sometimes she would be lifted aloft by a skating partner in a frosty pas de deux. (A special kind of freezable paint was added to the ice to make it opaque so that the refrigerator pipes wouldn't show.)*

candidate. The lighthearted pokes at politics American-style and the bright songs made the movie lively entertainment. *Sing, Baby, Sing* (1936) was suggested by Elaine Barrie's relentless—and headlined—pursuit of John Barrymore. The widely publicized "feud" between columnist Walter Winchell and bandleader Ben Bernie became part of an amiable Fox musical called *Wake Up and Live* (1937). Alice Faye starred in both films.

Alice Faye's other 1937 musicals avoided satire or topicality, for the most part, but were no less entertaining. After starring in *You Can't Have Everything* as a hopeful playwright who falls in love with a devious musical writer-director (Don Ameche), she appeared in *On the Avenue,* one of Fox's superior musicals of the period. She may have been relegated to a supporting role, but a reasonably amusing plot, expert direction by Roy Del Ruth, and especially the tuneful Irving Berlin score made it one of her more successful films. The story—with variations—had done service in many screwball comedies of the thirties: a headstrong heiress (Madeleine Carroll) is humiliated by a satirical sketch in the latest show of a thriving producer-singer (Dick Powell, back again from Warners). Eventually she turns the tables on him, but, to absolutely no one's amazement, they fall in love. Alice Faye was the show's singer who loved Powell in vain.

The screenplay has more than its share of bright lines, and supporting characters who would be worthy of a straight comedy. Still, it is the music that counts in *On the Avenue.* Irving Berlin contributed some of his best songs, including "You're Laughing at Me," "I've Got My Love to Keep Me Warm," and "This Year's Kisses," in which Faye uses all her familiar mannerisms: the quivering lower lip, the large, soulful eyes that brim easily with tears, the husky voice. The movie's largest production number is staged around the song "Slumming on Park Avenue."

Alice Faye was Fox's reigning musical queen of the thirties, but another blonde could lay claim to being its princess royal. (Betty Grable, the true heir to the throne, did not succeed to the title until the end of the decade.) This was a pert, dimpled, and eternally smiling girl from Norway named Sonja Henie. A skating champion in her own country at age fourteen, she had gone on to win gold medals in the women's figure-skating events in the Olympics of 1928, 1932, and 1936. Turning professional in 1936, she decided to pursue a career as an actress with a very specialized skill as a dancing skater. Her asking price of $75,000 per film discouraged most producers, but, undaunted, she rented a skating rink to demonstrate her skill and appeal. Darryl Zanuck, charmed by her winsome Scandinavian personality and amazed at her proficiency on the ice, signed her to a long-term contract.

She was immediately successful. In her first film, *One in a Million* (1936), she revealed a very modest acting ability, but she turned into a quicksilver apparition in the elaborate skating production numbers. She played a Swiss girl whose father (Jean Hersholt) enters her in the skating Olympics, but whose interest turns more to reporter Don Ameche. Uncertain whether her skating alone could sustain a film, Zanuck gave her sturdy support with the Ritz Brothers, Adolphe Menjou (playing yet another eccentric entrepreneur), Dixie Dunbar, and dour-faced Ned Sparks.

Audiences responded with enthusiasm, and for the rest of the decade and into the forties, Henie appeared in a series of

The Littlest Rebel *(Fox, 1935). Shirley Temple dances with her most famous partner, Bill Robinson. One of Shirley's biggest hits, the movie featured her meeting with President Abraham Lincoln, in which she pleads with him to save her father, a Confederate officer, from the firing squad.*

icebound musicals that steadily decreased in popularity. Her costars changed but the plots varied very little, inevitably calling for production numbers in which Henie would emerge as what the *New York Times* called "some Scandinavian goddess of wind and snow." Every film allowed for at least one spectacular number: in *My Lucky Star* (1938), she performed an ice version of *Alice in Wonderland,* and in *Happy Landing* (1938), she was the whirling center of a dazzling "Snow Maiden" ballet. In *Second Fiddle* (1939), she had the benefit of some Irving Berlin songs. By the early forties, Henie's popularity was waning. Although *Sun Valley Serenade* (1941) was one of her best and most successful musicals, her last films for Fox—*Iceland* (1942) and *Wintertime* (1943)—were poorly received, and failed at the box office. After a few films at other studios, she retired from the screen to become a wealthy producer of ice revues and sports spectaculars.

There may have been box-office gold in Alice Faye and Sonja Henie, but the studio's greatest treasure was dimpled, sunny Shirley Temple. She was that rare phenomenon, a child actress who could sing, dance, laugh, and cry on cue without inducing nausea in adults. With her fifty-five golden curls bouncing and her bright eyes sparkling with mischief or glee, she charmed her way through a series of mostly ramshackle Fox musicals. At the peak of her popularity she was an American original, a folk heroine adored by movie audiences who saw in her the ideal child: bright, cheery, and self-reliant. She was also imitated by scores of hapless little girls under the thumbs of their ambitious mothers. By 1937 she was the highest-paid actress in Hollywood.

Frequently adapted from stickily sentimental stories that had been filmed in the silent era, her movies tended to be skimpy in their sets and costumes, merely adequate in their direction, and predictable in their plots. All that mattered was Shirley: pouting and giggling, generous and affectionate, her chubby arms ready to embrace her benefactors. In *Shirley Temple,* film historian Jeanine Basinger describes the standard Temple movie: The "basic ingredient of the child alone was mixed together with crusts of old codgers, heaps of adoring adults, pinches of heartbreak, and generous helpings of cheerful poverty (which quickly melted into lavish living)—all stirred up with the subtlety of a McCormick reaper and garnished with a few songs and dances."

Shirley's forthright delivery of the tinkly tunes she was assigned made them charming and appealing. From her true entrance into feature films in *Stand Up and Cheer*—she had appeared in bit roles in five previous movies—her professionalism was apparent. Many of the numbers in her early films are part of movie lore: entertaining a group of flyers with "On the Good Ship Lollypop" in *Bright Eyes* (1934); dancing up and down a staircase with Bill Robinson in *The Little Colonel* (1935); joining gangly Buddy Ebsen in a memorable rendition of "At the Codfish Ball" on the street of a New England fishing village in *Captain January* (1936); or carrying off an intricate tap routine to "I Love a Military Man" in *Poor Little Rich Girl* (1936).

In several of her films, Shirley performs musical tours de force remarkable for a child: In *Curly Top* (1935), she does an elaborate number to "When I Grow Up," impersonating a teenager as well as an old woman in a rocking chair. In *Stowaway* (1936), she does impressions of Al Jolson, Eddie Cantor, and—with a male doll attached to her toes—the dance team of Fred

Captain January *(Fox, 1936). Shirley Temple sprints her way through a New England fishing village with Buddy Ebsen. The number displayed her astonishing skill as she leaped over barrels and boxes, or tap-danced down the stairs.*

above, right: Alexander's Ragtime Band *(Fox, 1938). Alice Faye sings as Tyrone Power leads the band. An enormously popular movie,* Alexander's Ragtime Band *prompted Fox to continue dipping into the musical past. For the next few years, many of their musicals were nostalgic valentines to American popular entertainment.*

above: Rose of Washington Square *(Fox, 1939). Onstage, Alice Faye sings "My Man," a torch song for her errant husband (Tyrone Power). The film was based, not too loosely, on the troubled marriage of comedienne Fanny Brice and Nick Arnstein. Brice sued the studio, but the case was settled out of court. One of the movie's principal attractions was Al Jolson, bellowing some of the songs for which he was noted.*

right: Lillian Russell *(Fox, 1940). Alice Faye in the title role of the famous turn-of-the-century singer. A lavish but tepid "biography," the film was inexplicably made in black-and-white.*

opposite: Tin Pan Alley *(Fox, 1940). Alice Faye and Betty Grable in another familiar but breezy and tuneful period musical. Faye, then the studio's top musical star, was teamed for the first and last time with Grable, its most important future attraction.*

Astaire and Ginger Rogers. *Heidi* (1937) includes a dream sequence in which she sings and dances in Dutch costume to "My Little Wooden Shoes" and, wearing an ornate eighteenth-century French gown and powdered wig, also dances a minuet. Under the budget restrictions, few of her songs received full treatment, but *Little Miss Broadway* (1938) closes with a mind-boggling production number in which Shirley, suddenly acquiring a tiara and ballet slippers, dances about a courtroom with George Murphy.

As Shirley Temple's popularity waned by the late thirties, Alice Faye remained the studio's most prominent musical star, and in her softer, more demure persona of the mid-thirties, she was the logical choice to play the leading role in what Zanuck regarded as one of his major films: a musical chronicle of America over the years as personified by the career and the songs of Irving Berlin. He would call it *Alexander's Ragtime Band* (1938).

Until that point, few major musical films other than *Show Boat* and *High, Wide and Handsome* had been set in America's past. Virtually all the offspring of *The Broadway Melody* took place in the fast-paced contemporary world of show business, and the Astaire-Rogers musicals until *The Story of Vernon and Irene Castle* were also strictly contemporary in their sophistication and elegance. Even the Jeanette MacDonald–Nelson Eddy operettas that took place in the America of another century evoked little sense of the American scene in the European-inspired music of Sigmund Romberg, Rudolf Friml, or Victor Herbert. It remained for Irving Berlin, with his distinctively American variety of singable, foot-tapping, frankly sentimental music, to popularize the kind of film musical that reconstructed and celebrated, in admittedly idealized terms, the shape of American life in other years.

The film spans many years in the lives of three people: Roger Grant (Tyrone Power), a classical musician who, under the name of "Alexander," organizes a ragtime band; Stella Kirby (Alice Faye), the band singer he transforms from a flashy honky-tonk type into a famous Broadway star; and Charlie Dwyer (Don Ameche), band member and faithful friend. As they go from San Francisco before World War I to the late thirties, Alec and Stella fall in and out of love, while Charlie waits patiently on the sidelines for Stella. Involved in their fortunes, good and bad, are a hearty singer named Jerry Allen (Ethel Merman) and affable Davey Lane (Jack Haley).

Later musicals would amply evoke American life in their dramatic incidents based on history, and in their meticulously reconstructed costumes and settings. But *Alexander's Ragtime Band* makes little effort in this direction, conveying only a suggestion of the country's changing life-styles over more than twenty years. Here the breezy, confident spirit of America resides squarely in the songs by Irving Berlin. From "The International Rag," sung by Faye, Haley, and Chick Chandler on one of their first band dates, to the final reprise of the title song as Alec and Stella are reunited, the score is a catalogue of delights, brimming with Berlin's enthusiasm for America's good cheer and hearty optimism ("Nothing but blue skies do I see"). Alice Faye is in top form, her smooth, unaffected style giving the songs just what they call for, no more and no less. In the more ladylike manner affected by Stella after Alec has forced her to have some "class," she sings a brisk "Everybody's Doin' It," and she gives a velvety reading of Berlin's new ballad "Now It Can Be Told."

Most of Berlin's rhythm songs go to Ethel Merman, and this inimitable singer belts out such songs as "Say It with Music" and "Blue Skies" with her usual vigor and authority. In Paris, she joins with chorus girls wearing devils' costumes in an ear-shattering performance of "Pack Up Your Sins." In the movie's last scene, at a Carnegie Hall band concert, she raises the temperature with her definitive reading of "Heat Wave."

The success of *Alexander's Ragtime Band* prompted Fox to continue dipping into the musical past. For the next few years, many of its musicals were nostalgic valentines to American popular entertainment, inevitably starring Alice Faye. Bedecked in lavish gowns, she impersonated a torch-carrying musical star in *Rose of Washington Square* (1939), a none-too-authentic *Lillian Russell* (1940) in a very loose "biography" of the famed singer, and half of a vaudeville sister act (Betty Grable was the other half) in *Tin Pan Alley* (1940). She also starred with John Payne and Jack Oakie in a salute to radio called *The Great American Broadcast* (1941). There were many similar musicals to come, and it would be some time before Fox or the other major studios would retire their period costumes.

Less ramshackle than Paramount's musical films, less opulent than MGM's, Fox's song-and-dance films in the thirties revolved about marketable personalities rather than the music or the production values. Lightly satirical or sweetly sentimental, they aimed at pleasing the public with the winning ways of their top musical stars: a throaty chanteuse, a goddess of snow and ice, and a little princess.

MGM Grandiose and Glittering Goldwyn

After introducing *The Broadway Melody* to delighted audiences, Metro-Goldwyn-Mayer had been caught up in the industry's frantic rush to produce "all-talking, all-singing, all-dancing" films. But the years 1931 and 1932 had been a dry musical period, as it had for the other studios. In fact, MGM had released no musical film in 1932.

The success of *42nd Street* early in 1933 did not go unnoticed at MGM. The triumphant hooting of the Warner brothers at their resuscitation of the musical genre must have irritated more than a few MGM executives. At the same time, Joan Crawford, one of the studio's biggest stars, was in trouble at the box office. Her two films after *Grand Hotel,* W. Somerset Maugham's *Rain* (1932), which she did on loan to United Artists, and a turgid war romance called *Today We Live* (1933), had fared poorly with critics and the public. It was decided to boost her sagging career with a musical extravaganza called *Dancing Lady* (1933).

Under Robert Z. Leonard's direction, Crawford was tossed, tap shoes and all, into a musical that was almost a blatant imitation of *42nd Street*. She played Janie Barlow, a tough-minded, ambitious chorus girl who becomes a dancing star under the reluctant tutelage of hard-driving director Patch Gallagher (Clark Gable). It was really a reworking of the familiar Crawford role: the girl from the lower rungs of the ladder whose goal is upward mobility at any cost. Though reputedly unhappy in his role, Gable created a reasonable facsimile of Warner Baxter, working the chorus line into a lather, badgering the determined Janie until he sees her star quality and, incidentally, her potential as a romantic partner. *Dancing Lady* even copied *42nd Street*'s snappy backstage banter and obligatory production numbers, elaborate beyond those of any real theater stage.

The intention was clear, but unfortunately, the execution left something to be desired. The musical numbers in *Dancing Lady* are gaudy and replete with camera trickery in the Berkeley style, but they lack the vitality and the brazen, amusing vulgarity of the Warners spectacles. And Crawford is far from being an authentic musical comedy star; her modest and tentative dancing, perched somewhere between the clumsiness of Joan Fontaine and the skill of Eleanor Powell, makes the acclaim she receives highly suspect. In "Heigh, Ho, the Gang's All Here," she does a fast dance with Fred Astaire, playing himself in an inauspicious film debut, then flies off with him on a magic carpet to a Bavarian beer garden, where, in peasant garb, they sing and dance to "Let's Go Bavarian." Another number is even more extravagant: a "then-and-now" fantasy to the tune of "That's the Rhythm of the Day." A chorus in elaborate eighteenth-century dress is exhorted by Nelson Eddy (in his second film) to stop their mincing minuet and dance to a jazzy beat. Everyone changes into modern costume, and the number's dazzling finale features a kaleidoscopic carrousel on which smiling chorines ride mechanical horses as they are photographed from all angles.

Since Joan Crawford was clearly not destined to become MGM's dancing darling, another performer assumed that role for the next few years. A talented tap dancer with a beaming smile and limited acting ability, Eleanor Powell had made her film debut in *George White's 1935 Scandals,* then signed a contract with MGM. Her first film for the studio, directed by Roy Del Ruth, was *Broadway Melody of 1936* (1935), an attempt to recall—if only in title—the landmark 1929 musical, *The Broadway Melody*. A group of entertaining musical numbers grafted onto a thoroughly silly plot, *Broadway Melody of 1936* starred Powell, Robert Taylor, and Jack Benny, with support from Buddy Ebsen and his sister Vilma. The production numbers, splashy but less inclined than Berkeley's to camera trickery or brash vulgarity, were built around the Nacio Herb Brown–Arthur Freed songs, which included "I've Got a Feelin' You're Foolin' " (with a vocal by Robert Taylor in his very own voice), "Broadway Rhythm," and "My Lucky Star." But the film's best numbers were the simplest: Powell's marvelous tap solo, done partially without music, and a genial, easygoing song and dance to "Sing Before Breakfast," performed on a New York rooftop by Powell and the Ebsens. Buddy Ebsen was especially engaging with his loose-limbed, eccentric dancing style.

The following year, Eleanor Powell was again directed by Roy Del Ruth, in *Born to Dance,* a musical whose virtues happily outweigh its faults, and the faults are not serious. The principal defect (a common one) is a foolish story that had Powell as an

ambitious young dancer coming to New York City to find fame and fortune. She succeeds, of course, and also finds romance with a sailor, played by James Stewart in his early "aw-shucks" style. But the movie had ample musical compensations, provided by Cole Porter in one of his better film scores. Porter had come to Hollywood in late 1935 and loved it immediately: "It's like living on the moon, isn't it?"

The most agreeable number teamed Powell and Stewart in a park setting. Stewart, in his own light but pleasing voice, sings "Easy to Love" to his new-found sweetheart, then Powell performs a lyrical dance to the song. Earlier, Stewart and Powell join friends Frances Langford, Buddy Ebsen, Una Merkel, and Sid Silvers in a rollicking rendition of "Hey, Babe!," and on an Art Deco rooftop, a dubbed Virginia Bruce, playing a temperamental musical comedy star, sings "I've Got You Under My Skin" to an embarrassed Stewart. The film's finale, using a nautical motif for the song "Swingin' the Jinx Away," is one of those mammoth MGM creations that, unlike Busby Berkeley's numbers, is too humorless and intent on its "big effects" to revel in its bad taste. The number was created by Roger Edens, the gifted composer and arranger who later became a vital member of the celebrated Arthur Freed Unit.

With little chance to rest her busily tapping feet, Powell was assigned to another *Broadway Melody* film, this one dated 1938 and released in the fall of 1937. Robert Taylor was again on hand, as was George Murphy, the bush-league Fred Astaire. Most of the footage was given to the musical numbers, and—in an odd fashion of the time—to specialty routines such as Robert Wilback's "sneezing" demonstration. Powell danced in the rain with George Murphy, in a boxcar with Murphy and Buddy Ebsen, and in a lavish finale. The movie's Freed-Brown score included "Feelin' like a Million," "Follow in My Footsteps," and "Yours and Mine."

This musical *Melody* also contained a footnote to film history in the presence of fifteen-year-old Judy Garland. An MGM contractee since 1935, she had appeared opposite Deanna Durbin in a one-reeler called *Every Sunday,* in which each girl had the chance to demonstrate her style of singing. Legend has it that Louis B. Mayer ordered, "Drop the fat one," meaning Garland, but Durbin was sent packing instead. At a party in February, 1937, Garland had sung Roger Edens's specially written tribute to Clark Gable on his thirty-sixth birthday: a version of "You Made Me Love You" with interpolated commentary to his photograph. It won applause, a kiss from Gable, and the opportunity to repeat the number in *Broadway Melody of 1938.* On screen the number was a showstopper. Her throbbing voice lends an unexpected touch of poignancy to the gushing lyrics.

By far the most extravagant MGM musical of the period— and the studio's most expensive film since *Ben-Hur* ten years earlier—was *The Great Ziegfeld* (1936). Overlong and top-heavy, it nevertheless combined the elements that appealed to audiences and impressed Academy members, who voted it the year's best film: a mostly fictionalized story concerning showman Florenz Ziegfeld; a star cast headed by William Powell, Myrna Loy, and an intense young Viennese actress named Luise Rainer; and, above all, production numbers astonishing in their lavishness. As a welcome added attraction, a number of Ziegfeld's greatest

Broadway Melody of 1936 *(MGM, 1935). Robert Taylor sings "I've Got a Feelin' You're Foolin'" to June Knight. Taylor sang in his own voice, but it was the only time he was given the opportunity.*

page 118: *Filming an extravagant production number for* Rosalie *(MGM, 1937). The studio's prodigious resources are very much in evidence.*

opposite: Dancing Lady *(MGM, 1933). Chorus-girl-turned-star Janie Barlow (Joan Crawford) dances to "Heigh, Ho, the Gang's All Here" with an established stage star named Fred Astaire (making his film debut). Seeing himself on the screen, Astaire exclaimed, "My God, I look like a knife!"*

Born to Dance (MGM, 1936). "Swingin' the Jinx Away," a stupendous number aboard an Art Deco battleship, ended with Eleonor Powell flipping into a standing salute, as the ship's guns fired directly into the camera. Years later, the number was called "an embarrassment of bad taste" by its creator, composer-arranger Roger Edens.

Broadway Melody of 1938 (MGM, 1937). Eleanor Powell, decked out in top hat and tails, leads the musical's finale.

stars either appeared (Fanny Brice) or were impersonated (Will Rogers, Eddie Cantor).

The film takes Ziegfeld from his early days as a sideshow promoter, through his ill-fated marriage to French singer Anna Held (Luise Rainer), his lavish and popular series of *Follies,* his happy marriage to stage actress Billie Burke (Myrna Loy), which, from all reports, was not always that happy, to his financial and physical decline and death. Episodic and rambling, the screenplay touches the high points in Ziegfeld's life, but seldom strikes any emotional sparks.

The movie's production numbers are truly spectacular, and one, on the New Amsterdam Roof, almost defies description. In a Busby Berkeley–like dormitory, chorus girls sprawl on beds and coyly cover themselves with blankets. They then proceed to open bottles of champagne and dance on top of the rhythmically moving beds. The number is as close as MGM ever got to matching Berkeley in spirit and intention. In the closing segment, the gaudily costumed girls parade to the song ''You Never Looked So Beautiful.''

The film's most awesome number takes place during one of the *Follies.* On a stage of vast proportions, Dennis Morgan (billed under his real name of Stanley Morner, and dubbed by Allan Jones) stands atop a high platform singing ''A Pretty Girl Is like a Melody.'' One delirious moment follows another in a Ziegfeldian mixture of ballet, opera, and spectacle. A viewer who can retain his sanity during this number will behold girls strutting in wildly exotic Oriental garb, an excerpt from *Pagliacci,* a dance performed to George Gershwin's ''Rhapsody in Blue'' by chorines in glittering black costumes, and (shades of Berkeley) chorus boys ''playing'' many pianos simultaneously. This overstuffed number won an Academy Award for its dance director, Seymour Felix.

Many other MGM musicals of the thirties were extravagant, but a higher budget did not necessarily spell higher achievement. It was as if all the lavish trappings were weighing down the proceedings, making them cumbersome rather than lighter-than-air in the best musical tradition. A case in point was another Eleanor Powell musical, *Rosalie* (1937), based on Ziegfeld's 1928 stage musical. All the credentials were present for a surefire hit. The story of a romance between an incognito princess (Powell) and a West Point cadet (Nelson Eddy) may have been absurd, but it was offset by some Cole Porter songs, especially the haunting ''In the Still of the Night,'' which were substituted for the original tunes by Sigmund Romberg and George Gershwin. The impressive supporting cast included Edna May Oliver, Ilona Massey (in her American film debut), Ray Bolger, and Frank Morgan in his original stage role. Yet somehow the movie was tedious, with a sluggish pace, two wooden leads, and musical numbers that seemed to stretch into infinity. It could not be rescued by an eye-popping finale for the wedding of Princess Rosalie and her cadet. Eight huge pipe organs join a sixty-piece orchestra and a chorus of one hundred voices to play the *Lohengrin* Wedding March. As Eddy sings the title tune, Powell dances down a staircase made of enormous bass drums of graduated sizes.

One MGM musical film of 1939 towered above the others, and indeed above most of the musical films of the decade and beyond. The previous year, Loew's Inc., MGM's parent company,

above: The Great Ziegfeld *(MGM, 1936). Florenz Ziegfeld (William Powell) steps out with his second wife, the beauteous stage star Billie Burke (Myrna Loy). Reportedly, their life together was not as idyllic as it was depicted in the film.*

top: The Great Ziegfeld *(MGM, 1936). Impresario Florenz Ziegfeld (William Powell) kisses the hand of his future star and wife, Anna Held (Luise Rainer). Most of the film's histrionics fell to Rainer, who acted with such an excess of winsomeness that a nonindulgent viewer might be tempted to throttle her. She did, however, win that year's Academy Award as best actress.*

opposite: The Great Ziegfeld *(MGM, 1936). A striking moment from this film's most spectacular production number. In the midst of all the musical activity swirling below her, Ziegfeld girl Audrey Dane (Virginia Bruce) poses serenely atop a revolving platform.*

Rosalie (MGM, 1937). Eleanor Powell and a horde of extras in one of the musical's overstuffed numbers. When Cole Porter's title song for the film was rejected by Louis B. Mayer, who asked him to write "a good old-fashioned honky-tonk number" instead, an enraged Porter composed a new version in three hours. Mayer accepted it, and the song was a great success. But Porter always considered it the dreariest tune he had ever written.

The Great Waltz (MGM, 1938). In her one film, Polish opera star Miliza Korjus performs in an operatic sequence. One of MGM's most costly films of the decade, the movie purported to be the story of "Waltz King" Strauss, played by Belgian actor Fernand Gravet. The film was heavy going, but it had one memorable sequence: Johann Strauss's composing of "Tales from the Vienna Woods" as he rides at dawn through the woodland with opera singer Carla Donner (Korjus).

had purchased the rights to L. Frank Baum's beloved children's stories of the land of Oz from Samuel Goldwyn. The stories, written by Baum between 1904 and 1919, had served twice before, in 1910 and 1925, as the basis for films. Now Louis B. Mayer and Arthur Freed, a studio songwriter and aspiring producer, were discussing a musical version of the property. Freed was finally made associate producer, with Mervyn LeRoy, recently brought over to MGM from Warners, as executive producer. At first the film's direction was assigned to Richard Thorpe, then to George Cukor (for two days), and finally to Victor Fleming. Judy Garland was cast in the leading role of Dorothy when Shirley Temple was unavailable.

Viewed more than four decades after its release, The Wizard of Oz remains an enchanting film with flaws that cannot seriously mar its durable delights. Dorothy's trip, as we follow her from her Kansas farm down the Yellow Brick Road to the Emerald City and back home again, is depicted with rare cinematic imagination and skill. At the beginning, we may wonder at the obvious falseness of the black-and-white Kansas setting, although the flat, arid landscape ultimately makes an effective contrast to the later scenes in Oz. But rationality disappears the moment Judy Garland, perhaps a shade too old for the role of Dorothy, strikes at the heart with her tremulous singing of "Over the Rainbow." And when Frank Morgan appears as Professor Marvel, we are captivated by his familiar bumbling charm.

Dorothy's entrance into the land of Oz remains one of the screen's most memorable moments, as the black-and-white scenes give way to Harold Rosson's glowing color photography. "I have a feeling we're not in Kansas anymore!" is her understated response as she enters Munchkinland. The sequence in Munchkinland, though beautifully designed, is actually a mixed blessing. Billie Burke is exactly right as the Good Witch of the North, and Margaret Hamilton is wonderfully shrill and repulsive as the Wicked Witch of the West. But the Munchkins themselves, midgets gathered from all over the world for the occasion, are rather off-putting with their wizened, prematurely old faces and chipmunk voices.

Once Dorothy meets her friends on the road to the Emerald City, all's right with the movie. The talents of Dorothy's friends —Jack Haley as the Tin Man, Ray Bolger as the Scarecrow, Bert Lahr as the Cowardly Lion—have been frequently celebrated, but their good humor and their shining humanity behind the grotesque makeup remain fresh forever. It is true that Lahr virtually steals the show with his inspired low-comedy performance as the Lion: we cherish his raucous "Put 'em up! Put 'em up!" when the travelers first meet him, his flapping tail when he is disguised as one of the Witch's guards, and—best of all—his unforgettable rendition of "If I Were King of the Forest." But Ray Bolger is also fine as the Scarecrow, forever stuffing hay into his innards, and Jack Haley gives the Tin Man a gentle sweetness that is totally disarming. Their scenes together, as they dance with Dorothy down the road to Oz, are the stuff of movie legend.

The subsequent scenes in the Emerald City, and in the Witch's castle, are studded with magical moments. Along with the delightful special effects—the Horse of a Different Color, the fraudulent Wizard's noisy contraptions, the Witch's skywriting

The Wizard of Oz *(MGM, 1939)*. *Friends forever, the Scarecrow (Ray Bolger), the Tin Man (Jack Haley), Dorothy (Judy Garland), and the Cowardly Lion (Bert Lahr) march down the immortal Yellow Brick Road. Toto is undoubtedly somewhere in the vicinity.*

The Wizard of Oz *(MGM, 1939). The Wicked Witch (Margaret Hamilton) spies on Dorothy (Judy Garland) and the Scarecrow (Ray Bolger) as they march down the Yellow Brick Road. Gale Sondergaard was scheduled to play the role, but director Mervyn LeRoy decided that a beautiful witch would disturb everyone who had read the book.*

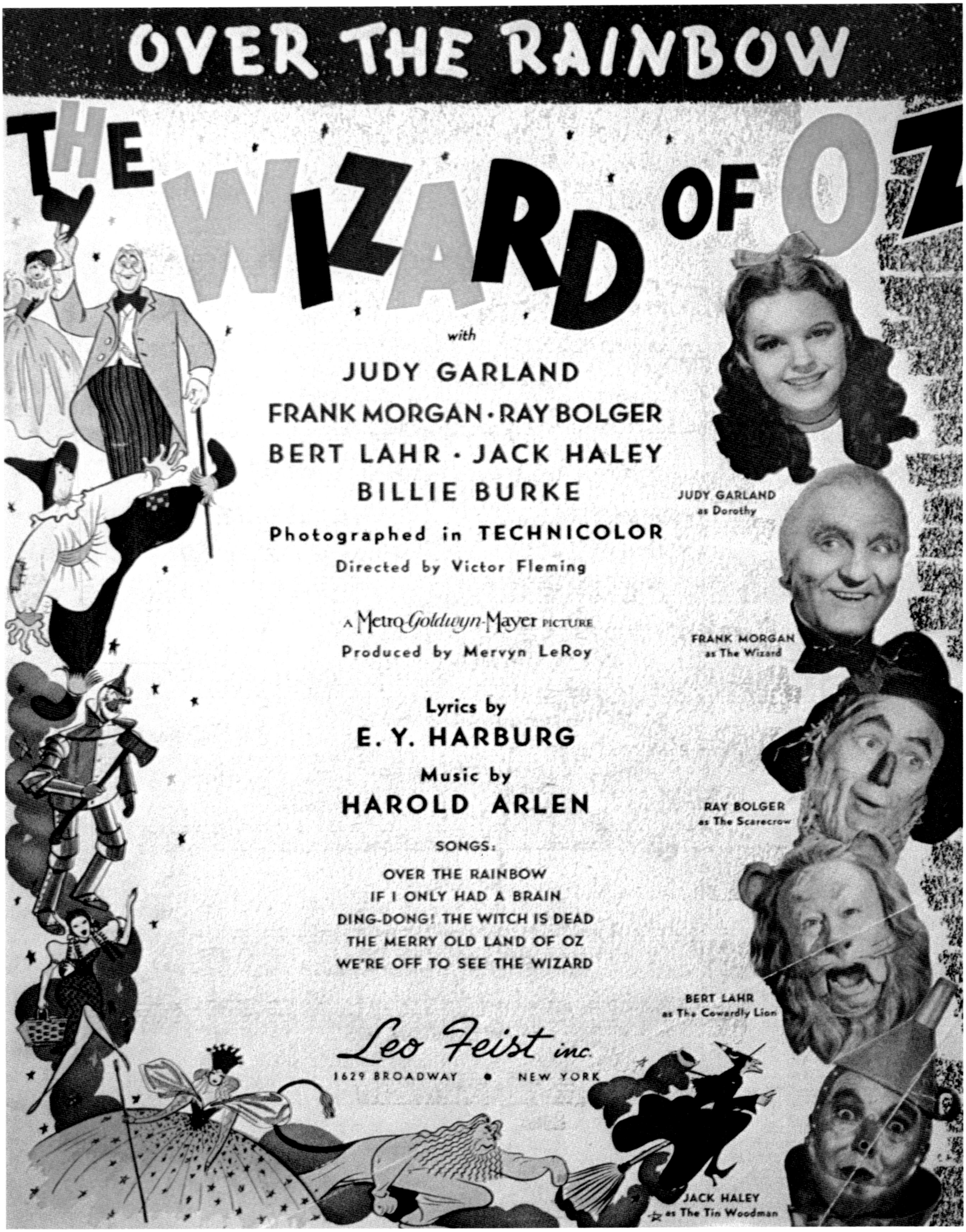

The cover of the sheet music to The Wizard of Oz *(MGM, 1939).*

of "Surrender, Dorothy"—the perennial viewer recalls Frank Morgan's adept playing of several roles, including the Emerald City gateman and the Cockney coachman, and the Wicked Witch's final moments as she melts into oblivion. After she has spent the entire movie threatening cataclysms at every turn, her last words are curiously poignant. "What a world! What a world!" she moans. "Who would have thought that a good little girl like you could spoil my beautiful wickedness?"

Although *The Wizard of Oz*, with a score of nearly a dozen songs, certainly qualifies as a musical, the music has never been the most important factor in its durable appeal. And yet the E. Y. ("Yip") Harburg–Harold Arlen songs are immutably bound into the fabric of the movie, adding to its charm and above all to our perception of the characters. "Over the Rainbow" may have become an indelible part of the Judy Garland legend, but it also expresses Dorothy's—and every child's—longing to move beyond one narrow corner of the world to a private and wonderful Oz. Bert Lahr's songs are inspired low-comedy turns in the best burlesque tradition, but they make the Cowardly Lion's false bravado even more endearing. ("What makes a Hottentot so hot? Courage!") The songs never stop the action: "We're Off to See the Wizard!" the friends sing—and so they are.

The Wizard of Oz is a joy forever, but, in the final analysis, one must question the simple homilies that it offers as its message. Dorothy finds all the happiness she would want in her own home—"my heart's desire" is in "my own backyard"—but, while comforting, this attitude would leave worlds undiscovered and lives unlived. Other of the movie's pronouncements, such as the Wizard's comment to the Tin Man that "a heart is not judged by how much *you* love, but by how much you are loved by others," are further examples of hollow sampler sentiment. Yet carping aside, there are few scenes that can match this film's final moment when the camera settles on Dorothy's face and she cries, "Oh, Auntie Em, there's *no* place like home!" Judy Garland's luminous sincerity in the role earned her a special Oscar for the year's most outstanding juvenile performance and made her an international star.

Why does *The Wizard of Oz* still glow, while other films of the period grow dimmer every year? It is unquestionably due to more than the sum of its sterling cast, winning songs, and lovely special effects, although the absence of these virtues has turned more than one "musical fantasy" into failures. It may be that when Dorothy steps from black-and-white Kansas into the bright colors of Munchkinland, she is taking everyone's first voyage of discovery. With the universality of the best fables, *The Wizard of Oz* has her learning about evil (the Wicked Witch), friendship (her companions on the road to Oz), and fallibility (the Wizard). And somehow children—and the child in all of us—like to see this voyage made repeatedly, every year on television. *The Wizard of Oz* has gone beyond popularity to become a ritual.

MGM's musicals in the thirties had begun by imitating Busby Berkeley without duplicating his flair, and ended with a musical film that no other studio could duplicate. In between, the studio had produced a number of musical films that tried to substitute size for style and inevitably failed. Grandiose and often elephantine, they sought to overwhelm moviegoers with their

The Wizard of Oz *(MGM, 1939). Having been roused by the Good Witch of the North from a dangerous slumber caused by the Wicked Witch, Dorothy and her friends head joyfully for the Emerald City.*

The Wizard of Oz *(MGM, 1939)*. *The Cowardly Lion (Bert Lahr),*
cheerful for once rather than terrified, enjoys his visit to the Emerald City
with his friends. Lahr's performance was the best in the film: broad,
hilarious, and totally irresistible.

opulence and proceeded to put them to sleep with their dullness. (Today, many of their musical numbers are considered so outrageous that the laughter keeps viewers from dozing.) There were incidental rewards: the expert tapping feet of Eleanor Powell, some Cole Porter tunes, the bracing presence of such past and future stars as Fanny Brice and Judy Garland. But most of the time the going was heavy, heavy.

Ironically, the next two decades would firmly establish MGM as the most outstanding and creative producer of musical films. In the forties, the emergence of the fabled Arthur Freed Unit, and the burgeoning talents of such musical performers as Judy Garland and Gene Kelly, would send the studio into orbit, from which it descended only when the musical genre lost its momentum in the late fifties. For MGM, the triumphant musicals were all in the years ahead.

By the thirties, the name "Goldwyn" had long been nothing but a hyphenate in "Metro-Goldwyn-Mayer." Many years before, edged out of the corporation he had formed with Metro Pictures and Louis B. Mayer Productions, he had founded his own company, Samuel Goldwyn Productions. Anxious to prove that he was a master showman, he began producing prestigious films, with strong, capable players and expensive production values. Many of his movies were romantic dramas, but following the stock market crash in 1929, Goldwyn decided that what audiences needed most was a healthy dose of music and laughter. At the center of his plan was one of Florenz Ziegfeld's leading comedians, the irrepressible and indefatigible Eddie Cantor.

Convinced that Cantor's stage appeal could be transposed to the screen, Goldwyn cast him in a series of six elaborate musical films between 1930 and 1936. The first, *Whoopee* (1930), was coproduced with Florenz Ziegfeld from Ziegfeld's 1928 stage show starring Cantor. Filmed in two-color Technicolor, which gave the movie an unreal but not unpleasing hue, *Whoopee* was set on an Arizona dude ranch overrun with cowboys and chorus girls. Cantor played a hypochondriac whose imaginary ailments did not keep him from making jokes or from breaking into song. Inevitably, his big number was the show-stopping "Makin' Whoopee." The film's most notable feature was its dances, staged by Busby Berkeley, a Broadway dance director new to films. A dance by Indian maidens (including Betty Grable) displayed the touches that were later to become his trademarks: the close formations in perfect symmetry, the kaleidoscopic views shot from overhead, and the close-ups of each smiling girl.

Berkeley also staged the dances for Cantor's next films, *Palmy Days* (1931), *The Kid from Spain* (1932), and *Roman Scandals* (1933). *Palmy Days* cast Cantor as a timid soul who is mistaken for an efficiency expert and becomes involved with a gang led by George Raft and with Charlotte Greenwood, a man-chasing amazon. Berkeley's direction was evident in the dances, and Cantor got to sing "My Baby Said Yes, Yes" and (in blackface) "There's Nothing Too Good for My Baby." *The Kid from Spain* had a larger budget than usual (one million dollars, high in those days), and the typical harebrained plot, including a slapstick finale with the comedian as a terrified bullfighter. Cantor's big song was "What a Perfect Combination."

Roman Scandals, written by George S. Kaufman and Robert

E. Sherwood after their abortive attempt to fashion a musical version of Shaw's *Androcles and the Lion* for the comedian, was Cantor's most elaborate musical of the period. As a down-and-out drifter in West Rome, Oklahoma, Cantor daydreams his way back to ancient Rome, where he becomes enmeshed in various low-comedy situations, including a climactic wild chariot race. This time, Berkeley moved perilously close to the censor's shears, especially in his "slave auction" number in which the chorus girls were nude, though strategically covered with their long hair. Cantor exhorted them to "Keep Young and Beautiful," and also cheered up the Depression community of West Rome with "Build a Little Home."

Kid Millions (1934) suffered from a barrage of mostly unfunny jokes and situations, and an inane plot that found Cantor as a none-too-bright young man who inherits a fortune from his archaeologist father and becomes the target for greedy types. Luckily, the musical numbers, delivered by Cantor, Ethel Merman, Ann Sothern, and George Murphy (in his film debut), had a degree of charm (especially Cantor's "When My Ship Comes In"), and the finale was a joyful surprise. The sequence, filmed in a pleasantly pastel three-color Technicolor, had Cantor fulfilling his dream of opening an ice cream factory for children. Cantor's last film for Goldwyn, *Strike Me Pink* (1936), was one of his weakest, a mediocre musical in which he played a timid mouse who becomes a raging lion in defending an inherited amusement park from the designs of slot-machine racketeers.

Like MGM's musicals of the thirties, Goldwyn's musicals of the period were exercises in extravagance, but once again their lavishness was usually more oppressive than exhilarating, with little of the audacity or wit that made Berkeley's movies for Warners and some of their imitations perversely entertaining. Whatever pleasure they afforded came in musical moments: a jaunty song by Eddie Cantor or Ethel Merman, or a musical number employing as much imagination as money, such as the fantasy sequence in *Kid Millions.* Goldwyn's later ventures into the musical genre would seldom match his dramatic films, nor did he approach the stature of Florenz Ziegfeld, despite his best efforts. Yet, if only as camp amusement, his musicals retain a measure of fun.

Their Voices Raised in Song

Apparently the movie-going audience of the thirties liked its stars in pairs: aside from that tiny international favorite, Shirley Temple, and a crooner named Bing Crosby, musical film stars of the day were singing sweethearts Dick Powell and Ruby Keeler, and the dance team of Ginger Rogers and Fred Astaire. There were two other performers whose popularity was phenomenal: redheaded singer Jeanette MacDonald and her newest costar, a blond baritone named Nelson Eddy.

After her sparkling musicals with Maurice Chevalier, plus a few songless comedies during the period in which musicals were in disfavor, Jeanette MacDonald had left for Europe on a strenuous concert tour. Her contract with Paramount had ended, but MGM had its eye on her, planning to star her in several musicals. Like Darryl Zanuck at Warners, Irving Thalberg believed that musical films would return to popularity—and Zanuck had already entered the market with *42nd Street.* Thalberg—and Louis B. Mayer—felt it was time to join the bandwagon. Persuaded by an offer she couldn't refuse, MacDonald signed a contract with MGM early in 1933. Following *The Cat and the Fiddle,* her first musical for the studio, she was given a plum assignment: the title role in a lavish remake of Franz Lehár's perennial operetta *The Merry Widow.*

The tribulations surrounding this sumptuous production have been well recorded. MacDonald was reluctant to appear in yet another frivolous operetta, and she was not pleased with costar Maurice Chevalier, whom she called ''the fastest derrière pincher in Hollywood.'' For his part, Chevalier disliked what he regarded as her prudishness and highhanded ways. As usual, Louis Mayer got his own way: he launched the film under the direction of Ernst Lubitsch, with MacDonald and Chevalier as his edgy stars. Lehár's music was embellished with new lyrics by Lorenz Hart and Gus Kahn.

The Merry Widow is a champagne cocktail that bubbles merrily from first sip to last. Its familiar plot is treated not with the mocking decadence of Erich von Stroheim's 1925 silent version but with the impudence and wit characteristic of Ernst Lubitsch at his best. The film even begins stylishly: a magnifying glass is held over a map to reveal the tiny Central European country of Marshovia. It is 1885, and the country's wealthiest widow, Sonia

(MacDonald), is planning to end her grieving and move to Paris. The move would ruin Marshovia's economy: after all, she owns 52 percent of the country. Captain Danilo (Chevalier), Marshovia's most dashing roué, is assigned to court her in Paris and bring her back home. Thus begins a series of amusing stratagems and deceptions in which Sonia pretends to be one of the available girls at Maxim's, Paris's gayest night spot, and Danilo finds himself entranced and bewildered by the lovely lady.

The film is studded with memorable moments: Sonia's black dresses, furniture, and dog suddenly turning white when she decides to end her period of mourning; Danilo's attempt to seduce Sonia in the private room at Maxim's; and Danilo's comic trial for treason, at which he wears handcuffs engraved with a message from one of his admirers. But of course it is the glorious music that lingers in the memory. By this time Chevalier had learned to restrain his strenuous mugging, and the result is delightful, especially in his jaunty ''I'm Going to Maxim's,'' and a joyful ''Girls! Girls! Girls!'' as he marches with his troops through the streets of Marshovia, or leaps about the dance floor with a cluster of Maxim's coquettes on each arm. MacDonald sings the lovely ''Villa'' from her balcony window and also beguiles with her rendition of ''Paris in the Spring.''

Inevitably, the film's most impressive sequence revolves about the ''Merry Widow Waltz.'' In Maxim's private dining room, a bewildered Danilo is suddenly enchanted by Sonia as she whirls about his table, singing the unforgettable melody of the waltz. Later, they begin to dance together in an empty ballroom, to be joined after a moment by dozens of couples who come pouring through the door to the music. As the music increases in tempo, the dancers fill the screen—and in one dazzling image, they waltz down a mirrored hall. The ''Merry Widow Waltz'' envelops them and the audience with a feeling of rapture seldom achieved in a musical number.

Although *The Merry Widow* failed to generate as much business as expected, Louis B. Mayer was enthusiastic about Jeanette MacDonald's future as one of the ''stars'' in his MGM ''heaven,'' and he revived a plan to make *Naughty Marietta* with her. Reputedly, MacDonald balked at playing the lead but

The Merry Widow (MGM, 1934). The widow Sonia (Jeanette MacDonald) entrances the dashing Captain Danilo (Maurice Chevalier) in a private room at Maxim's. The censor objected to MacDonald's "horizontal" position during this scene and insisted that she keep her feet on the floor at all times.

page 134: Maytime (MGM, 1937). Lovers Marcia Mornay (Jeanette MacDonald) and Paul Allison (Nelson Eddy) join in the festivities of a country fair. This idyllic sequence is one of the best-remembered in the MacDonald-Eddy musical romances.

opposite, below: Rose Marie (MGM, 1936). Mountie Nelson Eddy courts opera star Jeanette MacDonald, even though he is stalking her brother, a fugitive from justice.

relented when Mayer acted out the story for her, told her to put more feeling in her singing, and, as a demonstration, sang "Eli, Eli," a Hebrew lament, on bended knee. The studio casting office set out to find a new costar for MacDonald. On the lot since 1933 was a young baritone who had appeared in small roles in three musical films. With a background in opera and radio, Nelson Eddy had hoped for a concert career, but a tempting offer from Mayer convinced the singer to move to Hollywood. He was assigned to play opposite Jeanette MacDonald in a new version of the 1910 operetta by Victor Herbert and Rida Johnson Young.

At first glance the prospects for *Naughty Marietta* were not favorable. The budget for the film was not large. The male lead was an unproven singer whose acting experience was mostly confined to opera. And the director was not Ernst Lubitsch but W. S. ("Woody") Van Dyke, known as "One Take" Van Dyke for his ability to get through a production on time and without wasted effort. Yet *Naughty Marietta* (1935) became one of the largest-grossing musical films to that time, and MacDonald and Eddy were established as singing idols whose popularity extended into the next decade.

The plot, set in pre-Revolutionary America, remains airy nonsense concerning a disguised French princess (MacDonald) who is befriended—and ultimately loved—by the captain (Eddy) of a troop of mercenary scouts. After several narrow escapes and a number of songs, the pair head west to begin a new life. MacDonald plays Princess Marie (Marietta) with the tongue-in-cheek exaggeration that she used for her more sophisticated films with Chevalier, and although she resorts to the facial reactions that would become excessive in later films, she is a charming heroine. Eddy, however, is clearly ill at ease as Captain Warrington, his flat, wooden line readings making MacDonald seem all the more animated. (James Robert Parish, in *The Jeanette MacDonald Story*, recounts that director Van Dyke was reputed to have said, "I've handled Indians, African natives, South Sea Islanders, rhinos, pygmies, and Eskimos, and made them act— but not Nelson Eddy.")

Still, there is no resisting the Victor Herbert music, and few tried. By now the songs have become indelibly identified with the stars: "Tramp, Tramp, Tramp," " 'Neath the Southern Moon," "Italian Street Song," and "I'm Falling in Love with Someone" were mythologized by MacDonald and Eddy. Best of all is their performance of "Ah, Sweet Mystery of Life." At a ball, Marietta is asked to sing for the guests. She agrees, although she fears that her beloved captain will risk his life by showing up to spirit her away. She begins to sing "Ah, Sweet Mystery of Life," then starts to rush away in tears. Suddenly Warrington joins her in song, and their voices blend in a soaring duet.

Their next film, a second screen version of the popular operetta *Rose Marie* (1936), was also directed by "Woody" Van Dyke. This time the production was more expansive, the story line more substantial, and MacDonald's performance more relaxed than it had been in *Naughty Marietta*. She played Marie de Flor, a popular opera singer whose brother (James Stewart in his second film role) has fled into the Canadian wilderness after escaping from jail and killing a Mountie. Marie rushes to find him, but also meets a handsome Mountie (Eddy) who is relentlessly on her brother's trail. The old theme of love versus

Naughty Marietta *(MGM, 1935). Disguised as one of the Casquette Girls sent by King Louis XV to French Louisiana to marry the planters and trappers, Princess Marie (Jeanette MacDonald) encounters Captain Dick Warrington (Nelson Eddy), head of a troup of mercenary scouts.*

Maytime *(MGM, 1937). Lovers Marcia Mornay (Jeanette MacDonald) and Paul Allison (Nelson Eddy), with Paul's friend Archipenko (Herman Bing) and Marcia's fiercely jealous teacher and mentor, Nazaroff (John Barrymore). At left: Walter Kingsford. During the filming, Barrymore was drinking heavily and forgetting his lines. The director managed to extract a creditable performance by printing huge cards with the actor's lines and keeping them in view at all times.*

The Merry Widow *(MGM, 1934). Couples glide to the lilting strains of the "Merry Widow Waltz." The film's sumptuous décor won Oscars for art directors Cedric Gibbons and Frederic Hope.*

duty raises its familiar head, but all is resolved happily—at least for the hero and heroine; Stewart is returned to prison.

The Rudolf Friml–Oscar Hammerstein II songs, with additions by other hands, are lilting, but they have probably been subjected to more parody than any others from a MacDonald-Eddy musical. As he paddles across a lake in the moonlight, Eddy sings the title song to a rapt Jeanette. Later, they join forces in a full-throated duet of "Indian Love Call" ("When I'm calling you-ou-ou-ou-ou-ou-ou"), which is reprised at the film's end. Eddy leads the troops in a rendition of "Song of the Mounties." Allan Jones appears briefly as MacDonald's partner in several operatic sequences, but his role was trimmed when Nelson Eddy registered his strong objection.

The following year, they starred in a second film version of Sigmund Romberg's 1917 operetta, *Maytime*. In most respects, it is the best of their films. Smoothly directed by Robert Z. Leonard, lushly designed by Cedric Gibbons, and beautifully photographed by Oliver T. Marsh, the film has the effect of a lace-covered valentine: it is excruciatingly sentimental, and yet it is also affecting in its forthright appeal to the emotions. But its sweetness is relieved by the presence of the flamboyant, increasingly self-destructive John Barrymore. All in all, *Maytime* transcends easy ridicule as a lovely, fragrant curio of the past.

The film's story is told in flashback as a remembrance of a tragic love. At a May festival in 1906, Miss Morrison (MacDonald), a "sweet and sheltered" old lady, consoles an unhappy young girl who has to choose between her boyfriend and a singing career. Miss Morrison relates the tale—actually her own—of famed opera star Marcia Mornay, who enters into a loveless marriage with her adoring teacher and mentor, Nicolai Nazaroff (Barrymore). But she meets an ardent young American singer named Paul Allison (Eddy), and they fall passionately in love. They separate, but years later they are singing together in an opera, their love for each other as strong as ever. Insanely jealous, Nazaroff shoots Paul to death. Back in the present, old Miss Morrison expires and joins her lover for eternity, as they walk together in a shower of blossoms.

This dolorous story probably receives far lusher treatment than it deserves, but there are scenes in Noel Langley's screenplay that are difficult to forget. "I was very young. It was Paris—in the court of Louis Napoleon," Miss Morrison begins in her flashback, and in a startling moment, we are in the court of Louis Napoleon, at a lavish ball possibly only MGM could stage with such attention to detail. Marcia arrives in an extravagant gown, with a smirking Nazaroff at her side. The opera sequences are equally lavish, and one, for a mythical opera called "Czaritza," contained the first operatic music (by MGM's music director Herbert Stothart) ever written directly for the screen.

The film's most unforgettable sequence is the May Day country fair. Arriving at the height of the festivity, Marcia joins her lover Paul in singing "Santa Lucia," and they mingle with the May dancers. After a lovely montage of flowers, trees, and sun-splashed water, they sit by a blossoming tree, where he sings Sigmund Romberg's "Will You Remember (Sweetheart)," one of the songs with which they are most closely identified and the only song retained from the original stage version. Marcia tells him she must marry Nazaroff, but she reassures him, "I'll always

The Firefly *(MGM, 1937). As Nina Maria, the Spanish dancer who doubles as a spy during the Napoleonic Wars, Jeanette MacDonald entertains the troops.*

The Girl of the Golden West *(MGM, 1938). A romantic idyll for
Ramerez (Nelson Eddy) and Mary Robbins (Jeanette MacDonald).
MacDonald had wanted Allan Jones, her costar in* The Firefly, *to
play opposite her, but studio head Louis B. Mayer refused, partly
because he disliked the rebellious Jones and partly because Nelson
Eddy, still a valuable studio property, had insisted that he (Eddy)
was to be her only costar in the future.*

remember you and your song.'' She reprises ''Will You
Remember'' as the camera lingers on the idyllic scene.

As usual, MacDonald is somewhat overemphatic in her
approach to acting, and Eddy is rather desultory in his, but they
are at their most appealing in *Maytime*. Despite Barrymore's
disintegrating state, he dominates the film with his baleful manner
and glowering eyes. There is more than a touch of ham in his
performance, but he achieves some powerful moments, most
notably in the scene in which he shoots Paul Allison. ''I'm giving
Marcia her freedom, and you yours!'' he cries, just before he
fires. Paul dies in Marcia's arms, with one last reference to their
day at the fair: ''That day *did* last me all my life!''

Maytime was an enormous success with both the critics and
the public, but MacDonald was pleased when the studio signed
Allan Jones to be her costar in the film version of the Rudolf
Friml–Otto Harbach operetta *The Firefly* (1937). She liked Eddy,
but was slightly apprehensive about being identified as only half of
a singing team. With his handsome appearance and strong voice,
Jones was ideally cast as Don Diego, the dashing French officer in
disguise, who both loves and opposes Nina Maria, the Spanish
dancer engaged as a spy during the Napoleonic Wars.

The Firefly was expensively mounted in the grand MGM
tradition, but the plot, complicated and heavily melodramatic,
made far too many demands on the players. The score included
some of the original Friml-Harbach songs, such as ''Giannina
Mia,'' but the hit song was ''Donkey Serenade,'' which became
permanently associated with Allan Jones. Derived by studio
composers Chet Forrest and Bob Wright from one of Friml's
piano works, the catchy tune is first sung by Jones to MacDonald,
then to her mule, as he rides beside her stagecoach.

When *The Firefly* did not do as well at the box office as the
MacDonald-Eddy musicals, the message seemed clear: the
audience wanted their singing sweethearts back in each other's
arms. MacDonald and Eddy were reunited for five more films
that extended into the forties and became increasingly arch and
archaic. The radiance of *Maytime* faded as the team's films began
to resemble wedding cakes in a bakery window: lavish and
decorative on the outside but hollow at the center, and mostly
indigestible. With each film, their acting limitations became more
apparent: her coy and kittenish manner seemed inappropriate for
an obviously mature woman, and his portly figure and stolid line
readings made him an unlikely romantic lead.

They were first reunited in *The Girl of the Golden West*
(1938), a new version of the 1905 David Belasco melodrama that
had been filmed three times before without music. The Sigmund
Romberg–Gus Kahn score was melodious, but the story creaked
terribly, and the performances could be described charitably as
merely adequate. *Sweethearts* (1938) was considerably better, not
only the first MacDonald-Eddy musical to be filmed in
Technicolor, but also MGM's first all-color film since 1929. The
story about a bickering musical comedy team was serviceable, and
the Victor Herbert tunes were often hummable.

Unfortunately, their subsequent films grew steadily worse,
burdened by unsuitable stories, heavy-handed direction, and
awkward acting. In *New Moon* (1940), a new version of the 1928
Sigmund Romberg operetta, they seemed too old for their roles,
and their acting had not improved with time. Eddy's rendition of

"Stout-Hearted Men" furnished impressionists with fodder for many years. *Bitter Sweet* (1940) was the team's first financial failure. By 1942, when they were brought together for the last time in *I Married an Angel,* it was clear that audiences no longer responded to their romantic tribulations or their singing.

By now the team of Jeanette MacDonald and Nelson Eddy had become a source of mockery, an obsolete artifact of a more naïve time. Today, many of their films are viewed as amusing camp. Nevertheless, it is difficult to dismiss them entirely. The romantic aura they created in *Maytime* was almost palpable, and even now, as we watch them sing their love for each other at the foot of that MGM tree, the scent of blossoms lingers in the air. We can regret that their musical films never made adequate use of the piquant personality MacDonald displayed in her earlier films. We may even wonder whether more skillful directors might have made Eddy's performances more pliable. But the memory of those *Maytime* lovers, reunited in eternity, remains an indelible —and cherished—part of movie lore.

About the time that Jeanette MacDonald was sharing romantic bliss with Nelson Eddy, other sopranos were finding varying degrees of success on the screen. One of the more popular singers was Grace Moore, the blonde Metropolitan Opera diva. In 1934, she had been eager to play opposite Maurice Chevalier in MGM's planned remake of *The Merry Widow*. "I'll do it for nothing," she told Irving Thalberg. "The role was made for me—the music for my voice" (Parish, *The Jeanette MacDonald Story*). Several years earlier, however, an overweight, temperamental Moore had appeared in two disastrous operettas for the studio, and it was not about to take another chance—not with its newly signed soprano, Jeanette MacDonald, on the lot.

Ironically, Moore's failure to get the coveted role triggered a successful new career in films. She was signed by Harry Cohn, head of Columbia Pictures, and following the usual vacillation over what to do with her, she was cast in an original operetta called *One Night of Love* (1934). Cohn had serious misgivings about grand opera in the movies, and he insisted that the arias be embedded in a romantic story of a temperamental opera star and the music teacher she both despises and loves. A few popular songs were also added to lighten the musical load. Once again, his instincts were right. The film was a success, even winning an Oscar nomination as best picture. And Grace Moore, photographed with a diffused lens to soften her rather heavy features, became a major musical star for a few years.

One Night of Love was one more variation on the Trilby-Svengali theme, with Moore as Mary Barrett, a singer who places herself in the hands of ruthless, demanding teacher Giulio Monteverdi (Tullio Carminati). ("Work, work, work! Your life will be completely in my hands! You must learn to hate me!") After she becomes an opera star, they quarrel and separate, but are reunited when they realize that they need and love each other. The film is a charming though musty antique, but Moore is in strong voice, singing arias from *Carmen* and *Madama Butterfly,* two surefire operas for the more culture-minded filmgoer.

Her second film for Columbia, *Love Me Forever* (1935), was almost as popular as the first, mixing Moore's arias and popular songs with the story of an obsessive love. Leo Carrillo played

Sweethearts *(MGM, 1938). Musical star Gwen Marlowe (Jeanette MacDonald) in a scene from* Sweethearts, *the long-running stage musical in which she costars with husband Ernest Lane (Nelson Eddy). MacDonald looked radiant in Technicolor, and she acted with more spirit and vivacity than at any time since* The Merry Widow.

overleaf, above: Bitter Sweet *(MGM, 1940). Jeanette MacDonald in an operatic sequence. The movie, filmed in Technicolor, concerned the tragic romance of a struggling composer and his devoted sweetheart. The songs that were retained from Noël Coward's original score were charming, but the stars were clearly too old for their roles, and they were unable to cope with the heavy-handed, antiquated screenplay.*

overleaf, below: I Married an Angel *(MGM, 1942). Playboy Nelson Eddy dreams that he courts and marries an angel (Jeanette MacDonald). The leaden musical captured little of the charm or sophistication of the stage musical comedy, and not even the Rodgers and Hart songs from the original score (including "Spring Is Here" and the title song) could salvage it.*

page 143: New Moon *(MGM, 1940). Jeanette MacDonald as Marianne de Beaumanoir, a noblewoman in the French colony of Louisiana who falls in love with a rebel leader (Nelson Eddy). During the course of the film, the actress wore sixteen different costumes, including one that weighed eighty-five pounds. Despite the exceptionally beautiful score ("Lover Come Back to Me," "Wanting You," "Softly, as in a Morning Sunrise"), the film was poorly received, and the team's acting was generally criticized as inept.*

Steve Corelli, an illiterate but opera-loving gambler and restaurateur who devotes himself single-mindedly to the career of soprano Margaret Howard (Moore). Moore sang beautifully, especially in a scene from *La Bohème* with Michael Bartlett. Her next few films, however, were not well received, although they continued to attract audiences who enjoyed her singing. *The King Steps Out* (1936), a lighter-than-air conceit concerning a Bavarian princess who poses as a dressmaker, had stylish direction by Josef von Sternberg and several lilting songs by Fritz Kreisler. In *When You're in Love* (1937), Moore sang more popular selections than usual, including several songs by Jerome Kern and Dorothy Fields. She also performed Cab Calloway's ''Minnie the Moocher,'' designed to show that she could be as ''lowbrow'' as the next person. Her last movie for Columbia, *I'll Take Romance* (1937), was a dull affair, despite arias from *La Traviata, Manon,* and *Madama Butterfly*. By this time Moore's bland and rather metallic screen personality was much too evident, and there was little to sustain audience interest beyond the singing.

By the mid-thirties, it was clear: audiences enjoyed having a jigger or two of culture added to their movie cocktail. Singers with operatic backgrounds were welcome on the screen provided they were reasonably attractive and their high-toned arias were mixed with some homespun popular music. It also helped to ''humanize'' them by involving them in light romantic stories that placed little strain on their thespian abilities.

MGM had MacDonald and Eddy, Columbia had Grace Moore, and Universal had a sweet-voiced, sweet-faced teenager named Deanna Durbin. A protégée of comedian Eddie Cantor, she had gone to Universal Pictures after being rejected by MGM in favor of Judy Garland. Under the tutelage of producer Joe Pasternak, who would later work similar wonders at MGM with Jane Powell, she became not only the studio's leading attraction, but the personality who singlehandedly saved it from bankruptcy.

The Durbin musicals followed a pattern that audiences found irresistible, combining frivolous stories centering on the plucky, mischievous Durbin with a batch of songs rendered in her bell-like voice. Many of them were directed with charm and skill by Henry Koster. In her first feature film, *Three Smart Girls* (1937), she conspires with her two older sisters to keep their father (Charles Winninger) from a bad marriage and return him to his ex-wife. In subsequent movies, she spent her time singing and getting herself into—or out of—trouble. Typically, she succeeded in persuading conductor Leopold Stokowski to hire her down-and-out musician father (Adolphe Menjou) and his friends in *One Hundred Men and a Girl* (1937), or ''invented'' a dashing father (Herbert Marshall) for the benefit of her school chums in *Mad About Music* (1938). Her songs were either arias, American folk songs, or expressions of girlish *joie de vivre*. Growing into womanhood in the forties, Durbin became less of a singing phenomenon and more of a conventional leading lady.

One soprano sang on screen for only a short period, then went on to greater triumphs as a top-flight comedienne and dramatic actress. A popular musical comedy player of the twenties, Irene Dunne had come to Hollywood in 1930, after her appearance as Magnolia in the road-company production of *Show Boat*. For years she played regal or demure heroines in soapy romantic dramas, until she revealed a delicious comedy sense in

Love Me Forever (Columbia, 1935). Grace Moore and Michael Bartlett in a scene from La Bohème.

opposite, above: *A lobby card for* Sweethearts *(MGM, 1938).*

opposite, below: *A lobby card for* The King Steps Out *(Columbia, 1936).*

145

One Night of Love (Columbia, 1934).
Grace Moore, Jessie Ralph, Tullio
Carminati, and Mona Barrie in a scene
from the musical that finally brought
stardom to opera singer Grace Moore. It
also launched a cycle of musical romances
with operatic sequences.

opposite: Hitting a New High (RKO,
1937). Lily Pons sings an aria from the
mad scene of Lucia di Lammermoor in
the last of her three musicals for the studio.
Pons's voice was glorious, but her piquant
French personality never caught on in films.

One Hundred Men and a Girl (Universal,
1937). Deanna Durbin sings with Leopold
Stokowski and his orchestra. Durbin made
films into the late forties, but she never quite
regained the enormous popularity she had
known as a young girl. Long after she retired,
she wrote that the Durbin screen personality
"never had any real similarity to me, not
even coincidentally."

the mid-thirties with such films as *Theodora Goes Wild* (1936) and *The Awful Truth* (1937). For the rest of her career, she alternated between lighthearted comedy and genteel drama.

For several years in the thirties, however, she was given the opportunity to use her training as a singer. After singing three of Jerome Kern's lovely melodies in *Roberta,* she was assigned to repeat the role of Magnolia in Universal's 1936 version of the classic Jerome Kern–Oscar Hammerstein II musical play, *Show Boat.* Under the direction of James Whale—a definite change of pace for the director of *Frankenstein* and *The Bride of Frankenstein*—the film was the best of the three screen versions: a beautifully photographed and admirably cast musical that did full justice to the enchanting score.

Irene Dunne made a fetching Magnolia, whether in romantic tandem with Allan Jones as the riverboat gambler Gaylord Ravenal or doing a funny shuffle dance to "Can't Help Lovin' That Man." Singer Helen Morgan, already on the road to her own tragic destiny, was unforgettable as the ill-fated mulatto Julie, especially when her small, plaintive voice brought a heartbreaking validity to her rendition of "Bill." Charles Winninger, in his original stage role of Cap'n Andy, was especially memorable, giving the movie its emotional peak when he discovers Magnolia nervously making her nightclub debut and tearfully urges her on to a triumphant reception.

The following year, Dunne starred in *High, Wide and Handsome,* Rouben Mamoulian's second musical film after a four-year interim devoted to more dramatic efforts. More of a Western drama with musical interludes than a conventional musical, *High, Wide and Handsome* had a historic base: the struggle, in 1859, between Pennsylvania farmers who had discovered oil on their land and the railroad tycoons who wanted to keep them from completing the pipelines that would bring cheap oil to every American home. Against this background is set the story of the marriage between the daughter (Dunne) of a medicine show proprietor and a heroic young farmer (Randolph Scott). While their marriage languishes, Scott and his men battle the railroad forces. After many setbacks, there is a brilliantly staged climax in which Dunne and her father's carnival—midgets, clowns, elephants, roustabouts—join in saving the day for the farmers.

Though this film has many good moments, it is also oddly schizoid, the true rugged West existing side by side with the romantic West of song and legend. On one hand, we are given the gritty realism of the Western scenes, especially in the desperate clashes between the farmers and the railroad thugs. On the other hand, we have the patent unreality of Scott's farmhouse, complete with sparkling kitchen, ethereal apple orchard, and crusty but kindhearted grandmother (Elizabeth Patterson). Most of the musical numbers by Jerome Kern and Oscar Hammerstein II are performed in this idealized environment: the exquisite "Can I Forget You?" is sung by Dunne to Scott in the moon-dappled orchard, and, later, after they are married, she sings the beautiful "The Folks Who Live on the Hill," as they overlook the site of their dream house. A slightly more realistic note is sounded when William Frawley and the farmers sing a jaunty "Will You Marry Me Tomorrow, Maria?" at Dunne and Scott's wedding party, or when Dorothy Lamour, as a saloon girl befriended by Dunne, sings a torch song,

"The Things I Want," to the grizzled barflies. Yet even these songs have nothing to do with the farmer-railroad conflict, since Mamoulian probably recognized that it resisted musicalizing.

By the late thirties, the public's interest in operatic voices was on the wane. Attendance was falling off at the MacDonald-Eddy musicals, and Grace Moore was no longer making films. Other opera-trained voices were not drawing audiences. Audiences were expressing a preference for the more proletarian voices of Bing Crosby or Alice Faye, and they were beginning to listen attentively to the vibrant voice of young Judy Garland. As a musical theme, deathless romance was being replaced by more mundane concerns: putting on a successful show, or paying tribute to America's neighbors below the border. From here on, if "serious" music was to turn up in films, it would be in "biographies" of classical composers or in frivolous musicals that added a touch of class in the form of Jose Iturbi or Lauritz Melchior.

High, Wide and Handsome *(Paramount, 1937). In an idyllic scene from the Kern-Hammerstein musical, Irene Dunne sings about "The Folks Who Live on the Hill." Her bucolic boyfriend is Randolph Scott. The ethereal but artificial look of scenes such as this clashed with the robust realism of the Western action scenes.*

The Gay Desperado *(United Artists, 1936). Rouben Mamoulian's amusing musical spoof starred Ida Lupino as a runaway heiress and opera tenor Nino Martini as a singing caballero. Both are kidnapped by a Mexican bandit (Leo Carrillo) who has seen too many American gangster movies.*

Show Boat *(Universal, 1936). As the showboat roustabout Joe, Paul Robeson reprised his stirring version of "Ol' Man River" that had brought him an unprecedented ovation when the musical was first revived on stage in 1932. He was also given a new Kern-Hammerstein song, "Ah Still Suits Me."*

Show Boat *(Universal, 1936). The wedding of gambler Gaylord Ravenal (Allan Jones) and showboat soubrette Magnolia Hawks (Irene Dunne). This film version of the Kern-Hammerstein musical classic is the most enduring, superior in most ways to MGM's richly produced but juiceless production fifteen years later.*

BING
AND PARAMOUNT

Warners had Buzz, RKO had Fred and Ginger, Fox had Shirley
and Alice, MGM had Jeanette and Nelson—and Paramount
Studios had a pleasant-looking but not terribly handsome, jug-
eared, and mellow-voiced singer named Bing. Bing Crosby began
the thirties inauspiciously in Universal's *King of Jazz* (1930),
singing "A Bench in the Park" as a member of a group called the
Rhythm Boys. But by the end of the decade, he was Paramount's
leading star, one of the most popular figures on radio, and a
singer whose records sold phenomenally. By the time his career
was on the wane many years later, he had become the most
successful recording artist in the history of the industry.

When he came to *The King of Jazz*, Harry Lillis Crosby had
already been in show business since the mid-twenties. With
friends Al Rinker and Harry Barris, he had formed the Rhythm
Boys, who eventually joined Paul Whiteman and his orchestra
as an "added attraction." Before long, his smooth vocalizing,
with its unique throb, was very much in demand, and after
leaving Whiteman, he became a favorite singer in Los Angeles
nightclubs. His records, both solo and with the Rhythm Boys,
were widely circulated as he developed his warm, distinctive
singing style.

As their careers flourished, Crosby and his colleagues had
a few more fleeting brushes with the movies, providing the voices
for a rendition of "Three Little Words" by Duke Ellington's
musicians in *Check and Double Check* (1930), and appearing briefly
in *Confessions of a Co-Ed* (1931). Crosby, obviously the most
popular member of the group, even got to sing his first solo—
"When the Folks High Up Do the Mean Low-Down"—in the
Douglas Fairbanks comedy *Reaching for the Moon* (1930), and to
speak his first line on screen: "Hello, gang!"

About that time, Crosby also appeared in six musical
shorts for Mack Sennett, but a major role in a feature film was
inevitable. The movie was *The Big Broadcast* (1932), the first in a
series of Paramount musicals lightly spoofing the new medium of
radio. In a role obviously suggested by his off-camera life,
Crosby played a genial but irresponsible radio singer who loses
his girl and his job with a radio station. Going on a bender, he
meets wealthy and also lovelorn Stuart Erwin, who eventually

puts him back on the air. The plot was merely a frame for
appearances by radio stars who were currently popular on the
airwaves: Kate Smith, the Boswell Sisters, the Mills Brothers,
Cab Calloway and his band, and others. The score included three
of Bing's best-known tunes: "Please," "Here Lies Love" (sung
in an oddly morbid sequence), and the song that became his
trademark, "Where the Blue of the Night Meets the Gold of the
Day."

The pattern was set from the start: Crosby, easygoing,
debonair, and inclined to slough off trouble with a shrug, a
whistle, or a song, would become involved in what he might call
"a mild and inconsequential amatory dilemma," which was solved
within ninety minutes. He would caress a girl or a lyric with
equal aplomb, and his mellow voice, on screen or on radio,
became one of the most familiar of the decade.

His movies during the first few Paramount years were hardly
distinctive, but several of them were entertaining. *College Humor*
(1933) offered Crosby as a rather unlikely college professor who
was adored by coed Mary Carlisle. In addition to "Learn to
Croon" and "Moonstruck," his songs included the classic
"The Old Ox Road," staged in a romantic moonlight
setting. In *Going Hollywood* (1933), on loan to MGM at a
surprising two thousand dollars a week, he appeared as a movie
singer with another adoring fan, this time mousy schoolteacher
Marion Davies. His big number was a torchy "Temptation,"
sung in a Mexican bar to the hot-blooded Fifi D'Orsay rather than
the demure Davies. *She Loves Me Not* (1934) sent him back to
college as a Princeton student who gets mixed up with a
nightclub dancer (Miriam Hopkins), a murder witness on the
run. The comic frenzy stopped long enough to have Crosby sing
"Love in Bloom" and other tunes. In *We're Not Dressing* (1934),
a very free adaptation of Sir James M. Barrie's play *The Admirable
Crichton*, Crosby played a shipwrecked sailor who melts the icily
patrician Carole Lombard with such songs as "Love Thy
Neighbor" and "Good Night, Lovely Little Lady."

By 1935, there was a slight, but only slight, change in his
persona. The insouciance and relaxed air remained—they would
be part of his image until the fifties—but he became a little less

page 150: *The amiable, inimitable Bing Crosby, whose musical films in the thirties and forties helped greatly to maintain the financial health of Paramount Pictures.*

above: Pennies from Heaven *(Columbia, 1936). Hoping that their few chickens will soon multiply, Edith Fellows, Bing Crosby, Louis Armstrong, and Donald Meek stand guard at the coop.*

top: We're Not Dressing *(Paramount, 1934). From left to right: Carole Lombard, Ray (billed then as Raymond) Milland, Bing Crosby, Leon Errol, and Ethel Merman, all adrift on a musical comedy island.*

opposite, below: She Loves Me Not *(Paramount, 1934). Princeton student Bing Crosby chastises nightclub dancer Miriam Hopkins. This was the last film in which Crosby permitted the studio to glue back his prominent ears with a cosmetic device. The heat from the lighting caused them to pop out intermittently, and he finally insisted that they stay that way.*

Mississippi *(Paramount, 1935). Joan Bennett and Bing Crosby share a romantic moment aboard a Mississippi showboat. Not present is the star who walked away with the movie: the inimitable W. C. Fields.*

above: Anything Goes *(Paramount, 1936). Bing Crosby and Ethel Merman, decked out in Hollywood's idea of Chinese chic for the musical's finale. Some of Cole Porter's fine songs ("I Get a Kick Out of You," "You're the Top," and the title tune) were retained, but others were replaced with vapid songs by other hands.*

above, right: Rhythm on the Range *(Paramount, 1936). Martha Raye (in her film debut) and Bing Crosby sing for the cowpokes and others. At right, in a print dress, is heroine Frances Farmer. The movie's hit song was "I'm a Lone Cowhand."*

right: The Big Broadcast of 1938 *(Paramount, 1938). W. C. Fields, as millionaire T. Frothingham Bellows, steers the ocean liner Gigantic in its transatlantic race with another ship. This cluttered musical farce ran the gamut from songs bellowed by Martha Raye to an excerpt from* Die Walküre *sung by opera star Kirsten Flagstad.*

callow, a little less collegiate, and more postgraduate in his behavior. In *Here Is My Heart* (1935), one of his more appealing musicals of the period, he was a famous singer on a pleasure trip to Monte Carlo, who pokes fun at the haughty attitude of a princess (Kitty Carlisle). Inevitably, he also falls in love with her. His best-known song in the film was "Love Is Just Around the Corner." In *Anything Goes* (1936), Crosby joined Ethel Merman, Charles Ruggles, and Ida Lupino in a disappointing version of the Cole Porter stage musical. A few mediocre non-Porter songs were added to the original scintillating score.

In one film of the period, made away from Paramount at Columbia, Crosby amended his devil-may-care attitude long enough to help a down-and-out family. *Pennies from Heaven* cast him as an amiable vagabond, released from prison after being convicted on a false charge. He befriends the daughter(Edith Fellows) and father (Donald Meek) of an executed murderer, setting them up in a ramshackle mansion that he turns into a profitable café. Sentimental and curiously glum, *Pennies from Heaven* was one of the very few Crosby movies to acknowledge the Depression. The enormously popular title song became a popular selection for amateur singers everywhere.

It was not often that Crosby found himself out of the spotlight, but it happened in *Mississippi* (1935), a musical version of a Booth Tarkington story, in which his costar was another Paramount contractee, W. C. Fields. As a young Philadelphian in the Deep South who gets into deep trouble, Crosby sang several good Rodgers and Hart songs, including "It's Easy to Remember" and "Soon." But Fields stole the show as the disreputable owner of a Mississippi showboat, whether gazing with liquor-soaked eyes at some cigar store Indians, or finding himself in a poker game with five aces. Crosby also faced some competition from the inimitable Beatrice Lillie, but their film together, *Doctor Rhythm* (1938), was a slapdash affair with little to recommend it except some pleasant songs ("My Heart Is Taking Lessons," "On the Sentimental Side") and one famous Bea Lillie routine centering on her attempt to purchase "two dozen double-damask dinner napkins."

Crosby's most frequent costar during this period was brassy Martha Raye. A better-than-average singer and a comedienne with a gift for playing knockabout farce, she supported Crosby in *Rhythm on the Range* (1936), making her film debut as a rough-and-ready society girl who sets her cap for rodeo star Bob Burns. She sang "Mr. Paganini," which became one of her trademark tunes over the years, and bellowed her way through the movie with enthusiasm. She had less to do in *Waikiki Wedding* (1937), in which Crosby sang "Sweet Leilani," the Oscar-winning tune of that year. But in *Double or Nothing* (1937), she fared better as one of a quartet of people—Crosby, Andy Devine, and William Frawley were the others—who are caught up in a plot involving a millionaire's will. The story paused often enough to permit Crosby to sing, but Martha Raye stopped the show with a riotous spoof of a burlesque stripper called "It's On, It's Off." She was not around to help him in the last few years of the thirties, when his films lacked the lively spirit and sense of fun of his earlier musicals.

While Bing was the principal source of the flippant, lighthearted tone that permeated Paramount's musicals of the

Sing You Sinners (Paramount, 1938). On the set, cast and crew members listen to the singing Beebe brothers: Donald O'Connor, Bing Crosby, and Fred MacMurray. A sentimental comedy-drama with music, the film starred Bing as the ne'er-do-well in a poverty-stricken family who finally wins the day. The hit song of the movie was "Small Fry," by Hoagy Carmichael and Johnny Mercer.

above: College Swing *(Paramount, 1938). The kids at the malt shop go into their dance. Visible in the front line (next to the waitress) is Betty Grable. Paramount's college musicals were mostly ramshackle, but they had occasional rewards, such as Bing Crosby's mellow crooning of "The Old Ox Road" in* College Humor *(1933).*

opposite: Collegiate *(Paramount, 1935). With her shapely legs and winning smile already very much in evidence, young Betty Grable poses for a publicity shot. This film, her seventeenth movie, was another entry in the series of "college" musicals from Paramount and other studios in the thirties.*

right: Artists and Models *(Paramount, 1937). Blackfaced Martha Raye sings "Public Melody Number One." The number was staged by Vincente Minnelli, who worked briefly at Paramount that year, then returned to New York. A few years later, he was summoned back to Hollywood by MGM.*

thirties, his was not the only presence. (Sometimes, it only seemed that way.) Other performers, some of them from radio, turned up to star in musicals that were, in Paramount's fashion, largely variety shows, loosely tying strings of musical numbers to a thin plot. George Burns and Gracie Allen were often on hand to add their note of inspired lunacy, he as the sardonic, cigar-puffing foil to Gracie with her bird-brained non sequiturs. They appeared first with Crosby in *The Big Broadcast,* then spent the next few years leapfrogging from further *Big Broadcast* revues (dated 1936 and 1937) to unvarying college musicals. Somehow they were left out of *The Big Broadcast of 1938,* a totally insane musical which involved, among other things, a madcap race between two ocean liners, W. C. Fields's golf game and pool playing, Bob Hope and his three ex-wives, songs by Martha Raye, and an excerpt from *Die Walküre* by opera singer Kirsten Flagstad!

By some miracle, a few of these musical hodgepodges included memorable moments: Ethel Merman's earthshaking rendition of "The Animal in Me" in *The Big Broadcast of 1936;* a wonderfully absurd "Vote for Mr. Rhythm," sung by Martha Raye in *The Big Broadcast of 1937;* the startlingly beautiful close-ups of conductor Leopold Stokowski's face and hands in the same film; and the classic Bob Hope–Shirley Ross duet of "Thanks for the Memory" in *The Big Broadcast of 1938.* In a setting of utter asininity, the last song shone like a rare jewel, its clever lyrics of a lost but fondly remembered romance coming as a happy surprise.

In the years to come, Paramount continued its fondness for musical revues that used several of its contract players, confusing (as other studios did) a quantity of star power with simple quality. But in the thirties, there was little chance of confusing Paramount's musical films with cinematic art. Cheerful, foolish, and unpretentious, they wore their rather disheveled air without apology, disregarding the innovations wrought by Busby Berkeley's camera. (One of the studio's few attempts to use the camera in an imaginative way came a year before *42nd Street,* in *The Big Broadcast,* where "trick" effects were achieved in some sequences.) In Paramount musicals of the period, comedy and music were simply stirred together, sometimes in equal portions, with the sole purpose of keeping Depression audiences laughing and singing. And when they sang, chances are that the melodies belonged, lock, stock, and "boo-boo-boo-boo," to the man named Bing.

During the decade of the thirties, the musical film had not yet come of age, but it had made giant strides. In the first years, there had been the glittering operettas of Rouben Mamoulian and Ernst Lubitsch, topped by Mamoulian's *Love Me Tonight* and Lubitsch's *The Merry Widow.* But their mocking sophistication had eventually palled for earthbound, Depression-weary audiences. Another musical influence entered the scene in the person of an imaginative and adventuresome dance director named Busby Berkeley. Almost singlehandedly, he created a new genre of musical film, extravagant in its settings and audacious in its purely cinematic approach. With one camera, he conjured a fantasy world that, even today, never fails to delight or irritate audiences.

Even without these major influences, Hollywood musicals

of the thirties had clearly come a good distance from the early sound years, when the mere novelty of singing (and talking) performers had created a glut of musicals with only occasional evidence of style or musical talent. By the early thirties, the sound techniques were very much improved, if not perfected; the harsh and screeching voices had disappeared, and songs no longer sounded as if they had been recorded in someone's garage. The musical film had achieved at least some technical smoothness and proficiency.

In the matter of style, however, there was not much progress during the thirties. Certainly the musicals became less cumbersome, less self-conscious, more professional. Each studio also revealed a leaning toward its own type of musical. But, except for Lubitsch and Mamoulian in the first years of the musical, and Berkeley while at Warners, no one attempted to evolve a style that would put the stamp of a musical filmmaker on his work, and there was little interest in extending the boundaries of the musical film. That would come in the forties, when talented people such as Arthur Freed and Vincente Minnelli turned the musical film in the direction of art.

What the thirties musicals *did* have, as in no other decade, were the icons: figures endowed with mythic qualities by adoring audiences. All the art that the musical film could claim at that time resided in these figures and not in their films—from dimpled moppet Shirley Temple to easygoing crooner Bing Crosby, from the romantic ardor of Jeanette MacDonald and Nelson Eddy to the grace of Fred Astaire and Ginger Rogers. If Hollywood's musical films of that decade offered a safe though temporary haven from an almost intolerable world, the guides to that haven were the gods and goddesses of the screen.

By the end of the decade, Shirley Temple had reached the gawky stage, Astaire and Rogers were no longer appearing together, and Busby Berkeley had left Warners to work on a different sort of musical at MGM. Another turbulent decade lay ahead, but one that was turbulent in far different ways than the thirties had been. There would be world conflict, and destruction on an awesome scale. And paradoxically and perhaps ironically, the forties would be the greatest years of the movie musical.

PART III
THE
GLORY YEARS
1940~1949

Mickey, Judy and Others
Something for the Boys
Remembering the Past
The Music Makers
From Cover Girls to Gobs on the Town

MICKEY, JUDY, AND OTHERS

All the well-honed skills of Hollywood's filmmakers seemed to reach a peak in 1939, resulting in an honor roll of memorable motion pictures. It was the year of *Gone with the Wind,* David O. Selznick's perennial epic, and of *The Wizard of Oz.* Garbo laughed in Ernst Lubitsch's scintillating *Ninotchka,* and Bette Davis went to her poignant death in *Dark Victory.* Merle Oberon also expired, to Laurence Olivier's eternal grief, in Samuel Goldwyn's film version of *Wuthering Heights.* There were sturdy American heroes: James Stewart as naïve, idealistic Senator Jefferson Smith in *Mr. Smith Goes to Washington* and Henry Fonda as *Young Mr. Lincoln.* Many of these films have remained on the all-time-best lists of critics and the all-time-favorite lists of moviegoers.

At the same time, the musical genre was relatively dormant, undergoing changes that would not reach fruition until the middle of the new decade. The most significant changes were taking place at Metro-Goldwyn-Mayer, where new creative talents were beginning to assemble. While *The Wizard of Oz* was in production, Arthur Freed had approached Louis B. Mayer with the idea of a musical loosely based on the 1937 Rodgers and Hart stage show *Babes in Arms.* In the high-spirited musical about a group of youngsters who put on a show to help their ex-vaudevillian parents, he saw an ideal vehicle for Mickey Rooney and MGM's new star Judy Garland (they had already appeared together in two films). Mayer agreed, and Arthur Freed was assigned as producer, a turning point not only in his career but in the history of the film musical.

Production began on *Babes in Arms.* To direct the movie, Freed selected Busby Berkeley, hiring him away from Warners with a one-picture contract. (Berkeley, dissatisfied with his lot at Warners, stayed on at MGM.) Roger Edens, who would become an important member of the Freed Unit, was given the job of arranging and orchestrating the musical numbers. (Only two of the Rodgers and Hart songs were retained, and new and old songs by other composers were added to the score. This was frequently done, not only because the original music was considered unsuitable for the screen, but because the studio wanted new revenue from songs written expressly for the movie.) Others who worked on the film, and who made part of the

nucleus of the unit, were scriptwriter Jack McGowan and cameraman Ray June.

For Busby Berkeley, directing *Babes in Arms* was a new experience. Without the lavish budget he could expect at Warners, and confronted with a more intimate story than he was used to, he had to deal effectively with the characters' motivations and feelings. (He was lucky to have instinctive, "emotional" actors like Rooney and Garland, who could express much more in a line than either Dick Powell or Ruby Keeler could manage in an entire script.) His only opportunity to create a spectacular production number was with the staging of the Harold Arlen–"Yip" Harburg song "God's Country," which came at the film's end. Despite these restrictions, Berkeley managed to carry off a musical that pleased Freed, Mayer, and the filmgoing public.

However, the memories of the film's stars, especially Garland, are far from happy. Many years later, she recalled, "They had us working days and nights on end. They'd give us pep-up pills to keep us on our feet long after we were exhausted. Then they'd take us to the studio hospital and knock us cold with sleeping pills—Mickey sprawled out on one bed and me on another. . . . Half of the time we were hanging from the ceiling, but it became a way of life for us." She also claimed to have had a terrible time with Busby Berkeley: "I used to feel as if he had a black bull whip and he was lashing me with it" (Juneau, *Judy Garland*).

Whatever the cost to the performers, *Babes in Arms* was an enormous success; the showing in New York City brought such a stampede of customers that police protection was requested by the theater. The movie became the first in a series of lively films known as the "Mickey-Judy" musicals. Close friends offstage and beautifully matched on the screen, Rooney and Garland shared an enthusiasm, a lusty sense of humor, and a camaraderie that are evident in their films together, however dated they may seem four decades later. The private turmoil that Garland was undergoing in those years was not visible on film.

Although she sings several tunes in her best expressive style, Garland was really playing a supporting role in *Babes in Arms.*

Mickey Rooney and Judy Garland relaxing on the set of Babes in Arms *(MGM, 1939). Many years afterward, Rooney spoke about Garland and their relationship: "She could deliver a comic line with just the right comic touch, or say a poignant line slowly enough for the poignancy to hit hard but still stay short of schmaltz. . . . We were a couple of teenage kids, proud of our talent and our poise. . . . God, we had fun" (Rooney, i.e.).*

page 158: Meet Me in St. Louis *(MGM, 1944). Tootie (Margaret O'Brien), distraught at having to leave her "snow people" when the family moves to New York, has decided to "kill" them. She is consoled by her sister Esther (Judy Garland) in a scene that is one of the best-remembered in the movie.*

page 160: Girl Crazy *(MGM, 1943). Their energy boundless as usual, Mickey Rooney and Judy Garland whoop it up for a Busby Berkeley finale to the song "I Got Rhythm."*

Rooney dominates the movie with his inexhaustible zest. As Mickey Moran, a pint-sized dynamo determined to keep his friends out of the state work school and their parents from disgrace and indigence, Rooney performs with multitalented ferocity. (He even won an Academy Award nomination as best actor.)

Except for the wince-inducing "God's Country" finale, most of the musical numbers are pleasing. Mickey and Judy romp through the Arthur Freed–Nacio Herb Brown song "Good Morning" (reprised thirteen years later in *Singin' in the Rain*), and, as a bus takes her away from Mickey, she sings a plaintive version of "I Cried for You," adding the kind of emotional monologue she did in her famous "You Made Me Love You" number in *Broadway Melody of 1938*. The film's highlight is the staging of the title tune, in which Mickey, Judy, and a lumpish singer named Douglas McPhail lead their friends through the town, picking up more youngsters as they stride down the street, proclaiming their indestructibility. Suddenly, many of the kids are carrying torches, and in a troubling echo of Hitler Youth, they build a huge bonfire and march around it in a circle holding hands.

The success of *Babes in Arms* made Arthur Freed a full-fledged producer and turned Mickey Rooney and Judy Garland into a popular box-office team. Inevitably, there had to be a follow-up. It was decided to go with *Strike Up the Band* (1940), retaining only the title song from George and Ira Gershwin's innovative 1927 stage musical. A suitable new story was concocted, and a batch of new songs by Arthur Freed and/or Roger Edens replaced the original score. Busby Berkeley was again signed to direct. With little time to catch their breath, Mickey and Judy were tossed into the new film, allegedly with a fresh supply of the pep-up pills and sleeping pills that had kept them going through *Babes in Arms*.

Strike Up the Band followed the Mickey-Judy formula of *Babes in Arms*, but added a large dose of the maudlin sentiment favored by Louis B. Mayer. As before, Mickey is all energy and ambition. His goal this time is to win a dance band contest sponsored by Paul Whiteman. When one of the young band members becomes seriously ill, Mickey uses the band's money to pay for an operation. But no good deed goes unrewarded in Hollywood heaven, and the band gets its big chance after all. Who wins first prize? Correct. Judy is the band singer who dotes on Mickey.

Much of the footage is lugubrious, but happily the stars are given the opportunity to display their musical wares. Garland and Rooney sing "Our Love Affair" and perform with others in "Nell of New Rochelle," a seemingly endless burlesque of old-time melodrama. In "Drummer Boy," Rooney follows Garland's singing with an enthusiastic turn on the drums, and later a forlorn Garland, brooding about Rooney, sings one of her obligatory torch ballads with "I Ain't Got Nobody." In addition to a flag-waving finale to the title song, Garland is featured in a large-scale number, "Do the Conga," photographed in Berkeley's familiar style with a dizzying array of camera angles. For "Our Love Affair," a novel staging was devised in which pieces of fruit become musicians in an animated symphony orchestra. The idea came from a new boy on the block: a dance director named Vincente Minnelli. A well-known New York stage director and designer, Minnelli had joined MGM in 1940, but had been given no assignments to date.

Babes on Broadway (1941), the third in the Mickey-Judy series, retained Busby Berkeley as director. It used the not exactly fresh story of stagestruck kids who put on their own show in New York, against odds that might have stymied the Theatre Guild. As usual by now, the musical numbers ranged from delightful to embarrassing. On the credit side was Garland's exuberant version of Harold Rome's "Franklin D. Roosevelt Jones" (originally performed in the 1938 stage musical *Sing Out the News*), the Rooney-Garland duet of "How About You," and a lavish minstrel show finale, arranged by Roger Edens and staged by Busby Berkeley. Strictly on the debit side was an extended number called the "Ghost Theatre" in which the stars impersonated such celebrities of the past as Sarah Bernhardt and Harry Lauder. The movie's low point, however, was clearly designed to be one of its highest: as guests of the neighborhood kids, British refugee children relay a radio message to their beleaguered parents in London, after which Garland assails them with the song "Chin Up! Cheerio! Carry On!" Well-intentioned at the time, it now seems painfully patronizing.

Besides the obvious fact that they were less expensive—the budgets on these films were modest in comparison with the studio's "prestige" productions—the numbers Berkeley staged in his three popular Mickey-Judy musicals at MGM differed greatly in tone from those he had created during his halcyon days at Warners. With his emphasis on home-and-hearth family values, Louis B. Mayer could never countenance the leering, scantily clad chorines of Berkeley's Warners movies. (The girls dancing on top of their beds in *The Great Ziegfeld* must have generated a few angry memos; *Ziegfeld Girl*, released in 1941, had no such lapses in taste.)

Girl Crazy (1943), a new version of the Gershwin stage show that had been filmed in 1932, was the last of the Mickey-Judy musicals. This time the director was Norman Taurog; Berkeley was assigned to handle only the musical numbers. (Conflicting reasons have been given for the replacement, but the decision unquestionably involved Garland's continuing hostility toward Berkeley.) Rooney played Danny Churchill, Jr., a girl-chasing playboy who is sent out West by his exasperated father to impoverished Cody College. At Cody he meets and falls in love with Ginger (Garland), the dean's granddaughter, and helps her keep the college from closing. How? You guessed it. They will "put on a show"—a giant-scale Western rodeo that will somehow attract more admissions to good old Cody. Except for some dreary romantic complications that permit Garland to pout becomingly and sing a plaintive song to the moon, the plot is given the short shrift it deserves and is frequently cast aside for musical numbers.

These are mostly good: Garland singing "Bidin' My Time"; her delightful duet with Rooney, "Could You Use Me?"; her wistful rendition of "But Not for Me"; and the full-scale production number "Embraceable You." The finale, "I Got Rhythm," was staged by Busby Berkeley as another of his eye-popping spectacles. It is dominated by Berkeley's familiar military formations and bizarre camera angles. The most effective moment comes when Rooney and Garland simply dance together, but Berkeley cannot resist a smash closing. Here he goes berserk with

Babes in Arms (MGM, 1939). *Mickey Rooney impersonates President Franklin D. Roosevelt, and Judy Garland is Mrs. Roosevelt in the patriotic finale, "God's Country." Waving to them (at right) on the steps of the White House is singer Douglas McPhail.*

overleaf, above: Strike Up the Band *(MGM, 1940). Judy Garland sings "Drummer Boy," while Mickey Rooney drums away happily. William Tracy is at left.*

overleaf, below: Strike Up the Band *(MGM, 1940). Mickey Rooney and Judy Garland lead the gang in an exuberant if overlong performance of "Do the Conga," staged by Busby Berkeley. Berkeley rehearsed the number for thirteen days and then filmed it all in one take. His insistence on having an all-out number added almost $100,000 to the movie's budget.*

page 165: Babes on Broadway *(MGM, 1941). Busby Berkeley, standing atop the crane with a microphone, rehearses the minstrel show finale. The number was poorly received at the first previews, but then Roger Edens realized that the audience was unable to recognize Mickey and Judy in blackface. He did a retake showing the pair getting into blackface, and the number was a hit.*

whips and guns, and at the end, a cannon is fired directly at the audience. The final shot in this entertaining but foolish old-style musical is of a grinning Rooney and Garland.

During the period in which Rooney and Garland were MGM's box-office favorites, the studio did not lose its fondness for more extravagant musical films. Several movies were given expensive production values, not matching the opulence of *The Great Ziegfeld* but considerably dressier than the Mickey-Judy films. One was the latest—and the last—in the series of *Broadway Melody* musicals, this one dated 1940. (The title of *Broadway Melody of 1944* was changed to *Broadway Rhythm*.) In his first film for MGM since *Dancing Lady,* Fred Astaire was teamed with the studio's top musical star, Eleanor Powell. The match was not very compatible. Although she was a highly proficient dancer, and the two collaborated in the film's finale on one of the screen's best musical numbers, there seemed to be a distance between them. He always played—and danced—best when there was some tension, some give-and-take, between him and his partner. Ginger Rogers's tart and scratchy attitude toward him at the beginning made her later capitulation more complete, and even Rita Hayworth's haughty goddess stance made the resistance-and-surrender pattern reasonably believable. But here Astaire and Powell generate no sparks whatever, only admiration for their enormous skill.

Cole Porter contributed the score, and although it is not one of his best, it does contain a few of his loveliest songs. Astaire sings and dances to ''I've Got My Eyes on You,'' then joins Powell in an easy, graceful routine. ''I Concentrate on You,'' with its lyrical melody, is given an absurd production number featuring Astaire and Powell, masked and wearing harlequin costumes, dancing in lofty ballet fashion. (Astaire looks particularly uncomfortable.) In ''I Am the Captain,'' which resembles the ''Swingin' the Jinx Away'' number in *Born to Dance,* Powell is tossed about like a rag doll by the sailor chorus. George Murphy and Powell, dancing together to ''Between You and Me,'' create a memorable moment as they execute a dazzling quickstep across a huge ramp. Indisputably, the finest number in the movie is ''Begin the Beguine,'' which was originally written for *Jubilee,* the Cole Porter–Moss Hart stage musical of 1935. Highlighted by a staccato tap session without music, it is an altogether glorious display of dancing finesse and style.

The following year MGM released an even more elaborate musical film. Another attempt to exploit the Ziegfeld legend, *Ziegfeld Girl* (1941), directed by Robert Z. Leonard, was a lavishly produced movie that combined a stellar cast, splashy musical numbers, and a soap opera plot that followed the varying fates of three showgirls. (Inexplicably, it was filmed in black-and-white rather than the color it cried out for.) The girls were Sheila Regan (Lana Turner in one of her best early performances), an ambitious elevator operator with a taste for the high life; Susan Gallagher (Judy Garland), talented young daughter of an old vaudevillian (Charles Winninger); and Sandra Kolter (Hedy Lamarr), a stunningly beautiful brunette married to a struggling concert violinist (Philip Dorn). During the course of over two hours, they all make the Ziegfeld chorus line, but it is perky Susan who achieves stardom.

The only real diversion comes from the musical numbers,

A poster for Girl Crazy *(MGM, 1943).*

opposite: Girl Crazy *(MGM, 1943). Judy Garland sings the Gershwin tune ''Bidin' My Time'' with a group of overage cowboys who are laughably represented as students of Cody College. The filming was marked by many difficulties, including a sudden sandstorm and Garland's disappearance for a number of days from the company's location in Palm Springs. (Apparently, it was due to a romantic involvement in Los Angeles.)*

overleaf: Lady Be Good *(MGM, 1941). Eleanor Powell dances to ''Fascinatin' Rhythm'' in the finale created by Busby Berkeley. The score was by the Gershwins, but an added song by Jerome Kern and Oscar Hammerstein II attracted most attention. This was ''The Last Time I Saw Paris,'' a poignant reminiscence of the City of Lights before the German occupation, sung by Ann Sothern. It won that year's Academy Award as best song.*

167

staged by Busby Berkeley. He concentrated on two opulent production numbers: "Minnie from Trinidad," written for Garland by Roger Edens, in which she sings and dances to a calypso beat in a Caribbean setting, surrounded by a large number of chorus boys and girls; and the extravagant finale, "You Stepped Out of a Dream," the film's *pièce de résistance*. In this extraordinary number, Tony Martin sings as showgirls, including Garland, Turner, and Lamarr, parade in costumes by Adrian, each a vision in sequins, feathers, gauze, rhinestones, and what-have-you.

Musicals such as *Ziegfeld Girl* were merely extensions of the elephantine films that MGM had produced in the thirties. At the same time, however, creative seeds were being planted that would take root later in the decade. The emergence of Arthur Freed as full producer on *Babes in Arms,* the apprenticeship of Vincente Minnelli, who watched and learned on the sets of MGM's musical films, the developing gifts of composer-arranger Roger Edens, the maturing talents of Judy Garland—these were all auguries for a future of musical achievement at "The Studio of the Stars."

At 20th Century-Fox, the wave of nostalgic Americana that had started with *Alexander's Ragtime Band* was continued for several years in period musicals starring Alice Faye. At the same time, the studio was caught up in a new musical trend: one that moved to the much more contemporary rhythm of the rhumba and the samba. In keeping with President Roosevelt's "Good Neighbor Policy," Fox sought to pay tribute to the insinuating sounds and exotic sights of Latin America. As the thirties ended and a new decade began, Fox's south-of-the border world of movie fantasy was the setting for a cluster of their most popular musical films.

The first movie in this mode was *Down Argentine Way* (1940), and it was meant to star Alice Faye as a wealthy girl who has a romance with a dashing and equally wealthy Argentinian horse breeder, played by Don Ameche. When Faye had an attack of appendicitis, she was replaced by Betty Grable. Already a veteran of many films, mostly but not all musicals, she had made her debut as a chorus girl in *Let's Go Places* (1930). In this, her first starring role, she caught the public fancy and became the screen's "pinup queen" of the forties.

Except for its modest historical importance, *Down Argentine Way* is of no consequence, but as empty-headed nonsense, it is diverting. Fox's Technicolor of the period was gaudy to the extreme, but here the gaudiness is appropriate to the movie's never-never view of the Argentinian horsy set. Obviously no actress, Grable dispenses good cheer and radiance, and, alone or with Don Ameche, gets to perform the movie's pleasant songs. As Grable's happy-go-lucky aunt, Charlotte Greenwood, always a welcome sight, virtually steals the show, especially with her song and dance to "Sing to Your Señorita" during the obligatory fiesta.

In addition to making a star attraction of Betty Grable, *Down Argentine Way* introduced another musical phenomenon of the period. The movie begins with the first American appearance of the flamboyant, grotesquely attired Brazilian singer Carmen Miranda. Her arms waving, her eyes rolling, and her hips swaying in rhythm with the music of her own Bando da Lua, she sings "South ('Souse') American Way" with an energy that threatens

to topple the absurdly tall and elaborate hat from her head. A favorite in Brazil who had starred on Broadway in the Shubert musical *Streets of Paris,* she startled and delighted American moviegoers with her outrageous style. Her fruit-laden headgear, infectious songs, and fractured English became fixtures in Fox musicals of the forties.

With Betty Grable searching for a rich husband in *Moon over Miami* (1941) and then pausing for dramatic roles in black-and-white films, it was Alice Faye's turn to take up the "good neighbor" slack by starring in *That Night in Rio* (1941) and *Week-End in Havana* (1941). *That Night in Rio* reworked the story of *Folies Bergère,* with Don Ameche in the dual role of the aristocratic baron and the debonair entertainer, Alice Faye as the baron's confused wife, and Carmen Miranda as the entertainer's jealous girlfriend. The risqué quality of the 1935 Maurice Chevalier film was diluted by Ameche's much blander personality. Faye sang a few songs languidly, and Carmen Miranda delivered two of her best-known (and most imitated) songs, "Chica, Chica, Boom, Chic" and "I'yi, Yi, Yi, Yi (I Like You Very Much)." *Week-End in Havana* was more of the same, giving Faye the songs that induced audiences to doze, and Miranda the songs that woke them up. Both films benefited from the glittering sheen of the color that characterized Fox musicals at the time.

The first few years of the new decade had not been significant for the film musical. There had been some diversion in the Mickey-Judy musicals, and in the prismatic confections from 20th Century-Fox, but on the whole the song-and-dance films lacked style and artistry.

It would still be a few years before these qualities finally emerged. As America entered the war in December, 1941, all priorities changed, and all efforts converged on a single goal: victory. In the blazing light of a world conflagration, films might seem to cast a dim glow. But this was not the case during the war years. In a common cause, the studios began to produce documentaries and training films that filled a vital need. Many fiction films strove to deal in often hyperbolic fashion with the cosmic subject of war.

And the musical film? Let us see how it fared, and how its persistent goal of entertaining the masses survived the years of World War II.

above: Down Argentine Way *(Fox, 1940). Wealthy Charlotte Greenwood arrives in Argentina with her romance-minded niece Betty Grable. This frivolous but enjoyable musical launched Grable's long career as the studio's top attraction.*

above, left: A lobby card for Ziegfeld Girl *(MGM, 1941), showing Edward Everett Horton, Lana Turner, Hedy Lamarr, and Eve Arden.*

page 169: Broadway Melody of 1940 *(MGM, 1940). In their memorable dance to "Begin the Beguine," Eleanor Powell and Fred Astaire dance in Spanish costumes, then change into these more contemporary togs and join in a tap duet that has grace, ease, and brilliant footwork.*

opposite: Ziegfeld Girl *(MGM, 1941). Busby Berkeley's spectacular finale to the song "You Stepped Out of a Dream," with Hedy Lamarr, Tony Martin, and Lana Turner at front and center. Art director Cedric Gibbons created a sixty-foot-high spiral staircase in gold and silver for the occasion. The number probably exhausted the studio's supply of sequins and feathers.*

above: Down Argentine Way *(Fox, 1940). Carmen Miranda made her American debut in this "south-of-the-border" musical. She had no part in the story, but her garish costumes and lively music entertained moviegoers.*

above, center: Week-End in Havana *(Fox, 1941). Cesar Romero tries to appease a jealous Carmen Miranda, who has found him with tourist Alice Faye. Most of Miranda's roles called for a display of fiery Latin temperament.*

above: Down Argentine Way (Fox, 1940). Betty Grable in full regalia. After a decade of small roles, Grable became a major star with this musical film.

left: That Night in Rio (Fox, 1941). Carmen Miranda and Don Ameche entertain in a Rio nightclub with the song "Chica, Chica, Boom, Chic." Ameche hardly projected enough personality to fill one part, much less a dual role, but he sang pleasantly and made an adequate foil for his leading ladies.

SOMETHING FOR THE BOYS

During the first years of America's participation in the war, the film industry rallied to the cause. While actors joined the armed forces, many of them to serve with distinction, the producers sought to capture and inspire public feeling about the war in their movies. Films such as *Wake Island, Bataan,* and *Guadalcanal Diary* paid tribute to the courage and resilience of American servicemen, even in defeat, while films such as *Since You Went Away* and *The Human Comedy* recorded the fortitude of those on the home front. In *The Master Race, Hitler's Children,* and scores of similar films, the enemy was depicted as less than human, their evil unmitigated and remorseless.

But war-weary Americans craved more than an unvarying diet of war action films, "stiff-upper-lip" hearthside dramas, or hortatory denunciations of the enemy. They wanted to escape the war for a few hours, to be reassured that, despite the war, it was still possible to sing, dance, and tell jokes without feeling guilty. Throughout the early forties, the screen was flooded with musical films, few of them memorable, some of them embarrassing in retrospect, but most of them fired with a patriotic fervor, either casually implied or blatantly trumpeted.

For a while, the studios decided that the best way they could show their support for the country's war effort was to bring together their leading contract players and have them sing, dance, and play comedy in musical revues primarily designed for showing to the armed forces. (The last wave of all-star musical revues had been in 1929 and 1930, when sound was new.) It hardly mattered that some of these players could barely carry a tune, or that they had the terpsichorean ability of an elephant. Who cared that the material given to even established musical performers was far below their best? The list of participating stars was long and illustrious, and the intentions were honorable. Cinematic art would have to wait for better days.

Always favoring the variety show format, Paramount was first on the scene with *Star-Spangled Rhythm* (1942). Interspersed with the thinnest of plots were sketches and musical numbers by the studio's elite. Paulette Goddard, Dorothy Lamour, and Veronica Lake spoofed their movie personae with the song "A Sweater, a Sarong and a Peek-a-boo Bang," and Ray Milland, Fred MacMurray, Franchot Tone, and Lynne Overman burlesqued

women's ways in the George S. Kaufman sketch "If Men Played Cards as Women Do." A highlight of the film was Vera Zorina's lovely dance to the now-classic song "That Old Black Magic." Warner Bros. came out the following year with its own star-studded potpourri, called *Thank Your Lucky Stars.* Among the least embarrassing segments in the film were Bette Davis's amusing complaint about the shortage of men in wartime in "They're Either Too Young or Too Old," and Ann Sheridan's tart advice to a group of girls in "Love Isn't Born, It's Made."

About the same time that *Thank Your Lucky Stars* was playing in theaters, MGM released its own entry in the all-star sweepstakes, *Thousands Cheer* (1943). With so many genuinely talented musical stars under contract, this studio was able to turn out a reasonably diverting entertainment. The slender plot involved Kathryn Grayson's romance with reluctant soldier Gene Kelly. Most of the musical numbers and sketches were confined to the last reel, when Grayson put on the requisite show for the men at her colonel father's army camp. Although such performers as Judy Garland, Eleanor Powell, Lena Horne, Mickey Rooney, and Red Skelton were on hand, the most ubiquitous presence in the show was Jose Iturbi in his film debut, leading the army band in "American Patrol," playing the piano for a nervous Judy Garland, and, in the finale, conducting the orchestra in Dmitri Shostakovich's "United Nations Salute," accompanied by Grayson and a chorus of Allied nationals.

A few other MGM musicals of the period fortified their wartime stories with "guest stars." *Two Girls and a Sailor* (1944), one of the brighter films from Joe Pasternak's busy unit at the studio, embellished a harmless tale of two performing sisters in love with the same sailor with guest appearances that were, for a change, mostly enjoyable. Lena Horne sang "Paper Doll," Virginia O'Brien perched atop a piano to perform a somnolent "Take It Easy," and Gracie Allen lightly mocked the pretensions of classical concerts with her "Concerto for One Finger," led by distinguished English conductor Albert Coates. Fresh as a daisy as one of the lovelorn sisters, June Allyson sang "Young Man with a Horn," accompanied by Harry James and his orchestra. Later that year, she also starred in another Pasternak production, *Music for Millions* (1944). Both films were helped

above: Star-Spangled Rhythm *(Paramount, 1942). Bing Crosby ended this all-star revue with a salute to "Old Glory," filmed against a projected background of Mount Rushmore.*

page 174: Springtime in the Rockies *(Fox, 1942). Betty Grable poses prettily in another of her featherweight musicals. Grable received top billing for the first time, but other attractions were Carmen Miranda and Harry James and his orchestra, who played the hit song "I Had the Craziest Dream."*

opposite: Thank Your Lucky Stars *(Warners, 1943). Bette Davis sings "They're Either Too Young or Too Old," lamenting that the only available males in wartime are either "too gray" or "too grassy-green."*

right: Thousands Cheer *(MGM, 1943). Gene Kelly, in his fourth film, gave this multi-star musical its only memorable number. Soldier Kelly dances about the canteen of his army base, using a floor mop as a prop and leaping on top of a soda fountain for a round of taps. This energetic solo foreshadowed his numbers in later films.*

immensely by the warmth and charm of Jimmy Durante.

Wartime musicals often avoided the conflict altogether, merely putting the hero (and occasionally the heroine) into uniform, or adding a flag-waving patriotic number to the conventional musical mix. Limited by wartime restrictions on production and by players not always from the top echelon of talent, these musicals were, for the most part, undistinguished, although a number of them were entertaining. Several were close to the highest level. At the opposite ends of this four-year period were two musicals starring the two leading dancers in films. Released shortly before America's entry into the war, Columbia's *You'll Never Get Rich* (1941) was one of Fred Astaire's better films during the relatively dry period that extended from his last RKO film with Ginger Rogers to his first films at MGM. And *Anchors Aweigh* (1945), released some months before the end of the war, was one of Gene Kelly's major musical triumphs of the forties.

Since leaving RKO and Ginger Rogers, Astaire had danced with Eleanor Powell in *Broadway Melody of 1940* and with Paulette Goddard in *Second Chorus*. In *You'll Never Get Rich,* he had a new partner in Rita Hayworth: a lushly beautiful redheaded actress who was being groomed for stardom by Harry Cohn after six years in mostly low-budget films. (This was already her thirty-third movie.) She was a talented dancer who had worked with her family for many years in a vaudeville act called the Dancing Cansinos. Leery at first of her inexperience as a film dancer and also worried about her height, Astaire finally agreed to costar with her.

You'll Never Get Rich cast Astaire as Robert Curtis, a Broadway dance director who is drafted into the army. He becomes involved in an on-again, off-again romance with Sheila Winthrop (Hayworth), a beautiful chorus girl whose fiancé is a captain in the army. The not-very-interesting plot is often interrupted for musical interludes, composed by Cole Porter in one of his weaker periods. Astaire and Hayworth dance together twice—to the sensuous Latin beat of "So Near and Yet So Far," and in "The Wedding Cake Walk," a military finale which has a chorus of war brides and soldiers, plus the two stars, dancing atop a huge tank. They make an attractive dance team, although Hayworth seems a bit too formidable, too "grand" for Astaire's self-effacing style. Astaire also has several numbers without Hayworth: most notably, a dance in a guardhouse to the song "Since I Kissed My Baby Goodbye," in which he combines several kinds of dazzling footwork. The film is lightweight but amiable entertainment, and it kept Astaire dancing.

Anchors Aweigh, released almost four years later, was one of the most popular musicals of the period. Under the direction of George Sidney, it had the benefits of a handsome though not plush MGM production, a pleasant score, and—best of all—the services of Gene Kelly in his first true starring role at the studio. The year before, in Columbia's *Cover Girl,* he had revealed an innovative approach to dance on the screen, a light but agreeable singing voice, and considerable charm. In *Anchors Aweigh,* although he was billed under Frank Sinatra and Kathryn Grayson, he was laying the solid groundwork for his most rewarding years at MGM.

The film's story, a kind of dry run for *On the Town* four years later, follows sailors Kelly and Sinatra on shore leave in Hollywood, where they become involved in the affairs of an aspiring singer (Grayson) and her little nephew (Dean Stockwell).

Anchors Aweigh (MGM, 1945). "*Pomeranian*" *sailor Gene Kelly dances with cat Tom and mouse Jerry in a combination of animation and live action. The sequence took two months to film and required over ten thousand frames. Kelly claims that Stanley Donen, then an assistant choreographer, later his codirector, came to him with the idea at two or three o'clock in the morning.*

opposite, above: The Fleet's In *(Paramount, 1942). A contentious scene involving Dorothy Lamour, Betty Hutton, William Holden, and Eddie Bracken. A reworking of the old play* Sailor Beware, *this was a rickety musical highlighted by the popular song "Tangerine" and several hectic song routines by Hutton.*

opposite, below: You'll Never Get Rich *(Columbia, 1941). Fred Astaire and Rita Hayworth share some mild romantic tribulations in this Cole Porter musical.*

This Is the Army *(Warners, 1943). A rare screen appearance by Irving Berlin in the film musical adapted from his 1942 stage tribute to the army. Berlin sang "Oh, How I Hate to Get Up in the Morning" in a quavering voice.*

Grayson, it appears, has her heart set on an audition with conductor-pianist Jose Iturbi. She gets the audition, of course; Kelly gets Grayson after some misunderstandings; and Sinatra, a girl-shy Brooklyn boy, finds a kindred soul in Pamela Britton, billed only as the Girl from Brooklyn. The plot is conventional for the period but, regrettably, it now seems barely tolerable. Sinatra's behavior—he asks Kelly to teach him how to be a "wolf"—approaches feeblemindedness, and the central notion of Jose Iturbi as a lofty musical artist who deigns to give auditions for hopeful singers, and who secretly enjoys playing "boogie-woogie" on the piano, is sheer nonsense.

But then there is Gene Kelly, who dominates the movie with his agreeable personality. Perhaps he grins too much, but when he is permitted to dance, the film finally lifts off the ground. "I Begged Her," his early song and dance with Sinatra, is amusing and vigorous. Kelly has one fantasy number, now very dated and slightly absurd, in which he imagines himself as a bandit chieftain in a Spanish courtyard, wooing maiden Grayson with a flamboyant flamenco dance and some athletic Fairbanksian leaps. He also does a charming Mexican dance with little Sharon MacManus in the square of a Mexican settlement in Los Angeles.

The highlight of the movie, however, is Kelly's famous dance with the cartoon character Jerry the Mouse (of "Tom and Jerry" fame). Delightful and innovative, it skillfully combines live action and animation in its tale of a sad mouse king who refuses to allow music in his kingdom until Kelly, a sailor in the "Pomeranian Navy," wearing a striped shirt and a beret, shows him how to dance. "Look at me, I'm dancin'!" says the gleeful mouse king.

Inevitably, between *You'll Never Get Rich* and *Anchors Aweigh,* there were other musical films in which servicemen played important roles. Warners's *This Is the Army* (1943) was a film version of Irving Berlin's stage tribute to the military, which added a thin story line—picture Ronald Reagan as George Murphy's son—to the many songs and sketches that had stirred theater audiences in 1942. Berlin offered some pleasing tunes— "I Left My Heart at the Stage Door Canteen," "I'm Getting Tired So I Can Sleep," and the title song. RKO's *The Sky's the Limit* (1943) starred Fred Astaire as a reluctant Air Force hero who courts photographer Joan Leslie. He has one memorable solo to "One for My Baby," in which he smashes bar glasses with his hands and shoes in a frenzy of frustration.

Two films call for special attention. *The Gang's All Here* (1943) brought Busby Berkeley to 20th Century-Fox to direct his first Technicolor musical. With the complete film under his control, and with license from the producer to run rampant with his camera, Berkeley created a movie that is unique for the period: a perfectly dreadful and totally fascinating aberration with some of the director's most amazing and outrageous special effects.

The film's two spectacular production numbers are nearly beyond belief. "The Lady in the Tutti-Frutti Hat" is set on a South Seas island, where lightly clad chorus girls recline on the sand and monkeys chatter in the trees. Carmen Miranda, wearing a giant headdress made of fruits and flowers and seated on a bed of bananas, makes a startling entrance in a cart drawn by two live oxen, painted gold. The undulating girls dance with decidedly

Tonight and Every Night *(Columbia, 1945). Rita Hayworth assumes a "love goddess" stance in a production number.*

Tonight and Every Night *(Columbia, 1945). Rita Hayworth demonstrates the reason for her status as the screen's "love goddess" in the song "You Excite Me." This better-than-average musical concerned a gallant troupe of players who insist on carrying on with their musical show during the London "blitz." Hayworth was cast as one of the leading performers.*

The Gang's All Here (Fox, 1943). One of the most famous images *from the unfettered imagination of Busby Berkeley: Carmen Miranda, as "The Lady in the Tutti-Frutti Hat," wears a banana chapeau that seems to stretch into infinity. (It was actually thirty feet high.) During the filming of this number, there was a near disaster when Berkeley swooped down on the scene with his camera boom, overshot his mark, and dislodged Miranda's towering headpiece. The remnants of her hat lay strewn at her feet.*

opposite, above: You Were Never Lovelier *(Columbia, 1942). Rita Hayworth and Fred Astaire go into their dance. Astaire's dancing, singing, and acting have always been lighter than air, which is why Ginger Rogers's perky, no-nonsense realism always worked so well, keeping him moored to earth. But with Hayworth it is a case of Pegasus dancing with Juno. She is much too lush, too lofty in her "love goddess" stance to be really effective as Astaire's dancing partner.*

opposite, center: Best Foot Forward *(MGM, 1943). Gloria De Haven (left) and June Allyson are lifted aloft by the cadets of Winsocki Military Institute.*

opposite, below: Holiday Inn *(Paramount, 1942). Bing Crosby goes blackface for Irving Berlin's "Abraham" with Marjorie Reynolds, a musical sequence usually deleted from television showings.*

phallic bananas, and the final shot is an illusion of Miranda wearing a banana headdress that appears to stretch into infinity. The movie's last number, "The Polka Dot Polka," is an astonishing display of abstractions, using odd camera angles, kaleidoscopic effects, and of course many beautiful girls to create a cinematic hallucination possibly unmatched in film musicals.

Another film of the period worth recalling is Samuel Goldwyn's *Up in Arms* (1944), if only for its introduction of a new comedian, Danny Kaye, who had proven popular in nightclubs and in such stage musicals as *Let's Face It* and *Lady in the Dark*. Kaye was Goldwyn's choice for comedy stardom in the forties: a frenetic young man with a quicksilver delivery, a winning presence, and some freshly funny ideas. In *Up in Arms,* a loose version of a play called *The Nervous Wreck,* which had served Eddie Cantor fourteen years earlier for *Whoopee,* Kaye played a pill-popping, jittery hypochondriac drafted into the army.

Despite several amusing musical numbers, *Up in Arms* and Danny Kaye do not wear well. Where he once seemed an ingratiating original, he now comes across as noisy and unappealing, and the character he plays is something of a nuisance. Kaye's famous routines still have merit, however: a funny number in a theater lobby, in which he describes the movie showing inside and plays all the roles (including "Carmelita Pepita, the Bolivian Bombshell''), and the number "Melody in 4-F," which was one of his noted standbys. There is also a hideous dream sequence in which Kaye and Dinah Shore, joined by bizarrely gowned Goldwyn Girls, do a "jive" routine typical of the time. Subsequent Danny Kaye films for Goldwyn, including *Wonder Man* (1945), *The Kid from Brooklyn* (1946), and *A Song Is Born* (1948), contained patches of amusing slapstick and some bright musical numbers.

Other musicals of the war years were designed to keep the patriotic fires burning, but without enlisting the studio's complete star roster to do it. True to form, Irving Berlin provided one of the most effective home front musicals with Paramount's *Holiday Inn* (1942). Not a tribute to the motel chain but a celebration of American life as reflected in its holidays, *Holiday Inn* teamed Bing Crosby and Fred Astaire for the first of two times. They play song-and-dance men who vie for the same girl (Marjorie Reynolds) over the years. Crosby, as his usual lazy, easygoing self, decides to retire from the rigors of show business and keep an inn that will be open only on holidays. Predictably, he ends up with the girl and a successful Holiday Inn that thrives entirely on Irving Berlin melodies. Astaire is his disapproving friend.

The plot is forgettable but those melodies linger on. *Holiday Inn* is, in fact, a cornucopia of Berlin music, a reassuring reminder to wartorn Americans that it was still possible to believe in the simple verities of life. Thus, we have Crosby singing "Song of Freedom" with a wartime newsreel as the background, or paying tribute to President Lincoln with "Abraham," a rather tasteless blackface number which is usually deleted in television prints, or telling his audience on Thanksgiving Day, "I've Got Something to Be Thankful For." Crosby also gives his first screen performance of Berlin's classic "White Christmas," a song whose persistent popularity over the decades cannot diminish the poignancy of its lyrics. Astaire's best number is "Say It with Firecrackers," for the inn's Fourth of July celebration. He summons up all his old verve and dash to execute a dance in

Du Barry Was a Lady *(MGM, 1943). Lucille Ball as Madame Du Barry admires the necklace given to her by Louis XV, played by Red Skelton.*

page 185: Du Barry Was a Lady *(MGM, 1943). Lucille Ball in the title role of this tame version of Cole Porter's bawdy stage musical. The "lady" was actually a nightclub singer adored by a hatcheck boy (Red Skelton), who dreams he is back with her in eighteenth-century France. The movie marked the third appearance of an up-and-coming young dancer named Gene Kelly. The musical highlight was "Friendship," an uproarious spoof of hillbilly joviality under all circumstances, sung by Ball, Kelly, Skelton, and Virginia O'Brien.*

page 184, above: You Were Never Lovelier *(Columbia, 1942). Rita Hayworth and Fred Astaire share a quiet moment before launching their dance to Jerome Kern's uncharacteristic "boogie-woogie" tune, "The Shorty George."*

page 184, below: Bathing Beauty *(MGM, 1944). Esther Williams, MGM's all-American mermaid, poses at the center of a water spectacle staged by John Murray Anderson, in the first of her popular musicals for the studio.*

opposite: Billy Rose's Diamond Horseshoe *(Fox, 1945). Betty Grable, William Gaxton, and Beatrice Kay, as performers in the popular nightclub, take a curtain call after the musical number in which chorus girls wear hats topped with favorite desserts. Endearing in its absurdity, the number was typical of many in forties musicals.*

which his steps are punctuated by exploding firecrackers.

While many musicals were using home front war activities as a convenient background, many others chose to deny the war's existence, setting their stories and musical numbers in a contemporary never-never land that thrived on romance and hijinx. Mindless but often diverting, they served the purpose of making the conflict temporarily remote.

As expected, some of these musicals came from MGM. *Best Foot Forward* (1943), based on the musical that George Abbott had staged successfully on Broadway in 1941, was set at the fictional Winsocki Military Institute, where the big event is the annual dance. The story spun around a hapless cadet (Tommy Dix, repeating from the stage) who invites movie star Lucille Ball (Lucy, playing herself) to the dance and is startled when she accepts, for publicity reasons. The musical numbers included "The Three B's," sung by starlets June Allyson, Gloria De Haven, and Nancy Walker (Allyson and Walker in their film debuts), and Tommy Dix's surprisingly big-voiced performance of "Buckle Down, Winsocki," with which he had stopped the stage show.

One MGM musical of the time launched a career that flourished for the balance of the decade. A champion swimmer and a tall, strikingly pretty woman, Esther Williams had played small roles in two MGM films when she was starred in *Bathing Beauty* (1944). She played a swimming teacher at a girls' school whose husband (Red Skelton) enrolls at the school to be near her. The plot was merely an excuse for knockabout antics by Skelton and especially for Williams's aquacades. The pattern was fixed for the rest of the series of popular light musicals she starred in: Williams as a smiling mermaid moving balletically underwater to the strains of a lilting melody. *Bathing Beauty*'s finale was a lavish water spectacle staged by Broadway's John Murray Anderson, with the star as the focal point of intricate underwater formations.

Aside from MGM, other studios released musicals in contemporary settings calculated to keep the war at arm's length for roughly ninety minutes. At Columbia, Fred Astaire followed his bout with the army in *You'll Never Get Rich* with an excursion to an imaginary Buenos Aires in *You Were Never Lovelier* (1942). Costarred again with Rita Hayworth, he played a famous American entertainer who becomes involved with the family of a wealthy Argentinian (Adolphe Menjou), especially Menjou's coolly elegant, disdainful daughter (Hayworth).

The film works better than *You'll Never Get Rich* for several reasons. One is the Jerome Kern score, which is superior to Cole Porter's score for the earlier film. "Dearly Beloved" and the title song, in particular, have all of Kern's ear-caressing lyricism. Another reason is the setting, nearer to the posh locales of many of the Astaire-Rogers films and more suitable to the elegant Astaire and the haughty Hayworth than the army base of *You'll Never Get Rich*. Astaire doesn't get to dance as much as he should: he does a vigorous dance with a cane in Menjou's office, and he performs several duets with Hayworth. But director William Seiter seems more interested in Hayworth, photographing her in flattering close-up as she reprises "Dearly Beloved" or sings "I'm Old-Fashioned" in the moonlit garden of her home in a voice dubbed by Nan Wynn. Her sensuous dance with Astaire to the latter song is the best one in the film.

Pin Up Girl *(Fox, 1944)*. *Inevitably, Betty Grable—America's foremost "pinup girl" during the early forties—was starred in a musical with this title. However, with its nondescript music and an inane plot, it was one of her weakest vehicles.*

(Hayworth regards this film and *You'll Never Get Rich* as "the only jewels in my life." She has said, "They are the only pictures of mine I can watch today without laughing hysterically. And *Cover Girl,* too . . ."—Peary, *Rita Hayworth*.)

At 20th Century-Fox, the war years saw the continuation of the frothy Technicolor musicals that had dominated the studio's musical product from 1939 to 1941. But the contemporary settings were no longer south of the border, and the "good neighbor policy" was relegated to the background, along with the rhumba and the conga. Betty Grable was now the undisputed musical star at Fox, with movies that grossed millions and brought the star an astronomical salary and an average of ten thousand fan letters every week.

Grable's vehicles were all of a piece: giddy, lavish, and mindlessly entertaining musicals such as *Springtime in the Rockies* (1942) and *Pin Up Girl* (1944). The gaudiest of the lot was *Billy Rose's Diamond Horseshoe* (1945). Ostensibly a salute to the well-known nightclub, the film offered several extravagant musical numbers, including an outlandish opening routine in which the Diamond Horseshoe girls, starring in a show called "Revue à la Carte," wear hats bedecked with such desserts as cherries Jubilee, baked Alaska, chocolate cake, and banana split. Grable's song and dance to "Acapulco" and a razzmatazz version of "Play Me an Old-Fashioned Melody" by singer Beatrice Kay were livelier than usual.

One Fox musical worth recalling is *Orchestra Wives* (1942). Without Betty Grable, Technicolor, or a lavish production, it did more to summarize the popular musical taste of the time than many flashier films. It is, in fact, an icon of the Big Band era, with music (including "At Last" and "Serenade in Blue") provided by one of the Biggest Bands of all, Glenn Miller and his orchestra. In the film's finale, they perform the song that would be forever associated with the soothing Miller style: "I've Got a Gal in Kalamazoo."

Over at Paramount, there was little, as usual, to celebrate in the musical area. The popular series of "Road" movies with Bing Crosby, Bob Hope, and Dorothy Lamour occasionally interrupted the steady stream of gags for songs by Crosby and Lamour, but the films were much less musical than farcical. The studio's most unusual musical of the period was *Lady in the Dark* (1944), an elaborate but leaden version of the Moss Hart–Kurt Weill–Ira Gershwin stage show. With Ginger Rogers solemn and grim-visaged in the leading role of a troubled fashion editor, this film confined its musical sections to garish visualizations of Rogers's dreams. Her rendition of "The Saga of Jenny," the unfortunate lady who "*would* make up her mind," was merely adequate. Mitchell Leisen directed with a heavy hand.

In their search for musical entertainment on the screen, many war-weary moviegoers preferred not to dwell on the present, but to return to a peaceful and idealized past. In the midst of chaos it was comforting to view a Technicolor, turn-of-the-century America, all tied up with ribbons and bows and seemingly inhabited by demure ingenues or saucy soubrettes wearing colorful clothes, dapper young men in straw hats, and crochety but lovable oldsters. It was a cinema-created world in which singers, comics, composers, and song pluggers shared the same dream of

Lady in the Dark *(Paramount, 1944). Liza Elliott (Ginger Rogers), a deeply troubled magazine editor, relates her dreams (left) to her psychiatrist (Barry Sullivan). In the lavishly designed circus dream sequence (above), Ginger Rogers sings "The Saga of Jenny," the musical number that Gertrude Lawrence made famous on the stage. Visible on either side of Rogers are Ray Milland and Warner Baxter, two of the important men in her life. A set decorator and art director before becoming a full-fledged director, Leisen created many of the extravagant costumes for the film. But he was plagued by many problems, not the least being a leading lady ill-suited to the role.*

auditioning for Oscar Hammerstein or Florenz Ziegfeld, or playing the legendary Palace. The music was usually the simple and melodic kind that anyone could (and did) sing around the piano, mixed with a few contemporary-sounding ballads. In general, the backward-looking musicals of the war years were artless, amiable entertainments.

With leading ladies who looked especially fetching in period costumes, Fox took the lead in nostalgic musicals of the early forties. After a maternity leave, Alice Faye returned to the studio to star in *Hello, Frisco, Hello* (1943), a musical set in that favorite spot of filmmakers seeking a rowdy old-time setting: San Francisco's Barbary Coast at the turn of the century. Only a few months later, Fox released the first and one of the best of Betty Grable's period musicals, *Coney Island* (1943). Directed by Walter Lang with little wasted movement, and set in a mythical and devulgarized Coney Island of the early 1900s, the movie had the ingredients that helped to make Grable the "sweetheart" of Fox's forties musicals: a serviceable plot, concerning two warring saloonkeepers (George Montgomery and Cesar Romero) and the singer they both love (Grable), glittering Technicolor settings, and, especially, musical numbers that permitted Grable to sing and dance in abbreviated costumes.

Her numbers in *Coney Island* are best when their staging is the simplest and the songs are the oldest. Her rendition of "Cuddle Up a Little Closer," when she is forced into a slower, less flashy version by Montgomery, is highly appealing, and she sings "Pretty Baby" delightfully, accompanied by a "dancing horse." Unfortunately, some ghastly early-forties staging intrudes in a number such as "Miss Lulu from Louisville," in which, wearing a tight slit skirt and unflattering mulatto-like makeup, she performs some bumps and grinds. The delirious finale, "There's Danger in a Dance," moves from an old Southern plantation, with Grable being whirled about in a wide-skirted white dress, to an absurd climax involving hundreds of balloons and a gaudily dressed chorus dancing to a vaguely Latin rhythm.

Grable had one of her biggest successes with *The Dolly Sisters* (1945), joining with rising Fox blonde June Haver in a highly fanciful version of the lives of singing stars Jennie and Rosie Dolly. The production was lavish and the color excellent, but the drawn-out plot was not helped by the principals' merely adequate acting skills. The film was also burdened with two production numbers that embody the worst of the forties musical style. In "Don't Be Too Old-Fashioned," the Dolly Sisters sing this paean to the "new-style" woman, then chorus girls dressed as various forms of makeup emerge one by one, talk-singing their lines as Lady Lipstick, Patricia Powder, Rosie Rouge, and Patsy Powder Puff. A girl representing mascara appears, wearing a gown festooned with eyes! Can this number be topped? Yes. In a showy version of "Darktown Strutters' Ball," Jennie and Rosie sing the tune, then girls in dark makeup strut about a set with a gambling motif of cards and dice. The sisters turn up again wearing "pickaninny" dresses, and the entire fantastic number ends with a huge animated figure of a black trombonist. The simply staged reprises of the standard "I'm Always Chasing Rainbows" are much more effective.

Warner Bros. offered *Shine On Harvest Moon* (1944), a limp musical ostensibly based on the lives of vaudevillians Nora Bayes

(Ann Sheridan) and Jack Norworth (Dennis Morgan), but its most acclaimed musical biography of the period was *Yankee Doodle Dandy* (1942), directed by Michael Curtiz. Both a tribute to popular entertainer George M. Cohan and a patriotic salute to American vitality and heroism, badly needed in the country's first year of war, *Yankee Doodle Dandy* turned the life of a complex, sometimes controversial man into a mostly fictional story, but it presented a joyous parade of old tunes. James Cagney played Cohan as a self-assured writer-performer who is born into a show business family and rises to become one of the theater's leading lights.

Bustling with energy, bouncing from one musical number to the next, Cagney gives one of his best, most vigorous performances. From early scenes that show him performing with his father (Walter Huston), mother (Rosemary DeCamp), and sister (Jeanne Cagney) to his final little jig on a White House staircase after the long session with President Roosevelt that frames the film, he offers a perfect portrait of a man who never tired of appearing ''with a trunkful of songs and a heartful of confidence.'' His singing and dancing to such songs as ''Yankee Doodle Boy'' and ''Give My Regards to Broadway'' are exhilarating throughout, and even the flag-waving finale to ''You're a Grand Old Flag'' seems pertinent under the wartime circumstances. He won an Academy Award for his performance.

MGM's important contribution to the period musical would reach its peak in the years after the war, under the leadership of Arthur Freed, but in the early forties, there were only a few films in this subgenre emerging from the studio. The most notable was Busby Berkeley's *For Me and My Gal* (1942), not a good film by any means but a modest and tuneful expression of wartime sentiment, and the first to team Judy Garland and Gene Kelly. After Kelly's contract with David O. Selznick had been signed over to MGM, the studio was not at all sure how to use him, and some studio executives had been opposed to signing him. Playing a brash, ambitious young dancer opposite nineteen-year-old Garland's vaudeville singer, Kelly projected an appeal that almost negated the unsympathetic characteristics of his role—a World War I shirker who injures his hand deliberately to keep from being inducted before making his Palace debut. (He later proves his heroism and redeems Garland's love.)

Reportedly, Garland again had a difficult time adjusting to Berkeley's directorial style (it would be worse in the following year with *Girl Crazy*), but Kelly was fascinated by the director's techniques. Many years later, in a *New York Times* article, he said, ''Everything I know about moving a camera I picked up from him.'' Despite the on-the-set problems, the resulting film was a pleasant nostalgic entertainment. The score's many spirited old songs included ''Oh, You Beautiful Doll,'' ''When You Wore a Tulip,'' ''After You've Gone,'' and a group of patriotic World War I tunes. The film's most memorable moment came when Garland and Kelly pooled their talents to perform the title song in a restaurant. Garland's full-throated trouping and her obvious delight in doing the song blended felicitously with Kelly's easy charm and dancing grace. (Their recording of the song was one of the year's surprise hits.)

While the studios during the war years were harking back to a supposedly quieter and less troubled time in their nostalgic

The Dolly Sisters *(Fox, 1945)*. June Haver and Betty Grable starred as Rosie and Jennie Dolly, turn-of-the century entertainers who graduated from beer gardens to Broadway. June Haver was expected to be Fox's new blonde star after Grable, just as Grable had replaced Alice Faye, but she never reached the top echelon. She retired from films in 1953, and by that time the studio's top blonde was Marilyn Monroe.

opposite, above: Hello, Frisco, Hello *(Fox, 1943)*. June Havoc, Jack Oakie, Alice Faye, and John Payne perform a musical number. The musical's principal new song, ''You'll Never Know,'' was voted an Oscar as the year's best.

opposite, center: Sweet Rosie O'Grady *(Fox, 1943)*. As a Gay Nineties entertainer engaged in a ''now-I-hate-you,'' ''now-I-love-you'' running war with a reporter (Robert Young), Betty Grable looked delectable, as always, and gave her fans no more and no less than they expected. Here, in her bath, she is singing from the sheet music of ''My Heart Tells Me,'' the film's hit song.

opposite, below: Shine On Harvest Moon *(Warners, 1944)*. Ann Sheridan and Dennis Morgan as vaudevillians Nora Bayes and Jack Norworth, in a musical ''biography'' that bore no resemblance to the truth.

above: Yankee Doodle Dandy *(Warners, 1942)*.
*James Cagney as George M. Cohan gives his jaunty
rendition of the title song. Cohan would accept only
Cagney in the role, and Cagney, himself a song-and-
dance man in the early days of his career, leaped at
the opportunity. His vigorous performance, the
old-time Cohan songs, and Michael Curtiz's assured
direction made the film one of the most popular of the
period.*

opposite: Coney Island *(Fox, 1943)*. *Costars Betty
Grable and George Montgomery in one of the studio's
breeziest and most typical period musicals of the forties.*

right: My Gal Sal *(Fox, 1942)*. *Rita Hayworth sings
and dances as Gay Nineties musical star Sally Elliott.
The film purported to be the story of songwriter Paul
Dresser (brother of novelist Theodore Dreiser), but
more footage was given to Hayworth, who looked
radiant in Technicolor.*

For Me and My Gal *(MGM, 1942). Harry Palmer (Gene Kelly), a charming but devious entertainer, shines up to aspiring singer Jo Hayden (Judy Garland) in the years before World War I. Busby Berkeley directed this nostalgic musical—the first to give evidence of Kelly's star potential.*

musicals, one film that turned up in 1943 represented a marked departure from the norm, and foreshadowed the remarkable body of work that was to influence the shape and direction of the musical film in the next ten years. The film was *Cabin in the Sky,* a production of the burgeoning Freed Unit at MGM.

Cabin in the Sky had been a great artistic success on Broadway in 1940, hailed by the *New York Times* as an "original and joyous" musical fantasy, in which the magnificent Ethel Waters had given a sterling performance as the wife of an ingratiating rascal who is perched precariously between heaven and hell. The show, written by Lynn Root, with songs by Vernon Duke and John Latouche, had enjoyed a good run, but seemed an unlikely choice for filming. Despite disapproval by many MGM executives, Arthur Freed proceeded with the production. Ethel Waters was signed to repeat her stage role, but Dooley Wilson, who had played her husband "Little Joe" on Broadway and had recently scored a success as Rick's loyal friend Sam in Warners's *Casablanca,* was replaced by Eddie "Rochester" Anderson, a more recognizable box-office name. Lena Horne was cast as the wicked, seductive Georgia Brown. Freed had noticed the imaginative contributions of Vincente Minnelli to a number of films since 1940, and he chose him to direct. Minnelli approached his first full assignment as a film director with the knowledge that his Broadway reputation would be of little consequence.

Shot entirely in sepia, to give it what Minnelli has called "a soft, velvety patina," *Cabin in the Sky* proved to be a fascinating excursion into the realm of musical fantasy. It is probably the best of the handful of all-black musicals, more moving and less pretentious than *Porgy and Bess* and certainly more skilled than *Hallelujah!* The story is simple: Petunia Jackson (Ethel Waters) is the poor but loving, deeply religious wife of "Little Joe" (Eddie Anderson), a "backslidin'" sinner given to gambling. When Joe is critically wounded in a violent quarrel, he becomes the prize in contention between the forces of the Devil, headed by the Devil's very own son, Lucifer, Jr. (Rex Ingram), and the angels of the Lord, led by the General (Kenneth Spencer, natty in his white military uniform). Georgia Brown is sent by Lucifer, Jr., to seduce Joe into hell, but Petunia triumphs eventually, and Joe becomes (he says) a new and better man.

Despite elaborate disclaimers at the time the film was made and an opening legend that reads "A Story of Faith and Devotion," *Cabin in the Sky* cannot escape criticism for showing many members of the black race as shiftless, irresponsible, and highly sexed. Yet the movie has enough rewards to compensate for its patronizing attitude, including a delightful score, superb photography with what Minnelli called "a restless and inquisitive camera," and, above all, Ethel Waters. Her expressive face and soulful voice are perfectly joined with songs with which she became identified, and she does full justice to them: a lovely duet with Anderson of the title song, the moving "Happiness Is Just a Thing Called Joe" (written especially for the film by Harold Arlen and "Yip" Harburg), and, especially, "Taking a Chance on Love," which she endows with such an abundance of glad-to-be-alive feeling that the screen seems barely able to contain her joy. Anderson has his own good Arlen-Harburg solo, "Life's Full of Consequences," while Lena Horne, her eyes flashing and her body fairly dripping with jewelry, sings a sexy "Honey in the

Honeycomb,'' which Ethel Waters reprises later in the film.

In a period dominated by war-oriented musical films, *Cabin in the Sky*'s gentle fantasy seemed almost an anachronism. A transitional musical, it reflected the antiquated attitude of *Hallelujah!* and looked ahead to the future efforts of Vincente Minnelli. Already many of Minnelli's characteristics are apparent: the penchant for fantasy, the concern with décor, and the occasional stylistic excesses in which design (and, later, color) overwhelm the musical content. Most important, there was a hint of Minnelli's ability to create an overall tone and style that was uniquely his.

The director's great musical films were all ahead, and one, *Meet Me in St. Louis,* was just around the corner. With Minnelli as one of the guiding lights, the Hollywood musical was about to enter a new phase. Until now, the gold in the musical film was a small but precious lode, located mainly in the nimble feet of Fred Astaire, the throbbing voice of a young Judy Garland, or an inspired moment in a Berkeley extravaganza. Only rarely could it be found in an entire film such as *Love Me Tonight*. From the mid-forties and into the fifties, all the creative forces that went into the musical film converged on the films themselves, giving the best of them a glow that permeated every frame. There was dross, too —a great deal of it—and many musicals that were neither dross nor gold but were made of solid though nonprecious materials.

With the enthusiastic participation of many talented people, the Hollywood musical was about to sing and dance its way into the realm of film art.

Cabin in the Sky *(MGM, 1943). In this musical fantasy, "Little Joe" Jackson (Eddie Anderson) and his loving wife Petunia (Ethel Waters) arrive in heaven, where they are greeted by the General (Kenneth Spencer) in charge of the angels of the Lord. Waters's radiance dominated the film, as it had the original stage version.*

REMEMBERING THE PAST

The film musical that could arguably be called the first masterpiece in the genre for more than a decade was sparked by Arthur Freed's sentimental nature and his strong feeling for family ties. Sally Benson had written a series of charming stories for *The New Yorker* about a close-knit St. Louis family in the early years of the century, and they had been collected in a book called *Meet Me in St. Louis*. Freed believed that they could be adapted into a musical starring Judy Garland, but the MGM moguls were unimpressed. Where was the plot or conflict in the serene lives of these people? Fortunately, Louis B. Mayer, given a persuasive account of the Benson stories by Lillie Messenger, his favorite story editor, sided with Freed. A screenplay was finally approved, but not before many writers, sometimes at cross-purposes, had made their contributions. Vincente Minnelli was assigned to direct, pleased with the chance to re-create a special time and place on film.

The first stumbling block was that Judy Garland simply did not want to make the movie. She was certain that the youngest Smith sister, Tootie, was really the starring role, and, at the ripe old age of twenty-one, she was also not delighted at the prospect of playing a seventeen-year-old. But the persistence of Minnelli and Mayer—and the threat of suspension—changed her mind. The supporting cast was headed by six-year-old Margaret O'Brien, a phenomenally gifted actress who was the studio's prized juvenile since her sensational performance in *Journey for Margaret* in 1942. The Smith house at 5135 Kensington Avenue and the St. Louis sets were designed and constructed with the utmost care and attention to detail by Lemuel Ayers, Jack Martin Smith, and others. The costumes—the first created by Irene Sharaff for an entire motion picture—were made to blend artfully with the décor. And the musical structure was provided by Roger Edens. Vincente Minnelli, however, remained the guiding force.

The production itself was beset with problems. Judy Garland was frequently ill, and Margaret O'Brien's mother pulled her daughter off the set for ten days to have braces fitted for her teeth. Other cast members suffered from various ailments. A serious setback occurred when the studio was informed that the youngster had developed a cold and a sinus condition and would have to go to Arizona to recuperate. No amount of persuasion could change her mother's mind. The production resumed after two weeks.

Another problem was the difficulty in extracting a convincing emotional performance from little Margaret O'Brien. In *I Remember It Well*, Minnelli related one incident during the making of the film in which Margaret was unable to bring forth tears for a crucial scene. Her mother suggested to Minnelli that he tell Margaret that her little dog was going to be killed. Reluctantly, he approached the child, shivering on the cold exterior set, but still tearless. "Somebody is going to take a gun and shoot your dog," he told her. When there was no reaction at first, he embellished his story with graphic details of the animal bleeding and suffering terribly. The tears began to flow—and Minnelli ordered the cameraman to start shooting. After the take, Margaret skipped off the set happily, but Minnelli felt like a monster.

The film was released in the fall of 1944 to glowing reviews and huge business. It became MGM's second highest-grossing film (after *Gone with the Wind*) until that time—and small wonder. From first frame to last, *Meet Me in St. Louis* is delectable entertainment, a landmark musical that is also a beautifully evoked if romanticized view of turn-of-the-century America. For possibly the first time in a film musical, nostalgia was used in the service of art, and the result was enchanting. A series of vignettes concerning the Smith family of St. Louis during the course of a year, the film is virtually plotless in the conventional sense: the principal crisis is the father's decision to move his family to New York City. But as the seasons pass, there are changes and rites of passage: a romance, a proposal of marriage, and childhood adventures, all presented with tenderness and affection.

The film begins by introducing the Smith family in its gingerbread house in 1903: loving, understanding Mrs. Smith (Mary Astor, in a delicately shaded performance of quiet beauty), crochety but softhearted Mr. Smith (Leon Ames), and their five children: stuck-up Rose (Lucille Bremer), winsome Esther (Judy Garland), college-bound Lon (Hank Daniels), tomboy Agnes (Joan Carroll), and little Tootie (Margaret O'Brien). Also present is jovial Grandpa (Harry Davenport) and the no-nonsense spinster cook, Katie (Marjorie Main). With the Louisiana Purchase Exposition in the offing, the family sings about this exciting prospect, while domestic dilemmas are taking shape. Rose is expecting her beau to call from New York with a proposal of marriage. And Esther has a serious crush on their new next-door neighbor John Truett (Tom Drake). Five-year-old Tootie is blissfully happy: riding on the ice wagon with Mr. Neely (Chill Wills), she exults about the coming fair. "Wasn't I lucky to be born in my favorite city?" she remarks.

Judy Garland's first song sets the tone for the film. Esther gazes with longing at the impervious John Truett, then sings "The Boy Next Door." Photographed in loving close-up by George Folsey, she gives an expressive reading of the song. She examines herself in the mirror, does a little dance around the room, and then closes with a last lingering glance out of the window. There is a bewitching moment when the lace curtain falls across her face.

A series of superbly etched sequences takes us deeper into the placid lives of the Smiths. A going-away party for Lon brims over with youthful gaiety, as the guests sing and dance to "Skip to My Lou," and Esther joins with a nightgowned Tootie in a delightful little cakewalk to "Under the Bamboo Tree," complete with straw hats and canes. Later, after all the guests have gone, Esther manages to get John Truett to accompany her as she turns out the lights, rendering a sweet old song, "Over the Bannister," as she gazes at him with undisguised love. A few days later, Esther and her friends ride off merrily to a picnic at the fairgrounds, with Esther leading them in "The Trolley Song," one of the tunes with which Judy Garland became most closely associated.

Tootie is the center of the famous sequence that follows. On Halloween, she and Agnes venture out into the dark street, dressed in suitably grotesque costumes. Tootie is "a horrible ghost" who "died of a broken heart" ("I've never been buried"). They join other children around a huge bonfire and discover that nobody wants to "take" the local ogre, Mr. Braukoff. Tootie, brave beyond her years, volunteers for the job. Her task: to hit Mr. Braukoff in the face with flour and shout "I hate you!" The camera tracks in front of her as she walks stealthily to her victim's front door. Summoning all her courage, she succeeds in flinging the flour in his glowering face, shouts "I hate you, Mr. Braukoff!," shrieks, and runs off in terror. "I killed him!" she cries. "I'm the most horrible!" The children express their approval: "Tootie's the bravest of them all!" Impeccably directed by Minnelli, the scene is a matchless view of the demons that lurk in the shadows of sunny childhood.

The movie progresses to its main dilemma: Mr. Smith, offered an important job in New York City, announces that they will all leave St. Louis in a matter of months. The family is shocked and depressed at the thought of going away before the fair, and both Esther and Rose are desolate at having to abandon their romantic commitments. But family loyalty prevails, and in a touching scene, the members gather as Mr. Smith sings the Nacio Herb Brown–Arthur Freed song "You and I" (with voice dubbed by Freed!) to Mrs. Smith's piano accompaniment. Winter arrives, and on the night of the big dance of the season, Rose gets her

straying beau back, and Esther gets a proposal of marriage from John Truett.

The evening closes with a poignant scene that ranks with the Halloween sequence as one of the finest in the film. Going upstairs after the dance, Esther finds Tootie awake, waiting for Santa Claus. She gently places her wrap around the shivering child. Tootie sadly announces that she is taking everything with her when they leave, but she is obviously upset about the "snow people" she has built in their yard. Lovingly, her face tender and wistful, Esther sings "Have Yourself a Merry Little Christmas" to her sister. Sobbing, Tootie rushes out to the yard to destroy all her "people." "Nobody's going to have them," she cries. "I'd rather kill them!" The family wakes up, Tootie is bundled inside the house, and Mr. Smith calls a meeting. He has decided that they will *not* move to New York City after all.

In the spring, with all the Smith women sparkling in their white dresses, the family is off to the Louisiana Purchase Exposition. At the fair, Esther and John look at the expanse of glittering lights with awe. Esther cries, "I didn't dream anything could be so beautiful! It's right in our own back yard! I can't believe it! Right here where we live. Right here in St. Louis!"

Meet Me in St. Louis was only Vincente Minnelli's fourth film (*Ziegfeld Follies,* produced before *St. Louis,* was released afterward), but he was clearly in firm control throughout, investing every frame with his overall view of the film. Under his astute direction, the cast plays as an ensemble, although the star turns are given to Judy Garland. Despite her initial objections to the role, she plays it entrancingly, and she looks extremely fetching as well. The movie's most extraordinary performance, however, is given by Margaret O'Brien. Her Tootie is endearing but more than a little odd in her obsession with death and dying. She buries her dolls which die of mysterious ailments, accuses John Truett of trying to "kill" her when he pulls her from the path of an oncoming trolley, "kills" Mr. Braukoff on her Halloween adventure, and finally "kills" all her snowmen rather than leave them behind.

Just as the cast members work as a unit, so does the music fit seamlessly into the fabric of the movie. Beautifully tuned to the time and place, the songs, by Hugh Martin and Ralph Blane, never impede the action, as they so often did in past years ("time for a musical number"). Instead, they emerge naturally from the feelings of the characters, especially Esther. Her secret longing for John Truett, expressed in "The Boy Next Door," eliminates the need for dialogue. Her joy at the prospect of spending a day with him at the fairgrounds bursts forth in "The Trolley Song," and her sorrow at leaving St. Louis is tempered by compassion for her little sister in the warming "Have Yourself a Merry Little Christmas."

Meet Me in St. Louis marked a turning point, not only for MGM but for the Hollywood musical. For the first time since Rouben Mamoulian's *Love Me Tonight* in 1932, a musical film had not only been filtered through the vision of its director, Vincente Minnelli, but had fused all the elements that go into the making of a musical—score, performances, photography, costuming, and décor—in the service of that vision. The creative seed that Arthur Freed had planted in 1939, when he began to gather some of the studio's most talented people around him

page 196: Meet Me in St. Louis *(MGM, 1944). Esther Smith (Judy Garland) pines in song for the boy next door.*

Meet Me in St. Louis *(MGM, 1944). Esther Smith (Judy Garland) and John Truett (Tom Drake), her adored "boy next door," marvel at the wonders of the St. Louis fair.*

Meet Me in St. Louis *(MGM, 1944). Little Tootie (Margaret O'Brien) is volunteering to "kill" Mr. Braukoff, the neighborhood "ogre," in the celebrated Halloween sequence. When someone suggested that it be deleted because the film was running long, a horrified Minnelli waited while the film was run for Arthur Freed with the scene eliminated. "It's not the same picture," Freed decided, and the scene, happily, was restored.*

Meet Me in St. Louis *(MGM, 1944). The Smith family gathers solicitously about the "injured" Tootie (Margaret O'Brien). From left to right: Grandpa (Harry Davenport), Esther (Judy Garland), Mrs. Smith (Mary Astor), Rose (Lucille Bremer), and Katie the cook (Marjorie Main). The doctor was played by Donald Curtis.*

The Harvey Girls *(MGM, 1946)*. Selena Royle guides the demure Harvey waitresses, properly uniformed and ready for their jobs. Judy Garland *(at front left)* played the mail-order bride who becomes a Harvey Girl instead.

The Harvey Girls *(MGM, 1946)*. The Harvey waitresses, led by Judy Garland, model their finery. Cyd Charisse can be seen just behind Garland's shoulder, at the right.

as a unit, had now blossomed into the first musical masterpiece of the forties.

Many years later, Gene Kelly assessed the special quality of the Freed Unit: "The days in the 1940's and 1950's when I was at MGM were great days for all of those connected with the musical motion picture, because there was money enough and largesse enough that we could experiment. . . . We had the best musical people creatively, as far as performance goes, at MGM. As a result, we turned out to be a repertory company. We had one thing that the American theater has been searching for for years—the same fellows in the Music Department, the same fellows doing the arrangements, and all of us doing choreography, directing, and so forth. . . . We all got to know each other. We even got to know each other in our bad moments, when we were difficult with one another, or when we got too important, or when we'd be too stubborn and say, 'No, I can't do that.' You see, we knew each other, and that's a marvelous way to create a musical" (Knox, *The Magic Factory*).

While *Meet Me in St. Louis* was in production, Arthur Freed was planning another musical steeped in the nation's past. Impressed by Rodgers and Hammerstein's successful stage musical *Oklahoma!*, he decided to musicalize the stories about the Harvey girls, waitresses of the pioneer restaurant chain founded by Fred Harvey. These demure young women were brought out West to counteract the bad influence of the "loose ladies" usually found in public houses. With a screenplay by various hands (but largely by Samson Raphaelson) and a score by Harry Warren and Johnny Mercer, *The Harvey Girls* was launched under George Sidney's direction. Judy Garland was assigned to star as a mail-order bride who becomes a Harvey girl instead.

The Harvey Girls (1946), filmed partly on location in the San Fernando Valley, proved to be an entertaining though not top-grade musical film. It begins beautifully, with Judy Garland standing at the back of a train as it wends its way out West. Her face expressing awe and wonder, she sings "In the Valley When the Evening Sun Goes Down" in her tremulous style. Learning that her prospective bridegroom (Chill Wills) had the local saloonkeeper (John Hodiak) write his love letters as a joke, she opts for staying in town as one of the Harvey waitresses. Soon, a pitched battle develops between the forces of "wickedness," represented by Hodiak (but only temporarily), Preston Foster, and spangled saloon singer Angela Lansbury, and the forces of "civilization," headed by Garland. The Harvey restaurant is burned to the ground, but all ends happily, with Garland and Hodiak declaring their love.

The screenplay of *The Harvey Girls* is cluttered and predictable, but many of the musical numbers are engaging. Uncertain about the future, Judy Garland, Virginia O'Brien, and Cyd Charisse sing "It's a Great Big World" wistfully, as they shiver together in their nightgowns in the cold night air. Virginia O'Brien sings "The Wild Wild West" in her familiar deadpan style. The best number is a rousing rendition of the Academy Award–winning song, "On the Atchison, Topeka and the Santa Fe." It begins with the townspeople singing as they hear the whistle of the approaching train, and it opens into an elaborate production number involving many singers and dancers. There are numerous clever variations as the song gains in scope

and intensity, but Judy Garland remains the central figure in the number, without dominating it completely.

The following year, the Freed Unit produced a new version of *Good News,* a DeSylva, Brown, and Henderson 1927 stage show that had been filmed once before in 1930. Dusted off and dressed up in bright Technicolor, this quintessential college musical was the first full-fledged directorial job assigned to dance director Charles Walters. Heading the cast were June Allyson as the lovelorn heroine and Peter Lawford as the rather unlikely football hero of Tait College in the Roaring Twenties. (To Lawford's credit, he balked at playing the role, since he was not only British but couldn't sing a note. The studio persisted, however.) Betty Comden and Adolph Green contributed the screenplay—their first—and joined with Roger Edens, Hugh Martin, and Ralph Blane in refurbishing the original score and adding a few new songs.

With all these elements in its favor, it is surprising that *Good News* turned out to be merely average entertainment. Certainly the musical portions are not to blame: June Allyson sings such standards as "Just Imagine" and "The Best Things in Life Are Free" in her laryngitic style, and in the finale, all of Tait College cavorts in a lively rendition of "The Varsity Drag," staged by Robert Alton. Allyson and Lawford engage amusingly in a "French Lesson," and Joan McCracken, a delightful vixen from the Broadway stage, leads the college kids in a drugstore song and dance to "Pass That Peace Pipe." But the screenplay retains the musty old plot of the football hero who finally resists the class vamp and goes on to win the big game and the girl who always loved him. Unfortunately, the cheerful score could not surmount the triteness or the excruciating silliness of much of the dialogue. *Good News* was not bad news—but it got by more on energy than on talent.

One MGM period musical, *Summer Holiday,* was filmed in 1946 but shelved by the studio until mid-1948. In the mid-forties Arthur Freed had hired director Rouben Mamoulian, hoping to assign him to some musical project. Eventually, Freed suggested a musical version of Eugene O'Neill's affectionate comedy, *Ah, Wilderness!* Mamoulian went to work on creating what he regarded as a musical play rather than merely a musical. Determined to make the film a one-man vision, he took charge of all departments, from scenery and costume design to the screenplay and music. But as the months passed, troubles ensued, weakening and compromising Mamoulian's overall concept of the film.

On its release, *Summer Holiday* was largely dismissed by critics and the public, but the verdict was in error. In spite of its lapses, this much-maligned film remains one of the better musicals of the forties. True, it is clearly meant to emulate *Meet Me in St. Louis,* and in this respect it fails (as did other imitations). It is also true that Mickey Rooney was a poor choice for the leading role—he is too old, too rambunctious, too much like a superannuated Andy Hardy. Yet *Summer Holiday* is a lovely, beautifully observed piece of Americana. Part of its charm is due to its pleasing if rose-colored view of some American rituals: the graduation ceremony, the Fourth of July picnic, and others.

Adhering closely to the original play, the film begins well, as newspaper publisher Nat Miller (Walter Huston), in a

The Harvey Girls *(MGM, 1946). Angela Lansbury as Em, the pomaded dance hall queen who vies with Judy Garland for the affections of John Hodiak. Only nineteen at the time of filming, she was often cast as women much older than her years.*

opposite, above: Easter Parade *(MGM, 1948). Fred Astaire and Judy Garland enjoy a rip-roaring good time as a couple of tramps who like to think of themselves as "A Couple of Swells." In this number, Garland disports herself with such comic aplomb that she seems to have momentarily shed all her many off-camera burdens.*

combination of song and dialogue, introduces us to his family, particularly his middle son, Richard (Rooney). Romantic-minded and idealistic, Richard is in love with Muriel McComber (Gloria De Haven). Bitter at being forced to give Muriel up because of some "indecent" writings he has shown her, he dallies for a few innocent hours on the "bad" side of town with a bar girl named Belle (Marilyn Maxwell) and returns home roaring drunk. In one of the classic scenes in the American theater, his embarrassed father tries to tell him "the facts of life." But all ends well when Richard is reunited with Muriel, and even his alcoholic Uncle Sid (Frank Morgan) renews his longstanding courtship of prim Aunt Lily (Agnes Moorehead).

Summer Holiday derives its charm and poignancy from the O'Neill play, but the added musical numbers give it vitality and freshness, either enriching the period setting or expressing a character's emotions. Early in the film, Richard sings "You Mustn't Be Afraid to Fall in Love" to Muriel, and they dance across a green field with the uninhibited joy of young love. A production number to the song "The Stanley Steamer" is obviously modeled after "The Trolley Song" in *Meet Me in St. Louis*—the lyricist was the same on both—but it has its own infectious gaiety as the newfangled car chugs down the road with the proud, if apprehensive, family. At the Fourth of July picnic, the men sing "This Independence Day," leading to a high-spirited musical romp in which everyone participates. In the movie's most imaginative number, bar girl Belle attempts to seduce Richard with the song "I Think You're One of the Sweetest Kids I've Ever Met." As she sings, her appearance in the eyes of an increasingly sodden Richard changes from hooker to goddess. The combination of music and photography conveys Richard's state of mind more aptly than any dialogue.

Though hardly a masterpiece, *Summer Holiday* is worthy of kinder treatment than it has received in the past. Aside from some excessive mugging by Mickey Rooney, it does not violate the spirit or the intention of the O'Neill play, and in some cases, it improves on previous casting of the central roles. Walter Huston gives a sensitive, quietly authoritative performance as Nat Miller, and Frank Morgan brings a sadness and a rumpled charm to Uncle Sid that Wallace Beery missed in the 1936 film version of *Ah, Wilderness!* And little Jackie ("Butch") Jenkins, as the youngest child in the family, is adorable without being annoyingly cute.

As the forties waned, MGM's musicals continued to brighten the screen, but one inimitable presence was nowhere to be seen. Since making *Blue Skies* with Bing Crosby at Paramount in 1946, Fred Astaire had been in self-imposed exile, devoting his time to establishing a chain of dance studios and to breeding race horses. Always a self-effacing man, he was glad to be out of the spotlight. But then fate interceded and placed him back in front of the cameras. Before production began on MGM's *Easter Parade* (1948), another bouquet made up of Irving Berlin songs, Gene Kelly injured himself while playing softball with a group of children—he told Louis Mayer it was during rehearsals—and a replacement was urgently needed. Astaire was asked to assume the role opposite Judy Garland, and *Easter Parade* finally went into full production under the direction of Charles Walters. It turned out to be not only one of Astaire's best musicals in years, but also

left: Good News *(MGM, 1947). June Allyson and Peter Lawford lead the Tait College crowd in "The Varsity Drag." The song had been the big hit of the original 1927 stage show.*

below: Good News *(MGM, 1947). Tait College's football hero Peter Lawford courts coed and librarian June Allyson in this quintessential but only moderately effective college musical.*

overleaf, above: Summer Holiday *(MGM, 1948). The Miller family goes out for a ride in their brand-new Stanley Steamer. In the front seat: young Richard (Mickey Rooney) and his girl, Muriel (Gloria De Haven). In back: Aunt Lily (Agnes Moorehead), Mr. Miller (Walter Huston), and Mrs. Miller (Selena Royle). Taking up the rear: Tommy (Jackie "Butch" Jenkins).*

overleaf, center: In the Good Old Summertime *(MGM, 1949). Judy Garland and Van Johnson are employees in Oberkugen's music store. They are also—unknown to each other—devoted "pen pals."*

overleaf, below: Take Me Out to the Ball Game *(MGM, 1949). Frank Sinatra and Gene Kelly are baseball players "moonlighting" as vaudevillians. This amiable but routine movie marked their first teaming since* Anchors Aweigh *in 1945.*

203

one of the most successful musicals of the forties.

Still limber at forty-eight, Astaire played a 1912 vaudeville dancer who is cast aside by his ambitious partner (Ann Miller). He vows to make a virtual duplicate of her out of the very first girl he sees. Naturally, the girl turns out to be Judy Garland, a chorus girl with aspirations. She falls in love with him, but he is interested only in their work onstage, prompting her to accuse him of being "nothing but a pair of dancing shoes!" It isn't long before this Pygmalion discovers that his Galatea is a vibrant, talented woman with a style of her very own. He also comes to reciprocate her feeling for him.

Astaire and Garland act out this story with easy assurance, his reticence and professional élan blending surprisingly well with her more emotional approach. Happily, their disparate styles also blend well onstage, and they do several memorable numbers together: a duet of the deliberately "cutesy" "Snooky Ookums," a razzmatazz version of "When the Midnight Choo-Choo Leaves for Alabam'," and their classic "A Couple of Swells," in which, dressed as outlandish tramps, they gambol with genuine glee.

Separately, the two stars are also at their best in *Easter Parade.* In a toy store, Astaire goes "Drum Crazy," using his talented feet to beat an insistent rhythm on the drums, and he dances in slow motion to "Steppin' Out with My Baby." Early in the movie, he also dances about a hotel suite with Ann Miller to the Berlin ballad "It Only Happens When I Dance with You." (Miller, one of the screen's best tap dancers, reveals a surprisingly sinuous grace in this duet.) Garland, in good voice, sings the plaintive "Better Luck Next Time" at a bar, reflecting on Astaire's indifference to her (a recurrent onscreen problem of hers since her movies with Mickey Rooney), and also sings "I Wish I Were in Michigan." To add to the movie's musical riches, Ann Miller has a sizzling solo to "Shakin' the Blues Away."

Judy Garland's last film for the decade was also her next-to-last film for the studio at which she had started her career fourteen years earlier. A musical remake of Ernst Lubitsch's classic romantic comedy *The Shop Around the Corner, In the Good Old Summertime* (1949) changed the locale from old Budapest to Chicago in the early 1900s but kept the basic premise: two young people working in the same store (a parfumerie in the earlier film, a music shop in this one) share a mutual dislike without knowing that they are secret "pen pals" with much in common. By the time they discover the truth, they are genuinely in love.

The musical has a lovely bandbox setting in color (most of the film is set in wintertime, despite the title), a degree of charm, and several tinkly old tunes, but it settles too often for easy cuteness, amply represented by S. Z. ("Cuddles") Sakall as the store proprietor, Mr. Oberkugen. As the store manager and Garland's secret pen pal, Van Johnson plays with even more earnest boyishness than James Stewart had displayed in the earlier version. As Oberkugen's bumbling nephew, great silent comedian Buster Keaton has little to do, but he manages one hilarious pratfall in which he completely demolishes a violin.

In the role originally scheduled for a now-pregnant June Allyson, Judy Garland looks slim and attractive despite the severe strain she was under at the time, and she gives *In the Good Old Summertime* whatever freshness it can claim. Whether singing a melting "Meet Me Tonight in Dreamland" to demonstrate a harp, or a spirited version of "Put Your Arms Around Me, Honey," she is thoroughly appealing. Her best number comes at the party celebrating Oberkugen's engagement to Nellie, his cashier and longtime fiancée (Spring Byington). With not too much persuasion, she sings "Play That Barbershop Chord" with a quartet of mustachioed men, and does a version of vaudeville star Eva Tanguay's famous number "I Don't Care," complete with Garlandian gestures, that fairly explodes with energy and good cheer. Unfortunately, none of these musical numbers has any relation to the story. The movie ends with a small historical footnote: a postscript shows Garland and Johnson years later, now happily married. With the title tune in the background, they are strolling with their tiny two-year-old daughter, played by Garland's true daughter, Liza Minnelli.

Gene Kelly and Frank Sinatra starred in the Freed Unit's last musical for the forties, *Take Me Out to the Ball Game* (1949). This moderately entertaining musical involved another "last": it was Busby Berkeley's last assignment as a full director. Berkeley has related how he went to the office of Louis B. Mayer with Arthur Freed. Mayer, skeptical about Berkeley's ability to direct, asked him what made him think he was as good now as he had been in the past. Berkeley told him that he had learned something from all his troubles and quoted a favorite saying, "I have travelled a long way over sea and sod, and I have found nothing as small as me, and nothing as great as God." Mayer, whose piety was well known, was impressed. He turned to Freed and said, "Buzz will direct *Take Me Out to the Ball Game*" (Thomas and Terry, *The Busby Berkeley Book*).

Berkeley proceeded to make a musical film that falls squarely into the MGM mode, with only one musical number ("Strictly U.S.A.") that reveals signs of the Berkeley touch of old. The emaciated plot concerns a championship baseball team in the early years of the century, dominated by its three biggest drawing cards, Eddie O'Brien (Gene Kelly), Denny Ryan (Frank Sinatra), and Nat Goldberg (Jules Munshin). When the team is taken over by beautiful K. C. (Katharine) Higgins (Esther Williams on dry land), romantic and business troubles ensue.

Obviously derivative of *Anchors Aweigh* with its three-buddies-on-the-loose framework, *Take Me Out to the Ball Game* played like a worn retread, with Kelly again the suave, self-assured "wolf" and Sinatra repeating the painfully shy dimwit that was becoming tiresome. Even their duet early in the movie, "Yes, Indeedy!," is reminiscent of "I Begged Her" in *Anchors Aweigh*. The songs by Betty Comden and Adolph Green and Roger Edens are apportioned as expected: Sinatra gets a romantic solo ("She's the Right Girl for Me") and Gene Kelly sings and dances to "The Hat Me Dear Old Father Wore." The big production number, "Strictly U.S.A.," is a rowdy clambake that brings together the principals and a crowd of extras to prance through Berkeley's overbusy staging.

Since the late thirties, 20th Century-Fox had produced many period musicals, but they had been mostly frothy concoctions for Betty Grable or Alice Faye, mixing hummable old tunes with a few mediocre new songs, stirring in a few gaudy production numbers, and pouring it all into the movie theaters for instant consumption. There was no pretense at art or sophistication, or even a genuine interest in re-creating American life in other times. Betty Grable was the ideal heroine for these films: brash, curvaceous, artless, and enjoyable to watch.

But even Betty Grable could not remain locked in time, and by the mid-forties, she was approaching the age of thirty, ready to take advantage of the change in the musical film. In her earlier period films, she had usually played the spangled entertainer, but *Meet Me in St. Louis* had shown that musicals need not be set in the backstage world of two-a-day and could indeed celebrate the joys of the American past and the American family. Cheerfully adjustable as always, Grable played, in succession, a sensible turn-of-the-century business girl, the level-headed mother of two young girls, and the devoted wife of an entertainer on the skids.

Fox's first and most direct imitation of *Meet Me in St. Louis* did not star Betty Grable, however. With the Louisiana Purchase Exposition of 1904 locked up by the earlier film, *Centennial Summer* (1946) chose for its setting the Philadelphia Exposition of 1876. Obviously derived from *St. Louis,* the musical centered on a family caught up in the excitement of the Exposition. With a colorful setting, an attractive cast headed by Jeanne Crain and Linda Darnell, and a melodious if not top-flight score by Jerome Kern, *Centennial Summer* seemed likely to be a diverting musical. Regrettably, there were serious shortcomings: a tepid and rambling screenplay, and a director (Otto Preminger) with no previous experience at directing a musical film. The movie began well, with a charming Kern roundelay called "Up with the Lark," and dancer Avon Long turned up abruptly to perform "Cinderella Sue" in a pleasing solo. But the warmth and spirit of *Meet Me in St. Louis* were nowhere in evidence.

Another Fox period musical released that year was much better, and a nice surprise. *Three Little Girls in Blue* was yet another variation on that favorite theme: determined girls in search of rich husbands. Here the setting was Atlantic City in 1902, and the girls were three of the studio's most promising young stars: June Haver, Vivian Blaine, and Vera-Ellen. With little else on their minds but men and money, the damsels become involved in some predictable romantic adventures and end up with mates, only one of whom is actually wealthy. It was all very frivolous, but Bruce Humberstone's direction was brisk, the cast was pleasant, and the songs, including "On the Boardwalk" and "You Make Me Feel So Young," were easy to take. As icing on the cake, the movie marked the film debut of Celeste Holm, the talented singer-actress who had played Ado Annie in the original production of *Oklahoma!* As a dizzy, well-to-do Maryland girl, she brought theatrical flair and genuine gaiety to her role and to a song called "Always a Lady."

Betty Grable's first excursion away from her flashy-showgirl roles turned out to be aboard a sinking ship. *The Shocking Miss Pilgrim* (1947) cast her as the first woman "typewriter" in conservative Boston of 1874, who disrupts the business world of men and discovers romance with her young boss (Dick Haymes). Despite some clever satirical touches in George Seaton's screenplay (he also directed) and a not-bad score of recently uncovered and never published Gershwin songs, the movie was given exceptionally harsh treatment by the critics. Amusing supporting performances by Anne Revere as Haymes's militant suffragette

aunt and Allyn Joslyn as a bearded avant-garde poet passed unnoticed in the general condemnation. The few who were inclined to see the film might even have been surprised at having a passably good time.

Fortunately for Grable's reputation, she scored one of her greatest successes later that year with *Mother Wore Tights,* directed by Walter Lang. A sentimental curio concerning a devoted vaudeville couple and their two daughters, the film appealed to movie audiences as few other Grable musicals had in recent years, and it was an enormous box-office hit. The screenplay centered on the blissful marriage of schoolgirl-turned-chorus girl Myrtle McKinley (Grable) and vaudeville headliner Frank Burt (Dan Dailey, ingratiating in his first major movie for Fox). Myrtle retires for a while, but later the two resume as vaudeville stars, leaving their two growing daughters (Mona Freeman and Connie Marshall) unhappily at home. The older daughter's embarrassment at her parents' profession causes a family crisis, but everything is resolved through smiles and tears. Mom and Pop survive to get their very own old-age makeup.

Watching the musical portions of *Mother Wore Tights,* it is easy to see why Grable and Dailey were reunited for three more movies. They make a likable team, with talents that blend well in such songs as "Kokomo, Indiana." Several old tunes fall to Mona Freeman, and Grable gets her obligatory solo with "You Do," wearing a striking gown and carrying a feather fan. (One of the movie's unintentionally funny moments occurs when Mona Freeman, now tearfully proud of her parents, reprises the song at her graduation ceremony.)

Grable was reunited with Dailey a year later in *When My Baby Smiles at Me.* The third film version of the George Manker Watters–Arthur Hopkins play *Burlesque,* the movie worked familiar terrain in its story of a married small-time vaudeville team split asunder when the wife succeeds on her own and the husband becomes an alcoholic brawler. With their quarrels, separation, and ultimate reconciliation taking so much of the footage, there was not much time for musical numbers, and the movie contained only a few new and old songs. Since the film industry has always doted on portrayals of drunkards, Dan Dailey received an Academy Award nomination for his performance.

One Fox musical of the mid-forties had a contemporary setting, but its rose-colored, picture-postcard view of American life placed it squarely in the tradition of the period musical. This was *State Fair* (1945), the first screen collaboration of Richard Rodgers and Oscar Hammerstein II. It was launched with high hopes under Walter Lang's direction, with a cast headed by Jeanne Crain, Dana Andrews, Vivian Blaine, and Dick Haymes. The story centered on the Frake family of Iowa, and their adventures, romantic and otherwise, at the annual state fair. Daughter Marjy (Crain) meets and falls in love with a seasoned newspaperman (Andrews), who is not interested in settling down. Son Wayne (Haymes) has a brief, thwarted romance with Emily (Blaine), a married singer with a traveling band. Father Abel Frake (Charles Winninger) has temporary trouble with his prize-winning hog, Blue Boy. And mother Melissa Frake (Fay Bainter) wins first prize with her highly spiked mincemeat.

There is little wrong with this story line, but its execution conveys none of the pungency or excitement of a state fair. Nor

above: Mother Wore Tights *(Fox, 1947). The Burt family comes together for a session of songs around the piano: Mother Myrtle (Betty Grable), father Frank (Dan Dailey), and their daughters (Connie Marshall and Mona Freeman). Betty Grable's most financially successful movie,* Mother Wore Tights *was pleasant, unexceptional nostalgia, with some good backstage atmosphere, tinkly tunes, and a hearty dose of sentiment.*

top: Three Little Girls in Blue *(Fox, 1946). Vera-Ellen, June Haver, and Vivian Blaine—the girls of the title—pause in their search for wealthy husbands to sing and dance. One of Fox's better period musicals of the forties, the movie was lighthearted, agreeable entertainment.*

opposite: The Shocking Miss Pilgrim *(Fox, 1947). Betty Grable as Cynthia Pilgrim, the first woman "typewriter" in Boston of 1874. The musical was scorned by the critics and did little business, but it had some merit, including a charming Gershwin song called "Changing My Tune."*

When My Baby Smiles at Me *(Fox, 1948). Another teaming of Dan Dailey and Betty Grable, this time in the third film version of the 1927 play* Burlesque. *Dailey gave a commendable performance as a vaudevillian on the skids, whether behaving with drunken abandon or performing the title song in an imitation of Ted Lewis.*

does the score help. Although it includes some pleasant though not outstanding songs in the Rodgers and Hammerstein canon, it is presented on the whole in surprisingly flat and ordinary fashion. "That's for Me" and "All I Owe Ioway" are given dull bandstand renditions, although the latter song is expanded into a full-scale production number, and "Isn't It Kinda Fun?" is sung by Dick Haymes at a band party. Early in the movie, the lilting "It Might as Well Be Spring" is sung by Jeanne Crain (dubbed by Louanne Hogan) in a pretty but patently phony farm setting, and in the unimaginative staging of "It's a Grand Night for Singing," the melody is merely passed from couple to couple at different points on the fairgrounds.

At Paramount, musical nostalgia for America's past took the form of another cavalcade of Irving Berlin songs. Like Fox's *Alexander's Ragtime Band* in 1938 and Paramount's *Holiday Inn* in 1942, *Blue Skies* (1946) used a slender story as the basis for singing and dancing to a generous selection of new and old Berlin tunes. The movie made no bones about its intention: it began with Fred Astaire, as a dancer-turned-disk jockey, informing his listeners that he was about to tell a story using Irving Berlin songs that "reflect an epic of American life."

The story is rambling and tedious, but several of the songs and dances are first-rate, marred only in some instances by the typically ugly décor and costumes of many forties musicals. As expected, Crosby gets the best numbers, singing a cluster of Berlin songs including "All by Myself," "Always," the title tune, and even a reprise of "White Christmas." He also sings Berlin's lovely new ballad "You Keep Coming Back like a Song" as a recurrent romantic motif, and he serenades his little daughter with the charming tune "Running Around in Circles." Crosby only falters when he is obliged to sing one of the "military" songs Berlin often insisted on putting into his scores, this one called "I've Got My Captain Working for Me Now," originally sung by Eddie Cantor in *Ziegfeld Follies of 1919.*

In *Blue Skies,* as in *Holiday Inn,* Fred Astaire gets short shrift, joining Crosby in a clowning but overlong routine to "A Couple of Song-and-Dance Men," and taking a drunken fall off the bridge in an elaborate setting for a production number of "Heat Wave." However, his dance to "Puttin' on the Ritz" almost compensates for the cursory treatment he receives in the film. It is a virtuoso number in which his only prop is the cane he uses in syncopation with his machine-gun taps. A parted curtain and mirrored door reveal ten miniature Astaires, with whom he dances in dazzling counterpoint. A number that epitomizes Astaire's wit, inventiveness, and peerless style as a dancer, it was intended as a kind of valedictory to films. Mindful that Gene Kelly was now the favored screen dancer, and aware that too many ineffectual roles could diminish his popularity, Astaire announced his retirement. Ironically, two years later, he replaced Gene Kelly in *Easter Parade.*

Crosby followed *Blue Skies* with a minor period musical called *The Emperor Waltz* (1948). Set in late nineteenth-century Austria, the movie concerned a resourceful American salesman (Crosby) who is traveling through Europe with a newfangled contraption called a phonograph. During the course of the film, he wins the approval of Emperor Franz Joseph (Richard Haydn) and the hand of a beautiful countess (Joan Fontaine). The

screenplay, coauthored and directed by Billy Wilder, was often cleverly amusing, and the scenery—a snow-laden Canada substituting for old Austria—was lovely. Crosby didn't sing as much as usual; his only new song was "Friendly Mountains," which he croons at the film's beginning as he strolls down an alpine road. The following year he turned up in another period musical, a mildly entertaining version of Mark Twain's *A Connecticut Yankee in King Arthur's Court*. Crosby played the amiable Yankee, but Sir Cedric Hardwicke stole the film as a runny-nosed King Arthur.

In a short five years since the release of *Meet Me in St. Louis,* Hollywood studios (especially MGM) had produced a series of musicals that glowed with a warm, nostalgic feeling for a world that probably existed only in the imagination. The improvement in color techniques, the increased skill in re-creating the look and the attire of past eras, and the ripening talents of performers who had made their mark or had begun their careers in the thirties— all these elements helped to give the films a luster that emanated from the screen. Audiences were responsive—the postwar years were a time of healing and readjustment—and for a while it seemed infinitely preferable to celebrate an idyllic past than to confront an uncertain future. In the hoopskirts, the gaslights, the horseless carriages, and the honky-tonk saloons of a vanished era, there were comfort and serenity, set to song and dance. There would be other period musicals ahead to enjoy and remember. But in a dry season, the second half of the forties brought Technicolored oases of remembrance for which most moviegoers were grateful.

State Fair (Fox, 1945). At the fair, the Frake family gathers around the pen of their prize hog, Blue Boy: son Wayne (Dick Haymes), mother Melissa (Fay Bainter) daughter Marjy (Jeanne Crain), and father Abel (Charles Winninger). Seasoned veterans Winninger and Bainter gave the film a measure of distinction, but the most memorable character was little Donald Meek, who has one pricelessly funny scene as a judge at the mincemeat competition. He tastes Bainter's inadvertently spiked mincemeat and reacts with barely suppressed glee.

The
MUSIC MAKERS

During the immediate postwar years, while the studios were busily stuffing their leading players into period costumes or dipping them into Olympic-size pools, a subgenre of the musical film was taking shape. For many years, America's most popular composers had contributed songs—and a great deal of pleasure—to movie musicals. Though not a biography, *Alexander's Ragtime Band* had been virtually a musical chronicle of Irving Berlin's career from the pre–World War I years to the late thirties. But what about Jerome Kern, George Gershwin, Richard Rodgers and Lorenz Hart, and Cole Porter? Their captivating music could form a melodic background for frankly fictionalized versions of their life stories. And so, in the second half of the forties, the musical dealing with contemporary composers enjoyed a vogue that continued into the early fifties.

Warners began the trend with *Rhapsody in Blue* (1945). Ostensibly a biography of George Gershwin, it transformed the supremely gifted, egotistical composer into a colorless man obsessed by his music but unable to work out a satisfactory personal life. Gershwin, played woodenly by Robert Alda, was depicted as the object of awe and admiration of everyone. On hand at all times was Oscar Levant, one of Gershwin's closest friends, who plays himself in his familiar sneering style. Hobbled by a screenplay that captured little of Gershwin's personality or the reasons for his musical obsession, Irving Rapper directed this exceptionally long movie in routine fashion.

Gershwin's music receives mostly indifferent treatment in *Rhapsody in Blue*. As his mythical girlfriend Julie Adams, Joan Leslie turns such marvelous songs as " 'S Wonderful" and "Lady Be Good" into exhibitions of simpering girlishness, while pianist-singer Hazel Scott grimaces her way through "The Man I Love," "Fascinatin' Rhythm," "Clap Yo' Hands," and "I Got Rhythm." In his first movie since 1939, Al Jolson sings "Swanee" to a cheering audience at the Winter Garden. Gershwin's serious compositions are handled more effectively, with a performance of "Rhapsody in Blue" led by Paul Whiteman, and Oscar Levant's expert playing of the Concerto in F for piano and orchestra.

Warners's version of the life and times of Cole Porter, filmed in 1944 but released in 1946, was even worse. *Night and*

Day has the dubious distinction of containing one of Cary Grant's two worst performances in the forties. (The other was in *Arsenic and Old Lace*.) Curiously stiff and flat as the composer, Grant took Porter from his days at Yale, through his success as a composer and his marriage to Linda Lee (Alexis Smith), to his crippling riding accident. Comfort and support came from Monty Woolley, playing himself as the acidulous Yale professor-turned-entertainer, and from fictional admiring friends, played by Ginny Simms, Jane Wyman, Eve Arden, and others. The film's director, Michael Curtiz, was despised by Grant as a tyrant—possibly one reason for the actor's unconvincing performance.

Night and Day does a grave injustice to the composer's incomparable songs. They are either sung without regard for their wit and lyrical quality ("In the Still of the Night," one of Porter's most beautiful love songs, is chirped by caroling youngsters on Christmas eve) or staged in the hectic style of many forties musicals ("Begin the Beguine," a sensuous melody that can easily teeter on the edge of parody, is especially damaged by this treatment). One number stands out: Mary Martin, wearing a fur coat and apparently little else, reprises the rendition of "My Heart Belongs to Daddy" that brought her fame in the Broadway musical *Leave It to Me*.

With more accomplished musical performers under contract, MGM seemed a clear choice to improve on Warners's mediocre musical biographies, but its ventures into the subgenre were only marginally superior. In 1946, the studio released *Till the Clouds Roll By*, purportedly based on the life of Jerome Kern, and starring a great many leading MGM personalities. To play Kern, producer Arthur Freed, who idolized the composer, selected Robert Walker, a contract player who specialized in boyish charm. It was the first of many mistakes; Walker played Kern as a cipher in his early years and as a pompous old man by the film's end.

Given a life that was richly productive but apparently without the usual major traumas of the creative artist, the writers fashioned a dull screenplay that traced Kern's career, marriage, and lifelong friendships. Luckily, there was the Kern music to fall back on, and some of it is performed competently and even better than that. MGM stars keep turning up like

Night and Day *(Warners, 1946). One of the least satisfactory musical biographies of the period, the film suffered from Cary Grant's surprisingly awkward performance as composer Cole Porter and from the inept staging of many of Porter's witty songs. Among the exceptions: Monty Woolley's amusing talk-singing of "Miss Otis Regrets."*

page 210: Rhapsody in Blue *(Warners, 1945). Robert Alda as George Gershwin and Oscar Levant as himself play a duet on two pianos for admiring party guests. Visible among the guests (behind Levant): jowly Charles Coburn as music publisher Max Dreyfus.*

raisins in a pudding, helping to make the tedious stretches of plot tolerable. As Ziegfeld star Marilyn Miller, Judy Garland sings two numbers from *Sunny*: an expressive version of "Look for the Silver Lining," her face artfully smudged with dirt as she washes dishes, and "Who?" performed in a lavish circus setting. June Allyson succeeds in making her "cuteness" an asset rather than a liability as she sings the amusing "Cleopatterer" and joins dancer Ray McDonald in a charming performance of the title song. Even the long excerpt from *Show Boat* that begins the movie is bearable, although the principals—Kathryn Grayson, Lena Horne, Tony Martin, and Virginia O'Brien—make one long for another viewing of the 1936 version.

The movie's last musical segment begins well, as Kern watches MGM's stars perform a medley of his songs. But then a serious error in judgment pulls down the entire enterprise. Chorus girls emerge, and following a portentous drum roll, the audience beholds Frank Sinatra in a white tuxedo, standing on a platform as he sings a perfectly enunciated version of "Ol' Man River." Nobody seems to notice the disparity between his elegant appearance and Oscar Hammerstein's despairing lyrics. The camera pans back to show the full elaborate set, with Sinatra as its beacon at the center. It is one of the truly insensitive musical numbers in film history, and it climaxes a movie that has only one true virtue: it leaves the music of Jerome Kern undiminished.

Two years later, MGM produced *Words and Music* (1948), based on or, more accurately, loosely suggested by the lives and careers of Richard Rodgers and Lorenz Hart, and the results were similar: a weak story line wedded to splendid music, unevenly performed. The songwriters were played by Tom Drake, Esther Smith's devoted "Boy Next Door" in *Meet Me in St. Louis* and colorless as Rodgers, and by Mickey Rooney, whose performance as the tormented, witty Lorenz Hart was simply excruciating. Since virtually all of the film's "drama" rested in the tragic disintegration of Hart, the hapless viewer was subjected to Rooney's scenery chewing for much of two hours. Juggling dates to fit the story, the screenplay ranged from his early teaming with Rodgers to his premature death.

The film's single attraction is, of course, the wonderful music, and some of it is well handled in Robert Alton's staging. Judy Garland belts out "Johnny One-Note" with much of her customary force, and she joins Mickey Rooney in a spirited duet of "I Wish I Were in Love Again." Lena Horne is elegance personified in her two numbers, "Where or When" and "The Lady Is a Tramp." There are also a few pleasant surprises. June Allyson is delightful singing "Thou Swell" with the Blackburn Twins (who almost wreck the number with their forced grinning), and Ann Sothern, charming in a bright yellow dress, performs "Where's That Rainbow?" agreeably. Perry Como is on hand to sing "Mountain Greenery" and "Blue Room" in his familiar "laid-back" style.

Songwriters Bert Kalmar and Harry Ruby fared much better in MGM's *Three Little Words* (1950). Although not in a league with Kern or Rodgers and Hart, they did create a catalogue of hummable tunes that includes "Thinking of You," "Who's Sorry Now?," and the title song. Fred Astaire was cast as Kalmar, a hoofer-turned-songwriter and an aspiring magician, and Red Skelton, unusually subdued, as Ruby, an ardent baseball

above: Till the Clouds Roll By *(MGM, 1946). Judy Garland, as Ziegfeld star Marilyn Miller, sings Jerome Kern's "Who?" in a circus setting. Pregnant at the time of filming, Garland was directed in this and her other numbers by husband Vincente Minnelli.*

top: Till the Clouds Roll By *(MGM, 1946). In one of the film's most pleasing musical numbers, June Allyson and Ray McDonald sing and dance to the title song. This star-heavy musical was temporarily halted in mid-production when Kern died, and the screenplay had to be rewritten.*

above: Words and Music *(MGM, 1948). Vera-Ellen and Gene Kelly dance in Rodgers and Hart's jazz ballet "Slaughter on Tenth Avenue." Introduced as the grand finale in the 1936 stage musical* On Your Toes, *the ballet originally had a comic emphasis. For this movie it was turned into steamy melodrama.*

top: Words and Music *(MGM, 1948). June Allyson and the Blackburn Twins have a merry time performing Rodgers and Hart's song "Thou Swell" from their 1927 stage musical,* A Connecticut Yankee.

Three Little Words *(MGM, 1950). Fred Astaire as composer Bert Kalmar and Vera-Ellen as his girlfriend (and later wife) Jessie Brown step out to the music of "Where Did You Get That Girl?"*

opposite: The Jolson Story *(Columbia, 1946). Larry Parks, as entertainer Al Jolson, assumes the familiar Jolson pose during a musical number. This phenomenally popular musical originated when Columbia's head Harry Cohn, a worshipful Jolson fan, outbid Jack Warner for the rights to the singer's life and music.*

fan. The slender plot touches on their unexpected partnership, their romances and marriages (Astaire to Vera-Ellen, Skelton to Arlene Dahl), and their bitter separation and ultimate reconciliation. With a screenplay that had few dramatic high points and performers not given to emoting on screen, the movie touched off no sparks, but it also avoided embarrassment and boredom, to its definite advantage.

Somewhat more modestly scaled than MGM's previous biographical musicals, *Three Little Words* leaned musically on its leading players, with mostly happy results. Debbie Reynolds turns up midway through the film as "boop-boop-a-doop" singer Helen Kane and chirps "I Wanna Be Loved by You," dubbed by Kane in her little-girl voice. But usually Astaire and Vera-Ellen take front and center, dancing with genuine romantic ardor to "Thinking of You," and performing "Mr. and Mrs. Hoofer at Home," an amusing and clever routine in which they take married dancers through a typical day. Astaire also has one effective solo with a cane. By replacing grandiose effects and star power with an amiable low-key story and some authentic musical talent, *Three Little Words* managed to be more successful than its predecessors.

Occasionally, the biographical musical of the period veered away from the composer to focus on the entertainer. Betty Hutton played twenties nightclub queen Texas Guinan in Paramount's *Incendiary Blonde* (1945), but the movie was much more Hutton than Guinan. It touched fancifully on the entertainer's rise from a rodeo rider to the raucous owner of a string of Prohibition nightclubs, where her trademark, "Hello, suckers!," could be heard nightly. Hutton sang many old-time songs in her strident style.

The most widely attended musical biography of the forties dealt with the all-time favorite entertainer, Al Jolson. Columbia's *The Jolson Story* (1946) was a phenomenon: a huge but unexpected success that began an entirely new career for the sixty-year-old performer, who had been long out of the spotlight. To play Jolson, the studio selected a contract player named Larry Parks, who seemed most able to mime the flamboyant Jolson style. Alfred E. Green, a veteran of the silent era, was assigned to direct. Shooting on the film began without a completed screenplay and with the writers often supplying scenes on the day before they were to be filmed. Gradually, the pieces fell into place, with Jolson, not very happy at being passed over for the role, supplying the singing voice for Parks's mimicry. (Jolson can be seen as himself in a long shot during the "Swanee" number.)

From the first week of its release, *The Jolson Story* was a sensational success. However, few moviegoers noticed, or cared, that it was not a superior musical film. Its story line is so banal that an alert viewer could spend his time counting the musical clichés: the vaudeville partners who have to separate because only one is wanted by a leading producer; the warmhearted family complete with doting mother and loving but crochety father; the man who sacrifices his marriage to his career; and so on. Despite good trouping by Evelyn Keyes as Julie Benson (a surrogate for Ruby Keeler, who refused to have her name used), Ludwig Donath and Tamara Shayne as Papa and Mama Jolson (Yoelson), and especially William Demarest as Jolson's vaudevillian friend, the plot limps and wheezes to a preordained conclusion: Jolson,

alone, singing his heart out as Julie walks out of his life.

The music is, however, the truly important factor, and it brings *The Jolson Story* fitfully to life. The movie overflows with songs: "Mammy," "I'm Sitting on Top of the World," "You Made Me Love You," "California, Here I Come," and others, all delivered with the Jolson exuberance that thousands of viewers found entrancing and others found exhausting. His contribution to *The Jazz Singer* is sloughed over, but there are good versions of his most popular film songs, including "A Latin from Manhattan" and "About a Quarter to Nine," and one of his best-remembered stage songs, "The Spaniard Who Blighted My Life." One surefire sequence reaches an apogee of sentimentality when Jolson-Parks sings "The Anniversary Song" to his adoring parents, to mark their many years of wedded bliss. Three years later, Columbia filmed a pointless and self-congratulatory sequel, *Jolson Sings Again* (1949), which made much ado about Jolson's "comeback" after the earlier film was released. But the success of *The Jolson Story* was not repeated.

In the years ahead, entertainers would dominate the biographical musical with problems that composers never seemed to acquire, at least in movie lore. There would be instances of alcoholism, mental breakdown, crippling disease, and marital anguish. The biographical musicals of the forties had no truck with such distasteful subjects. In their Technicolored world, it was only the music that mattered, and their "songbooks" gave us the glorious best of America's popular composers. Art? No, and in some cases not even cinematic competence. But when the warmth of the music that was (and is) part of all our lives washed over us, we were glad to bask in the melodies. And we sang and danced to them all the way home.

From Cover Girls to Gobs on the Town

In 1944, the same year in which *Meet Me in St. Louis* was released by MGM, another musical turned up to alter the direction of the genre. It was not intentional: Columbia Pictures, under the leadership of coarse, profane Harry Cohn, merely wanted to create a lavish vehicle for Rita Hayworth that would make a major box-office attraction of the beautiful redheaded actress. He chose to star her in an elaborate musical called *Cover Girl*.

With so much at stake, it was surprising that Harry Cohn gambled on so many "firsts" with this production. To act as the film's producer, he assigned composer Arthur Schwartz ("Dancing in the Dark," "Alone Together"), who had never produced a film before. A baffled Schwartz accepted after firm persuasion by Cohn. Charles Vidor, a Hungarian-born director who had never worked on a musical film, was named to put Rita Hayworth and a large cast through their paces. And then there was the choice of Hayworth's leading man. Schwartz suggested Gene Kelly for the role, arguing that the young dancer had made something of an impression in his few MGM films. At first Cohn was violently opposed, shouting, "That tough Irishman with the tough Irish mug! You couldn't put him in the same *frame* as Rita!" But a closer viewing of Kelly on film apparently changed his mind, and Kelly won the role that made him a star. Other *Cover Girl* components were first-rate: songs by Jerome Kern and Ira Gershwin, glittering forties photography, principally by Rudolph Maté, and hilarious sideline commentary by sharp-tongued Eve Arden.

The result was perhaps the quintessential musical film of the forties, a movie perched squarely between past and future. *Cover Girl* looks backward in its foolish backstage plot and in some of its conventional musical numbers. Yet it also looks forward to the late forties and beyond in the emergence of Gene Kelly as an important film dancer and in the unforced exuberance and innovative style of other of its musical numbers. The new and the old rattle together in a loose framework that makes the movie both dated and ahead of its time. *Cover Girl* also created one of the film icons of the decade in Rita Hayworth.

The movie's plot is the sort of nonsense that might have served Betty Grable a few years earlier. Hayworth plays Rusty

Parker, an ambitious showgirl who becomes a famous cover girl while conducting a seesaw romance with a Brooklyn nightclub owner, Danny McGuire (Gene Kelly). Phil Silvers plays their friendly sidekick, Genius. Eve Arden was the acidulous assistant to the magazine publisher (Otto Kruger) who once loved Rusty's grandmother.

With little of interest in the screenplay, *Cover Girl* must rely on its musical interludes. Several of them are amusingly campy in the brash forties style: the opening number, "The Show Must Go On," introducing the beautiful but not conspicuously talented Cover Girls (reputedly Gene Kelly hated the number and even shows his disapproval in a quick backstage shot), and Phil Silvers's song with the girls, "Who's Complaining?," in which he bemoans the rationed wartime shortages ("Because of Axis trickery/ My coffee now is chicory"). One of the film's best sequences was built around the lovely ballad "Long Ago and Far Away," which received an Oscar as the year's best song. Together after hours in Danny's club, Hayworth and Kelly, sensing that they are about to part, do a wistful rendition of the song. Kelly is especially effective as his face, combined with his thin yet appealing voice, expresses his sadness and longing. (Hayworth's voice was dubbed again by Nan Wynn.) They dance together amorously, kiss, and move quietly out of the scene.

Cover Girl's status as an important transitional musical rests on two of its musical numbers. Devoted friends, Rusty, Danny, and Genius spend much of their time at a neighborhood bar, ritually looking for a pearl in their order of oysters. Convinced that their future is bright, they sing and dance to "Make Way for Tomorrow." As the number spills into the street, it uses props and passersby to convey an exuberance rare in traditional musical numbers. The street may have the stylized, claustrophobic look of a movie set, but the joyful mood foreshadows the innovative open-air feeling of the truly original *On the Town* of five years later.

The movie's most famous number is Gene Kelly's "Alter Ego" dance. Having lost Rusty to fame, Danny is angry and bitter, and he begins to argue with his reflection in a store window. His alter ego steps down from the window, and both figures dance together in a dazzling display of the evolving Kelly

right: Cover Girl *(Columbia, 1944). Phil Silvers, Rita Hayworth, and Gene Kelly sing "Make Way for Tomorrow" as a testament to their faith in the future. The number was one of the first to convey the "outdoor" feeling that later flourished in such musicals as* On the Town.

page 216: Rita Hayworth, the lustrous "love goddess" of the forties, was a dancer and actress for a number of years before Harry Cohn, head of Columbia Pictures, groomed her for superstardom with Cover Girl.

below: Cover Girl *(Columbia, 1944). A ravishing "Pied Piper," Rita Hayworth leads the chorus boys across a long ramp, as clouds billow above her head. In her clinging gold gown, with her red hair cascading behind her, she became an instant movie goddess.*

style: original, imaginative, and quite different from the style of Fred Astaire—more athletic, more aggressive, and possibly a mite more ambitious and pretentious. In a *New York Times* article many years later, Kelly remarked that it was his first chance to "fit a three-dimensional art into a two-dimensional medium." He also said, "All the technicians said it was impossible because you had to pan and dolly and double expose. I showed them how I would do it, and it was successful." Like Fred Astaire, Kelly usually choreographed his own numbers. In this case, it was devised with the help of his friend and later codirector Stanley Donen.

As expected, many of the contemporary musicals came from those busy folks at MGM. Aside from the Freed Unit's efforts to advance the art of the musical film, the studio divided its musical productions, as it had for a number of years, between Joe Pasternak, who had come to MGM after producing the successful Deanna Durbin musicals at Universal, and Jack Cummings, who had worked at MGM since the silent era. Both men would continue to work prolifically into the fifties.

Inevitably, with his Durbin musicals behind him, and a well-known fondness for classical music, Pasternak was assigned to oversee the career of a new teenage soprano named Jane Powell. Pretty, vivacious, and a capable singer, Powell had come to MGM at age seventeen, after making two minor musicals elsewhere. Under Pasternak's production banner, she starred in a series of featherweight musical entertainments as a chirruping maiden with family or mildly romantic problems. Her first for MGM, *Holiday in Mexico* (1946), cast her as the daughter of the American ambassador to Mexico (Walter Pidgeon). Lightheaded and cheerful, she runs her motherless home and has a puppy-love affair with young Roddy McDowell. Received with favor by film audiences, Jane Powell was kept busy by her studio, appearing in such films as *Three Daring Daughters, A Date with Judy,* and *Luxury Liner,* all released in 1948. There were only incidental pleasures in these musicals: a few bright songs and production numbers and, in *A Date with Judy,* the exhilarating presence of Carmen Miranda.

In furthering the career of another MGM musical star, Joe Pasternak shared his production umbrella with Jack Cummings. Esther Williams had made her starring debut in 1944 in *Bathing Beauty,* proving that audiences would accept an exhibition of swimming to music as a bona fide musical number. The rich-hued color, the dreamlike underwater atmosphere, the lithe figure swimming gracefully to the music, all conspired to lull most viewers into the belief that they were being entertained. Add a frivolous plot and a few musical numbers by other hands, and the pattern was set for the Esther Williams musicals, produced by either Pasternak or Cummings in the second half of the forties. *Thrill of a Romance* (1945) enhanced Esther Williams's underwater ballet with arias and other songs by Metropolitan Opera singer Lauritz Melchior in his film debut (MGM's latest stab at culture). *Easy to Wed* (1946) had two virtues: a screenplay adapted from a funny 1936 MGM comedy called *Libeled Lady,* and the comic presence of Lucille Ball in the role previously played by Jean Harlow. *This Time for Keeps* (1947), *On an Island with You* (1948), and *Neptune's Daughter* (1949) offered more of the same, pausing at intervals to let Williams take the obligatory plunge.

By the last year of the decade, MGM continued to hold the

Down to Earth (Columbia, 1947). Rita Hayworth and Marc Platt (an excellent dancer from the Broadway stage) dance to "People Have More Fun." Hayworth played the true *goddess Terpsichore, who assumes human guise in order to appear in (and change) a "vulgar" stage musical about the Greek muses being produced by Larry Parks. The film used characters from the popular 1941 fantasy* Here Comes Mr. Jordan, *but they failed to bolster a preposterous plot. The musical numbers, though splashy, were dull.*

right: A Date with Judy *(MGM, 1948). Elizabeth Taylor offers a spoonful of ice cream to a lovestruck Jane Powell. A popular young singer in the Deanna Durbin mode, Powell starred in a number of light musicals produced largely by Joe Pasternak, who had performed the same function earlier for Durbin. As before, the public responded favorably to winsome girlishness and a trilling soprano voice.*

high cards as the foremost producer of musicals, and Joe Pasternak still had one ace up his sleeve. Having introduced Lauritz Melchior and Jose Iturbi to films, and having turned Jane Powell into a major box-office attraction, he now launched the brief but skyrocketing career of a young tenor named Mario Lanza. Lanza, gifted with an unusually powerful but untrained voice, had been singing for a number of years at concerts and on RCA recordings, when he was heard by Louis B. Mayer and his assistant Ida Koverman at a Hollywood Bowl concert. He was signed to a seven-year contract and was cast in Joe Pasternak's production of *That Midnight Kiss* (1949), with Kathryn Grayson.

The film was an enormous success as audiences responded, not to the short, stocky, unprepossessing Philadelphian with minimal acting ability, but to the richness and emotional force of his singing voice. *That Midnight Kiss* was carefully calculated to display that voice, and, although Lanza's face occasionally turned bright red with the strain of his efforts, he was impressive singing arias from *Aida, L'Elisir d'Amore,* and *Cavalleria Rusticana.* While critics deplored Lanza's lack of subtlety or finesse, moviegoers clamored for more of his singing. He was costarred again with Kathryn Grayson in *The Toast of New Orleans* (1950), which repeated the combination of a light, untaxing story with a generous number of arias, this time from *Martha, La Traviata, Carmen,* and *La Gioconda.* He also sang a popular tune, "Be My Love," which became a big hit.

By this time Lanza was a box-office phenomenon, and it was no surprise when the studio announced that he would star in a biography of the great tenor Enrico Caruso. The volatile, egocentric Lanza virtually *demanded* the role, exclaiming to the press, "There is nobody but me who can play that role! I *am* Caruso!" *The Great Caruso* (1951) was one of MGM's largest-grossing attractions of the year, doubly impressive in view of the public's aversion to grand opera on screen since the waning days of Jeanette MacDonald and Grace Moore. Lanza sang fifteen of Caruso's favorite arias in a mostly fictionalized story that took the tenor from his apprentice days in Italy to his premature death. Under Richard Thorpe's direction, Lanza and Ann Blyth (as Mrs. Caruso), with singer Dorothy Kirsten in prominent musical support, struggled with a cliché-ridden screenplay. But Lanza's voice remained the lure, and it rang out with ear-shattering power in theaters across the nation.

Lanza's next film, *Because You're Mine* (1952), was also popular, but the singer made it under duress. Hating the script, he showed up on the set drunk, continually ate too much, and behaved lewdly toward costar Doretta Morrow. By now, his personal problems were getting out of hand. His explosive personality was triggering fierce battles at the studio, and his excessive eating and drinking caused him to balloon to nearly three hundred pounds. Crash diets and barbiturates were seriously affecting his health. When he walked out on *The Student Prince* (1954), the studio cast Edmund Purdom in the leading role and used Lanza's already recorded songs. Lanza's contract was canceled, and he never returned to MGM.

His aggressive and irrational behavior grew worse as his career plummeted. He was replaced as the lead in Paramount's *The Vagabond King* (1956), and an engagement at a Las Vegas nightclub had to be canceled when he took an overdose of

That Midnight Kiss *(MGM, 1949). Kathryn Grayson and Mario Lanza join in a duet. Lanza was given a seven-year contract after Louis B. Mayer heard him sing at a Hollywood Bowl concert.*

opposite: Neptune's Daughter *(MGM, 1949). Ricardo Montalban and Esther Williams pose atop a gaudy and improbable riverboat. This extravagant entry in the series of waterlogged musicals designed for Esther Williams had only one claim to fame: the Oscar-winning song "Baby, It's Cold Outside."*

The Great Caruso *(MGM, 1951). Mario Lanza as celebrated tenor Enrico Caruso and Ann Blyth as his wife Dorothy. This enormously popular film established Lanza as a major star, but personal problems seriously damaged his career, and he was dead by the end of the decade.*

seconal with champagne. His last two films, *The Seven Hills of Rome* (1958) and *For the First Time* (1959), were not successful. In October, 1959, weakened by pneumonia, phlebitis, and more dieting, he died when a blood clot in his leg moved to his heart.

Years later, Dore Schary, head of production at MGM during Lanza's years at the studio, responded to the charge that the singer had been destroyed by Hollywood and the studio system: "Good heavens, this man was catered to! He was given all sorts of thoughtful, believe me, very thoughtful training and thoughtful care. And somebody writes he was destroyed by Hollywood. He was not. He was *not*. It's within the nature of men and women to destroy themselves" (Knox, *The Magic Factory*).

As Mario Lanza was beginning his career brightly in 1949, another MGM contractee, older and more durable than Lanza, marked his own auspicious occasion. The year before, Fred Astaire had replaced Gene Kelly in *Easter Parade,* scoring his first major success at the studio opposite Judy Garland. Eager to reunite the stars in a new musical, MGM had Betty Comden and Adolph Green fashion a screenplay concerning two married musical comedy stars who are in perfect harmony onstage, and in perfect disharmony when the curtain comes down. *The Barkleys of Broadway* had started production under Charles Walters's direction when Garland, ill and exhausted from filming *Easter Parade,* was forced to leave the cast. Arthur Freed had an inspired idea: why not use an admittedly sad occurrence as a springboard to a happy event—the first reunion in nearly a decade of the legendary dance team of Ginger Rogers and Fred Astaire? Astaire was excited by the prospect, and Rogers was most willing.

The Barkleys of Broadway turned out to be a reasonably diverting but not truly magical reunion for the team. As Josh and Dinah Barkley, Fred and Ginger certainly look fit enough as they play out a story that is curiously close to their own: he as a song-and-dance star content to stay in the musical mold, and she as the partner determined to make it on her own as a dramatic actress. Nearing fifty, Astaire may seem a bit worn, and Rogers is somewhat lacquered and artificial in her later high-toned style, but they can still strike a few sparks together.

When they dance, which is fairly often, they provide some of the old pleasure to faithful viewers. Their Scotch-flavored song and dance to "My One and Only Highland Fling," one of the new Harry Warren–Ira Gershwin songs in the score, is a wee bit too whimsical, and they tend to get lost amid the chorus in a too brief "Manhattan Downbeat" finale. But even the sight of their dancing feet behind the opening credits makes the pulse quicken, and the stars are given a few pearly musical moments. They do a romantic dance to "They Can't Take That Away from Me," correcting the grievous error that deprived them of a duet to this song in *Shall We Dance.* Astaire sings a heartfelt "You'd Be So Hard to Replace" to Rogers, echoing the evident fact that she *was* hard to replace. They also do a lighthearted tap routine in rehearsal clothes to "Bouncin' the Blues." *The Barkleys of Broadway* was not a superior musical, but it showed that the passage of time had not appreciably dimmed the glowing rapport of Astaire and Rogers.

With *Meet Me in St. Louis,* Vincente Minnelli had shaped a musical close to perfection in its nostalgic evocation of the American past.

The Barkleys of Broadway *(MGM, 1949)*.
Filming Fred Astaire's solo, "Shoes with Wings
On." Astaire plays a cobbler bewitched by dozens
of pairs of animated dancing shoes.

The Barkleys of Broadway *(MGM, 1949)*.
Ginger Rogers and Fred Astaire, together for the
first time since 1939, dance in the film's finale,
"Manhattan Downbeat."

223

However, his principal experience before coming to Hollywood had been in stage and costume design, and in creating musical numbers with fantastic, even surrealistic elements. (He had staged surrealistic ballets in New York City with George Balanchine.) Excited by the innovative possibilities of color, and by the chance to use design as a dramatic element in a musical film, Minnelli veered from the homespun, idealized reality of St. Louis into new areas that expanded the horizon of the genre. With the backing and support of Arthur Freed and his team, he became the architect of a new and imaginative form of musical film.

In his first assignment after St. Louis, he was named principal director of MGM's extravagant new production of Ziegfeld Follies. Virtually every major star on the lot was enlisted to appear in a collection of sketches, songs, and lavish musical numbers in the Ziegfeld style. As the film took form, scores of problems emerged: shooting that had to be arranged around the busy schedules of the stars, complex and expensive set construction, and numbers that had to be constantly rearranged, recast, or deleted. Costly sequences were filmed and later scrapped. Others were retained, for reasons that were never quite clear. Out of confusion, helter-skelter decisions, and occasional pandemonium, a musical revue finally emerged, but one so buffeted by the winds of change that it could not be released until February, 1946, nearly two years after production began.

Small wonder that the completed film was an uneven musical revue, mixing numbers of striking beauty and originality with numbers that are almost unbelievably inane. After an introductory section with William Powell, playing his old role of Florenz Ziegfeld in an MGM view of heaven (all pastel and fluffy, like a surrealist nursery), the numbers then unfold, beginning with one, directed by George Sidney, that is both sublime and outrageous. Singing "Bring on the Beautiful Girls," Fred Astaire introduces chorus girls elaborately dressed in pink costumes, with ballerina Cyd Charisse spinning in their midst. Smiling in their best Ziegfeld Girl manner, they ride on a lavishly designed carrousel. The number then turns bizarre, as a haughty Lucille Ball wields a whip on a "menagerie" of caged girls dressed in black panther costumes.

One number tumbles on the other, comedy sketch followed by musical number in bewildering succession. Esther Williams does one of her water ballets which is neither true ballet nor swimming exhibition but an odd hybrid of both. An excerpt from La Traviata with James Melton and Marion Bell is virtually destroyed by the garish décor; Red Skelton does the "Guzzler's Gin" monologue that had been his vaudeville staple for many years. Fred Astaire and Gene Kelly, in their only joint screen appearance before That's Entertainment, Part 2, perform "The Babbitt and the Bromide," which the Gershwins had written for Astaire and his sister Adele to perform in Funny Face in 1927. Judy Garland appears in "The Great Lady Has an Interview," a somewhat too precious takeoff on Greer Garson's lofty pretensions (Garson had been asked to do the number, but declined). Other comedy sketches involve Fanny Brice, Keenan Wynn, Victor Moore, and Edward Arnold. In an unintentionally hilarious finale, Kathryn Grayson sings "There's Beauty Everywhere" as chorus girls emerge from a sea of billowing

Ziegfeld Follies (MGM, 1946). Lucille Bremer dances with Fred Astaire in Vincente Minnelli's stunning "Limehouse Blues" sequence. The song had been delivered memorably by Gertrude Lawrence in Charlot's Revue, and the set used in the beginning and closing sequences of the number had been used previously in The Picture of Dorian Gray.

opposite: Ziegfeld Follies (MGM, 1946). Fred Astaire introduces Cyd Charisse in the lavish opening number, "Bring on the Beautiful Girls."

Ziegfeld Follies *(MGM, 1946). Lucille Bremer in the sequence built around the song "This Heart of Mine." Her diamonds and her beauty are both irresistible to jewel thief Fred Astaire.*

colored soap bubbles and drape themselves about the set.

Aside from Lena Horne's sultry rendition of "Love" in an exotic but sleazy Martinique café, the movie's two best numbers feature Fred Astaire. In "This Heart of Mine," against a background of surrealistic props, he plays a suave jewel thief scouting potential victims at a ball. He comes upon Lucille Bremer, whose beauty is almost as dazzling as her jewels. Courting her with the Arthur Freed–Harry Warren song, he coaxes her into a dance in a setting of what seem like bizarre petrified trees. He steals her bracelet, but then she willingly gives him her necklace, revealing that she knew of his intentions all along. They embrace ardently. The number is a stylized vision in which voices are represented by various musical instruments: for example, a flute and a piccolo imitate the chatter at the ball.

The movie's most successful number, and one of Minnelli's most perfectly realized musical sequences, is "Limehouse Blues." It is a dazzling fantasy, brilliantly designed and staged in Chinoiserie style—not Chinese but the French idea of Chinese style. Dressed entirely in black (except for white socks), Astaire plays an ill-fated Chinese coolie in a London slum who is stunned by the beauty of Lucille Bremer. When he goes to buy her the fan she admired, a robbery ensues and he is mortally wounded in the shooting. In his dying fantasy, conceived and designed by Irene Sharaff, he sees himself followed by figures in huge grotesque masks, then pursuing an elusive fan as blue-lit Oriental figures swirl around him. He dances with Bremer, their red velvet costumes in startling contrast to the setting. (Their dance with fans is beautifully choreographed by Robert Alton.) He regains consciousness briefly, reaches for the fan, and then dies. The lecherous man who had attempted to pick up Bremer earlier agrees to buy her the fan, but she drops it in distaste, seeing it is stained with Astaire's blood. The number is a perfect example of Vincente Minnelli's creative imagination as well as his penchant for running riot (and occasionally to excess) with color and design.

Both sides of Minnelli emerged even more conspicuously in his next film, *Yolanda and the Thief* (1945), which was produced after but released before *Ziegfeld Follies*. *Yolanda* was based on a tale by Belgian-American author Ludwig Bemelmans, and even drew in part on Bemelmans's paintings and illustrations for its settings and costumes. The movie, essentially an exotic fairy tale, has developed a cult following over the years. It concerns a con man (Fred Astaire) down on his luck in the mythical South American country Patria who comes upon a beautiful, wealthy, and sheltered girl (Lucille Bremer) praying to her guardian angel. Out to get her money, he pretends to be her angel come to earth to protect her. Inevitably, he falls in love with her, while the girl's *true* guardian angel (Leon Ames) makes an appearance to resolve matters.

Yolanda and the Thief spins its gossamer tale in a setting of lush beauty, and there is no denying the visual enchantment of Jack Martin Smith's décor and Irene Sharaff's costumes, particularly in the musical sequences. The first view of the pampered Yolanda is bewitching, and Mildred Natwick makes an early and welcome appearance as Yolanda's addled aunt, then virtually vanishes from the movie. But all too soon the charm begins to fade, the story becomes arch and absurd, and a torpor

Ziegfeld Follies *(MGM, 1946). Lucille Ball "tames" a menagerie of caged "panthers" as part of the bizarre opening sequence of this all-star musical revue.*

The Pirate *(MGM, 1948)*. *Gene Kelly as the irrepressible Serafin.*
Playing in the Douglas Fairbanks–John Barrymore style, Kelly
appeared to be enjoying himself immensely, despite the production's
many vicissitudes.

Yolanda and the Thief *(MGM, 1945)*. *Fred Astaire has a vision of*
Lucille Bremer in the fantastic dream setting inspired by artist Salvador
Dali. In this ballet, Astaire is torn between his greed and his growing
love for Bremer.

settles on the film from which it never recovers.

The screenplay is only partly to blame. There is also the inappropriate casting. Fred Astaire is unable to project the devious, often reprehensible behavior of an experienced con man—it is difficult to believe that he would deliberately deceive so naïve a girl. Gene Kelly, whose screen persona frequently included a touch of the larcenous, would have been a better choice for the role. Lucille Bremer is all wrong as Yolanda, her cool, lofty manner at odds with the sweet, trusting girl she is playing. In *Ziegfeld Follies,* she and Astaire danced well together, and here they do get a few chances to display their musical rapport. But their romance is unconvincing and also dull.

The film's cult status is largely due to its two production numbers, choreographed by Eugene Loring. In a surrealistic dream ballet, Astaire finds himself torn between his usual mercenary attitude and his growing love for Bremer. Wandering at night into the village square, which becomes progressively unreal, he is caught up in a fantastic setting influenced by artist Salvador Dali. He dances out his confused feelings in this rather bold but ultimately tiresome number. His duet with Bremer to ''Coffee Time'' is much better: an exuberant song and dance performed in a striking setting highlighted by a pavement of wavy black-and-white stripes. It is the most successful number in a film that tries to be different but sinks under the weight of its own pretensions.

Minnelli's next musical, *The Pirate* (1948), was planned as his most extravagant production to date. Adapted from the 1942 play by S. N. Behrman that had starred Alfred Lunt and Lynn Fontanne, the tongue-in-cheek musical romance, set in the West Indies of the 1830s, concerns a flamboyant strolling player who pretends to be a notorious pirate, and the pliant young girl taken in (at first) by his ruse. Gene Kelly, who saw in the role of Serafin the entertainer the chance to cavort and swashbuckle in the best Douglas Fairbanks style, was enthusiastic about the project. Judy Garland, assigned to play the naïve Manuela, began with high hopes that *The Pirate* would not only be one of her best films but that it would show her mettle as a comedienne in a class with Katharine Hepburn and other MGM stars. Cole Porter, whose last few Broadway musicals had not been successful, was hired to write the score.

There are those who believe that *The Pirate* is a glittering tour de force by Minnelli, and one of his best musical films. This estimate places undue emphasis on its considerable merits and disregards its equally considerable faults. Aside from the sumptuous physical production and the often clever screenplay that never takes itself seriously, *The Pirate* records one of Gene Kelly's most virtuosic performances. He strains a little too hard at playing the Fairbanks-Barrymore romancer, and his thin, reedy voice, so effective when he sings, hampers the kind of florid play-acting called for by the role of Serafin. But he looks marvelous with his black curly hair and jaunty mustache, and he is in splendid form when he sings and dances. He is at his best in ''Niña,'' the Porter song that introduces Serafin as a tireless singer, dancer, juggler, conjurer, and womanizer. Porter's clever lyrics (with rhymes like ''Niña/ neurasthenia''), the gaudy Port Sebastian setting, and Kelly's dashing, flamenco-style dance get the movie off to a heady start.

The Pirate (MGM, 1948). Manuela (Judy Garland) moves bravely through the town, having agreed to ''sacrifice'' herself to the notorious pirate Mack the Black. The ''pirate'' is actually the roguish entertainer Serafin (Gene Kelly), making the most of the mistaken identity.

On the Town *(MGM, 1949)|. A moment from the innovative dance
number "A Day in New York."*

opposite, above: On the Town *(MGM, 1949). Their hopes and spirits
soaring, sailors Frank Sinatra, Jules Munshin, and Gene Kelly burst from
their ship, docked in the Brooklyn Navy Yard. The logistics of filming
on actual locations in New York City were staggering in their complexity.
It was not only difficult to synchronize the actors' movements and voices
with the music and the action, but other problems also arose: changing
weather, curious crowds, and hazardous conditions for the cameramen
and crew.*

opposite, below: On the Town *(MGM, 1949). Sailors Frank Sinatra
and Jules Munshin discover the wonders of New York City with their new
girlfriends, taxi driver Betty Garrett and anthropologist Ann Miller.*

Serafin, having convinced the town of Calvados that he is Mack the Black Macoco, holds all its citizens in his thrall. The adoring Manuela imagines a fantasy ballet in which he is the principal figure. In black tights and wielding a sword, Serafin-Macoco leaps, dances, and battles aboard his pirate ship, as fires and explosions break out all around him. Toward the end of the film, when he is exposed as a mere entertainer, he asks to give one last performance before he is hanged. During the course of his dance, he hypnotizes the *real* Mack the Black into revealing himself. He turns out to be Don Pedro (Walter Slezak), the mayor of the town and Manuela's intended husband.

It may well be that Kelly's role in the film was strengthened to offset Garland's deteriorating state. (She was often absent due to illness, and when she appeared she was either extremely tense or incoherent due to pills.) In any case, Kelly makes the stronger impression throughout the movie. Garland, looking quite beautiful in her ornate gowns, is in strong voice, but her performance is edgy and slightly overwrought. When Serafin intentionally hypnotizes her with his mirror, she sings a fervent "Mack the Black," her arms extended with abandon and her bright red hair flowing behind her. Serafin kisses her, and she wakes up horrified. Her other songs, "You Can Do No Wrong" and "Love of My Life," are medium-drawer Cole Porter, but her voice throbs with much of the familiar unfettered emotion of earlier years.

Garland may have disliked "Be a Clown"—she quarreled bitterly with Cole Porter over the number—but it closes the movie on a merry note. In their clown costumes—Minnelli designed them himself—Kelly and Garland seem to be enjoying themselves immensely as they perform one knockabout gag after the other. After all the *Sturm und Drang* surrounding the film, and some last-minute reshooting and editing, *The Pirate* finally went into release. The critical and public response was largely apathetic. Today, the film has many champions, and it deserves serious consideration for its virtues. Yet it still suffers from a tone that is too self-conscious, too strident, and its "arent't-we-being-clever" approach is slightly off-putting. Among the blooms in Arthur Freed's bounteous garden, it is the hothouse flower, beautiful to look at and admire but also too delicate to survive the years.

The Pirate had given Gene Kelly the chance to create some of his most imaginative dances (aided by Robert Alton). Ahead, however, were his greatest triumphs on film: musicals that crystallized the achievements of the genre and blended all the elements that make up a musical film into a perfect (or near-perfect) entity. These films would mark the final flowering of the genre before its decline.

The first of these movies closed out the decade for the Freed Unit and also opened the first new vista for the musical since 1944. *On the Town* (1949) burst upon theater screens in time for the Christmas holiday season and was quickly acclaimed the freshest and most innovative musical in a long time. In its use of actual outdoor locations in New York City for many of its scenes, and in its integration of dance into the story, it was cited as an important step forward for a genre that was finally reaching maturity.

Actually, the journey of *On the Town* from stage to screen had been quite bumpy. The original Betty Comden–Adolph Green–Leonard Bernstein stage musical, conceived and directed by Jerome Robbins, had been a hit on its opening in December, 1944, and MGM had bought it for filming. But the studio did nothing to put it into production, since Louis B. Mayer disliked it intensely, and Arthur Freed was not happy about the stage show's book or music. Four years later, however, Freed was ready to move, intrigued by the notion of having Gene Kelly codirect his first musical with friend and dance director Stanley Donen. Freed asked Betty Comden and Adolph Green to write an entirely new book, and also to write a cluster of new songs with Roger Edens. The production got under way, with Kelly, Frank Sinatra, and Jules Munshin as the three gobs on leave, and Vera-Ellen, Ann Miller, and Betty Garrett as the girls the sailors meet on their jaunt around New York City. Alice Pearce was signed to repeat her hilarious stage role as Lucy Shmeeler, Vera-Ellen's roommate and the girl with the permanent head cold.

Kelly and Donen wanted to shoot the entire film in New York City, but when that was ruled out as impractical, it was decided to send the first unit to New York to shoot many exterior scenes with the six principal players. It would be the first time that actual locations were used for musical numbers, and the exhilarating result is on film for all to see. *On the Town* grips the audience immediately, as a view of the Brooklyn Navy Yard at dawn is followed by a lone worker singing "I Feel like I'm Not Out of Bed Yet" as he heads for his job. A ship's whistle sounds, and three sailors—Kelly, Sinatra, and Munshin—tumble off their ship for their twenty-four-hour leave in New York City. They crow "New York, New York!" as they set off on their excursion into "a helluva town." As in *Anchors Aweigh,* Kelly is the grinning "wolf" and Sinatra is the shy "lamb" (less feebleminded than in *Anchors Aweigh*), and with Munshin along for goofy support, they touch the city's high spots. The refreshing open-air feeling of these scenes is never achieved again in the movie, but its influence is evident in everything that follows.

Inevitably, the sailors meet the girls—in Kelly's case, meets, loses, and then finds the girl—and there is not much more than that to the musical's plot. But it allows for a number of songs, and especially for dances that are original, imaginative, and, most important, directly related to the situation. Munshin meets anthropologist Ann Miller in the fictional Museum of Anthropological History, giving Miller the opportunity for a sizzling song and dance to "Prehistoric Man," with the other principals in support. Taxi driver Betty Garrett tackles Sinatra with her brash "Come Up to My Place." And Kelly's special problems with Vera-Ellen give rise to the film's most ambitious musical numbers. He first spots her on a subway poster as the month's "Miss Turnstiles" and falls in love with her instantly. In a style that would be repeated a few years later with Leslie Caron in *An American in Paris,* he imagines Vera-Ellen demonstrating her qualifications for "Miss Turnstiles" in dance. When he meets her, they discover that they are from the same hometown, and they perform an engaging duet to "Main Street." The most elaborate number comes when Kelly, certain that he has lost Vera-Ellen forever, recalls the day's events in dance. A stylized dream sequence, with music composed by Leonard Bernstein toward the end of filming, "A Day in New

York" runs through an array of moods as Kelly and Vera-Ellen, with surrogate dancers for Miller, Munshin, Sinatra, and Garrett, dance out their joys and frustrations. With this one number, Kelly extended the boundaries of dance in musical films.

On the Town is not a complete delight, however, and more than three decades after its release, some of its portions are trying indeed. This is especially true of several of the songs composed for the film, such as Garrett's "You're Awful" ("awful nice to be with"), sung to Sinatra atop the Empire State Building. Much of the dialogue is foolish in the worst forties manner, and the final chase, in which the group is pursued by the police to Coney Island, is more frantic than funny. Also, the physical production apart from the actual locations is not very attractive. Still, *On the Town* remains a landmark musical that brought new vitality to the genre.

The forties had seen the flowering of the musical film as creative men and women responded enthusiastically to the many new directions in the genre. They were discovering that color could be used to enhance and even convey musical moods and emotions, and that filming at actual locations could open new vistas for musical expression. They were also rediscovering what Ernst Lubitsch, Rouben Mamoulian, and a few other moviemakers had known many years earlier: that songs and dances could emerge from character and need not be grafted forcibly onto the film, and that screenplays for musical films could have their share of wit and sophistication. At the same time, talented performers, both new and established, were sharpening their skills on new approaches to song and dance. At MGM particularly, the Arthur Freed Unit nurtured its gifted people, allowing them to send their imaginations soaring.

This flowering had come only after a fallow period in the early forties. The first half of the decade had seen a marked falling off in the musical's quality, due to the more urgent concerns of the war, more stringent budgets, and the need to turn out a great many more escapist films for war-weary audiences. For a musical artist such as Fred Astaire, it meant marking time away from RKO, where he had made musical film history with Ginger Rogers. His new dancing partners were not always compatible, and he was even relegated to virtually supporting status opposite Bing Crosby. He left the screen for two years, then returned to assume a prominent place on MGM's musical roster. By the end of the decade, he had teamed with Judy Garland for the first time, and danced with Ginger Rogers for the tenth.

For another major musical star of the thirties, the forties had meant continuity and a few surprises. Bing Crosby had continued to make the lighthearted musicals he had popularized in the thirties, but also veered into gag-laden knockabout farce with Bob Hope, and he had won an Academy Award playing a genial priest in *Going My Way* in 1944. Crosby sang in all of them, but the films were actually comedies or comedy-dramas with music. The strictly musical stars came, not surprisingly, from MGM, where Judy Garland's emotion-charged voice and Gene Kelly's tirelessly dancing feet were showcased at the peak of the stars' artistic powers. Together with stars of lesser rank—Jane Powell, Kathryn Grayson, Howard Keel, and others—they moved into the fifties with varying success.

One musical star was just beginning her film career at the end of the forties. A popular band singer for many years, Doris Day had arrived at Warner Bros. to replace the pregnant Betty Hutton in the musical *Romance on the High Seas* (1948). The blonde singer-actress pleased moviegoers with her smooth voice and piquant manner, and began a series of musical films that continued into the fifties. (Later, she emerged as a highly competent comedienne and dramatic actress.)

Musical milestones had arrived in the forties, first with *Meet Me in St. Louis* and *Cover Girl,* and then with *On the Town.* They brought a freshness and a vitality to musical films that reverberated in the years ahead. There would be greater musicals in the fifties, followed by a sad but steady decline. But during the mid- and late forties, a group of people had shown us what was possible with talent, craftsmanship, and a joyous involvement in their work. The movies they made, and the songs and dances they created, are woven into the fabric of memory, and they refuse to fade with time.

above: Where Do We Go from Here? *(Fox, 1945). In this curious and sometimes clever original musical, Fred MacMurray played a 4-F civilian in wartime who is transported back to various crucial moments in world history by a confused genie. Here he finds himself in colonial times, in a Valley Forge inn with Joan Leslie. The score was by Kurt Weill and Ira Gershwin.*

PART IV
THE
SUMMIT & DECLINE
1950~1959

The Final Flowering
In the Tradition
Stage to Screen
Set It to Music
Let Us Entertain You

The Final Flowering

Ironically, the finest achievements in the musical film were created at a time when the genre itself was beginning to fade. In the fifties, with a decline in attendance largely caused by the popularity of television, with trimmed budgets that resulted in firings and production cutbacks, the studios could no longer afford to produce extravagant musical films. Musicals were becoming an indulgence, and besides, most Americans seemed to prefer songs and dances on the small screen. Yet at MGM—with Gene Kelly, Fred Astaire, Judy Garland, Kathryn Grayson, Howard Keel, and Cyd Charisse under contract—the musical film was still indispensable, especially in the first years of the decade. While Hollywood declined, the units of Arthur Freed, Joe Pasternak, and Jack Cummings continued to thrive. And one of them, the Freed Unit, was responsible for the most memorable series of musical films ever produced within a concentrated period of time.

The Freed films—*An American in Paris, Singin' in the Rain,* and *The Band Wagon* in particular—represented the final maturation of a group of talented, imaginative people who worked together to achieve an overall vision of the musical genre. In the best of these movies, there is a unity of tone, style, and structure that pervades every aspect, from the costumes of the extras to the design of the most elaborate production numbers. In addition, a palpable delight in putting together the elements that go into a musical entertainment, a pride in the gifts of the performers, and a respect for the intelligence of the audience shine in every frame. The Freed musicals of the early fifties were not perfect—some concepts are dated and pretentious, and occasionally the aspiration exceeds the execution—but to a great extent Freed helped to turn a cheerful commodity into a durable art, challenging good people to be better than they had ever hoped they could be.

The first Freed productions released in the fifties were solidly entertaining: a large-scale filmization of Irving Berlin's *Annie Get Your Gun* and an agreeable Fred Astaire vehicle called *Royal Wedding.* But then came *An American in Paris* (1951), an ambitious and, in its time, daring musical production that rose above its considerable faults to win unprecedented acclaim.

From the very first, Arthur Freed had conceived of the film as an all-Gershwin musical which would conclude with a ballet to the composer's "An American in Paris." Between the idea and the finished print, there were more than the usual number of complications, setbacks, and disappointments, along with an occasional triumph. It was not difficult to assemble the principal participants: Alan Jay Lerner had discussed the project with Freed from the beginning, and he was signed to write the screenplay. Vincente Minnelli, who had not directed a musical since *The Pirate* in 1948, was the inevitable choice to oversee a stylish movie set in Paris. Gene Kelly was the logical star, and Oscar Levant, a close friend of George Gershwin, would add his piano artistry and his waspish wit. The part of the heroine went to Leslie Caron, a teenage dancer with the Ballet des Champs-Élysées who impressed Freed and Kelly with her ability and her winsome personality.

Some of the film's problems were fundamental: constructing an entire section of Paris on the MGM lot, selecting songs from the vast Gershwin catalogue, coping with personalities—Caron's shyness or Levant's temperament—and juggling the constantly spiraling budget. But most of the difficulties centered on the unprecedented ballet planned for the film's ending. The idea of a seventeen-minute ballet without songs or dialogue to close a musical film was considered foolhardy at the time. But Freed never wavered in his decision to do it, and production head Dore Schary, backed by Louis B. Mayer, remained firm in his approval, convinced that it would make the difference between an ordinary musical film and a great one. He proved to be right. When *An American in Paris* was released in the fall of 1951, to general acclaim, it was the ballet that was most often singled out for praise.

Most of the critics were impressed by the film's brilliant design and its use of color. If there was one common objection, it was to Alan Jay Lerner's screenplay, generally considered the weakest feature of the film. It is serviceable but no more than that as it tells of the bittersweet romance between American artist Jerry Mulligan (Gene Kelly) and young shopgirl Lise Bourvier (Leslie Caron), which unfolds amid the wondrous sights of Paris.

An American in Paris (MGM, 1951). Georges Guetary and Gene Kelly, unaware that they love the same girl (Leslie Caron), sing a jubilant " 'S Wonderful" on a street in the Latin Quarter.

page 234: Singin' in the Rain (MGM, 1952). One of the durable treasures in the history of Hollywood musicals: Gene Kelly's rhapsodic dance to the title song.

page 236: An American in Paris (MGM, 1951). Gene Kelly, Leslie Caron, and dancers on the Place de la Concorde, designed à la Raoul Dufy. The money required for the number—over half a million dollars— sent the moguls at MGM's parent company, Loew's Inc., into shock.

opposite: An American in Paris (MGM, 1951). Leslie Caron and Gene Kelly dancing in the Renoir flower market section of the ballet.

The impediment to their love affair turns out to be one Henri Baurel (Georges Guetary), a musical favorite in Paris, who has been Lise's friend and protector for many years, and to whom she owes a great deal. Jerry, on the other hand, has become involved with Milo Roberts (Nina Foch), an attractive but possessive patron of the arts whose interest in him goes beyond his paintings. There are some bright lines, and a generally friendly air, but the script lacks substance and sparkle.

As a musical, however, An American in Paris often glitters as brightly as the City of Lights itself. Most of its musical numbers contain moments of shimmering beauty and striking originality, and surprisingly, considering the thinness and triteness of the story, many of the songs flow smoothly from the events and the characters, in the best musical fashion. The first musical sequence, for example, introduces the elfin, enchanting Leslie Caron to the film—and to the moviegoing public. With "Embraceable You" as the background song, Henri Baurel describes his beloved Lise to Adam (Levant), and as he explains her many moods, she dances on screen, changing costumes to match each mood. The number leads to the delightful "By Strauss," in which Jerry, Henri, and Adam frolic merrily with the local citizens. Later, Kelly does one of his best-remembered numbers, dancing to "I Got Rhythm" for the benefit of a group of French children.

Almost all of Gene Kelly's films include at least one solo expressing his jubilation, and one "falling-in-love" duet with his leading lady. In this respect, An American in Paris does not disappoint. He has met Lise at a café, and he is so entranced with her that his feet cannot possibly remain still. To the Gershwin tune "Tra-La-La," he dances joyfully about Adam's room, leaping on top of the piano at one point for a round of taps. It is an amiably goofy, inventive dance that captures his mood. Afterward, he meets Lise and they walk along the banks of the Seine, holding hands. He expresses his love for her with the tender lyrics of "Love Is Here to Stay," and they begin to dance. The number is pure enchantment. She dances with her head on his shoulder; she tries to run away from him several times, to no avail. They move backward, away from each other, then pause and rush toward each other to embrace. The theme of resistance-and-surrender recalls the dances of Fred Astaire and Ginger Rogers, but the setting, the muted color, and the fully expressed ardor of the dancers give this number a more romantic, less formalized feeling than the Astaire-Rogers duets of the thirties.

The film's weakest numbers are those that bear little relation to the story. In one, Oscar Levant, a concert pianist self-described as "the world's oldest prodigy," imagines himself both leading and playing all the instruments in an orchestra, and even applauding his own performance afterward. It is a clever photographic gimmick, but it impedes the flow of the film. Georges Guetary also performs in an elaborate musical number, "I'll Build a Stairway to Paradise," flanked by lavishly gowned chorus girls. It is both a tribute to and a spoof of the Folies Bergère style, for which Georges Guetary's florid music-hall tenor is entirely appropriate. He is much better served in a charming duet with Gene Kelly to " 'S Wonderful," sung and danced in a street of Kelly's Latin Quarter neighborhood. A magnificent last high crane shot takes in the entire street as the men move off in different directions.

An American in Paris concludes with the extravagant ballet that is both the *pièce de résistance* of the film and its principal claim to fame. It is everything that its defenders and detractors have claimed over the years: imaginative, audacious, spectacular, pretentious, and too ambitious for its own good. It is Jerry Mulligan's fantasy of his lost love and of his feelings about Paris, as viewed through the artistic styles of some of France's most celebrated painters. Designed by Irene Sharaff and Preston Ames, choreographed by Gene Kelly, and directed by Vincente Minnelli, the number sums up the film's boy-meets-girl, boy-loses-girl story, as Kelly pursues the elusive Caron through a continually changing, stylized Paris. The tour includes a Raoul Dufy–like version of the Place de la Concorde, with a huge fountain at the center, a Montmartre street as it might be designed by Maurice Utrillo, a flower market in the style of Pierre-Auguste Renoir, and the Place de l'Opéra as it might be seen by Vincent van Gogh. Kelly dances with (and without) Caron in an extraordinary variety of styles; in one segment, he struts in a striped blazer and straw hat in a Rousseau-like square, in another, he joins Caron in a smoky *pas de deux*. He even does an impression of ''Chocolat,'' Henri Toulouse-Lautrec's dancing friend, in a representation of the artist's Moulin Rouge. After a while, the ballet becomes a blur of colors, images, and dancing figures, to the extent that a benumbed viewer might be inclined to yell ''uncle'' or possibly ''*oncle*.'' When it is over, and Jerry Mulligan is happily reunited with his Lise (Henri Baurel has nobly decided to give her up), we are almost relieved to have the film end on a restful panoramic view of Paris.

At the Academy Award ceremonies in March of 1952, *An American in Paris* was the surprise winner, edging out such movies as *A Place in the Sun* and *A Streetcar Named Desire*. It also garnered six other Oscars, including an honorary award to Gene Kelly ''in appreciation of his versatility as an actor, singer, director, and dancer, and specifically for his brilliant achievement in the art of choreography on film.'' But barely a week after the festivities, the Freed Unit and Kelly topped this triumph with the release of a musical film that has been widely regarded as the best ever made. With no premonition of its exalted status, and with all the woes and mishaps attendant on the production of any musical film, *Singin' in the Rain* (1952) was created by masters of the Hollywood musical at the peak of their powers.

The story of the making of *Singin' in the Rain* has been related by its talented authors, Betty Comden and Adolph Green. Urgently summoned to Hollywood in May of 1950—their last film, *On the Town,* had opened to wide acclaim some months before—they were told by MGM that they had been assigned to write an original story and screenplay using songs from the catalogue of Arthur Freed (ex-lyricist, now producer) and Nacio Herb Brown. Their first decision came after hearing such Freed-Brown songs as ''Broadway Rhythm,'' ''Fit as a Fiddle,'' and ''You Were Meant for Me.'' The vitality of the songs was infectious, but they were also indelibly a part of the time in which they were written. Comden and Green agreed to set their story in the late twenties, during the hectic period in which silent movies gave way to sound.

Drawing on their deep knowledge of the history of movies, and an even deeper love for its colorful lore, they fashioned the screenplay of *Singin' in the Rain*. To their joy and delight, both Gene Kelly and Stanley Donen read and adored the script, and decided to codirect the film, with Kelly as the star. Two decades later, Comden and Green wrote in their introduction to the published screenplay: ''In addition to their outstanding skill in integrating all the elements of a musical film, our old friendship with them, and their knowledge of our work from our early performing days made it easy for them to use many ideas and visual details that might have seemed irrelevant or a total mystery to anyone else.''

With Kelly in the lead, the rest of the cast was quickly set. To play Kelly's friend and sidekick, Cosmo Brown, Arthur Freed favored Oscar Levant, but, wisely, all other parties insisted on a dancer for the role, and Donald O'Connor was signed. A performer for many years, O'Connor had started in films as Bing Crosby's ''Small Fry'' brother in *Sing You Sinners,* and had lent his fast-stepping feet and engaging manner to many minor musicals at Universal Studios. Jean Hagen, under contract to MGM, was selected to play the inimitable silent-screen star Lina Lamont, and the role of the heroine, Kathy Selby, was given to Debbie Reynolds, the pert nineteen-year-old who had caught the public eye as singer Helen Kane in *Three Little Words* and as Jane Powell's kid sister in *Two Weeks with Love.*

Singin' in the Rain begins with a glittering 1927 premiere of Monumental Pictures's newest hit, *The Royal Rascal,* starring those ''romantic lovers of the screen,'' Don Lockwood (Gene Kelly) and Lina Lamont (Jean Hagen). Stars dressed in the outer limits of chic are introduced by gushing gossip queen Dora Bailey, to the wildly enthusiastic response of a horde of fans. Keeping Lina firmly away from the microphone, Don proceeds to tell his story ''from the beginning.'' In a sly parody of the standard studio puffery about its stars, he recites a genteel, dignified (''Dignity, always dignity'') tale of his rise to fame, while the images on screen negate his words hilariously. For example, he talks about playing in ''the finest symphonic halls,'' while we see him scratching out a paltry living with Cosmo in tacky vaudeville houses.

The tone has been set for a merry spoof of twenties Hollywood, and the pace never flags as the explosion of sound rocks the movie colony and sends every studio into an emergency conversion to talkies. (Actually, there was some doubt about the permanency of sound.) With silent films becoming obsolete, Monumental Pictures must convert its latest Lockwood-Lamont epic, *The Duelling Cavalier,* into a talkie. There is one serious problem: the lovely Lina Lamont has a preposterously nasal, shrill, ear-splitting voice. (Don succeeds in keeping her quiet at the premiere until we hear her first screeching remark, ''F'heaven's sake, what's the idea—can't a girl get a word in edgewise? They're my public, too!'') At the same time, Don is discovering that he loves a pretty, aspiring starlet named Kathy Selby.

Don's on-again, off-again romance with Kathy is the conventional center of the film, but it is surrounded by so many delicious satirical jabs at moviemaking in the late twenties that it never interferes with the general enjoyment. On the silent set of *The Duelling Cavalier,* Don and Lina exchange ardent embraces while a furious Don actually mouths invectives at her (''Why,

An American in Paris *(MGM, 1951). Georges Guetary sings "I'll Build a Stairway to Paradise" in a lush production number that both emulates and pokes fun at the style of the Folies Bergère.*

An American in Paris *(MGM, 1951). In the film's unprecedented ballet, the Renoir-like flower market sets an appropriately lyrical mood for the amorous dance of Gene Kelly and Leslie Caron.*

Lili *(MGM, 1953). Leslie Caron enjoys a relaxed moment with Mel Ferrer, as the usually morose puppeteer, and his friendly puppets Carrot Top and Reynardo. In her first good role after* An American in Paris, *Caron played a wistful French orphan who joins a carnival. A beguiling, becomingly small-scaled movie,* Lili *was not very musical—Caron danced in a few ballet scenes and sang the appealing "Hi-Lili, Hi-Lo"—but the film established a reputation that has lasted to this day. Caron received an Academy Award nomination as best actress.*

opposite, above: Singin' in the Rain *(MGM, 1952). In the "Broadway" ballet, sexy gun moll Cyd Charisse perches hoofer Gene Kelly's hat atop one well-curved leg. This was her first teaming with Kelly.*

opposite, below, left: Singin' in the Rain *(MGM, 1952). Aspiring actress Debbie Reynolds has unintentionally flung a custard pie into the face of Jean Hagen, that "shimmering, glowing star in the cinema firm-a-mint," to use her very own words. Gene Kelly registers dismay, possibly mixed with satisfaction.*

opposite, below, right: Singin' in the Rain *(MGM, 1952). Donald O'Connor and Gene Kelly in midair during their song and dance to "Moses Supposes." The two dance about the room and atop tables, finally piling chairs, drapes, lamps, and anything else they can move on the head of the stunned diction coach.*

you rattlesnake, you!"), recalling the illicit thrill that lip-reading moviegoers occasionally enjoyed. The nonstop influx of diction coaches to help speech-defective stars is spoofed in coach Phoebe Dinsmore's desperate attempt to get Lina ready for sound. ("Rrround tones. Rrround tones.") And in one of the movie's funniest sequences, a frantic director (Douglas Fowley) tries to record Lina's voice by concealing a microphone in every conceivable place. Later, Cosmo Brown offers the ultimate comment on Lina: "She can't act. She can't sing, and she can't dance. A triple threat!"

If the screenplay of *Singin' in the Rain* is a superb example of what an original musical book can be when informed by wit, craftsmanship, and affection, then the music matches it every moment of the 103-minute running time. (The film's length is an object lesson to the bloated two-and-a-half and three-hour musicals of recent years.) The songs either reinforce the satire, heighten the euphoria with explosions of exuberance, or give the film a romantic glow that is necessarily missing from the tongue-in-cheek book. Even the "throwaway" songs are part of this structure.

There are many musical highlights: Donald O'Connor's inspired comedy routine, "Make 'Em Laugh," certainly one of the funniest numbers ever recorded on film, in which he does what Comden and Green aptly described, in their introduction to the published screenplay, as "zany gymnastic clowning and surrealistic vaudeville" (at one point he prances with a dressmaker's dummy to hilarious effect, and he ends the number with a mad leap through the wall of a set); "Moses Supposes," in which O'Connor and Kelly drive Don's diction coach to distraction; Kelly, O'Connor, and Reynolds performing a spirited "Good Morning" in Kelly's living room, during which they use a number of props, including three raincoats; Kelly and Reynolds in a deserted studio, dancing to the strains of "You Were Meant for Me." In the last, Kelly converts the bare and sprawling stage into a magical setting for a musical number, complete with lights and special effects.

Gene Kelly's dance to the title song is now a movie legend, but its lofty status as perhaps his finest solo number on screen can never dim the pleasure it induces at every viewing. (When asked what he would do for the number, he replied modestly, "A simple dance.") Happy and in love, Don Lockwood strolls down the street in the rain with his closed umbrella at his side. He begins to sing ("The sun's in my heart and I'm ready for love!"), then starts to dance, using his umbrella as a prop. When he finally opens the umbrella, his joy is boundless, and he whirls about the street with such glee that he threatens to lift off the ground. He splashes in puddles until a policeman looks at him suspiciously. Grinning broadly, he saunters off, singing the last lines of the song. Kelly's performance makes our spirits soar as do few other numbers in the entire history of the Hollywood musical.

Before the resolution of the story—Lina's well-deserved comeuppance, the success of Monumental's first talkie, *The Dancing Cavalier*, and the happy ending to Don and Kathy's love affair—*Singin' in the Rain* offers an elaborate "Broadway" ballet. Although it may be somewhat too extravagant for the movie's tight overall structure, it is also less pretentious and

Singin' in the Rain *(MGM, 1952)*. *In the climax of the film's "Broadway" ballet, Gene Kelly and a massive chorus dance joyfully against an impressionistic background of signs on the Great White Way. During production, the cost of this fifteen-minute sequence leaped from $80,000 to about $600,000.*

Singin' in the Rain *(MGM, 1952)*. *For his dance to the title number, Kelly had the studio dig holes in the ground so that the water would form puddles he could splash in.*

ultimately less wearying than the ballet in *An American in Paris*. It traces the rise of a gawky, bespectacled young hoofer (Kelly) from his arrival in New York ("Gotta dance! Gotta dance!") to his stardom in *The Ziegfeld Follies*. Along the way, as the ballet continually spoofs movie conventions, the hoofer meets the girl of his dreams. In a speak-easy, he is singing and dancing to "Broadway Rhythm" when a long, long leg appears abruptly on screen and tips the straw hat from his head. The leg belongs to gangster's moll Cyd Charisse, who, with her short green dress and long cigarette holder, is both comical and gloriously sexy. She dances seductively around him, after tossing his eyeglasses to the floor and smashing them with her foot. Later, Kelly sees her as an idealized vision, wearing a long white scarf that billows behind her. Their dance together is lyrical but also rather self-consciously "arty." Forlorn after she rejects him, he goes off to the huge Broadway set that opened the number. When he sees another eager young hoofer arriving in town, his spirits are revived, and he leads the chorus in a large-scale closing to "Broadway Melody."

Kelly's performance in *Singin' in the Rain* is adroitly tuned to the spirit of the film, as are the performances of Donald O'Connor and Debbie Reynolds. (Reynolds had minimal acting ability at the time, but her Kewpie doll appeal made her the perfect choice for the role.) By general agreement, the movie's truly classic performance is contributed by Jean Hagen, who makes the most of every quotable line she is given. Believing every word of the studio's publicity, she invests herself with superhuman status: "People! I ain't people! I'm a shimmering, glowing star in the cinema firm-a-mint!" "Why—I make more money than—than—Calvin Coolidge—put to*gither*!" she informs the harried studio head R. F. Simpson (Millard Mitchell). When Don, Cosmo, and Simpson happily pull the curtain that will expose Lina as a fraud—Kathy has been dubbing for her—it is a gratifying moment of retribution.

Why is *Singin' in the Rain*, a classic musical film, frequently cited on all-time-ten-best lists? There may never have been a musical as funny, but others have been more beautiful, more extravagant, or even more imaginative. It may be that the movie, in its eternally fresh, impudent, and lighthearted way, *defines* the Hollywood musical: that combination of creative and technical skills in which story, setting, and especially music converge in an effusion of joy. Perhaps more than any other American musical film, *Singin' in the Rain* exudes confidence without cockiness, secure in its professionalism and delighted to share its myriad pleasures with moviegoers at every viewing. Three decades after its release, *Singin' in the Rain* remains a life-enhancing film, imparting a sense of well-being that lingers long after the final shot. When Gene Kelly dances in the rain, we can share his euphoria. "What a glorious feelin'" indeed.

After the success of *Singin' in the Rain*, codirector Stanley Donen was given a few minor films. But in 1954, he was assigned to direct another important film for the studio, and it turned out to be one of the best Hollywood musicals of the fifties: a winning and totally charming movie called *Seven Brides for Seven Brothers*.

After producing a number of musical films rooted in homespun Americana during the late forties, MGM had veered into more sophisticated areas in the early years of the fifties. But

Seven Brides for Seven Brothers reverted to the nostalgic world of buckskin and crinoline, of barnyards and rustic kitchens. Taken from a Stephen Vincent Benét story called "The Sobbin' Women," it dealt with a rugged young Oregon farmer (Howard Keel) in 1850 who takes a comely wife (Jane Powell) and then convinces his six lonesome brothers to do the same—only by force. Conveniently in love with six girls of the town, the rambunctious boys carry them off to the farm, following the example in Plutarch's story of the Sabine women. When an avalanche keeps the girls imprisoned for the long winter, they squeal in maidenly protest, but by the time spring arrives, they naturally decide to go ahead with a group wedding.

It is hardly the sturdiest of stories, and the production was far from lavish in the MGM manner, but the film has a freshness and a buoyancy that make it irresistible. The Gene de Paul–Johnny Mercer songs are well above average, and with much of the singing done by Howard Keel and Jane Powell (in her best screen performance), they are in good hands. Keel sings a robust "Bless Your Beautiful Hide" while contemplating the town's candidates for his bride, and Powell chirps an engaging "Wonderful, Wonderful Day" as she welcomes what she expects will be a new life with Keel. She demonstrates the techniques of dancing and genteel behavior to her awkward brothers-in-law in "Goin' Courtin'," and the brothers and their thawing sweethearts sing a cheerful tribute to "Spring, Spring, Spring."

Unquestionably, the most outstanding feature of *Seven Brides for Seven Brothers* is its dancing. All the players move rhythmically throughout the film, with a grace and an ease that keep the situations from sinking irretrievably into coyness. Not coincidentally, the roles of Keel's brothers were cast largely with professional dancers, including Jacques d'Amboise, Tommy Rall, Marc Platt, and Russ Tamblyn, and they dance up a storm at every opportunity. The highlight—and one of the great musical numbers in films—is the barn-raising sequence. It begins as a "challenge" dance—a truly breathtaking display of acrobatic leaps and ballet steps—in which the brothers compete for the girls with the more "urbane" men of the town, and it ends inevitably in an all-out brawl as the men actually try to raise the barn. Acclaim for this and all other dances in the movie was deservedly given to choreographer Michael Kidd.

The year after Gene Kelly reached the summit in *Singin' in the Rain*, Fred Astaire did the same in his best MGM musical, *The Band Wagon* (1953). Whereas his films with Ginger Rogers had focused on their dances together, achieving an intimacy that could never be duplicated, *The Band Wagon* is a true musical comedy in which the dances, even Astaire's dances, are only one element of the many that fuse together to make a near-perfect entity. *The Band Wagon* combined Betty Comden and Adolph Green's witty screenplay, stylish performances by most of the leading players, imaginative sets by stage designer Oliver Smith (his first for films), and a superb score by Howard Dietz and Arthur Schwartz, taken from their copious portfolio, into a delectable film. Under the assured direction of Vincente Minnelli, and with Roger Edens supervising the film's musical material, *The Band Wagon* was a major musical triumph of the period.

The movie is Comden and Green's affectionate tribute to the theater that nourished and sustained them in their beginnings.

Seven Brides for Seven Brothers *(MGM, 1954). Adam Pontipee (Howard Keel) is banished to a tree by his new bride Milly (Jane Powell).*

Seven Brides for Seven Brothers *(MGM, 1954). Pontipee brother Matt Mattox astonishes everyone with a breathtaking leap during the "challenge" dance that precedes the barn-raising. The film received an Academy Award nomination as best picture and won an Oscar for the best scoring of a motion picture.*

(The characters played by Oscar Levant and Nanette Fabray are their obvious surrogates.) They depict an enclosed world in which talent soars and tempers flare, sometimes simultaneously, where hits are born and flops are stillborn with agony, pride, and boundless hope. The authors' brisk and observant dialogue manages to catch the dedication and the obsession of "putting on a show." Although there is some idealization of theater life, the screenplay is still miles—and more than two decades—removed from the backstage musicals of the thirties, even from Julian Marsh's oppressive badgering in *42nd Street*. In his autobiography, *I Remember It Well,* Minnelli claims that "all the out-of-town scenes, the moment when things go wrong on a first night, were terribly authentic, autobiographical."

Fred Astaire plays one of his best roles: a skidding, once-great film star named Tony Hunter who comes to New York City for a visit and ends up starring in a musical show written by his friends Lily and Lester Marton (Nanette Fabray and Oscar Levant). Astaire's lonely entrance into the railroad station provides him with one of his most magical moments on screen: sauntering down the platform in that unique dancer's manner, he sings a rueful but never self-pitying chorus of "By Myself." Gallantry, understated longing, and vulnerability pervade his rendition.

Once Tony becomes involved with the Martons' show, *The Band Wagon* plunges him into the maelstrom of the theater. He finds himself under the direction of the celebrated Broadway figure Jeffrey Cordova (Jack Buchanan), a flamboyant, self-styled madman with artistic pretensions. Another problem for Tony is that his costar is Gabrielle Gerard (Cyd Charisse), a haughty ballerina who is not only too tall for him but who also has undisguised contempt for his style of dancing. After their show is a calamitous failure on the road, Tony removes the arty barnacles and turns it into a solid success. He also comes to love Gaby, who reciprocates the feeling.

One of the reasons that *The Band Wagon* works so well is that the staging of the musical numbers retains and matches the confident theatrical style of the nonmusical portions. Early in the movie, Astaire dances to "Shine on Your Shoes" in a Forty-second Street penny arcade that is patently unreal, but his zest and humorous aplomb, especially his enthusiastic duet with genuine bootblack LeRoy Daniels, turns the number into a memorable tour de force. The Central Park setting in which Tony and Gaby discover their love for each other is also an obvious studio interior, but once the two begin their elegant and graceful leaps and swirls to the haunting melody of "Dancing in the Dark," the artifice vanishes. Later, when the cast assembles after the show's grim out-of-town opening, Tony and the Martons cheer them up with a lively rendition of "I Love Louisa" (the movie's original title). The score is so prodigiously rich that a truly lovely song like "High and Low" is played only as background music as Astaire and Charisse first enter the park and gaze at the passing couples.

In a way, *The Band Wagon* is the conventional backstage musical of the thirties and forties brought to a new peak of skill and sophistication in the fifties. Some of the musical numbers are performed as part of the show in which everyone is involved, a device often used in earlier years. But Vincente Minnelli stages them with such brio and flair that they seem eons removed from

above: The Band Wagon *(MGM, 1953). In "Triplets," Fred Astaire, Nanette Fabray, and Jack Buchanan play obnoxious, fratricidal baby siblings who "hate each other very much." To make it seem as if they were dancing on infant legs, specially made leather boots were molded to fit over their knees. Baby shoes were added to the bottom of the boots, and the boots were then strapped to their knees.*

top: The Band Wagon *(MGM, 1953). In a Central Park pavilion, to the bewitching melody of the Howard Dietz–Arthur Schwartz song "Dancing in the Dark," Fred Astaire and Cyd Charisse discover that they really care for each other. The number is one of Astaire's best "falling-in-love" dances.*

247

The Band Wagon *(MGM, 1953)*. *Cyd Charisse and Fred Astaire in the "Girl Hunt" ballet suggested by the literary efforts of Mickey Spillane. Charisse, a seemingly virtuous blonde who is actually the gang's "Mr. Big," is dying in the arms of tough private eye Rod Riley, Charisse also played the slinky brunette proprietor of a high-fashion salon. ("She came at me in sections. She was bad. She was dangerous.") The narration for the ballet was written by Alan Jay Lerner without credit or payment.*

opposite: Funny Face *(Paramount, 1957)*. *The enchanting Audrey Hepburn sings "How Long Has This Been Going On?" in the Embryo Concepts Book Shop, where she works as a clerk (but not for long).*

the standard behind-the-footlights musical. A couple of the numbers ("Louisiana Hayride" and "New Sun in the Sky") are adequate and nothing more. But "Triplets" is simply hilarious, and there is consummate pleasure in watching Astaire and Buchanan suavely dismiss a lost romantic opportunity with "I Guess I'll Have to Change My Plan." Buchanan's disastrous attempt to stage "You and the Night and the Music" as an "artistic" number filled with explosions and colorful lights is an amusing poke at Minnelli's own occasional penchant for busy staging, as in *Ziegfeld Follies*. *The Band Wagon* concludes with "The Girl Hunt," a jazz ballet cleverly conceived by choreographer Michael Kidd in close collaboration with Roger Edens. Primarily a broad takeoff on Mickey Spillane's lusty, hard-boiled detective novels, it is also a sly poke at Gene Kelly's more "serious" ballet endeavors.

When Jeffrey Cordova is trying to convince Tony to join the show, he launches into "That's Entertainment," a song that celebrates the diverse forms of show business. (It was written expressly for the film by Dietz and Schwartz.) As Astaire, Levant, and Fabray join him in the song, it becomes an anthem to all the tenacious, hopeful, and talented people who work at entertaining us. When they reprise it at the very end of the film, we can appreciate their proclamation that "a show that is really a show/ Sends you out with a kind of a glow." *The Band Wagon* "sends you out with a kind of a glow," and the glow has not faded over the years.

After completing *The Band Wagon,* Fred Astaire was dealt a tragic blow with the death of his wife Phyllis in September, 1954, but he was determined to ease the pain and grief of his loss with hard work. He plunged into Fox's production of *Daddy Long Legs,* and then later agreed to costar with Audrey Hepburn in Paramount's stylish Gershwin musical, *Funny Face* (1957). In a way, he was not leaving MGM at all to make *Funny Face:* the producer (and the composer of added songs) was Arthur Freed's longtime assistant Roger Edens, and the director was Stanley Donen, who had guided Astaire through *Royal Wedding* in 1951. Astaire played a high-fashion photographer for *Quality* magazine who helps to transform a bookish young Greenwich Village girl (Audrey Hepburn) into an exquisite fashion model. Of course, he also falls in love with her.

Funny Face dates—its mild spoof of bohemianism is now pointless, and the chic apparel of more than two decades ago is bound to look rather outlandish today—but it also dazzles, blending all the right ingredients into a first-rate musical entertainment. It is also one of the most colorful of fifties musicals; photographer Richard Avedon was hired as the movie's visual consultant, and he drenches the screen with so much color, so many vivid shades, hues, and tones, that the impression is dizzying, but delightful. *Funny Face* uses color to startling effect, even from the very first number, in which *Quality* magazine's editor Maggie Prescott (singer-composer-arranger Kay Thompson in her first major film role) announces that the new fashion edict is "Think Pink!" and the screen is soon crowded with everything from pink clothing to pink toothpaste and shampoo.

Funny Face moves from number to number with the clear assurance that how it *looks* is as important as how it *sounds*. Few musicals have ever been so conscious of color effects. When Hepburn dances to "How Long Has This Been Going On?" in

248

her bookstore, she wears a bright orange and yellow hat, and there is one glorious moment in which the green ribbons on her hat billow behind her. Astaire sings "Funny Face" to her in his darkroom, and they dance together with the glow of a red lightbulb as their only illumination. Later, in an idyllic park setting, Astaire dances with Hepburn on the greenest of green grasses to the beautiful Gershwin song "He Loves and She Loves." Hepburn is wearing the white wedding dress in which she was posing for him.

Color is so essential to *Funny Face* that one might be tempted to minimize the other elements—the story, performances, décor, and music—were it not for their outstanding quality. True, the plot line is thinner than most of the fashion models in the film, but Leonard Gershe's screenplay has a degree of wit, and it fits snugly into the movie's background of *haute couture* in Paris. Fred Astaire is not exactly convincing as a fashion photographer and, now in his late fifties, he is even less convincing as a romantic leading man. But there is still a spring in his step as his Dick Avery falls for Jo Stockton, a clerk in the Embryo Concepts Book Shop, who may have "character, spirit, and intelligence" but whose ravishing face and figure qualify her to be turned into "the *Quality* Woman." Jo, however, is more concerned with Professor Flostre (Michel Auclair), "the greatest living philosopher," whose theory of "Empatheticalism" is influential in her life. In Paris, she discovers that Flostre is more womanizer than philosopher, and that the man of her dreams has been taking her photograph right along.

Singing in her own light but appropriate voice, Audrey Hepburn gives the film an aura of enchantment, whether running with balloons in the rain, looking pensive in a railroad station, or floating down the steps in the Paris Opera House. Astaire is in fine fettle, too, joining Hepburn and Thompson in a joyful greeting to Paris ("Bonjour, Paris!"), or singing and dancing to "Clap Yo' Hands" with Thompson when they pose as beatniks in Professor Flostre's salon, or dancing with his old panache in front of Hepburn's window. After singing a heartfelt "Let's Kiss and Make Up" to her, his feet simply will not behave (when did they ever?), and, using his umbrella as a prop, he dances as vigorously as he did over two decades earlier. The rhythm turns Spanish, and Astaire becomes a matador, with the umbrella as his sword and the red lining of his raincoat as his matador's cape. He kills the "bull," turns his umbrella back to a mere prop for dancing, and saunters from the scene.

Gene Kelly had scored a double triumph with *An American in Paris* and *Singin' in the Rain* in the early fifties, but three of his later musical films for MGM also had substantial merit that placed them well above the routine level. *It's Always Fair Weather* (1955), which Kelly codirected with Stanley Donen, had more in common with *On the Town* than just its directors. Its book and lyrics, like those of the earlier musical, were written by Betty Comden and Adolph Green—for the first time on screen, all the lyrics were theirs—and it also concerned three servicemen who vow to be friends for life. In this case, however, the innocence and naïveté of the forties were replaced by a touch of cynicism in the fifties. When the friends meet a decade after their discharge, they discover to their chagrin that they not only have

Funny Face *(Paramount, 1957). Disguised as "beatniks" in order to gain entree to the salon of Professor Flostre, the high priest of "Empatheticalism," Fred Astaire and Kay Thompson amuse the guests by performing "Clap Yo' Hands."*

opposite, above: Funny Face *(Paramount, 1957).* Quality *Magazine's editor Maggie Prescott (Kay Thompson) proclaims the new fashion edict, "Think Pink!"*

opposite, below: Funny Face *(Paramount, 1957). On one of her photographic stops around Paris, Jo Stockton (Audrey Hepburn) poses in the Louvre, in front of the statue of the* Winged Victory of Samothrace. *Throughout this entire sequence, Hepburn is the breathtaking epitome of high-fashion glamour, and worlds removed from her Greenwich Village bookstore.*

It's Always Fair Weather *(MGM, 1955)*. *Drunk and deliriously happy at returning home, soldiers Michael Kidd, Gene Kelly, and Dan Dailey dance on a New York City street with garbage-can lids on their feet.*

Invitation to the Dance *(MGM, 1956)*. *In the "Sinbad the Sailor" sequence, Gene Kelly is caught up in an animated Arabian Nights world. Actually made in England four years before its release, this was a three-part dance film conceived by Kelly in a variety of styles and moods. "Sinbad the Sailor" combined live action and animation in much the same way that the "Jerry the Mouse" number had in Anchors Aweigh. The movie's relative sophistication, lack of continuous story content, and experimental nature put off most audiences.*

nothing in common but they actively dislike each other besides. Before they decide that they can still be friends—this is, after all, a musical comedy—they share some experiences, and one of the trio discovers romance. Since the plot involves an attempt to exploit their reunion on television, the screenplay also manages some barbed attacks on the idiocies of the medium.

The wartime buddies are played by Kelly, Dan Dailey, and Michael Kidd, the prominent choreographer in his first role before the camera. Since all three are agile dancers, they join in performing one of the film's best numbers, an exuberant dance across the streets of New York. The number even suggests the characters they play: Kelly as a hustling prize-fight promoter, Dailey as an unhappy advertising man, and Kidd as an easygoing owner of a fast food stand.

For his obligatory solo, to the tune of "I Like Myself," Gene Kelly dons roller skates. He dances about the city streets with such speed and athletic grace that he almost makes the Astaire-Rogers roller-skating dance in *Shall We Dance* look like slow motion. There are other gratifying musical moments in the film: Cyd Charisse, as the advertising girl Kelly comes to love, does a splendid dance in Stillman's Gym, accompanied by a group of muscular fighters, to the song "Baby, You Knock Me Out." Dan Dailey mocks the jargon and glib emptiness of the advertising game in his song "Situation-Wise." And singer Dolores Gray, bearing the brunt of much of the satire as an effusive television hostess, exudes musical comedy talent as she sings and dances to "Thanks a Lot but No Thanks." (The score was composed by MGM's musical director André Previn, his first for the screen.) There was a clever attempt to surmount the loss of intimacy created by the wide CinemaScope screen by masking it into three sections to convey simultaneous action. However, it was too distracting and gimmicky a device to come into general use.

Coming at a time when musical films were at their lowest ebb in many years, Gene Kelly's last musical for the decade should have been one final glowing tribute to the genre he had done much to change and develop. As it is, *Les Girls* (1957), although it stands head and shoulders above many of the musicals of the fifties, was further evidence that the Hollywood musical had fallen on hard times. Directed by the masterly George Cukor, *Les Girls* had an amusing premise, attractive stars, and songs by Cole Porter. What it lacked to a great extent was the sense of exultation and delight that permeates the best screen musicals. Its heart was certainly in the right place, but it was beating more faintly.

The story is undoubtedly different: Dancer Angele Ducros (Taina Elg) is suing Lady Sybil Wren (Kay Kendall) for slander, claiming that Lady Wren's book *Les Girls* paints a damaging picture of her when she and Sybil were members of a dance group called Les Girls. Both Angele and Sybil, along with Joy (Mitzi Gaynor), the third member of the group, were amorously involved with Barry Nichols (Kelly), their manager and leader. In a series of *Rashomon*-like flashbacks, Angele and Sybil relate completely different accounts of what happened, with Sybil characterizing Angele as giddy and promiscuous, and Angele portraying Sybil as an out-of-control alcoholic. Barry goes on the witness stand to tell the truth—both girls' "suicide" attempts out of frustrated love were really caused by a gas leak in their apartment—and he goes off with the girl he really loved: Joy.

Much of the dialogue is wryly amusing, but John Patrick's screenplay is unfortunately not matched by Cole Porter's music. The sophisticated, world-weary air and the ingenious rhyming are intact, and Porter could have few better interpreters of his style than the beautiful and splendidly funny Kay Kendall, but his score has too many stale and slightly tiresome reminders of past endeavors: "You're Just Too Too," sung by Kendall and Kelly, is another of his litanies of mutual admiration; "Ça, C'est l'Amour" has distinct echoes of "C'est Magnifique" from *Can-Can,* his 1953 stage musical; and "Ladies in Waiting" is ribald Porter, toned down for the screen and made to seem funnier than it is by Kendall's assured comedy playing.

Gene Kelly gets several chances to shine. In the opening song and dance, wearing a tuxedo and a straw hat and carrying a cane, he introduces Les Girls in his best jaunty style. In this number, George Cukor uses the wide CinemaScope frame intelligently and without gimmickry, avoiding the feeling that the filming is taking place in a giant stadium. Later, Kelly does a takeoff on Marlon Brando's 1955 motorcycle melodrama, *The Wild One,* wooing Mitzi Gaynor in dance to the song "Why Am I So Gone About That Gal?" Both are dressed in black as they wind about each other in a variety of shifting moods. Because Kelly's appearance and manner are so closely linked to the specific character of Brando's arrogant hood, this number dates badly, as opposed to the general spoof of Mickey Spillane's novels in *The Band Wagon.*

The year after *Les Girls,* MGM went Parisian again with *Gigi* (1958), its last great musical of the fifties. Adapted from Colette's famous short novel, the movie met with a major obstacle on the way to production. In 1955, the Code Office had sent Arthur Freed a memorandum objecting to the "immoral" elements in Colette's story of a family of Paris courtesans. Freed finally arrived at a treatment that would meet with Code Office approval, and launched the production, under Vincente Minnelli's direction.

Arthur Freed's decision to film all of the exteriors and some of the interiors in Paris and its environs created many difficulties. Paris officials were reluctant to give permission for filming in and about the city; they had had many bad experiences with filmmakers. The private citizens whose property had to be used for certain scenes were not very enthusiastic either. Ultimately, all gave their consent. But severe problems, including unsteady weather, the logistics of moving complicated equipment into famous Paris locations—the shooting at Maxim's was especially complex—and the usual quarrels and intrigues attendant on any major production put the movie close to half a million dollars over the budget.

The problems were far from over, however. The first preview was a disaster that stunned everyone connected with the movie. Funds to reshoot roughly one-quarter of the picture were approved, and the cast was reassembled. Dialogue was rewritten, new lyrics were inserted, and parts of some songs were refilmed under the direction of Charles Walters. After innumerable arguments, compromises, and last-minute decisions, *Gigi* was finally ready for release. Despite all the setbacks, *Gigi* emerged as a triumphant film that swept the Academy Awards as

no other film had since the awards were inaugurated. It won a total of nine Oscars, including best picture of the year and best director. The reviews were almost unanimously enthusiastic, although a number of critics took the trouble to point out its resemblance to *My Fair Lady*.

Perhaps only those who were close to the production could detect the occasional imitation-Paris aspects of the film. Most viewers are persuaded that they are watching Paris in the year 1900, from the moment that Honoré Lachaille (Maurice Chevalier) appears on screen to announce himself as ''a lover and collector of beautiful things,'' mostly women. He sings ''Thank Heaven for Little Girls'' with all of the insouciance and winking humor that kept him an international favorite for four decades. Honoré's exuberance for life, even in his mature years, is contrasted with the world-weariness of his nephew Gaston (Louis Jourdan), who, in the song ''It's a Bore!,'' expresses his total indifference to absolutely everything.

Soon we are swept into the private world of Gigi (Leslie Caron), the impish teenager who is being taught by her elegant Aunt Alicia (Isabel Jeans) to be the latest in a long line of courtesans. Gigi is learning the refinements and graces of her family's exalted profession, along with some of Aunt Alicia's basic truths: ''Bad eating habits have broken more households than infidelity.'' ''Wait for the first-class jewels. Hold on to your ideals.'' Above all, marriage is to be avoided until the last possible moment. ''We don't get married at once,'' her aunt tells Gigi. ''We get married at last.''

Gigi's progress from gawky girl to elegant, assured young woman is lightly traced in the screenplay, but it does not happen in the way that her aunt and her grandmother, Madame Alvarez (Hermione Gingold), expect. Gaston, a longtime friend of the family, regards Gigi as a child, until he realizes that she is a budding young lady and offers to make her his mistress. Gigi, in love with Gaston, shocks and upsets everyone by refusing to become his latest conquest. To her, ''the glory of romance, the eternal music of lovers,'' is not enough. ''What about kindness, sweetness, benevolence?'' she asks. She changes her mind only when she realizes that she would rather be miserable with him than without him. When Gaston understands how much he loves Gigi, and how wrong the life of a courtesan would be for her, he proposes marriage, to the relief of everyone.

Gigi's story may have originally prompted some concern in the Code Office, but it is really quite tame, even by 1958 standards, and Alan Jay Lerner's screenplay handles it without the suggestion of a smirk or a leer. It also serves as an appropriate framework for the film's principal virtues: Joseph Ruttenberg's dazzling color photography, Cecil Beaton's richly elegant costumes and settings, the enchanting score by Lerner and Frederick Loewe, and the performances of the leading players. Leslie Caron is an ideal Gigi, adorable and impudent, and Maurice Chevalier's aging boulevardier launched him on an entirely new career in films. But too little attention has been paid to Louis Jourdan, whose Gaston Lachaille is a marvelous blend of worldly cynicism and romantic idealism. His bearing, his demeanor, and even his singing voice (his own) are perfectly suited to the character.

Maurice Chevalier's presence in *Gigi* cannot help but remind us of his appearance in the Lubitsch and Mamoulian musicals of

top: Gigi (MGM, 1958). A memorable moment in this enchanting musical occurred when Madame Alvarez (Hermione Gingold) and Honoré Lachaille (Maurice Chevalier) sang ''I Remember It Well.'' His gallant attempt to remember the happy times of their romance many years ago is touchingly balanced by her delicate correction of his faulty memory. Only the obviously painted backdrop marred this exquisite number.

above: Gigi (MGM, 1958). Gigi (Leslie Caron) learns the art of walking gracefully from her aunt Alicia (Isabel Jeans).

opposite: Les Girls (MGM, 1957). ''Les Girls'' themselves pose for the camera: Kay Kendall, Taina Elg, and Mitzi Gaynor.

255

the early thirties. Like the earlier films, *Gigi* is informed by this presence: the saucy, wicked man about Paris for whom love is all. But the difference between the two Chevaliers—one young and bursting with vitality, the other aging but well-seasoned—is shared by the films themselves. *Love Me Tonight* and *The Smiling Lieutenant* have the exuberance, the cheekiness, and the occasional awkwardness of youth, pleased at being able to use the new toy of sound. *Gigi* has the glittering assurance of professionals who have honed their skills over long years of hard work. If this perfection implies a loss as well as a gain, a too careful application of the cinematic arts, it is hardly noticeable in the gaiety and beauty of *Gigi*.

Gigi's score has all the wit and the romantic aura of the best songs in the Lubitsch and Mamoulian operettas, with the added gloss provided by Lerner and Loewe's Broadway know-how. The songs are perfect reflections of the characters who sing them. At Maxim's, Gaston sings knowingly of his waning romance with the fickle Liane (Eva Gabor) in "She Is Not Thinking of Me." Watching young lovers in the park, Honoré sings of the relaxed and comfortable feelings that come with old age in "I'm Glad I'm Not Young Anymore." In the deepening twilight, Honoré and Madame Alvarez recall their past romance with "I Remember It Well."

Most memorable is Louis Jourdan's rendition of the title song. Leaving Gigi's house after her grandmother has carefully planted the idea of the girl as his new companion, Gaston reacts indignantly, but then he begins to realize that he is attracted to her. In a beautiful park setting, he begins to sing "Gigi," moving, in Lerner's brilliant lyrics and Loewe's shimmering melody, from anger to a wistful appreciation of her charms. Impeccably performed by Jourdan, the song has all the elements of a classic song in a musical film: it expresses the character's emotions far better than any dialogue, it envelops the movie audience in its words and music, and it bewitches the eye with its staging. The song provides the film's most memorable sequence, but, appropriately, *Gigi* ends not with the married Gaston and Gigi driving down the boulevard but with Honoré reprising "Thank Heaven for Little Girls" and then walking jauntily away from the camera.

If virtually all the first-rate musicals of the fifties came from MGM, there was at least one with some distinction that emerged from Samuel Goldwyn's studio: *Hans Christian Andersen* (1952), the first of his three musicals for the decade. Danny Kaye, one of the producer's major stars in the forties, had not made a film for him since *A Song Is Born* in 1948. Now he returned to appear as the Danish storyteller in one of Goldwyn's most attractive color productions. Moss Hart's screenplay made no pretense of being a biography of Andersen—it was frankly intended as a fanciful account of a Danish cobbler (Kaye) with a propensity for relating fairy tales who comes to Copenhagen, where he falls in love with a temperamental—and married—ballerina (French dancer Jeanmaire). Kaye played the role with surprisingly little color or variety, but the film excelled in its lovely candy-box sets and especially in Frank Loesser's melodious score. Some of the songs ("The Ugly Duckling," "Thumbelina," "The Emperor's New Clothes") were based on Andersen's tales. The major production number was an elaborate ballet derived from the

Andersen fable of "The Little Mermaid," which Jeanmaire danced under the direction of Roland Petit, choreographer of the Ballets de Paris. Only Kaye's listless performance and a sluggish, rambling script kept the film from the top echelon.

In the years after the handful of great musical films in the fifties—notably, *An American in Paris, Singin' in the Rain, The Band Wagon,* and *Gigi*—other superior musicals would come to the screen. But they would never achieve the consummate professionalism, the confidence, pride, and sheer love of movie-making that are present in every frame of these films. The seeds of talent planted in the early years of the forties had blossomed forth in the late forties and early fifties. For a brief but exhilarating period, the flowers thrived, and the musical film was finally bearing fruit.

opposite: Gigi *(MGM, 1958). In her new role as courtesan to Gaston (Louis Jourdan), Gigi (Leslie Caron) tests the quality of his cigar.*

IN THE TRADITION

The musical successes of the early fifties had brought the genre to the peak of achievement at a time when the genre itself was beginning to wane. Still, the business of making movies, even musical movies, continued apace, and if there were far fewer song-and-dance efforts on the screen, there were some more than respectable films in the established musical tradition. The decade even saw the full emergence of two new musical stars in Doris Day and Elvis Presley. Musical stars of the forties—Fred Astaire, Bing Crosby, Judy Garland, Gene Kelly, and others—kept on making films, and although few of them could match the best of the Freed musicals, a handful had considerable merit. A number of them, especially those from Joe Pasternak's group, working concurrently with the Freed Unit at MGM, were highly entertaining.

For Judy Garland, the fifties marked the beginning of a painful, deeply troubled period in which disaster followed triumph with dizzying speed. In personal appearances she would bring crowds to roaring adulation, but on screen there was only sporadic evidence of the glowing, tremulous actress and singer of the forties. Most of the time, it seemed as if the joy and warmth that had always surged through her singing had evaporated, leaving only the frightened girl surviving on nervous energy. After her suspension from MGM for failing to report for further work on *Annie Get Your Gun,* she took a long rest at a Boston sanitarium, where she gained considerable weight. She was finally summoned by the studio to appear opposite her old friend Gene Kelly in a musical called *Summer Stock* (1950), directed by Charles Walters. In a way, it represented a reversion to her Mickey-Judy days, for the plot involved a troupe of aspiring performers laboring to "put on a show" in the barn of Garland's farm. Kelly was the troupe's director who comes to appreciate and love Garland.

The film proved to be one of the lesser teamings of Garland and Kelly, a likable but uninspired musical. As a hardworking farmer who is astonished to find her place overrun with actors— her frivolous sister (Gloria De Haven) is the company's leading lady—Garland plays with her usual brisk humor. (She was always an underrated comedienne.) She is also in good voice, singing "If You Feel like Singing, Sing!," "Happy Harvest," and an appealing ballad, "Friendly Star." Her best scene with Kelly— one with something of their old magic—comes when they are alone in the theater. Kelly explains the smell of greasepaint, the meaning of hokum. He sings "You Wonderful You," then begins a "nice, easy dance," in which she joins him tentatively. They finish together at full throttle, and Garland giggles in that nervous, affecting fashion that was one of her trademarks. Kelly also has one brilliant solo in which he dances on the bare stage of the barn theater, incorporating the rustling sound of sheets of newspaper and a squeaking board in the barn floor into the dance.

At the staging of the troupe's big show in Garland's barn, she has her finest moment in the film: a rendition of "Get Happy," backed by a number of dancers. Filmed long after the movie was completed, the number reveals a suddenly trim Garland in black tights, a perky black hat perched on her head at a fetching angle. She is the vibrant performer of old, so electrifying in her voice and manner that a viewer has no time to reflect on the irony of the lyrics: "Forget your troubles. Come on, get happy!"

She rested again after *Summer Stock,* but was abruptly recalled to the studio to replace pregnant June Allyson opposite Fred Astaire in *Royal Wedding* (1951), a new musical from the Freed Unit. When she again failed to show up for rehearsals, she was dropped unceremoniously from the film and replaced by Jane Powell. Racked by illness, both physical and mental, confronted with a disintegrating marriage to Vincente Minnelli, and removed from a movie opposite a costar she admired enormously, Garland attempted suicide. No longer a tenable property, she was let go "for her own best interests" by the studio that had nurtured and developed her from her teenage years.

Meanwhile, *Royal Wedding* went into production under Stanley Donen's direction, his first solo assignment. Alan Jay Lerner, whose stage reputation was largely due to his lovely 1947 musical fantasy, *Brigadoon,* contributed his first screenplay. Fred Astaire, now happily residing at MGM after the success of *Easter Parade, The Barkleys of Broadway,* and *Three Little Words,* had discarded the idea of retirement and was keeping his dancing shoes polished and ready for action. Suggested by the long ago

The Belle of New York *(MGM, 1952)*. *Fred Astaire and Vera-Ellen dance on and around a horse-drawn trolley to a song called "Oops!" At one point, they perform some fancy steps on the poor horse's back with the aid of trick photography. (One wonders why the screen's foremost dancer would permit camera trickery to dominate the style or compromise the elegance and sophistication of any of his dance numbers, rather than have the camera subservient to the dance, as in his earlier films.)*

page 258: Summer Stock *(MGM, 1950)*. *Judy Garland sings "Get Happy," her last musical number for MGM.* Summer Stock *also marked her last appearance in a film until* A Star Is Born, *four years later.*

opposite, above: Royal Wedding *(MGM, 1951)*. *Fred Astaire dances on the wall of his London hotel room. To achieve the startling effects in this number, the room was placed inside a barrel, as in an amusement park, with all the furniture firmly nailed to the floor. As the room was turned inside the barrel, the camera turned with it, giving the impression that an upright Astaire was defying and actually breaking the laws of gravity.*

opposite, below: Two Weeks with Love *(MGM, 1950)*. *In the film's highlight, young Debbie Reynolds, bursting with vitality, sang "Aba Daba Honeymoon," a 1914 vaudeville tune, with gawky Carleton Carpenter, making a bid for stardom and also gaining a popular recording.*

marriage of Fred's sister Adele to Lord Cavendish, and especially by the marriage of England's Princess Elizabeth to Prince Philip a few years earlier, *Royal Wedding* concerned a sister and brother song-and-dance team who discover romance in London at the time of the gala event.

Royal Wedding is cheerful, colorful, and undistinguished. The screenplay was hardly one of Alan Jay Lerner's brightest, but his lyrics, to superior music by Burton Lane, were pleasing. (A longtime Hollywood composer, Lane had written the music for the 1947 stage hit *Finian's Rainbow*.) And the teaming of Astaire and Jane Powell was not as incompatible as one might suppose. Powell suppressed some (but by no means all) of her *Date with Judy* girlishness to keep up with Astaire in two amusing numbers. Aboard an ocean liner, they entertain the passengers until a sudden storm turns the ship into a turbulent seesaw. Later, Astaire, dressed as a flashy Brooklyn type, and Powell, as his raffish girlfriend, romp through "How Could You Believe Me When I Said I Loved You When You Know I've Been a Liar All My Life?"—one of the longest song titles on record.

Astaire was also given several solos, as well as a lavish production number in a Caribbean setting to the tune "I Left My Hat in Haiti." In his best-remembered number, he dances on the walls and ceiling of a hotel room in a burst of romantic exhilaration, to the song "You're All the World to Me." The effect was astonishing, but it made one long again for the Fred Astaire of earlier years who needed only his irrepressible feet and the stimulating presence of Ginger Rogers to create dancing miracles.

Astaire's first film after *Royal Wedding* was one of his least successful of the period. *The Belle of New York* (1952), loosely adapted from the 1897 musical that had been the first American musical to play London's West End, was placed in production under Charles Walters's direction. Astaire was an irresponsible man about old New York who falls in love with a Salvation Army girl (Vera-Ellen). Patently too old for the role, he was miscast as a playboy, but Vera-Ellen, his costar in *Three Little Words,* was at her most appealing, dancing with grace and pixieish charm.

The movie's principal troubles were a flat screenplay and an excess of labored fantasy. Many musicals have coped with and even triumphed over an inferior book, but few could survive a coy conceit that has the lovers literally walking on air as a sign of their devotion to each other. Instead of lifting the film to the skies, as intended, the device causes it to sink under the weight of the whimsy. When Astaire dances over New York's rooftops and on top of Washington Square arch, sharing his happiness with the pigeons, we may smile, but when the sky-walking is repeated incessantly, we can only wince. At one point the movie offers a series of colorful Currier & Ives tableaux, but the best musical sequence is provided by Astaire, sans gimmickry, sans special effects, informing us blithely that "I Want to Be a Dancing Man."

Jane Powell turned up in a number of other MGM musicals of the early fifties that took advantage of her soprano voice and her vivacious if slightly cloying personality. As she left her teens, the pattern of her movies varied little from those of the late forties, involving her in romantic moonings and misunderstandings that allowed her to chirp both sad and happy songs. The films were decorative and inoffensive, and occasionally they were graced with sideline contributions that were more memorable than the movies themselves. A minor period musical called *Two Weeks with Love* (1950) centered on Powell's girlish infatuation with a romantic South American (Ricardo Montalban), but the film was stolen by Debbie Reynolds as Powell's younger sister. The movie's musical numbers were staged by Busby Berkeley in his first MGM assignment after directing *Take Me Out to the Ball Game*.

Berkeley also staged two unusual musical numbers in *Small Town Girl* (1953), another Jane Powell musical of modest dimensions. In one, Ann Miller does a sizzling tap dance while only the arms of the accompanying musicians are seen, protruding from holes in the stage floor as she dances around them. The disembodied effect is both Berkeleyesque and Daliesque. In the second number, Bobby Van, as a young hoofer hoping to reach the heights of show business, dances across town by taking a series of kangaroo-like hopping steps. The number is simple but somehow memorable. Jane Powell was eclipsed by all this lively musical activity.

In the early fifties, MGM's swimming star Esther Williams retained her franchise on underwater musicals. Her first few movies in the new decade were given more condescending treatment than usual by critics weary of their sameness, but audiences continued to enjoy the lavish aquacades, the color and songs, and Williams's lithe, suntanned, and fresh-from-the-pool appearance. Apart from playing famous swimmer Annette Kellerman in a highly fictionalized version of her life called *Million Dollar Mermaid* (1952), she continued to star in the sort of Technicolor baubles her fans had come to expect, including *Duchess of Idaho* (1950), *Pagan Love Song* (1950), and *Texas Carnival* (1951).

By far the most elaborate of these films was *Easy to Love* (1953), photographed in part at the lush playground of Cypress Gardens at Winterhaven, Florida. The film's undeniable highlight was a water spectacle on Lake Eloise, involving Williams and scores of intrepid young swimmers in intricate acrobatics. Dangling at the ends of swiftly towed ropes, they formed amazing and seemingly life-threatening patterns on their water skis, with Williams as their goddess-like leader. (At one point, Williams, standing on a trapeze which dangled from a helicopter, leaped from a height of eighty feet into a formation of water skiers traveling swiftly across the lake!) This awesome number bore the unmistakable stamp of Busby Berkeley, who had created another aquatic extravaganza in *Footlight Parade* two decades earlier.

For musical stars of longer lineage than either Jane Powell or Esther Williams, the fifties brought an inevitable dwindling of their box-office popularity, less frequent appearances, and a maturing of their images. A slightly riper but still effervescent Betty Grable appeared in musical remakes of her own or other films, and for a while she was able to hold her own against the competition of Fox's newest blonde star, Marilyn Monroe. She continued to find a compatible costar in Dan Dailey, appearing with him in *My Blue Heaven* (1950), a soggy musical concerning the not necessarily related topics of television and motherhood, and in *Call Me Mister* (1951), which used only the title and a few

songs from the 1946 Broadway revue. By 1955, however, she had made her last film for Fox, and Monroe was the studio's top attraction. (In 1954, Monroe starred in an unendurably vulgar large-scale musical called *There's No Business like Show Business,* which wasted two of the country's natural resources, Ethel Merman and Irving Berlin, and did little good for costars Dan Dailey, Donald O'Connor, and Mitzi Gaynor.)

Bing Crosby was no less admirable in his fifties musicals than he had been two decades earlier, nor did the few added lines in his face change the fundamentally carefree attitude he usually projected in films. One of his most popular films of the period, and one of the most profitable in his long career, was Irving Berlin's *White Christmas* (1954). The movie used the title of the perennial Berlin song, which Crosby had introduced in *Holiday Inn,* for a story that suggested the earlier movie in its use of a country inn as the focal point. Teamed for the first time with Danny Kaye, after both Fred Astaire and Donald O'Connor had turned down the costarring role, Crosby played a singer who discovers that his beloved old wartime general (Dean Jagger) has fallen on hard times as the owner of a failing New England inn. He schemes with his partner (Danny Kaye) and two singing sisters (Rosemary Clooney and Vera-Ellen) to reunite the general's old division at the inn, and to have the event shown on national television. The story lines of many earlier Crosby musicals had been featherweight intervals between songs, and as such, they had been endurable. *White Christmas,* however, with a plot so unbearably sticky that it could serve as flypaper, failed to pass the tolerance test.

Fortunately, Irving Berlin's capacity to turn out cheerful tunes had not deserted him, and *White Christmas* contains some diverting songs that keep the treacle from becoming excessive, including "Count Your Blessings," "Love, You Didn't Do Right by Me," and "The Best Things Happen While You're Dancing." The movie is also brightened by the presence of Vera-Ellen, whose expert dancing and piquant personality offset the overall blandness. She joins Rosemary Clooney in a duet of "Sisters," dances to Berlin's old favorite, "Mandy," and joins Danny Kaye and a chorus in the movie's best number, an amusing tribute to "Choreography." Kaye, whose popularity waned after his peak years with Samuel Goldwyn, gets little opportunity to shine. He merely reprises his familiar "bumbling oaf" routine.

One musical star who came into her own in the early fifties was Doris Day. Her blonde prettiness and velvet voice appealed to the public, and her studio, Warner Bros., cast her in a series of musical movies that seldom required more than these assets to achieve popularity. Aside from an occasional dramatic part, she was cast in fresh-faced roles that kept her smiling and singing despite a few moments of mild adversity. Her early fifties musicals were all spun sugar, strongly flavored with nostalgia. Lacking the flair, the style, and the musical talent that MGM and even Fox, at its best, could bring to their musical valentines to the past, Warners frequently invested its period musicals with a heavy touch. Anachronisms abound—the ambiance is sometimes pure fifties—and even when the period is accurately recorded, there is a sense of strain. *Tea for Two* (1950), loosely adapted from the twenties musical comedy *No, No, Nanette,* cast Doris Day as a 1929 Long Island heiress who gets her uncle (S. Z. Sakall),

Texas Carnival (MGM, 1951). A seemingly disembodied Esther Williams floats dreamily under water. Comedienne Fanny Brice was alleged to have said about Williams, "Wet, she's a star. Dry, she ain't."

opposite: Small Town Girl *(MGM, 1953). Ann Miller meets Busby Berkeley. She sings and dances to "I've Gotta Hear That Beat," around the eighty-six musicians that Berkeley has arranged so that only their arms and their instruments are visible, protruding from holes drilled in the stage.*

White Christmas *(Paramount, 1954). Danny Kaye and Bing Crosby as army buddies who rally to the aid of their wartime commander.*

opposite, above: There's No Business like Show Business *(Fox, 1954). The principals assemble backstage. Left to right: Ethel Merman, Dan Dailey, Mitzi Gaynor, Donald O'Connor, and Marilyn Monroe.*

opposite, below: The Glass Slipper *(MGM, 1955). Cinderella (Leslie Caron) arrives at the ball in this retelling of the classic story. Caron danced with the Ballets de Paris under the direction of her mentor, Roland Petit. Charles Walters handled the narrative with a proper awareness of its fragile fairy-tale quality.*

recently ruined in the stock market crash, to invest in a show. Despite the efforts of Day, Gordon MacRae, and Gene Nelson, this *Tea for Two* was tepid. *Lullaby of Broadway* (1951) was more of the same.

One of Day's most popular period musicals was *On Moonlight Bay* (1951), a nosegay to small-town American life of the past, vaguely derived from Booth Tarkington's *Penrod* stories. Clearly influenced by *Meet Me in St. Louis,* it even offered Leon Ames repeating his *St. Louis* role as the stern family patriarch, and Doris Day, in an auburn wig not unlike Judy Garland's, falling in love with her own "boy next door" (Gordon MacRae). The resemblances end there. While *Meet Me in St. Louis* was a classic musical film that richly evoked an idealized yesteryear, *On Moonlight Bay* is all self-conscious quaintness. Its characters behave with depressing predictability: Doris Day goes from sports-loving tomboy to demure young miss the moment she is kissed by MacRae, who undergoes his own transformation from college "radical" to responsible young man on the rise, by way of the armed forces. The movie was so popular, however, that it prompted a sequel, entitled *By the Light of the Silvery Moon* (1953).

Day's best Warners musical until *The Pajama Game* in 1957 was *Calamity Jane* (1953), directed by David Butler. Although it had an obvious antecedent in *Annie Get Your Gun*—early Doris Day often resembled Betty Hutton at her most strenuous—this was still that *rara avis* of film musicals: one with an original screenplay and musical score. If the plot was absurd, and if the Sammy Fain–Paul Francis Webster songs were often derivative of not only *Annie Get Your Gun* but also *Oklahoma!,* there was still reason to applaud the movie's colorful production and irrepressible high spirits. Even the setting was well handled, neither so realistic that we expect to see herds of cattle stampeding down the street nor so stylized that it resembles a cardboard backdrop. And with Day giving the title role both barrels, *Calamity Jane* was better than average entertainment.

Her "Calam" is a roughhewn, ornery, and buckskinned stagecoach driver who switches her affections from a dashing young army lieutenant (Phil Carey) to her old rival, "Wild Bill" Hickok (Howard Keel), turning ladylike in the process. From her first appearance aboard the stagecoach, singing "Deadwood Stage," Day dominates the movie in exuberant—possibly too exuberant—fashion, with strong assistance from Howard Keel and his virile baritone. Returning home from a visit to Chicago, she gives her account of the "Windy City" in a song that suggests *Oklahoma!'s* "Kansas City" in more ways than the title. Her quarrelsome duet with Wild Bill—"I Could Do Without You"—echoes Annie Oakley's competitive duet with Frank Butler in *Annie Get Your Gun.* But one song is all Day's—and the film's—very own: walking through the countryside on a beautiful morning, Calam realizes that she loves Bill, and in a voice exuding warmth and tender feeling, she sings the Academy Award–winning song "Secret Love." (It is amusing to hear her perfect diction after an hour of her Western twang, but such are the vagaries of the musical film.)

Another musical performer who first achieved popularity in the fifties was a young Mississippi singer with an alarmingly gyrating pelvis, a sullen pout, and a throaty voice that combined

to send his legion of fans into hysteria. A sensation on records and on television, Elvis Presley began making musical movies in 1956. His most interesting films of the first five years were those that attempted, even if only glancingly, to probe an inch below the surface: *Jailhouse Rock* (1957), in which he played a churlish convict who becomes an even more churlish rock star; *King Creole* (1958), a film version of Harold Robbins's novel *A Stone for Danny Fisher*, featuring Presley as a hustling New Orleans musician who tangles with gangsters; and *Flaming Star* (1960), an almost songless Western drama with Presley as a brooding half-breed Indian.

As the years passed, his surly, antisocial behavior faded, and he took on the image of a brash, fun-loving young man not likely to threaten anyone. Most of his later films, which continued well into the sixties, became formula efforts—lightweight vehicles, tailor-made for Presley, mixing colorful backgrounds, pretty but interchangeable girls, many Presley songs, and an inconsequential story.

Although the Doris Day and Elvis Presley musical films of the fifties could claim no special virtues, most of them were at least written directly for the screen, with no roots in either the stage or a previous film. Several films in the first half of the decade, led by *Singin' in the Rain*, had brought the original screen musical to a new level of achievement, but few others qualified as an advance in the genre. In many of them, originality was no guarantee of success.

One fifties film, Paramount's Western musical, *Red Garters* (1954), attempted a fresh and inventive approach to musical conventions. A completely stylized screen musical with not even the slightest pretense of reality, it was a noble experiment that failed. The main feature was the décor, a series of symbolic, deliberately unrealistic sets (mostly disembodied store fronts), each designed in a single primary color. The performers, dressed to coordinate with the sets, frolicked with frankly musical comedy airs. The screenplay lightly mocked the characters of the traditional Western, including the stalwart young cowboy, the flashy, good-hearted saloon singer, and the nasty desperado all in black. Unfortunately, the result was more forced and distracting than innovative, since the basic nature of film as photographed realism clashed fatally with the patent unreality of the movie.

If the Hollywood musical was beginning its decline by the start of the fifties, the genre was far from dormant during the decade. Even as many moviegoers deserted the large screen for the small box, or as producers dropped the musicals on their schedules for more profitable ventures, there was musical fare to be seen and enjoyed in the nation's theaters. Apart from the last surge of creativity from MGM's Freed Unit, the active teams of producers Joe Pasternak and Jack Cummings were turning out agreeable light musicals with Jane Powell or Esther Williams. Audiences were responding to the fresh-scrubbed appeal of Doris Day, the galvanizing presence of Elvis Presley, or the enduring talents of Judy Garland, Gene Kelly, Bing Crosby, and Fred Astaire, even in their second-best vehicles.

The golden days may have been ending, but there was at least a trace of gold in the musical films that aspired not to greatness but to entertainment.

Calamity Jane (Warners, 1953). *Doris Day in the title role exchanges bar conversation with Howard Keel as "Wild Bill" Hickok. Probably Day's best musical of the fifties, the movie was clearly bent on imitating* Annie Get Your Gun, *but it had its own virtues, especially a tuneful and diverting musical score.*

opposite, above, left: On Moonlight Bay *(Warners, 1951). Marjorie Penfield (Doris Day) and her boyfriend Bill (Gordon MacRae) attend a carnival in this spun-sugar musical that tried to emulate the warm nostalgic feeling of* Meet Me in St. Louis.

opposite, above, right: By the Light of the Silvery Moon *(Warners, 1953). In this sequel to* On Moonlight Bay, *Marjorie Penfield (Doris Day) tries to prevent an altercation between boyfriend Bill (Gordon MacRae) and persistent suitor Chester Finley (Russell Arms). The movie reunited the Penfield family for new problems and a new round of pleasant songs and dances.*

opposite, below: By the Light of the Silvery Moon *(Warners, 1953). Doris Day leads the cast in the production number "Chanticleer."*

Red Garters *(Paramount, 1954). Rosemary Clooney and the girls entertain the rough-and-ready men in a Western saloon. An unsuccessful attempt at stylized musical satire, the movie used deliberately artificial sets, each designed in a single primary color. The songs were acceptable, even amusing, but the cast was much too bland for such a tongue-in-cheek effort.*

Jailhouse Rock *(MGM, 1957). Elvis Presley and his merry band of fellow "convicts" enjoy a musical spree in a production number to the title song.*

STAGE TO SCREEN

With the erosion of the musical genre, studios began to rely with increasing frequency on the stage for the handful of musical films they could afford to produce. At the beginning of the sound era, the studios, in search of material to satisfy their customers, raided the Broadway theater for musical properties, including some best left to gather dust. But in the fifties, the musical stage was tapped for an entirely different reason: for hard-pressed studios it offered the enticing prospect of a guaranteed audience which had either seen or read about the long-running Broadway hits. Many musical plays that had opened a decade earlier and had worn out several touring companies and innumerable stock productions finally came to the screen.

Although they often did solid business, the film adaptations were generally disappointing. Some of them faltered through miscasting of central roles, or through excessive reverence for the legendary stage production. But there were deeper lapses in judgment, reflecting an inability of the filmmakers to come to grips with the transference from stage to screen. Occasionally, a musical adaptation would open up the stylized stage backgrounds to awesomely real settings, violating the intention of the original material. (The grandiose filming of the charmingly small-scaled *Oklahoma!* is a case in point.) Others, like the film version of *Guys and Dolls,* simply went the other way by ignoring the idea of film as essentially photographed realism and opting for a deliberately unreal milieu. The result was equally distracting. (The less pretentious musical films of the forties never had this problem: they *knew* that the musical film was basically unreal, and simply heightened their reasonably authentic settings and costumes with bright, bright color, broad, larger-than-life characters, and a blithe acceptance of the musical's conventions. It often worked, not as art but as entertainment.)

In their haste to bring stage successes to the screen, the producers also failed to realize that not everything was equally transferrable. Group songs and dances that may have stopped the show on stage often flattened out on the screen and merely marked time until the principals could reappear. For years, dancing stars like Fred Astaire and Gene Kelly had labored to accommodate their three-dimensional dances to the two-dimensional screen, but in the stage adaptations, cinematic

considerations were usually sacrificed for sheer size. More important, essential differences between stage and screen were ignored. Where music and pageantry could be quite enough to stir up a palatable theatrical dish, moviegoers required a stronger narrative as one of the ingredients to whet their appetites. On the screen, pageantry without character involvement had a deadening effect. Also, a number of the most successful stage musicals of the forties, such as *Kiss Me, Kate,* had story lines that were frankly theatrical conceits designed to bolster the show's songs and dances, and their greasepaint contrivances were evident in the film versions of the fifties. Interestingly, the most successful fifties film version of a Rodgers and Hammerstein musical, *The King and I,* was the only one derived from a film (*Anna and the King of Siam,* a popular movie of the forties).

Of the many musical films that were adapted from Broadway hits, the majority was produced by MGM, which had more than ample production resources to buy many top stage successes for expensive screen versions. Fox was a close second. If there were lapses in judgment and creative imagination that made many of these musical adaptations less than what they should have been, if there was a recurrent failure to understand the changes that needed to occur in the transition from stage to screen, there was some compensation in the glorious theater music that poured forth from the screen.

MGM's first-released musical adaptation for the decade was Irving Berlin's *Annie Get Your Gun* (1950), produced by the Freed Unit. MGM had bought the musical for Judy Garland at a price higher than any other in movie history, but once again her depressed mental state had made it difficult if not impossible to get the film under way. (Other delays were caused by leading man Howard Keel's broken ankle and by the death of Frank Morgan, originally cast as Buffalo Bill.) Another problem was the longstanding friction between Garland and the director, Busby Berkeley, that went back to the Mickey-Judy days of the early forties. Finally, a letter chastising Garland for her constant lateness sent her reeling into hysteria, and she refused to return— or was incapable of returning—to the filming. She was fired and replaced by Betty Hutton.

It is, of course, futile to speculate on what a healthy and

Annie Get Your Gun *(MGM, 1950). Annie Oakley (Betty Hutton)
is inducted into the Sioux tribe in the outsize number "I'm an Indian
Too."*

page 270: *The King and I (Fox, 1956). One of the film's most
exhilarating moments: Deborah Kerr and Yul Brynner whirl about the
room to the strains of "Shall We Dance?"*

vibrant Judy Garland might have brought to *Annie Get Your Gun*. (She had recorded some of the songs, but in photographs of wardrobe tests, she looks ill and exhausted.) Still, she might have given the role of Annie Oakley the combination of rambunctiousness and vulnerability—a prairie chicken who longs to look like a swan—that Betty Hutton achieves only in part. Ethel Merman's leather-lunged brassiness had been perfectly scaled for the original stage version, but Hutton's frenetic style and frontal attack on the songs divest the character of necessary warmth and make her seem a mite mechanical.

Yet, under George Sidney's direction—he replaced Busby Berkeley after production resumed—*Annie Get Your Gun* is bountiful musical entertainment. Its serviceable story of the romance and rivalry between a sharpshooting, unlettered backwoods girl and the equally sharpshooting stellar attraction at Buffalo Bill's Wild West Show was fleshed out with colorful production numbers and with Irving Berlin's marvelous score, one of the most tuneful of his long career. The songs are astonishingly varied, from Annie's wistful ballad "They Say It's Wonderful" to "Doin' What Comes Natur'lly," her unabashed tribute to her family's straightforward approach to life's basic urges, which Hutton renders with more energy than humor. Hutton also rattles the scenery with her version of "You Can't Get a Man with a Gun." As Frank Butler, Annie's adored rival, Howard Keel (in his film debut) is ideally cast, vigorously singing "The Girl That I Marry" and "My Defenses Are Down," and joining Hutton in the challenge duet "Anything You Can Do." The finale, staged to Berlin's anthem "There's No Business like Show Business," is a rodeo of massive proportions.

For the next few years, MGM confined its musical adaptations to musical plays of older vintage whose scores were perennially popular. In 1951, the studio released a new version of *Show Boat,* the Jerome Kern–Oscar Hammerstein II classic. Filmed in color for the first time, and with most of its music intact, the hardy *Show Boat* sailed down the Mississippi once again. It proved to be a reasonably durable vehicle, with a few noticeable leaks. Directed by George Sidney, but with Roger Edens carefully overseeing the musical portions for Arthur Freed, it was still basically Edna Ferber's sentimental tale of the folks on the *Cotton Blossom,* especially the romance and marriage of Cap'n Andy's daughter Magnolia and the gambler Gaylord Ravenal. *Show Boat*'s principal glory had always been its score—one of the best ever produced for the musical theater—and here it sustained and enriched a faulty production. With such rapturous melodies as "Make Believe" and "Why Do I Love You?" on the soundtrack, it was possible to disregard the lacquered look of the film, which conveyed little if anything of the raffish but colorful lives of showboat people, and to accept, if not forgive, the miscasting of some of the central roles. Howard Keel is a persuasive Gaylord Ravenal, every bit as good as Allan Jones had been in the 1936 version, and Joe E. Brown, as Cap'n Andy, has the sense not to overplay the sentiment. But Kathryn Grayson is coy and shrill as Magnolia, lacking the charm and the delicate touch that Irene Dunne had brought to the role. As the showboat's resident dancers, Marge and Gower Champion are entirely too sophisticated, so expert in their dance turns that they seem incongruously out of place aboard the *Cotton Blossom.*

above: Show Boat *(MGM, 1951). Cap'n Andy (Joe E. Brown) acknowledges the attraction between his beloved daughter Magnolia (Kathryn Grayson) and Gaylord Ravenal (Howard Keel).*

top: Annie Get Your Gun *(MGM, 1950). Buffalo Bill (Louis Calhern) declares Annie Oakley (Betty Hutton) the winner of a shooting match between her and Frank Butler (Howard Keel, looking glum). Benay Venuta and Keenan Wynn are interested observers.*

Show Boat *(MGM, 1951). The* Cotton Blossom *is greeted by the townspeople as it comes into port. One of the most expensive props ever made, the showboat actually sailed—not down the Mississippi, but down what was known as the Tarzan Jungle Lake, on MGM's back lot.*

William Warfield sings "Ol' Man River" splendidly, but the innate dignity of his voice and bearing works against any true characterization of the shiftless roustabout Joe.

As Julie, the mulatto singer whose mixed marriage forces her to leave the showboat, Ava Gardner is surprisingly effective when she mimes her songs (her voice was dubbed by Annette Warren), especially "Bill," and moving when she traces the character's descent into alcoholic defeat. She disappears from the film for a long stretch but when she returns at the end, worn, shabby, but still beautiful, she manages to reunite Magnolia and Ravenal. In a movie that lacks the warmth, the emotional resonance that any production of *Show Boat* should have, Gardner contributes the only truly affecting moment. Standing at the levee, watching the *Cotton Blossom* moving down the river, she blows one last kiss to the people—and the life—she once knew and loved.

After costarring in *Lovely to Look At* (1952), a mediocre remake of Jerome Kern's *Roberta,* with a fashion show finale created and directed by Vincente Minnelli, Kathryn Grayson and Howard Keel were teamed in their most prestigious film to date: MGM's 1953 version of Cole Porter's Broadway musical success *Kiss Me, Kate.* The original production, opening on December 30, 1948, had marked the return of Porter, after years in relative decline, as the master composer whose ingenious, sophisticated lyrics and sinuous melodies were an ornament of the theater and films.

For a long time, Porter had shuttled between the two worlds of film and the stage, contributing either original scores for the screen *(Born to Dance, Broadway Melody of 1940, You'll Never Get Rich, The Pirate)* or chic and complex scores for the musical theater *(Nymph Errant, Leave It to Me, Jubilee).* Occasionally, his more successful stage musicals were transferred to the screen, but in many cases the studios excised all but a few of his songs, seeking new revenue with freshly composed songs by other hands. (Little was left of his inimitable and sometimes risqué scores for *Anything Goes, DuBarry Was a Lady,* or *Panama Hattie.*) *Kiss Me, Kate* would be the first Cole Porter musical to retain most of the songs from the original stage version.

These songs are dazzling indeed: a collection of wry, wickedly funny, or romantic tunes spun around a frail plot concerning Fred Graham (Howard Keel), a vainglorious actor who is costarring with his temperamental ex-wife Lilli Vanessi (Kathryn Grayson) in a musical version of Shakespeare's *The Taming of the Shrew.* Backstage scenes, in which the couple bickered, made up, and then bickered again, alternated with onstage scenes from their show, set in a frankly stylized Venice, where Petruchio goes about bringing his tempestuous Kate to heel. Appearing in both the contemporary story and the musical *Shrew* were Lois (Ann Miller), a bubbly singer-dancer, and her errant, gambling boyfriend Bill (Tommy Rall). Produced by Jack Cummings's busy unit and directed by the untiring George Sidney in one of his last films for MGM, *Kiss Me, Kate* should have been one of the studio's musical triumphs.

However, the film had several serious shortcomings. Its most glaring handicap was caused by the wrongheaded decision to shoot the movie in the new 3-D process, in which the audience, wearing special glasses, was assaulted by three-dimensional objects hurled at their heads. Apparently, the inappropriateness of using

above: Kiss Me, Kate *(MGM, 1953). Brash and hearty as always, Ann Miller sings and dances to "Too Darn Hot" for the amusement of Ron Randall (playing Cole Porter in an ill-advised opening scene), Kathryn Grayson, and Howard Keel.*

top: Kiss Me, Kate *(MGM, 1953). A "team of strolling players" sings about its upcoming tour of Italy ("We Open in Venice") in* Cole Porter's *witty and melodious musical. The players (from left): Tommy Rall, Ann Miller, Kathryn Grayson, and Howard Keel.*

the device for a sophisticated musical comedy never occurred to MGM's moguls. Also, the Sam and Bella Spewack book, with its purely theatrical concept, turned forced and affected under the camera's scrutiny. Another glaring error was the casting of Kathryn Grayson as Lilli Vanessi. Endurable in bland heroine roles, she was clearly out of her depth playing a quick-tempered stage star, and she transformed the leading lady, in the person of both Lilli and Katherine, into a petulant scold. She was easily surpassed by Howard Keel, who offered a reasonable facsimile of Alfred Drake's original performance as the flamboyant Fred and the swaggering Petruchio.

The pleasures of Cole Porter's score were almost (but not quite) enough to offset the film's faults. It is composed on two different levels, and both levels work admirably. On one hand, there are the songs written for the contemporary backstage scenes, mostly given to Ann Miller in probably the best role of her career: her plaintive query to boyfriend Tommy Rall, ''Why Can't You Behave?,'' her sizzling tap solo to ''Too Darn Hot,'' and her sly account of amatory dalliances in ''Always True to You in My Fashion.'' There are also Grayson and Keel's soaring duets to ''So in Love'' and ''Wunderbar.'' (The script's comic gangsters, played by James Whitmore and Keenan Wynn, and their song ''Brush Up Your Shakespeare,'' are emphatically *not* among the assets.) On the other hand, there are the songs composed as part of the *Shrew* musicalization, suggested by lines from Shakespeare's play. Graced with some of Porter's deftest and most marvelously intricate lyrics, they range from Grayson's vehement ''I Hate Men!'' to Keel's rousing ''Where Is the Life That Late I Led?'' and the beautiful ballad ''Were Thine That Special Face.'' In the colorfully designed *Shrew* sections, Ann Miller also does some first-rate, vigorous dancing, notably with Tommy Rall and Bob Fosse.

Kiss Me, Kate raises the question of Cole Porter's music on the screen. Although the score is one of the composer's brightest creations, it may possibly be *too* brittle and *too* witty to succeed as movie music. The uncluttered charm of Irving Berlin or the gentle lyricism of Jerome Kern work better in films. The music of a composer like Harry Warren, who has written almost exclusively for movies since the early thirties, may work best of all, since it is perfectly scaled to the screen's requirement for songs that are simpler, less intricate, more unabashedly melodic than those of the stage. The problem extends to Porter's lyrics as well. A great many of the lyrics of Ira Gershwin and Lorenz Hart have wit equal to Porter's but less of Porter's ultrarefined sophistication, which seems most dry and airless when it comes from a stage work like *Kiss Me, Kate*. Porter's music has always been most effective when rendered by theatrical personalities such as Alfred Drake or Ethel Merman, and has always suffered most when sung by strictly movie personalities, as in most of *Night and Day* and all of the later film *At Long Last Love* (1975). Ironically, his most successful film songs have been those that have been least characteristic of his style, such as the title tune of *Rosalie* and ''True Love'' in *High Society*.

By the mid-fifties, as the Hollywood musical continued to feel the impact of spiraling costs, dwindling markets, and the inroads made by television, MGM's stage adaptations seemed to lose their momentum. Most inexplicably, Vincente Minnelli's

1954 version of the Alan Jay Lerner–Frederick Loewe musical *Brigadoon* was a disappointment, a surprisingly drab and dispirited film that conveyed little of the play's magic. The elements for success were certainly there: the winning and melodious score; a whimsical book that managed to tiptoe through the minefield of fantasy without blowing up; a talented director whose last previous musical had been *The Band Wagon*; and a good cast headed by Gene Kelly, Cyd Charisse, and Van Johnson. The opening scene is enchanting: a Scottish village emerges from the shadows and the townspeople join in a lively rendition of ''Come Ye to the Fair.'' Yet *Brigadoon* seldom lifts off the ground.

As the American who becomes lost in the highlands of Scotland and comes upon Brigadoon, a village that comes to life only one day every hundred years, Gene Kelly sings and dances with his customary charm and skill. His lyrical dance with the lithe and beautiful Cyd Charisse to ''The Heather on the Hill'' rises above the obvious falseness of the setting, and his one important solo, to ''Almost like Being in Love,'' makes clever use of a hat and a coat as props. The rest of the cast goes through its paces with professional ease. Yet something is wrong: something that portends the decline of the musical film. The problem lay not only in the stifling soundstage ''exteriors'' or the off-putting distance between the audience and players created by the wide CinemaScope screen. It was more fundamental: a viewer could almost sense a lack of conviction in the material, a diluting of the creative juices that had made earlier musicals such a pleasure. (Reportedly, Minnelli was not happy with the assignment, and frequently differed with Kelly on interpretation.)

MGM's last stage-adapted musical of the fifties succeeded in restoring some of the quality that seemed to have vanished from this subgenre. In 1955, *Ninotchka*, Ernst Lubitsch's classic Greta Garbo comedy, had been turned into a moderately successful stage musical (called *Silk Stockings*) by George S. Kaufman, his wife Leueen McGrath, and Abe Burrows, with a score by Cole Porter. Since MGM had first refusal on the screen rights, Arthur Freed decided to produce the film version, costarring Fred Astaire and Cyd Charisse. His choice of a director alarmed the studio executives: Rouben Mamoulian had caused countless problems as the director of *Summer Holiday* back in 1946, and the movie had been a dire failure. But Freed insisted on Mamoulian, and the musical went into production. Janis Paige, Peter Lorre, Joseph Buloff, and Jules Munshin were assigned to other major roles, and Cole Porter contributed two new songs—''Fated to Be Mated'' and ''The Ritz Roll 'n' Rock''—to his original score.

The resulting musical, although several notches below the studio's best musical efforts, has definite virtues, the foremost being Fred Astaire. Although he worried about being too old for the role of a movie director in Paris who defrosts and falls in love with a forbidding lady Communist (Charisse), he was ageless when he danced, and he was still reasonably convincing in his love scenes. He sings ''All of You'' to Charisse with all of his old ardent feeling, dances athletically with her in a deserted movie studio to ''Fated to Be Mated,'' and joins Janis Paige, playing ''America's Swimming Sweetheart,'' in Cole Porter's clever ''Stereophonic Sound.'' His solo to ''The Ritz Roll 'n' Rock,''

Kismet *(MGM, 1955). In old Baghdad, the roguish Poet (Howard Keel) is entertained by the harem girls, while Lalume (Dolores Gray), the Wazir's seductive wife, looks on. Adapted from the stage musical,* Kismet *had an extravagant* Arabian Nights *setting and some lushly beautiful songs derived from the music of Alexander Borodin. But Vincente Minnelli's listless direction failed to make more of the musical than an overdressed pageant.*

Brigadoon *(MGM, 1954). Gene Kelly and Cyd Charisse dance to Lerner and Loewe's entrancing song "The Heather on the Hill." Unfortunately, in this instance the hill resembled papier-mâché.*

in which he wears his trademarked top hat and tails, is another display of his unchanging dancing agility.

For all its merits, *Silk Stockings* has an elegiac air about it, not only because of the waning dance careers of its stars. At a time when movie audiences preferred their musical films, when they preferred them at all, to be either folksy in the Rodgers and Hammerstein style or twitchy in the Elvis Presley mode, *Silk Stockings* had a degree of elegance and sophistication, and a deep interest in the dance, that made it seem already dated. There would be other film versions of stage shows ahead, many of them in the sixties, and some of them would be superior to *Silk Stockings* in many ways. But as Astaire danced his way through this Mamoulian film, he seemed like one of the last of a vanishing breed.

At 20th Century-Fox, the emphasis in adaptations of stage musicals was largely on the work of Richard Rodgers and Oscar Hammerstein II. The team that had altered the direction of the musical theater with *Oklahoma!* back in 1943 had since written a number of hugely successful musical plays characterized by Hammerstein's abundant sentiment (some said sentimentality) and good cheer, bounteous and flowing Rodgers melodies, and an occasional touch of social awareness. The balletic dances in these musicals, innovatively begun by Agnes de Mille in *Oklahoma!*, reflected or interpreted the musical's story. They were far removed from the precision tap dances by a beaming chorus, or the ballroom elegance of the Astaires. Above all, the Rodgers and Hammerstein musicals had a radiance, an optimism, and a whistle-clean innocence about them that brought entire families back into the theater. (One conspicuous exception was attributed to Hammerstein alone: the 1954 adaptation of his 1943 stage musical *Carmen Jones,* which Otto Preminger directed for Fox. Hammerstein's florid updating of the Bizet opera starred Dorothy Dandridge as the wicked Carmen and Harry Belafonte as her fatally infatuated lover.)

It took a number of years for the Rodgers and Hammerstein musicals to reach the screen—there could be no film versions until the last touring companies were disbanded—but by the time they did, they were ideal vehicles for the mid-fifties. Although many social critics deplored the complacent, "button-down" mood of the public in the Eisenhower years, it seemed a good time for Hammerstein homilies set to Rodgers melodies. Besides, these musicals were surefire properties that would certainly appeal to audiences who had been humming their songs for many years. It turned out to be not quite so simple.

Until *Carousel,* Fox's first-released Rodgers and Hammerstein adaptation, the studio had produced several versions of Broadway shows that merely accommodated their leading stars. *Gentlemen Prefer Blondes* (1953) leaned heavily on the obvious allure of Marilyn Monroe and Jane Russell, omitting (as the stage version had) most of the sly humor of Anita Loos's original story. In Irving Berlin's *Call Me Madam* (1953), Ethel Merman repeated her lusty Broadway performance as Mrs. Sally Adams, the "hostess with the mostes' on the ball," who becomes the American ambassador to the tiny mythical country of Lichtenburg. "You're Just in Love," Merman's show-stopping duet with her moonstruck press attaché, played here by Donald O'Connor, was reprised for the movie.

Silk Stockings *(MGM, 1957). Fred Astaire dances with Janis Paige in Cole Porter's musical version of* Ninotchka. *A vivacious redhead, Paige had done yeoman service in Warners musicals of the forties, then starred on Broadway in* The Pajama Game. *The role in* Silk Stockings *was her best in films.*

opposite: Silk Stockings *(MGM, 1957). In Cole Porter's title number, the very grim Ninotchka (Cyd Charisse) turns into a very alluring woman, entranced by her first pair of silk stockings.*

279

above: Carousel *(Fox, 1956). At Mrs. Mullin's carousel, barker Billy Bigelow (Gordon MacRae) attracts everyone's attention, especially that of Julie Jordan (Shirley Jones) and her friend Carrie (Barbara Ruick).*

opposite: Gentlemen Prefer Blondes *(Fox, 1953). Despite the glitter of their apparel (not to mention their bumps and grinds), Loreli (Marilyn Monroe) and her friend Dorothy (Jane Russell) insist musically that they are merely "Two Little Girls from Little Rock."*

left: Where's Charley? *(Warners, 1952). Ray Bolger repeated his acclaimed stage performance in this musical version of the perennial farce* Charley's Aunt. *Once again he was the frantic Oxford undergraduate who is forced to pose as his maiden aunt. Here he sings "Once in Love with Amy," the show-stopping number he had performed onstage. Frank Loesser wrote the score for this minor but enjoyable enterprise.*

The film version of *Carousel,* directed by veteran Henry King, appeared early in 1956 to captivate audiences with its superlative score and its touching story of Billy Bigelow, a bragging circus barker, and Julie, the wistful girl he loves and marries—Ferenc Molnár's *Liliom* transferred to New England in the 1870s. The original musical play, the team's first after *Oklahoma!,* had been applauded for songs that either established a time and place ("This Was a Real Nice Clambake," "June Is Bustin' Out All Over") or deepened and explained the characters ("If I Loved You," "You're a Queer One, Julie Jordan," or "Soliloquy," the seven-minute number in which Billy Bigelow meditates on his dreams and fears as an expectant father).

The movie *Carousel* has an abundance of riches, from the opening "Carousel Waltz," which sweeps the audience up with the irresistible lilt of its music, to the sentimental but touching climax in which the dead Billy returns to earth to make a mystical contact with his wife and daughter. The hectic activity of a "real nice" Maine clambake, the unfettered joy of a bright June day are beautifully realized in the settings, the costumes, and the entrancing Rodgers melodies. Also, Shirley Jones makes a fetching and poignant heroine and sings with charm and grace.

However, the film does have serious flaws. As Billy Bigelow, Gordon MacRae misses some of the character's swaggering but inwardly vulnerable nature, but he is acceptable. Much more damaging is the movie's tendency to mix pictorial styles in a confusing fashion. Scenes of pure fantasy, such as Billy's confrontation with the Starkeeper in a surrealistic movie heaven, mingle with sequences filmed on location, such as the number built around "June Is Bustin' Out All Over," shot on an actual dock in Boothbay Harbor, Maine. The problem of setting an appropriate pictorial style for a musical film—should the sets be purely stylized and unrealistic, or should they be actual locations, filmed exactly as they are?—has troubled many a producer. *Carousel* seems to have opted for both styles, with disconcerting results. (*Singin' in the Rain* had what appears to be the best solution: a slightly heightened, slightly stylized reality that tells the viewer immediately that he is inhabiting the special world of the musical film.) Complete stylization, as in *Guys and Dolls,* is usually distractingly ugly, and complete authenticity, as in *Oklahoma!,* can make the musical portions faintly ludicrous— why are these people singing and dancing on the open plains?

Some months after *Carousel,* Fox released its production of Rodgers and Hammerstein's musical play *The King and I.* Derived from Margaret Landon's book and a 1946 film, both titled *Anna and the King of Siam, The King and I* concerned a genteel Englishwoman who comes to Siam in the 1860s to tutor the many children of the autocratic but intellectually curious king. Before the king dies, Anna has learned to temper her outrage at his peremptory behavior toward her and at his primitive idea of justice with respect and admiration for his agile mind, and has come to feel an affection that borders on love. She has also learned something about the crucial differences between Eastern and Western ways of life, and about the meanings of pride, tolerance (and intolerance), and human limitations. Graced with a rich and singularly beautiful score, and skillfully directed by playwright John van Druten, *The King and I* was a major hit of the 1951 theater season.

South Pacific (Fox, 1958). "I'm Gonna Wash That Man Right Outa My Hair!" nurse Nellie Forbush (Mitzi Gaynor) exults. And so she does, while her colleagues watch in amusement.

preceding page: The King and I (Fox, 1956). Anna Leonowens (Deborah Kerr) attends the King of Siam (Yul Brynner) in his palace as he strives to understand another of the world's "puzzlements." A forceful and magnetic actor of mysterious ancestry, Brynner has never been given a role as fully rounded as that of the King.

opposite: South Pacific (Fox, 1958). Caught up in the spell of the islands, Lieutenant Cable (John Kerr) and Liat (France Nuyen) share a romantically idyllic moment. Unlike the tragic young lovers of The King and I, whose story tends to impede the action, this pair of doomed lovers provides an emotional counterpoint to the central romance of the story.

The studio had the good sense to cast Yul Brynner in his original stage role of the king. Brynner made the role his own, his imperious, stiff-backed stance and fierce, magnetic eyes denoting a royal leader who cannot be questioned or denied. Deborah Kerr was perfectly cast as Anna, conveying all the tenacity and melting compassion of the character. The production was sumptuous, capturing all the opulence of the Siamese court without overwhelming the story.

Under Walter Lang's direction, The King and I proved to be the best of the Rodgers and Hammerstein adaptations, for reasons that involve the transference of musical material from stage to screen. On the stage the musical was a lavish pageant; on the screen this pageantry is more expansive, drawing on the studio's bountiful resources. But in films pageantry is not enough: the mind can become benumbed by the constant extravagance of sets and costumes. A film requires a strong and viable narrative more than a stage play does. The King and I has such a narrative, and it forms a solid base that never crumbles under the weight of the pageantry.

The story also benefits from the subtle relationship between the leading characters. As they interact amid all the splendor of the court, we see two people of very different backgrounds drawing apart and then together, culminating in that most moving and triumphant of moments: when they dance together for the first time. The book permits us to enter into the complex mind of the king and into the feelings of an intelligent woman puzzled, intrigued, and deeply irritated by this man. The narrative is not perfect; the tragic subplot of the king's young concubine Tuptim and her secret lover may be necessary to dramatize the king's rigid code, but their clandestine meetings and their musical duets tend to impede the action. Yet the book of The King and I has a substance admittedly rare in a musical film.

The score is one of the treasures of the musical theater, and the film does it full justice. Dubbed by Marni Nixon, Deborah Kerr luminously recalls Anna's past in "Hello, Young Lovers," joins the king's children in the charming "Getting to Know You," and helps to make her dance with the king ("Shall We Dance?") a memorable sequence indicating their mutual admiration and sexual attraction. Yul Brynner gives "A Puzzlement" the proper mixture of arrogance, wonder, and confusion. As his head wife Lady Thiang, Terry Saunders expresses a familiar but dubious Hammerstein sentiment—love your man even when he is behaving badly or foolishly—in "Something Wonderful." The musical's set pieces, the delicious "March of the Siamese Children" and the ballet "The Small House of Uncle Thomas" (a Siamese version of Uncle Tom's Cabin), are staged with flair and a lavish hand. Yul Brynner was given an Academy Award as best actor, and the film was honored for its art direction, costume design, and music scoring.

Rodgers and Hammerstein's South Pacific, perhaps the most eagerly awaited filming of the team's musical plays, finally found its way to the screen in 1958. Produced on the stage two years before The King and I, South Pacific had received a tumultuous reception on its opening in 1949. Adapted from James Michener's Tales of the South Pacific, it offered an irresistible blend of ingredients: a wartime romance between a French planter (Ezio Pinza) and a young American nurse (Mary Martin); comic

cavortings by Seabees stationed on a Pacific island; a tragic subplot involving a young lieutenant and a native girl; and, of course, a cornucopia of Rodgers and Hammerstein songs.

The film version, however, was a severe letdown. Certainly all signs pointed to a reasonable facsimile of the original: an adaptation of the stage book by playwright Paul Osborn, the same director—Joshua Logan—who had guided the first stage production to success, and two perfectly acceptable stars in Mitzi Gaynor as nurse Nellie Forbush and Rossano Brazzi as planter Émile de Becque. (His singing voice was dubbed by Giorgio Tozzi.) Happily, Juanita Hall was signed to repeat her stage role as the pragmatic, ribald Bloody Mary, although her voice was dubbed by Muriel Smith, reportedly at the insistence of Rodgers and Hammerstein. Much of the film was shot on the Hawaiian island of Kauai, in settings that captured the lush beauty of the Pacific Islands.

Then what went wrong? Most of the blame for the film's failure has been placed on the photographic method used by Leon Shamroy, the principal cinematographer, who was responsible for a great many outstanding color films at Fox over the years. He chose to intensify the moods induced by the various songs by saturating the musical scenes with rainbow hues. Thus, when Juanita Hall sings "Bali Ha'i," the screen is bathed in green and purple colors filtered over the natural beach setting. Or when the leading players sing "Some Enchanted Evening" on a terrace facing a beautiful panoramic view of the island, the scene becomes distractingly unreal when a golden yellow fog covers everything in view. This photographic gimmickry not only made much of what had been entrancing on stage seem unnatural and hollow on the screen, it also served to call undue attention to the musical's faults: the Rover Boy antics of the Seabees, the preachiness and fuzziness of some of Hammerstein's sentiments, and the behavior of the island natives, which often seemed lifted from an old Dorothy Lamour South Seas movie. To this day, Joshua Logan deplores and repudiates the color experiment, calling it one of the worst mistakes of his career.

The one major Rodgers and Hammerstein musical film of the fifties that did not come from the Fox studios was *Oklahoma!* (1955), which the team had adapted from Lynn Riggs's folk play *Green Grow the Lilacs*. Produced by Arthur Hornblow, Jr., in the Todd-AO widescreen process, *Oklahoma!* was released a dozen years after the original production had opened to an acclaim that none of its creators expected. Today, its innovative qualities—the sunny radiance of the score, with its simple opening number of a cowboy on horseback praising the beauty of the morning, the unpretentious charm of the production, and Agnes de Mille's gay and spirited dances—are part of the *Oklahoma!* legend. In 1943, the musical was welcomed as an important step forward in the American musical theater.

The film version had several virtues but many more failings. There was still the unblemished beauty of the score, including the rousing title song, the cheerful bounce of "The Surrey with the Fringe on Top," the raucous humor of "I Cain't Say No," and the principal love ballad, "People Will Say We're in Love," which, in Hammerstein's usual fashion, avoids any direct statement of romantic feeling ("If I Loved You" and "Some Enchanted Evening" are two others). Some of the numbers are attractively staged, particularly Gene Nelson's singing, dancing, and rope-twirling to "Kansas City." The dances of Agnes de Mille are very much in evidence.

The first serious error was the selection of Fred Zinnemann as the director. Zinnemann had achieved a strong reputation for his direction of two important films of the early fifties, *High Noon* (1952) and *From Here to Eternity* (1953). But except for a brief stint in the early thirties as an assistant to Busby Berkeley in staging the dance numbers in *The Kid from Spain,* he had never directed a musical film, and his inexperience is evident in the cumbersome, unimaginative handling of many sequences that should have been light and airy. (Years later, Zinnemann admitted to Joshua Logan, who recorded it in his book *Movies, Real People and Me:* "I didn't do a good job. It was my first musical and I was in awe of Dick and Oscar. But I shouldn't have been. After all, this was their first film production [actually, *State Fair* was their first, in 1945], and I had had years of experience. I should have followed my own instincts, not theirs.")

The plot of *Oklahoma!*—who should take Laurey to the social: Curly, the cowboy who loves her, or Jud, the sinister farmhand?—is virtually nonexistent, and Zinnemann attempts to give it some weight by emphasizing its psychological undertones. These dark shadings are indeed present in the sunny original, but Zinnemann makes them even darker in his direction. This is especially true in his handling of Rod Steiger, who plays Jud with so many brutish snarls and leers that Laurey's terrified flight from him on the way to the social is like Fay Wray fleeing King Kong. Steiger is much too formidable an actor for a musical such as this—possibly for any musical—and he makes the character not only menacing as intended, but also unpleasantly pathological. In the dream ballet, whereas Curly and Laurey are represented by surrogate dancers, Jud is played by Steiger, making the dance's already heavily Freudian tone even more so, and giving an unnecessarily nightmarish cast to his imagined fight with Curly.

An even more serious error than choosing Fred Zinnemann as director was the decision to shoot much of the film on location, against actual outdoor settings. The grandeur of the scenery, impressive as it was in the Todd-AO process, worked against the nature of the show, turning a stylized, essentially small-scale musical fable into a Western epic. All at once the characters, familiar to most audiences from the years of touring companies, seemed slightly foolish against these awesome backgrounds, hopelessly quaint in their speech ("medder" for "meadow," "purty" for "pretty"), and coy in their ways. And when they sang and danced, a "feller" had to wonder, "What fer?" It had worked beautifully on the stage; on screen it looked phony and patronizing. The musical world is not the real world, and combining the two so arbitrarily only succeeded in diminishing both of them.

Other studios in the fifties, with less of an interest in the Broadway musical than either MGM or Fox, still turned occasionally to the stage for their more important releases. In 1957, Warners offered its film version of *The Pajama Game,* which had been one of the brightest hits of the 1954 theater season. A typical creation of the masterly George Abbott in its swift pace and boundless vitality, it revolved about the

The Pajama Game *(Warners, 1957). John Raitt, Doris Day, and the employees of the Sleep-Tite Pajama Factory model their product in the musical's colorful finale.*

opposite, above: Oklahoma! *(Magna, 1955). Cowboy Curly (Gordon MacRae) exclaims "Oh, What a Beautiful Mornin'" in the opening scene of this Rodgers and Hammerstein musical. On the stage, this scene, as simple and as straightforward as the song itself, heralded a historic change in the musical theater.*

opposite, center: Oklahoma! *(Magna, 1955). The cast assembles for a group photograph. Happily, the lyrical score of this musical remained intact, but Fred Zinnemann's direction had a heavy touch, some of the key roles were miscast, and the on-location photography was much too grandiose for such a charming but small-scale folk musical.*

opposite, below: Oklahoma! *(Magna, 1955). Gene Nelson as cowboy Will Parker has his doubts about the faithfulness of his flirtatious girlfriend, Ado Annie (Gloria Grahame). Nelson was a genial, able dancer from many Warners musicals. Grahame usually played pouting, sultry types, and this was her first major comedy role.*

The Pajama Game *(Warners, 1957). At the annual picnic of the Sleep-Tite Pajama Factory employees, Carol Haney gets carried away during the dance to "Once-a-Year-Day." Haney, an expert dancer and promising comedienne, was repeating her acclaimed performance in the original stage version. Her premature death was a loss to the theater and films.*

opposite, above: Pal Joey *(Columbia, 1957). Nightclub owner Joey Evans (Frank Sinatra) meets socialite Vera Prentice-Simpson (Rita Hayworth). The best feature of this scrubbed and only intermittently effective version of the stage musical was the profusion of fine songs by Rodgers and Hart, not all from the original score.*

opposite, below: Pal Joey *(Columbia, 1957). Frank Sinatra, at the piano, intimidates and fascinates socialite Rita Hayworth as he sings to her.*

Damn Yankees *(Warners, 1958). "Whatever Lola Wants, Lola Gets," Gwen Verdon sings to Tab Hunter—and she means it. This musical fantasy by the authors of* The Pajama Game *concerned a star baseball player (Hunter) in thrall to the Devil and his seductive emissary (Verdon).*

shenanigans at a pajama factory when a strike is called and the romantic leads, a union head and the factory superintendent, find themselves on opposite sides of labor-management relations. The amusing book by Abbott and Richard Bissell (from Bissell's novel *7 1/2 Cents*) was complemented by Richard Adler and Jerry Ross's first-rate score.

The usual Broadway-to-Hollywood routine was changed in that all but one of the central roles were cast with the original stage players: John Raitt as superintendent Sid Sorokin, Eddie Foy, Jr., as Vernon Hines ("Hinesy"), the wildly jealous factory timekeeper, Carol Haney as Gladys, his long-suffering girlfriend, and Reta Shaw as the ample secretary to the factory boss. To play heroine Babe Williams, the studio inevitably selected not Janis Paige, who had played the role on Broadway, but its leading musical star, Doris Day, a somewhat more mature and restrained actress-singer than the blonde hoyden who had made her debut nine years earlier.

The movie hewed closely to the original, except for an expanded picnic sequence. It showed surprisingly little cinematic flair for a musical codirected (with George Abbott) by Stanley Donen. Crisply and energetically, but without the added spark that ignites a truly superior film musical, it covers the essential territory: the arrival of handsome Sid Sorokin as the new superintendent of the Sleep-Tite Pajama Factory; the fracas over a seven-and-a-half cents pay increase; the tangled love affair of Sid and Babe Williams; and the final happy resolution of both the labor and romantic problems. Hinesy's unbridled jealousy and his proclivity for knife-throwing are not half as funny as intended, but the book is more than serviceable for a lighthearted musical comedy.

Choreographed by Bob Fosse, as they had been on the stage, the production numbers in *The Pajama Game* meet all the requirements for size, color, and variety: the "Once-a-Year-Day" picnic for Sleep-Tite employees, with scores of dancers gamboling across the greener-than-green grass; Carol Haney's show-stopping "Steam Heat" number with two partners at the union meeting; the cleverly staged song and dance at "Hernando's Hideaway," using lighted matches to good effect. The movie also manages a number of effective small-scale moments, such as the delightful soft-shoe dance of Eddie Foy, Jr., and Reta Shaw to the song "I'll Never Be Jealous Again," John Raitt's deeply felt rendition of the hit song "Hey, There," and his high-spirited duet with Doris Day, "There Once Was a Man."

Day is the film's one revelation, and she gives the best musical performance of her career. By now she had demonstrated her skill as a dramatic actress, but except for *Love Me or Leave Me* in 1955, she had not been given a role for years that made good use of her musical talent. Aptly cast as the no-nonsense but actually soft-natured union leader, she seems relaxed and glad to have the chance to sing. Performing "Small Talk" with John Raitt, she conveys a sense of amorous longing that is far removed from the "bland virgin" image she acquired in the early sixties, and her tearful reprise of "Hey, There" is a fine example of emoting through song.

The authors of *The Pajama Game* were not served nearly as well by the movie adaptation of their second stage success, *Damn Yankees* (1958). This musical fantasy concerned a middle-aged fan of the Washington Senators baseball team whom the Devil (Ray Walston) turns into a young hitting sensation (Tab Hunter). The amusing plot and a fairly good score all evaporated before the sizzling presence of the show's original star, Gwen Verdon. As the Devil's seductive emmissary Lola, she set an otherwise lukewarm musical to boiling, particularly with her inflammatory song "Whatever Lola Wants, Lola Gets." Like *The Pajama Game,* this musical was codirected by George Abbott and Stanley Donen.

The damage that can occur when a classic stage musical of one era is adapted as a film musical in another was demonstrated in Columbia's production of *Pal Joey* (1957). The original Rodgers and Hart musical, with a book by John O'Hara based on stories he had written for *The New Yorker,* had generally impressed Broadway in the fall of 1940, but some critics, including Brooks Atkinson of the *New York Times,* had been repelled by its cynical tone and its leading character, a disreputable nightclub entertainer. The show's brilliant score, however, had been widely praised. In turning *Pal Joey* into a vehicle for Frank Sinatra, Columbia removed most of the bite and turned Joey Evans from an opportunistic heel into a brash, "ring-a-ding" Sinatra-type swinger with a soft spot he tries to conceal.

The key role of the rich, predatory, and not-so-young Mrs. Prentice-Simpson was given to Rita Hayworth (Mae West was considered for the part), who gives a performance that is a swan song to her career as a sex goddess. Her biggest number, "Bewitched," dubbed by Jo Ann Greer, is photographed as a homage to her exalted status in the forties. She wakes up, and after stretching languorously across her bed in an echo of her old pinup photographs, she begins to move about the bedroom. She looks in the mirror admiringly, drapes herself across a chaise longue, and then takes a shower. All the while she is singing a slightly scrubbed version of Lorenz Hart's wittily suggestive lyrics. The last image is of her arms raised in the shower, the suggestion of her bare breasts showing through the glass door.

Pal Joey sensibly confined its score to Rodgers and Hart songs, although some of them ("I Didn't Know What Time It Was," "My Funny Valentine," "The Lady Is a Tramp") were not from the original musical play. Sinatra sings most of them extremely well, but his deliberate misinterpretation of "The Lady Is a Tramp," sung to Hayworth as a taunt to her "society bitch" manner, robs this song of all its wit and point. For all of its good music and its beautiful color photography of San Francisco, *Pal Joey* is thin gruel compared to the hearty stock of the original.

Producer Samuel Goldwyn's few film productions in the fifties included several musical stage adaptations. His 1955 version of the long-running musical *Guys and Dolls* had much in its favor. The original Jo Swerling–Abe Burrows book concerning Damon Runyon's fairy-tale Broadway world of sharpies and showgirls was transformed by Joseph L. Mankiewicz (who also directed) into a generally diverting screenplay, nicely flavored with the stylized Runyonesque patois. Most of Frank Loesser's excellent score, including "Fugue for Tinhorns," "Luck Be a Lady," and "Take Back Your Mink," was sensibly retained, and Michael Kidd re-created his flashy, vigorous dance routines.

On the whole, however, *Guys and Dolls* was something of a misfire. Aside from Joseph Mankiewicz's surprisingly pedestrian

direction and garish, stylized sets that failed to match the mood of Runyon's fable, the movie suffered from the miscasting of the leading male roles. As gambler Sky Masterson, who romances the Salvation Army "doll" Sarah Brown (Jean Simmons), Marlon Brando was heavy-handed and ill at ease, although he sang passably in his own voice. And Frank Sinatra, who would have made a persuasive Sky Masterson, played Nathan Detroit without conviction, missing all of the warm and likable quality that Sam Levene had brought to the role on Broadway. Only Vivian Blaine, repeating her stage role as Adelaide, gave an outstanding performance; her musical "Lament" about the psychosomatic symptoms caused by her fourteen-year engagement to Nathan is particularly fine.

Samuel Goldwyn's 1959 version of George Gershwin's folk opera, *Porgy and Bess,* closed out the decade. Gershwin, along with his brother Ira and DuBose Heyward, had fashioned the story of Catfish Row into a sensational but controversial stage success in 1935. Filmed in the widescreen Todd-AO process, the movie caught the teeming intensity of life in the black Charleston slum, and extracted every ounce of melodrama from the story of the crippled Porgy and his doomed love for Bess. Director Otto Preminger's heavy hand was evident in too many scenes (he had replaced the original stage director Rouben Mamoulian, who was discharged by Goldwyn), but the glorious music—"Summertime," "Bess, You Is My Woman Now," "It Ain't Necessarily So"— remained largely intact. In the leading roles, Dorothy Dandridge (dubbed by Adele Addison) and Sidney Poitier (dubbed by Robert McFerrin) were attractive, but somewhat too sophisticated. Diahann Carroll (dubbed by Loulie Jean Norman), Pearl Bailey, Brock Peters, and especially Sammy Davis, Jr., as an insinuating Sportin' Life, gave commendable performances.

Among the many stage-originated Hollywood musicals of the fifties, there were unquestionably a number that offered a high degree of entertainment. Yet even at their best there was a sense of constraint, of obeisance to the original material. Above all, there was a general failure to come to grips with the problems that invariably arise in transferring a stage musical to the screen. Characteristics of the stage version that may have made adaptation difficult—a thin or almost nonexistent plot line, or a heavily stylized physical production—were either ignored or mishandled when the camera took over. Many musical numbers that inspired ovations from theater audiences became wearisome on the movie screen. Too often there was a confusion of style and tone.

If there were few complaints from moviegoers, it was due in large part to the theater music that flooded the screen with melody: the seductive strains of Cole Porter, the heart-lifting romanticism of Richard Rodgers, the lilting enchantment of Jerome Kern, as well as the treasured wit and grace of lyricists such as Oscar Hammerstein II and Lorenz Hart. There was also the music of more contemporary composers such as Frank Loesser, Frederick Loewe, and Richard Adler. Many of them would continue to work actively into the sixties, enriching our lives with their words and music. We may point out the deficiencies of their creations, or the shortcomings of those who brought their work to the screen, but we can never deny the durable beauty of their art.

Set It to Music

Confronted by reduced production schedules and tighter budgets, the studios turned not only to the surefire properties from the musical stage but also to their own libraries of past successes, many of them nonmusical. They looked for films with tried-and-true story lines that could be easily musicalized (or so it seemed), as well as musical films that enjoyed a longstanding reputation as audience favorites. A new cast and a few new songs could be added to the ready-made screenplay, and lo, a new musical film was born for the fifties.

It all sounded reasonable, but more often than not the results were no improvement on or were worse than the original. This was especially true of the musical versions of comedy films in which the situations and the dialogue that had made the original movies so diverting were diluted or condensed to make room for the obligatory songs and dances. Moviegoers who could accept, and revel in, the delicious absurdity of a screwball comedy—a runaway heiress and a reporter hitchhiking on the highway, a husband doggedly pursuing his ex-wife—balked at seeing the same situations set to music. Also, the specialized comedy style of the original players—the tongue-in-cheek airiness of Irene Dunne and Jean Arthur, or the casual urbanity of Cary Grant and Melvyn Douglas—could not be matched by the more earthbound performers of the fifties.

The new versions of old musical films at least had the built-in advantage of the familiar songs, but they also had the inevitable disadvantage of being compared to well-loved original versions. There was the additional danger that the fifties audiences would be less responsive than audiences of two decades earlier to the attitudes and contrivances of the original: the pressed-flower romanticism of *Rose Marie,* for example, or the slightly musty merriment of *The Merry Widow.* Nevertheless, despite all these pitfalls, the studios persisted in remaking their old properties.

The leader in dressing old films in new musical garb was unquestionably Warner Bros. Time and again, it resuscitated its popular movies of the past, but the results were mostly negligible. The studio even went back to the birth of sound for an updated version of *The Jazz Singer* (1953), retaining the moss-laden plot of the cantor's son (Danny Thomas) who breaks his father's heart by going into show business. Since singer Peggy Lee played the hero's loyal girlfriend, there was time for some refreshing songs amid the copious tears. Often, Warners turned to its old comedy films for new musical treatment, hoping that added songs and color would suffice to give them a fresh look. Its hopes were in vain: *Brother Rat* (1938), the boisterous military farce, became a dismal film called *About Face* (1952). *A Slight Case of Murder* (1938), one of the funniest comedies of the thirties, was remade into *Stop! You're Killing Me!* (1952), in which such nonsingers as Broderick Crawford and Claire Trevor were ruthlessly forced to croak some tunes.

In 1938, *Four Daughters,* a sentimental but skillfully made drama concerning the romantic and familial troubles of four young girls, had been one of Warners's greatest successes of the year. The film had been most notable for introducing John Garfield as the cynical, ill-fated composer husband of one of the girls. Sixteen years later, Warners decided to set the story to music as a vehicle for its top star, Doris Day. To play the John Garfield role, the studio signed Frank Sinatra, who had recently revitalized his career with his Academy Award–winning performance in *From Here to Eternity*. The flippant, chip-on-the-shoulder attitude required by the character seemed a natural for Sinatra.

The movie, retitled *Young at Heart,* turned out to be a mistake. Reducing the number of daughters to three, it retained the story of a devoted New England musical family, and especially the involvement of one daughter (Doris Day) with a bitter, lonely piano player (Frank Sinatra). Despite the glowing color photography and several good songs, the movie seemed so lacquered and lifeless that it made the original look like *cinéma vérité*. Day and Sinatra were noticeably ill-matched, her cheerful effervescence failing to mesh with his brooding self-pity. The film's one strong note was Frank Sinatra's singing, especially his sensitive rendition of ''Just One of Those Things.''

Warners's most outstanding musical version of an old film was also released in 1954. Out of films since *Summer Stock* in 1950, Judy Garland had been interested for some time in starring in a musical treatment of David O. Selznick's *A Star Is Born*

above: A Star Is Born *(Warners, 1954). In one of her finest moments on film, Judy Garland gives a powerful, mesmerizing rendition of "The Man That Got Away."*

page 292: A Star Is Born *(Warners, 1954). With great warmth and tenderness, Esther Blodgett (Judy Garland) sings "It's a New World" to her new husband, Norman Maine (James Mason). Her performance in the film won her a well-deserved Academy Award nomination as best actress, but she lost to Grace Kelly in* The Country Girl.

right: A Star Is Born *(Warners, 1954). Judy Garland sings "Swanee" during the famous "Born in a Trunk" sequence, written for her by Roger Edens and Leonard Gershe, that was added after the film was completed. It made the film so long that twenty-seven minutes had to be cut from the original print to appease exhibitors.*

(1937), the Hollywood drama concerning a film star and her alcoholic husband. She finally acquired the rights, and after several traumatic personal setbacks, she began work on the film under George Cukor's direction. (Cukor had directed a little-remembered version of the story back in 1932, entitled *What Price Hollywood.*) The screenplay was written by Moss Hart, and Harold Arlen and Ira Gershwin composed six new songs. Roger Edens, Garland's mentor from her MGM days, was assigned to supervise the musical numbers.

Still heavily dependent on pills, Garland worked feverishly on *A Star Is Born,* word-perfect on one day and incoherent on another. At times it was impossible to get her to the studio, and nobody could shake her from her deep depression. Just when hope was abandoned, she would reappear and give one of her most expert, most astonishing performances. Costs mounted, and although not all the delays were due to Garland's fluctuating condition, she bore the largest burden of responsibility.

In its 1937 version, *A Star Is Born* had been an appropriate vehicle for winsome Janet Gaynor. Later, in 1976, it became a self-indulgent display for superstar Barbra Streisand. But at no time had the film's story been anything more than the ripest of corn. In Judy Garland's 1954 version, however, the corn is so well cooked and deliciously seasoned that it is irresistible. Moss Hart's full-bodied screenplay and George Cukor's adroit direction combine with all other elements to create a musical drama of power and conviction.

The first part of the film, in which Norman Maine (James Mason), the famous but skidding actor deep in the grip of his private demons, turns Esther Blodgett (Judy Garland) into movie star Vicki Lester, is rich in subtleties that are surprising for what is basically a Hollywood rags-to-riches fable. Esther's feeling for Norman—amusement turning to affection growing into love—is depicted skillfully and played by Garland with delicacy and humor. We also come to understand and appreciate Esther's great talent, not only in her performances but in her attitude toward her special gift. After a session at an after-hours club, she says, "I somehow feel most alive when I'm singing," and we believe her. Norman's pride in Esther is counteracted by his dangerous volatility.

Norman's descent, paralleled by Esther's rise to stardom, forms the emotional core of the film. At the Academy Award banquet, he makes an embarrassing drunken appearance while Esther is accepting her award, confirming his belief that he has "a genius—an absolute genius—for doing the wrong thing." Desolate at having to stand by helplessly as he destroys himself, Esther has a long, tearful speech—one of Garland's finest moments on film—to producer Oliver Niles (Charles Bickford) in her dressing room. Wearing a straw hat and painted freckles, she pours out her feelings with wrenching pain: "What is it that makes him want to destroy himself? . . . Love isn't enough . . ." From this point, Norman's downfall is swift, leading inexorably to his suicide. His funeral is a Hollywood nightmare, the screams of hysterical fans finally submerged by Esther's single scream of grief and anguish. The famous ending, when Esther appears at the benefit, may smack of glossy sentiment, but there is a cathartic release for the audience in her final lines: "Hello, everybody. This is Mrs. Norman Maine."

above: A Star Is Born *(Warners, 1954). An incredulous Esther (Judy Garland), now indisputably transformed into film star Vicki Lester, learns that she has won the Academy Award. At right: Charles Bickford.*

top: A Star Is Born *(Warners, 1954). Esther (Judy Garland) and Norman (James Mason) announce their engagement to producer Oliver Niles (Charles Bickford) and publicity man Libby (Jack Carson).*

James Mason's performance as Norman is among his finest, from his delight in Esther's remarkable voice to his last moments, as he listens with unbearable pain to her decision to give up her career. As the final vestiges of pride and dignity desert him, he achieves a kind of tragic grandeur. Garland also gives one of her best performances, one that runs the gamut of emotions with extraordinary skill. As usual, her nerve endings are almost too painfully exposed, but her professionalism never deserts her.

Garland's musical numbers are also superb, her audacious gestures, her throbbing voice, and her sense of showmanship all meshing beautifully under Roger Edens's guidance. Each number is like a miniature drama: her eloquent version of "The Man That Got Away" that makes the song a definitive hymn to lost love; her hushed and moving rendition of "It's a New World" to Norman on their wedding night; and her eighteen-minute, tour-de-force performance of "Born in a Trunk." Singing such familiar tunes as "Melancholy Baby" and "Swanee," she spoofs the sentimental Hollywood conception of how stardom is achieved, proving at the same time that Esther Blodgett *deserves* to become Vicki Lester. Later, for Norman's delectation, she performs a complete number in their living room, using the furnishings as props. It is an amusing and clever takeoff on grandiose production numbers, and it demonstrates, once again, Garland's gift for tongue-in-cheek comedy. The entire movie was a special triumph for her, the last time she could summon all her considerable resources and muster all her strength and tenacity for a performance that is quintessential Garland.

Twentieth Century-Fox also drew on its old films for musical fodder. *Wabash Avenue* (1950) was a lively, virtually scene-by-scene remake of *Coney Island,* starring Betty Grable in the role she had played eight years earlier. Looking none the worse for the intervening years, she was again the dance hall queen fought over by rival saloonkeepers, played with gusto by Victor Mature and Phil Harris. The settings of gaslight Chicago, replacing turn-of-the-century Coney Island, were properly gaudy, and the musical numbers were happily devoid of the elements that frequently turned *Coney Island* into forties camp. In her best and brassiest style, Grable sang "Wilhelmina," "Walking Along with Billy," and "I Wish I Could Shimmy like My Sister Kate."

In 1955, Fred Astaire appeared in his first (and only) Fox film, a musical remake of the venerable Jean Webster story *Daddy Long Legs.* He played a carefree millionaire who anonymously befriends and comes to love a young French orphan. Filmed in 1919 as a vehicle for Mary Pickford and again in 1931 with Janet Gaynor and Warner Baxter, the story seemed more than a little quaint for the mid-fifties. As usual, the studio gave it a lavish production to hide its age, gussying it up in De Luxe Color and photographing it in CinemaScope. Leslie Caron was cast opposite Astaire as the orphan waif.

Astaire and Caron dance together on several occasions, but not always successfully. It is not the difference in their ages but their contrasting styles that cause the lack of rapport. Astaire's elegant and uncluttered ballroom manner clashes too often with Caron's leaps and pirouettes, or, more specifically, with the highfalutin concepts of her mentor Roland Petit, who staged her numbers. They are relaxed and assured performing "The Sluefoot," another of the new dances that Astaire introduced over

above: Young at Heart *(Warners, 1954). Doris Day sings to Frank Sinatra in this musical remake of the popular 1938 film,* Four Daughters. *An incompatible team, the stars tried but failed to make something real of their characters' courtship and troubled marriage.*

top: The Jazz Singer *(Warners, 1953). Danny Thomas comes home to his parents, doting mother Mildred Dunnock and cantor-father Eduard Franz. The plot had served well enough for the landmark 1927 film, but now it creaked badly, and all the emotional carryings-on appeared hollow and dated.*

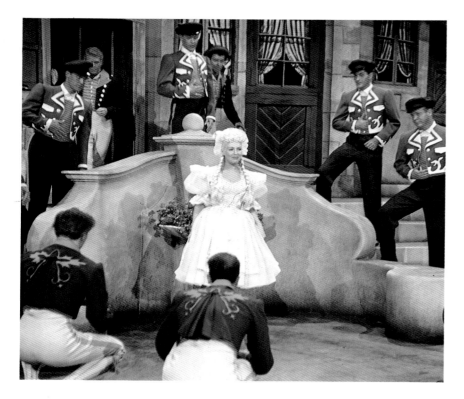

Wabash Avenue *(Fox, 1950)*. *Betty Grable sings "Wilhelmina" in this remake of her earlier musical film,* Coney Island.

Daddy Long Legs *(Fox, 1955)*. *Fred Astaire appears as a dapper aristocrat in Leslie Caron's dream, one of several guises he assumes in the ballet choreographed by Roland Petit.*

Daddy Long Legs *(Fox, 1955)*. *Fred Astaire and Leslie Caron danced together in this musical version of Jean Webster's story about a millionaire and the orphan he befriends anonymously. As a dance team, they were not well matched, but later, in his autobiography* Steps in Time, *Astaire praised Caron as "a fine artist, conscientious, apt, serious."*

opposite, below: My Sister Eileen *(Columbia, 1955)*. *Kurt Kasznar, Betty Garrett, Janet Leigh, and Dick York sing "We're Great but No One Knows It" on a Greenwich Village street. Those beleaguered sisters from Ohio—Ruth and Eileen Sherwood—have gone through many versions of Ruth McKenney's stories, originally published in* The New Yorker, *including a 1942 movie and a 1953 stage musical. There was even a short-lived television series in 1960.*

the years, but in a lavish and strikingly designed dream ballet, they seem to be incompatible. Caron, however, dances beautifully, in a variety of styles and moods. Astaire turns up briefly in a second Petit ballet, looking almost relieved to have so little to do. His best number is his song and dance to the marvelous Johnny Mercer song "Something's Gotta Give."

At Columbia Studios, the trend was to musicalize its most famous screwball comedies of the thirties, but judging from the results, it was a trend that should have been strenuously resisted. In 1953, the classic marital comedy *The Awful Truth* (1937) was set to music as *Let's Do It Again,* with Ray Milland and Jane Wyman trying gamely but vainly to duplicate the deft comedy performances of Cary Grant and Irene Dunne. *Too Many Husbands,* a 1940 Columbia comedy teaming Jean Arthur, Fred MacMurray, and Melvyn Douglas, was turned into the musical *Three for the Show* in 1955. Only some good Gershwin tunes kept Betty Grable, Jack Lemmon, and the dancing Champions, Marge and Gower, from sinking without a trace. Poor Jack Lemmon also had to contend with a ghastly song-and-dance version of the celebrated 1934 comedy *It Happened One Night.* Entitled *You Can't Run Away from It* (1955), it had Lemmon and June Allyson grappling hopelessly with the Clark Gable and Claudette Colbert roles, with no help from a few nondescript songs. Allyson was especially wrong, playing Ellie Andrews more like a pouty schoolmarm on a holiday than a flighty heiress on the run.

Jack Lemmon's luck in musical remakes was not all bad. In 1955, he played a leading role in Columbia's musical version of *My Sister Eileen,* based on the 1942 film starring Rosalind Russell and the 1940 stage play by Joseph Fields and Jerome Chodorov. The new movie retained the plot concerning two Ohio sisters (Betty Garrett and Janet Leigh) who arrive in Greenwich Village and become involved in a series of madcap adventures. Ruth (Garrett), the older, sharper, and supposedly less attractive sister, even finds romance with a magazine editor (Lemmon). In this case, the original play's structure proved to be sturdy enough to support the musical interpolations, and the Jule Styne–Leo Robin songs were better than average. Garrett and Leigh made a charming pair of sisters (Garrett's alleged plainness was clearly nonsense), and they sang and danced with considerable verve. Even Jack Lemmon got to sing a ballad with Garrett called "It's Bigger than You or Me." A standout in the cast was Bob Fosse, in one of a handful of appearances in fifties films as an actor and dancer. Agile and ingratiating, he demonstrated the skill that would emerge fully in later years.

As might be expected, MGM's hardworking production units also turned out either new versions of their familiar old musical warhorses or song-and-dance versions of their popular comedy films from the past. In doing so, however, they made two grave mistakes: testing and challenging the long memories of film buffs who revered the original films, and casting the films with performers who could not measure up to the earlier players in popularity or charisma. Too often in these remakes, dialogue or songs that had once sparkled like champagne became *vin ordinaire.*

An example was *High Society* (1956). Philip Barry's *The Philadelphia Story* had been a stage success for Katharine Hepburn in 1939, and she was equally triumphant in MGM's 1940 film version. The movie was a witty and silken-smooth romantic

On the Riviera *(Fox, 1951)*. *Danny Kaye is frolicsome as Bobo the Puppet in a musical number. The film was the third version of a French play that had served as the basis for* Folies Bergère *in 1935 and* That Night in Rio *in 1941. Kaye played both a financier and a nightclub entertainer, whose identities are shuffled about during the course of one evening. The musical highlight was Kaye's rendition of "Ballin' the Jack."*

above: The Opposite Sex *(MGM, 1956). Ann Miller and Dolores Gray get into a furious tussle, with June Allyson and Agnes Moorehead trying to separate them. In the original nonmusical film,* The Women, *the participants in the tug of war were Paulette Goddard and Rosalind Russell, with Norma Shearer and Mary Boland as the referees. This musical version of* The Women *extracted some of the venom from the original play and film and substituted bland musical numbers.*

opposite, below: The Opposite Sex *(MGM, 1956). Dressed to the nines and taking a brief respite from their constant warfare are (from left) Joan Collins, Dolores Gray, June Allyson, Ann Miller, and Ann Sheridan.*

comedy concerning a haughty, rich Philadelphia girl who discovers humility while rediscovering the virtues of her ex-husband. In the role that had been tailored for her, Hepburn was at her radiant, eccentric best, and her costars were perfectly cast: Cary Grant as her ex-husband, and James Stewart as the writer, disdainful of the rich, who finds Hepburn an irresistible revelation.

The 1956 musical version changed the setting to a very posh Newport, retained much of the original Barry dialogue, and added a Cole Porter score. It then proceeded to negate all these virtues by the miscasting of the central roles. To play the reluctant "goddess" Tracy Lord, the studio chose Grace Kelly, lovely indeed and to the manner born, but with a coolly elegant air that often resisted defrosting. In scenes that required the softening of her unyielding nature, she still seemed aloof. As her bemused and still loving ex-husband C. K. Dexter-Haven, Bing Crosby was woefully miscast, his patented casual air missing all the subtlety and irony of the role. Frank Sinatra was unconvincing as the smitten writer, his flip style making it seem unlikely that he had ever written a sentence.

In spite of these shortcomings, there were incidental pleasures in *High Society,* mostly in Cole Porter's score. Crosby and Sinatra (how potent a box-office combination that must have seemed to MGM) team up for a clever spoof of party mores in "Well, Did You Evah?," and Sinatra and Celeste Holm sing "Who Wants to Be a Millionaire?" as their awed reaction to the Lord mansion. Sinatra's songs to Kelly, "You're Sensational" and "Mind if I Make Love to You?," are first-rate examples of seductive Porter ballads. Crosby's songs are the least impressive, although the simplistic "True Love," sung with Grace Kelly in a flashback, was a popular hit. He also joined with Louis Armstrong, on hand for a Newport Jazz Festival, in a musical jazz lesson called "Now You Has Jazz."

That same year, MGM compounded the felony by releasing a musical version, entitled *The Opposite Sex,* of its 1939 comedy *The Women.* Clare Boothe's acid stage play had originally been turned into one of the studio's all-star features, which retained a surprising amount of the play's rampant bitchiness and wide-spreading venom. The new version, brightly Technicolored and featuring a display of fifties fashions, cast June Allyson as the devoted wife who sees her marriage wrecked. To explain the addition of five songs, she played a former singer who could still belt out a tune with Harry James's band. Once again, the material resisted musicalizing—the songs seem detached from the story and merely slowed the movie's rapid pace to a crawl. The film's only true amusement came from the actresses supporting Allyson, notably Ann Sheridan and Agnes Moorehead, who obviously knew their way about a sardonic line.

For a while in the fifties, MGM seemed intent on reviving vintage operettas in lavish new Technicolor versions, hoping to reach romantic-minded moviegoers who loved their music and who had never seen, or had forgotten, earlier editions. The first to appear was an opulent new production of *The Merry Widow,* the perennial Franz Lehár operetta. The 1934 film had been a stunning achievement with both Jeanette MacDonald and Maurice Chevalier at the peak of their forms. The 1952 version starred Lana Turner, a glamorous actress with no evident musical talent, as the widow Sonia, who bewilders and bewitches the dashing

left: High Society (MGM, 1956). Frank Sinatra sings "You're Sensational" to Grace Kelly.

opposite, above: High Society (MGM, 1956). Bing Crosby is an unwelcome arrival on the day before the upcoming wedding of his ex-wife (Grace Kelly). Louis Calhern, as Kelly's delightfully "wicked" uncle, observes the exchange of words. Despite a handsome production and some good Cole Porter songs, the musical failed to erase the memory of the glowing original, The Philadelphia Story.

The Merry Widow *(MGM, 1952)*. *Lana Turner as the resplendent widow Sonia and Fernando Lamas as dashing Count Danilo in a beautifully designed but rather lifeless fifties version of the warhorse musical.*

Count Danilo. Most of the songs fell to her costar, Argentine actor Fernando Lamas.

The resulting film *looked* marvelous, with sumptuous décor and lavish costumes that dazzled the eyes. This time there was little doubt that the widow Sonia *was* the richest person in Marshovia. And Turner and Lamas make a glittering romantic couple in the best Hollywood tradition, dancing to the familiar refrain of the "Merry Widow Waltz" amid swarms of elegantly attired couples in a giant ballroom. But off the dance floor they fail to convey even a hint of the sparkle and sophistication that MacDonald and Chevalier brought to their roles. Although the decadence that Erich von Stroheim suggested in his silent version is wisely avoided, little is offered in its place. Lamas provides a touch of Latin elegance, and he gives good renditions of "I'm Going to Maxim's" and "Girls, Girls, Girls" in a strong baritone. But Turner makes an inexpressive Sonia, appearing rather like a gorgeously gowned mannequin in a museum display of period clothing for the very wealthy.

Another fifties operetta from MGM was Sigmund Romberg's *The Student Prince,* which had been filmed by Ernst Lubitsch in 1927 with Ramon Novarro as the young prince whose love for a barmaid causes royal flutterings. The new film (1954) retained the most popular songs from the original 1924 stage musical, filling theaters with the schmaltz-laden sounds of "Serenade" and "Deep in My Heart, Dear." (Three new songs by Nicholas Brodszky were added to the score.) The movie attracted attention from the press when its original star, Mario Lanza, was removed from the cast due to his thickening waist and deepening emotional problems. He was replaced by a handsome young British actor named Edmund Purdom, who mouthed the songs to Lanza's prerecorded voice. As the barmaid, Ann Blyth joined him in several duets.

During the fifties, the studio archives proved to be not very fruitful as a source of new story material for musical films. Too often the popular or prize-winning comedy movie of the past resisted musicalizing. Caught up in their romantic or marital problems, the characters seemed to have no compelling reason to burst into song or to begin dancing. (*Carefree,* which could have been played as a screwball comedy without music, was one of the weakest Astaire-Rogers musicals.) The songs merely held up the action without embellishing it. The men and women inhabiting the memorable comedy films of the thirties and forties used words as tools for seduction, or as weapons to wound each other. Why bother to sing or dance? But the characters in the best musical films wanted to—*had* to—sing and dance. Words were simply inadequate. And therein lay the crucial difference.

Judging by the evidence, it was no easier to remake old musical films with much success. The earlier singers, sanctified by time and memory, hovered like ghosts over the new players, putting them at a disadvantage. Also, in a time when moviegoers were more sophisticated and more attuned to realism, it proved difficult for them to accept the floridly romantic conventions of the venerable operettas.

Yet film producers are forever dauntless, and we may expect some day to see a new film version of *The Vagabond King* entitled *Oh, François!,* or perhaps a musical version of *Animal House* called *Slobs Go Collegiate.* In the world of movies, anything is possible.

opposite, below: Rose Marie *(MGM, 1954)*. *On a cliff, lovers Fernando Lamas and Ann Blyth watch a tribe of Indians dance to "Totem Tom-Tom," staged by Busby Berkeley in one of his last assignments for MGM. (Note the* papier-mâché *look of the studio "mountain.") In this musical remake, neither Ann Blyth nor Howard Keel (as the Mountie) could remove the indelible image of Jeanette MacDonald and Nelson Eddy in the 1936 movie. Rudolf Friml contributed a few new songs, and the color and CinemaScope photography added pictorial values, but the result was hardly worth the effort.*

The Student Prince *(MGM, 1954). The ardent prince (Edmund Purdom, singing in Mario Lanza's voice) serenades the enchanted barmaid (Ann Blyth) in Sigmund Romberg's operetta. The brief operetta cycle in the mid-fifties ended with a film not from MGM but from Paramount—a new production of Rudolf Friml's* The Vagabond King *(1956), starring Kathryn Grayson and a tenor from Malta with the single professional name of Oreste.*

LET US ENTERTAIN YOU

The forties had given us highly fictionalized musical films on the lives and careers of the great popular composers, but most of the "biomusicals" of the fifties veered in another direction. To compete with television which, in the fashion of forties musicals, could easily offer up a string of tunes as a "testimonial" to any composer, the studios turned to the leading entertainers, past and present, whose lives were far from the serene plateaus of Jerome Kern or Richard Rodgers. Not every entertainer qualified for this dubious immortality. He or she would have to have had a career marked by personal tragedy, scandal, or at least serious setbacks. Romances and even marriages could be invented—and were—but it was helpful if there were a goodly number of songs associated with the entertainer. Select a star who may not bear the slightest resemblance to the subject, but who could sing or mime the material with conviction, wrap the entire package in bright color, and you had a biomusical for the movie-going public of the fifties.

There were a few biographical holdovers from the forties. Several of the major composers who had been passed over in other years were given their just due in the fifties. Gus Kahn, who had written the words for many popular songs until his death in 1941, was eulogized in a better-than-average Warners musical called *I'll See You in My Dreams* (1951). The Kahn songs were plentiful and tuneful, Danny Thomas played Kahn with becoming restraint, and Doris Day as his wife Grace gave many of the tunes the benefit of her lyrical, delicately shaded renditions. At MGM, composer Sigmund Romberg's "story" was used as an excuse to assemble an expensive "guest star" musical called *Deep in My Heart* (1954), directed by Stanley Donen. Jose Ferrer played the Vienna-born Romberg who arrives in America and proceeds to delight and impress leading show business figures of the day. Romberg songs were staged with variable success for Gene Kelly, Cyd Charisse, Jane Powell, Ann Miller, Metropolitan Opera star Helen Traubel, and Rosemary Clooney, who was Mrs. Ferrer at the time.

Fox contributed several others: *Stars and Stripes Forever* (1952), which transformed "March King" John Philip Sousa into testy Clifton Webb; *The I Don't Care Girl* (1953), suggested by the career of vaudeville star Eva Tanguay (Mitzi Gaynor); and *The Best Things in Life Are Free* (1956), concerning the careers of songwriters DeSylva (Gordon MacRae), Brown (Ernest Borgnine), and Henderson (Dan Dailey). But in view of the emerging interest in frank "confessional" literature, which would continue throughout the decade and into the sixties, it seemed wiser and more profitable to set aside the comparatively bland composers and concentrate on performers whose lives were fraught with inspirational drama. Of course, if the upbeat ending could be preceded by sordid or melodramatic details, all the better. Some of these problems had been touched on decorously in biomusicals of the forties (Cole Porter's riding accident, Lorenz Hart's drinking), but now they were placed squarely in the open, at the center of the entertainer's emotional turmoil.

Hollywood had always preferred to place the burden of life's dilemmas and traumas on the heads of women, and so women entertainers drew the brunt of the emotional upheavals in fifties biomusicals. On two occasions, Susan Hayward, a capable actress with the slightly hard edge that made her a good choice to play tough, resilient women, starred in musical dramas concerning entertainers who survived adversity. In *With a Song in My Heart* (1952), she played singer Jane Froman, who had suffered crippling injuries when her plane carrying entertainers to the men in service crashed during World War II. The story sketched in the singer's early success, then focused on her helplessness and despair after the near-fatal accident. Her ordeal in trying to overcome her handicap and resume her career was covered in a banal screenplay that reached the height of mawkishness in a scene where crippled Froman sings for a shellshocked paratrooper (Robert Wagner) and restores his powers of speech. But the film was also a musical, after all, and Jane Froman's full-bodied, somewhat overripe voice was used for a number of fine old songs, including "That Old Feeling," "Blue Moon," and the title song, while Hayward mimed the appropriate gestures convincingly.

Three years later, Susan Hayward was in deep trouble of a different kind, playing singer-actress Lillian Roth in a film version of Roth's best-selling book, *I'll Cry Tomorrow* (1955), which she had written with Gerold Frank and Mike Connolly. Starred or

Deep in My Heart *(MGM, 1954). Gene Kelly and his brother Fred sing and dance to Sigmund Romberg's "I Love to Go Swimmin' with Wimmen." At the extreme right in the chorus of bathing beauties is Barrie Chase, who danced with Fred Astaire in the sixties on several award-winning television specials.*

page 304: Love Me or Leave Me *(MGM, 1955). Doris Day in an uncharacteristic role as singer Ruth Etting. Her new, more mature approach to her songs and her impressive acting ability in a basically serious role won praise from the critics.*

opposite: With a Song in My Heart *(Fox, 1952). Susan Hayward as Jane Froman raises her voice in song. She received an Academy Award nomination for her performance but lost to veteran actress Shirley Booth (Come Back, Little Sheba).*

featured in films of the late twenties and early thirties, Roth had revealed a pert personality and a hearty singing voice, but a series of personal crises had led her to excessive drinking. An out-of-control alcoholic, she had plummeted to a life of degradation and despair. With the help of Alcoholics Anonymous, and an ex-alcoholic who befriended and finally loved her, she was able to begin the long way back to a normal existence.

Roth had told her story candidly and without self-pity, and the film version, directed by Daniel Mann, sought to be equally honest, with a minimum of Hollywood sugarcoating and an absence of color or widescreen photography. Hayward was Roth's own choice for the role—she had found the actress to be a kindred spirit, feisty, emotional, and resilient. "It was almost like looking in a mirror," she remarked later (Doug McClelland, *Susan Hayward*). Strengthening her performance with visits to jails, hospitals, and AA meetings, Hayward gave no quarter in depicting a once proud, talented woman in the throes of alcoholism, her voice raspy and liquor-soaked as she twitched, shuddered, and ranted her way toward near-oblivion. She was also impressive singing (in her own voice) many tunes associated with Roth.

The career of Ruth Etting, the popular singer of the twenties and thirties, was dramatized by MGM in *Love Me or Leave Me* (1955), one of the better biomusicals of the period. Etting, who gave definitive renditions of many songs in her smooth and distinctive voice, had had a stormy relationship with a Chicago gangster named Marty ("The Gimp") Snyder, and that relationship became the basis for the film's unusually sharp screenplay. The central role called for an actress who could be alluring, tenacious in the face of repeated emotional blows, and capable of singing or at least miming a large number of songs. The studio made a surprising choice in Doris Day, calling upon her to play emphatically against type.

She came through with one of her most effective performances, playing Ruth Etting as a tough, ambitious woman who becomes the total obsession of Marty Snyder (James Cagney), a crook who forces his way into Chicago's speak-easies and insists on their using his laundry service. The film traces Etting's rise from a dime-a-dance hostess to acclaimed star, her shaky marriage to Snyder, her growing feeling for a pianist (Cameron Mitchell) who has always loved her, and the final outcome when Snyder, insanely jealous, shoots the pianist (now a music conductor at a Hollywood studio) and goes to prison. Etting, out of a sense of obligation, pays Snyder's bail and agrees to star in his nightclub.

Day holds her own with Cagney, whose typically intense, vibrant performance as Snyder dominates the film. (It was the first time since 1931 that he was billed after his leading lady.) In their explosive exchanges, she removes virtually all the softness that marked her earlier, cheery-ingenue performances. His rough treatment of her, despite his slavish devotion, and her inability to escape his powerful hold on her life make their relationship exceptionally candid and even bold for a fifties film. Musically, Day is superb, not only giving her expected silken renditions of twenties standards associated with Etting, such as "You Made Me Love You," "Shaking the Blues Away," and the title song, but adding a sexiness indicating that the girl next door

I'll Cry Tomorrow *(MGM, 1955). As the trouble-plagued Lillian Roth, Susan Hayward sang in her own voice. Suspecting that she might be able to do her own singing, MGM's music supervisor Johnny Green had her make a recording and was pleased with the result. ("She sounded great! I played the tape for the big brass and at my suggestion they decided to let her do her own songs.")*

I'll Cry Tomorrow *(MGM, 1955). Susan Hayward as singer-actress Lillian Roth belts out "Sing, You Sinners" in a production number. (Roth had performed the song in the 1930 musical* Honey.) *Nominated for an Academy Award for the fourth time, Hayward lost again, this time to Anna Magnani in* The Rose Tattoo.

Love Me or Leave Me *(MGM, 1955). At the bottom of the ladder and on her way up, ambitious singer Ruth Etting (Doris Day) is one of the dance hall hostesses she later immortalized in the song "Ten Cents a Dance." The movie marked the birth of a new Day, torchy, sensual, and not above giving as good as she got.*

Love Me or Leave Me *(MGM, 1955). Doris Day performs as singer Ruth Etting.*

had been getting out of the neighborhood. It was Cagney, however, who received an Oscar nomination as best actor.

Apart from the music and the sterling performances by Day and Cagney, *Love Me or Leave Me* was not always successful. Charles Vidor's direction sagged noticeably in the second half of the film, and he was unable to make Day's relationship with Mitchell seem anything but dull. The movie also made clumsy use of the CinemaScope screen (a common failing). Still, the movie was extremely popular and won strong reviews that commented mostly on Day's new adult look and impressive acting ability in a dramatic role.

Another singer of Ruth Etting's era received indifferent treatment in Warners's *The Helen Morgan Story* (1957). Morgan's haunting voice, her pathetic vulnerability, and her increasingly ravaged appearance due to alcoholism should have been the components for a sturdy musical drama. But the film failed to capture her special qualities, settling for mostly fictionalized soap opera. Ann Blyth played Morgan without much conviction (Gogi Grant dubbed her songs), and Paul Newman, in his fourth film, played the cheap and abusive bootlegger she cannot help loving.

Not all the women performers whose lives were dramatized were self-destructive slaves to passion or liquor. *Interrupted Melody* (1955) was more in the vein of *With a Song in My Heart*: the inspirational drama of the person who rises above a severe physical handicap and triumphs in his/her profession. This entry dealt with Marjorie Lawrence, the opera singer who was stricken with polio at the peak of her career. Eleanor Parker played the singer with the requisite chin-up attitude, bringing Lawrence from a farm in Australia to the opera scene in France and in America, where she made a triumphant debut at the Metropolitan Opera. The movie covers her marriage to a doctor (Glenn Ford), the attack of poliomyelitis that almost ended her life, and the painful, racking struggle to resume her career. A number of operatic excerpts were well-staged, with Parker "singing" in the voice of soprano Eileen Farrell. With a persuasive performance by Parker that earned her an Academy Award nomination, a superior screenplay by William Ludwig and Sonya Levien, and direction by Curtis Bernhardt that kept the soapsuds under control, *Interrupted Melody* was sturdier than many other bio-musicals. It was infinitely better than the banal *So This Is Love* (1953), which professed to be the life story of opera and film star Grace Moore, played by Kathryn Grayson.

Apparently, few male entertainers suffered the vicissitudes that seemed continually to plague the ladies. *The Eddie Cantor Story* (1953), produced by Hollywood columnist Sidney Skolsky for Warners, merely skimmed across the highlights in the half-century career of Cantor. There were some pleasant nostalgic touches in the screenplay, and a good number of Cantor's familiar songs, sung by the comedian himself, but Keefe Brasselle was painfully inadequate as the adult Cantor, and the frail story—performer pursues success at the expense of his home life—was tattered beyond repair. A similar idea of the entertainer who must double reluctantly as a family man didn't help *The Seven Little Foys* (1955), Paramount's film about vaudevillian Eddie Foy and his band of sibling troupers. Bob Hope sang, danced, and even emoted strenuously as Foy, but the movie's highlight was his amiable dance with James Cagney, briefly appearing as

The Seven Little Foys *(Paramount, 1955). Bob Hope as Eddie Foy goes off on a picnic with his seven none-too-happy children.*

opposite: Interrupted Melody *(MGM, 1955). Eleanor Parker as singer Marjorie Lawrence, in a scene from Camille Saint-Saëns's opera* Samson et Dalila. *Her voice was dubbed by Eileen Farrell.*

sixties musical star was cool and impeccable Julie Andrews.) The best musical film directors were either largely inactive or confining their work to dramatic films, leaving the field to either nonmusical or stage-trained directors.

The most popular musical film of the sixties was *The Sound of Music*. But the sound of music was growing fainter.

George M. Cohan.

One of the most widely attended musical films to focus on an entertainer was Universal's *The Glenn Miller Story* (1954), a tribute to the bandleader whose mellow sound had been hugely popular in the early forties. Miller and his orchestra had appeared in several Fox musicals during that period, and then Miller had

PART V
THE FADING
SOUNDS OF MUSIC
1960~1980

By the sixties, the musical film was already a faint echo of what it once had been. The cost of producing a musical was now astronomically high, and yet with dubious logic many filmmakers believed that only giant-size musicals could lure audiences away from their television sets. As the money poured into individual musicals increased, the total number of musical films diminished. At the same time, many of the major studios began converting to television production, knowing that films for television not only had manageable budgets but could also claim an assured audience. In addition, the overseas market for Hollywood musicals had dwindled considerably, especially in Western Europe, where television was becoming all-pervasive.

As in the late fifties, most of the musicals made in the sixties were adapted from stage successes. They were expensive and carefully produced, usually cast with certified box-office attractions who may or may not have been ideal for the roles, and launched with the appropriate ballyhoo. They were "prestige" productions in every sense. Yet even more discernibly than in the fifties, these musicals often lacked the breath of life. Some of them, such as *My Fair Lady* and *Hello, Dolly!*, were visually stunning examples of the skills at which Hollywood's technicians excelled. Many of them brimmed with melodies that gladdened the heart with their beauty. Occasionally a performance would quicken the pulse of a musical, such as Robert Preston's energetic tour de force in *The Music Man*. But, in general, for all the dazzle and glitter, the sixties musicals seemed preserved rather than produced, with the meticulously created but lifeless and vaguely unsettling look of figures in a wax museum.

It is only possible to speculate on the reasons. Certainly caution played a part—with so much money and prestige at stake it was safer to give the public a careful reproduction of the musical play that many of them had seen and loved. Caution was also responsible for casting the central roles with "bankable" stars rather than with performers who may have created the parts on stage.

Yet it was more than caution that turned the Hollywood musical from a singing and dancing sprite, bursting with vitality, into an overdressed mannequin. The sixties musicals, on the whole, lacked the cinematic daring, the enthusiastic belief in the possibilities of the musical film that made earlier musicals so exciting. Too often their directors were either men of high reputation in the film industry who had seldom or never worked in the musical genre (William Wyler, Fred Zinnemann), or men whose major credits were in the theater or television (Joshua Logan, Morton Da Costa). Though undeniably skilled, they seemed incapable of stretching these skills to meet the special demands of the musical film. They were also handicapped by having to work with widescreen processes which permitted little rhythmic cutting and a minimum of varying camera angles. Even those directors who had proven themselves in musicals over the years were unable to approach their best work: Vincente Minnelli's only musical for the decade, *Bells Are Ringing* (1960) was markedly inferior to his forties or fifties films. Gene Kelly's *Hello, Dolly!* (1969) was hardly in a class with *On the Town* or *Singin' in the Rain*.

With the exception of *West Side Story,* the stage-adapted musicals of the sixties broke no new ground in their approach or subject matter. Some familiar themes regularly emerged: the nostalgic pleasures, whether real or imagined, of American life in supposedly more innocent days, especially the old-time show business world; the quirks, fashions, and obsessions of the contemporary American scene; and the civilized grace and eccentric ways of Great Britain. (The last theme had been popular for many years in nonmusical films, but the huge Broadway success of *My Fair Lady* in 1956 precipitated a taste for British-based musicals that carried over to the screen throughout the sixties.) There were isolated other subjects as well. But the changes in musical theater that extended to films would come later, especially with the infiltration of a new, more contemporary musical sound.

There would always be room on stage or screen for a celebration of old-fashioned American virtues, and certainly the juiciest slice of musical Americana to be filmed in the early sixties was Warners's adaptation of Meredith Willson's *The Music Man* (1962). A longtime composer and musical conductor, Willson (collaborating on the story with Franklin Lacey) had written a loving comic valentine to pre–World War I America, embellished with a group of his unpretentious, lilting songs. With Robert

Preston as its galvanic star, *The Music Man* had opened to acclaim in the fall of 1957. It was hardly an advance in the art of musical comedy, but its wholesomeness and bright American spirit appealed to theatergoers.

Five years later, the film version, with Preston repeating as the star and Morton Da Costa again in charge of direction, opened to an equally favorable reception. In truth, there is little reason to resist the honest blandishments of *The Music Man*. Cheerful and bandbox-pretty, it tells of one "Professor" Harold Hill (Preston), a crafty traveling salesman who arrives in River City, Iowa, in 1912 with the intention of convincing the townspeople to buy the instruments and uniforms for a boys' band that he says he will train and lead. Actually, Professor Hill cannot read a note of music. Before he is found out, he manages to fall in love with the town's librarian, Marian Paroo (Shirley Jones), and he also transforms River City into a singing and dancing community. An adoring Marian convinces the townspeople to forgive him.

The undernourished plot of *The Music Man* is rightfully concealed under the many colorful musical numbers that spring up at every opportunity. Inevitably, Robert Preston's Harold is given the best of them: the irresistible "Trouble" in which he persuades the River City folks that their boys are heading for damnation ("We've got trouble—right here in River City!"); the splendid "Marian the Librarian," in which his seductive attentions to a not-overly-reluctant Marian in her library lead to an expertly staged dance by her patrons; and, of course, the musical's biggest hit song, "76 Trombones," which Preston makes virtually his own with every confident stride and strut. The musical's ensemble numbers are also energetic fun. "The Wells Fargo Wagon," involving the entire town in a joyous welcome to a wagon laden with goods, is not unlike "The Atchison, Topeka and the Santa Fe" from *The Harvey Girls* or "The Deadwood Stage" from *Calamity Jane*. Led by the mayor's wife (Hermione Gingold), the ladies of the town cluck disapprovingly over Marian in the song "Pick-a-Little, Talk-a-Little." And Buddy Hackett, playing Harold Hill's confederate, Marcellus Washburn, joins the women in a lively song and dance to "Shipoopi."

The Music Man is undeniably entertaining, and yet it lacks the staying power that characterized the best period film musicals of other years. As engaging as the characters are, they are cartoon-like figures out of some antique rural comedy: the Officious Mayor, the Incorrigible Boy, the Demure Librarian. Given to excruciatingly cute and often-repeated expressions such as "You watch your phraseology" and "Ye gods! Great hog!," they have no basis in reality, which is as the authors intended and which is perfectly acceptable in a broad, affectionate spoof of small-town life in 1912 Iowa. They are not, however, the material out of which truly memorable musical films are created. The few attempts at conveying genuine emotion are patently phony: for example, the bad lisp of Marian's little brother Winthrop, which has turned him into a lonely, withdrawn boy, seems merely a setup for him to sing a cheerful "Gary, Indiana" when the lisp disappears. There is no real feeling for the fears or tribulations of childhood, as there was in the depiction of little Tootie in *Meet Me in St. Louis*.

Robert Preston is so persuasive, so dynamic as Professor Harold Hill that he all but overpowers the movie's calculated corniness. His performance is a miracle of energy and drive, perfectly in key to the style and intention of the film. He seems to be in motion even when he is standing still, and he uses his crisp, authoritative delivery to good advantage, in both speech and song. Whether raising the citizens of River City to fever pitch, or serenading the lovestruck Marian, or leading the boys' band in full regalia, he is the epitome of the "music man," a flesh-and-blood man among animated figures.

Another musical by Meredith Willson, this one with a colorful old Western setting and a heroine in the tradition of Annie Oakley and Calamity Jane, turned up on screen in 1964. *The Unsinkable Molly Brown* was a moderately successful musical play of 1960 about a boisterous girl who meets and marries a roughhewn young miner, and then crashes Denver society when he strikes it rich. (The true Molly Brown survived the sinking of the Titanic, hence the "unsinkable" reference in the title.) For the screen version, directed by Charles Walters, the title role went to Debbie Reynolds, who played it with such ferocious enthusiasm that the scenery seemed in imminent danger of toppling over. (Inexplicably, she received an Academy Award nomination as best actress.) Harve Presnell, rugged and strong-voiced in the Howard Keel mode, repeated his original stage role. The film's best songs were those that had made the stage version lively entertainment, notably the spirited march "I Ain't Down Yet" and the rowdy tune "Belly Up to the Bar, Boys." Peter Gennaro's dances, re-created for the film, also helped to make the movie enjoyable.

It took much longer for another Western musical play, Lerner and Loewe's *Paint Your Wagon*, to come to the screen, and when it did, a viewer had to wonder why anyone had bothered. One of the authors' minor works, the 1951 musical had offered some attractive songs, rousing dances by Agnes de Mille, and a feeble book centering on an old prospector (James Barton) and his daughter (Olga San Juan) during the peak of the California gold rush in 1849. For undetermined reasons, the makers of the movie version in 1969 saw fit to discard the original book for an even feebler, faintly distasteful screenplay by Paddy Chayefsky concerning a Western *ménage à trois*. They then proceeded to compound the felony by casting the leading roles with performers (Lee Marvin, Clint Eastwood, Jean Seberg) who could barely sing, and by entrusting the direction to Joshua Logan, who had directed many stage plays with distinction but whose style for films was heavy-handed and unimaginative.

The stage show's best songs—"Wand'rin' Star," "I Still See Elisa," and "They Call the Wind Maria"—were kept, but except for the last song, which Harve Presnell sang impressively in the pouring rain, the renditions were indifferent or worse. "Wand 'rin' Star" was croaked by an obviously uncomfortable Marvin, and "I Still See Elisa," which James Barton had sung movingly on stage, was inexplicably given to Eastwood, turning an old man's tender remembrance of a long-lost love into a young man's idle fancy. Joshua Logan, whose direction made a glum project even glummer, used the beautiful Oregon location to some advantage, but the movie sank as quickly as No-Name City, the hotbed of gambling, crime, and lust which, at the end of the film, sinks into the mud under the weight of its sinfulness.

The lure and the lore of the American entertainment world in past decades also remained a popular musical theme. On screen, the dazzle, the glitter, the bumptious bravado of show business had served as a musical source for many years. From tacky two-a-day vaudeville to the opulence of Ziegfeld, it offered color, vigor, and ample opportunities for songs and dances. In the sixties, several musical plays with theatrical themes came to the screen, years after their original productions.

In 1959, Ethel Merman had scored a resounding success on Broadway in *Gypsy,* a "musical fable" suggested by the lives of ecdysiast-actress-author Gypsy Rose Lee, her sister June Havoc, and their indomitable mother Rose. There was little truth in the narrative of Rose's brazen, aggressive campaign for the success of her girls, but the Arthur Laurents book and the Jule Styne–Stephen Sondheim score were unusually strong, with nuggets of bitterness and cynicism embedded in all the hard-driving show business razzmatazz. Merman's full-bodied performance was unforgettable, and in her ultimate number, "Rose's Turn," she conveyed all the rage, frustration, and unquenchable ambition of the all-too-human monster called Mama Rose.

Despite some virtues, Warners's 1962 film version failed to match the headlong excitement of the stage production. Many of the fine songs were intact, and the Technicolor cameras captured much of the gaudy atmosphere of vaudeville and burlesque. The show-stopping stage number in which three strippers prove that "You Gotta Have a Gimmick" to get ahead in burlesque was performed hilariously by Roxanne Arlen, Faith Dane, and Betty Bruce. As Gypsy, Natalie Wood was surprisingly good, making the transition from lonely, neglected waif to proud burlesque queen seem entirely convincing. Karl Malden was likable as Herbie, Rose's road agent and perennial suitor, who both loves her and is exasperated by her.

Only a star performance was missing, but it was a fatal gap. As Rose, Rosalind Russell went through the requisite motions, bullying her daughters and Herbie, badgering theater owners into giving her girls a chance, clawing her way relentlessly to success on her terms. ("We are an advancing army on the big time.") But the note of stridency and belligerence was unvarying, inflexible, and ultimately monotonous. When she sings "Some People" (her songs were partly dubbed by Lisa Kirk), we can sense her determination to rise above the crowd, but her big song, "Everything's Coming Up Roses," gets nowhere near the surging confidence and faith exuded by Ethel Merman. Her "Rose's Turn" is a game effort to crystallize the mother's heartbreak and defiance, but it lacks the intended emotional impact.

The circus formed the background for MGM's production of *Billy Rose's Jumbo.* Rose's original 1935 stage extravaganza had included over thirty actual circus acts, a lilting score by Richard Rodgers and Lorenz Hart, and an inimitable, lovable star in Mr. James Durante. Durante, nose and all, was on hand when MGM decided to use the title twenty-seven years later for its 1962 circus musical. (Rose insisted that his name be part of the title.) Doris Day was starred as Kitty Wonder, bareback rider and trapeze artist with the Wonder Circus, which is always on the edge of bankruptcy due to the haphazard bookkeeping and gambling proclivity of its owner, Pop Wonder (Durante). The

Gypsy (Warners, 1962). The ever-optimistic Mama Rose, backstage with her daughter Louise (Natalie Wood). No longer the ugly duckling, Louise is now the swan known as Gypsy Rose Lee.

page 314: My Fair Lady *(Warners, 1964). The transformed Eliza Doolittle (Audrey Hepburn) makes her first public appearance at the Ascot races. Hovering near her solicitously as she takes the stage is her teacher and mentor, Professor Henry Higgins (Rex Harrison).*

page 316: The Music Man *(Warners, 1962). A smashing finale for an entertaining slice of Americana: "Professor" Harold Hill (Robert Preston) and Marian (Shirley Jones) lead the spanking new River City Boys Band in "76 Trombones." Twirling a baton behind them is Timmy Everett.*

page 317: The Unsinkable Molly Brown *(MGM, 1964). The rambunctious, unstoppable Molly (Debbie Reynolds) joins the barflies in singing and dancing to "Belly Up to the Bar, Boys." They turn the number into a fine Western whoop-de-do.*

Billy Rose's Jumbo *(MGM, 1962)*.
Doris Day, Martha Raye, Jimmy Durante,
and Stephen Boyd in the finale, "Sawdust,
Spangles and Dreams." In the background,
bedecked for the occasion, is Jumbo himself.

Billy Rose's Jumbo *(MGM, 1962)*.
Doris Day and Stephen Boyd fall in
love in a colorful old-time circus setting.

opposite: Gypsy *(Warners, 1962)*. *Ecdysiast*
Gypsy Rose Lee (Natalie Wood) performs one
of her artful strip routines.

plot involved Kitty's romance with Sam Rawlins (Stephen Boyd), who claims to be a circus roustabout but who is actually the son of Pop Wonder's chief rival, John Noble (Dean Jagger). Eventually, she forgives his deception and takes him back. At the same time, Pop finally resolves his lifelong courtship of the tenacious Madame Lulu (Martha Raye) by marrying her.

Under Charles Walters's direction, *Billy Rose's Jumbo* is generally diverting entertainment. Despite its stage origins, it is really an original screen musical. With a fresh cinematic eye, it makes colorful use of the old-time circus backgrounds, permitting the camera to catch the hectic atmosphere and exuberance of circus life. (Some of this cinematic flair could probably be attributed to the film's second-unit director, Busby Berkeley, who worked closely with Walters.) The skill is most evident in the staging of the musical number ''Over and Over Again.'' It begins as Doris Day sings to a girl practicing on the trapeze, then opens up to a series of shots showing the rehearsing performers hard at work. As the waltz melody is reprised, the number increases in intensity until it ends with a CinemaScope shot of all three rings whirling with activity.

As the perennially engaged couple, Jimmy Durante and Martha Raye make an endearing pair, his air of permanent bafflement and astonishment meshing nicely with her good-sport rowdiness. The movie's most unforgettable moment comes when he reprises a chorus of ''The Most Beautiful Girl in the World'' to her at their aborted wedding ceremony. Durante even repeated his famous line from the original *Jumbo* production: trying to lead his beloved pachyderm Jumbo off the circus grounds, he is spotted by creditors and asked where he is going with the elephant. A look of total surprise comes over his face. ''*What* elephant?'' he asks.

The musical, however, is dominated by Doris Day, who plays her first musical role in five years with an assurance that reveals how far she had come from her blonde hoyden days at Warners. As usual, she is given a romantic ballad (''My Romance'') and a torch song (''Little Girl Blue''), both of which she sings with feeling and restraint. As they sit at the back of their wagon at the close of the day, she and Martha Raye perform a melancholy duet, ''Why Can't I?,'' one of the movie's best numbers. *Billy Rose's Jumbo* misses the top echelon of musical films because of a rather dull screenplay and a slightly lethargic air. Yet the film leaves the viewer exhilarated as the principals join in a finale called ''Sawdust, Spangles and Dreams,'' which captures the special magic of the circus.

One show business musical of the sixties brought superstardom to a phenomenon named Barbra Streisand. In March of 1964, after several years of attracting unusually wide attention as an odd- but striking-looking singer with a vibrant, richly expressive voice, Streisand opened in the Jule Styne–Isobel Lennart–Bob Merrill musical *Funny Girl,* playing Fanny Brice, the gifted comedienne and singer. Although the musical itself was heavily criticized, especially for its sentimental book concerning Brice's romance with gambler Nick Arnstein, Streisand was a sensation, attracting adulatory audiences who responded to her offbeat, Jewish-flavored personality and the all-out brilliance of her singing. She became one of the most popular entertainers of the time, with record albums that sold phenomenally well and

television specials that won high ratings. Inevitably, she was destined to repeat her role of Fanny Brice on the screen, but the question persisted: could she duplicate her impact in films?

The film version of *Funny Girl,* directed by William Wyler, was released in 1968. It began with a back view of Streisand as Fanny Brice as she walks to her theater, a fur collar high around her neck. She stops at a mirror, and we see her face for the first time. ''Hello, gorgeous!'' she says to her reflection—and from that moment, the question was answered, and Barbra Streisand's fame was assured. In flashback, the movie takes Fanny Brice from her early days as an aspiring actress with much more talent than beauty, through her meeting of and love affair with elegantly stylish gambler Nick Arnstein (Omar Sharif), to her triumph with *The Ziegfeld Follies.* The screenplay records their troubled marriage as Fanny's star rises and he goes to prison for embezzlement.

The story of *Funny Girl,* however much it is based on the truth, remains frayed and worn—it was not any better when Fox used it in disguised form in *Rose of Washington Square* in 1939— and the dialogue seldom rises above such lines as ''I want a personal life—and I'm going to have it,'' or ''We're just not good for each other.'' Nor does William Wyler, directing his first musical film, give the soggy dramatic portions any particular flair. Yet occasionally, Streisand, by the sheer force of her personality, makes several of the incidents palatable and even memorable. When Nick invites Fanny to a private (*very* private) dinner party, Streisand's combination of nervousness and willingness, even eagerness, to surrender, and her reactions to Nick's seductive maneuvers, are extremely funny. Years later, when Nick has been arrested, Fanny is forced to confront the press. In a scene that Streisand plays with remarkable assurance for a screen novice, she jokes with the reporters, tries to make light of Nick's predicament (''My dope was an innocent dupe!''), and insists on being called Mrs. Arnstein. She rushes away, with tears streaming down her face.

Streisand's best songs in *Funny Girl* are those that have dramatic resonance in the story or that reveal some facet of Fanny's character. In her first song, ''I'm the Greatest Star,'' she is funny, touching, and eloquent in her emotional directness as she outlines the self-evident reasons for her star quality. When she sings her lovely, feeling rendition of ''People'' to Nick, she expresses the longing of someone who, out of overriding ambition, has never been able to make an emotional commitment to others. In the movie's most remarkable sequence, she sings ''Don't Rain on My Parade'' as an affirmation of her new independence. The film ends with Streisand's compelling rendition of ''My Man,'' after leaving Arnstein for good. Eschewing the simple, direct approach of Fanny Brice herself (except for the stark black dress), she reaches for the bravura effects, beginning with a tentative and shaky voice as she summons all her resources to make it through the number. Her voice gains in strength and power until its throbbing intensity fills the theater. When the song ends with a light on only her face and hands, the audience knows that it has witnessed the emergence of a major film star.

Although she has remained a star of the top rank, Streisand has yet to find a role as suitable as that of Fanny Brice.

Her first film after *Funny Girl* was one of her most ill-considered choices. *Hello, Dolly!*, a musical version of Thornton Wilder's play *The Matchmaker,* had opened on Broadway in 1964. Written by Michael Stewart and Jerry Herman, it starred Carol Channing as Dolly Levi, a matchmaking widow in old New York who cleverly manipulates Horace Vandergelder, one of the wealthiest citizens in Yonkers, into a proposal of marriage. A bountiful, tuneful entertainment, the show received strong notices. The lengthy song and dance to the title tune became one of the most celebrated numbers in theater history.

There were many actresses eager to play Dolly Levi on film, but Barbra Streisand, riding the crest of her triumph in *Funny Girl* and her shared Academy Award with Katharine Hepburn, won the role. With a total absence of logic or reason, but with eyes fixed firmly on the box office, Fox cast the twenty-seven-year-old actress in a role calling for someone at least fifteen years older. Without being able to fall back on the audience-pleasing eccentricities of Carol Channing or of Ruth Gordon, who had played the title role of *The Matchmaker* on the stage, or the seasoned warmth of Shirley Booth, who had acted *The Matchmaker* on the screen, Streisand opted misguidedly for an impression of Mae West, waving her hips and giving an insinuating inflection to many of her lines. She sang with her customary brilliance, but the role was clearly wrong for her.

On stage and screen, *Hello, Dolly!* has been one of the most maligned musicals of recent years. The seemingly interminable run on Broadway and in touring companies, the relentless repetition of the title song on radio and television made the show a sitting target and ultimately persuaded many critics and viewers that it was basically worthless. (Apparently the glowing notices it originally received from most major critics were forgotten or ignored.) The criticism was inevitably extended to the film version which, despite some friendly reviews, was largely dismissed as an overproduced, miscast, lumbering dinosaur of a musical. Since it was the most expensive musical film produced to that date, it was not expected to regain its astronomical cost for a very long time, if ever, but the disappointing business caused alarm in Fox's executive suites.

It should be noted that the film does have a number of glaring faults. For one, the extravagant production, with its detailed re-creation of the streets, parks, and restaurants of New York City around 1890, is much too overpowering for the slender story. We were given pageantry without point or purpose, and the result weighed heavily on the screen. Worst of all was the rather cumbersome direction and the surprisingly uninventive dancing—surprising since the film's director was one of the masters of the screen musical and of dance on film: Gene Kelly. An indifferent costarring performance by Walter Matthau as Horace Vandergelder, and merely adequate supporting performances by a large cast (Tommy Tune was a notable exception as the gangly suitor of Vandergelder's niece) were additional handicaps.

Still, there are some purely musical pleasures in *Hello, Dolly!* that salvage it from failure. Contrary to some critical contentions, it is not a one-song musical; a number of the songs have the charm and the lilt of good if not superior theater music. ''Put on Your Sunday Clothes'' begins quietly, as Dolly summons Vandergelder's

Funny Girl (Columbia, 1968). On her way to join lover Nick Arnstein, Fanny Brice (Barbra Streisand) sings "Don't Rain on My Parade" at the bow of a tugboat. In the extraordinary last shot of this number, the camera pulled back to take in all of New York City's harbor, including the Statue of Liberty. The entire number was staged brilliantly, with Streisand singing as she hurries from a railroad station to a taxi to a tugboat and finally into Nick's waiting arms.

overleaf, left, above: Funny Girl (Columbia, 1968). Fanny Brice, a self-described "bagel in a plate of onion rolls," attracts attention in a burlesque chorus on roller skates by entering dressed in purple tights, with a huge purple bow in the rear. Spreading havoc with her clumsiness, she maneuvers herself into the position she has always wanted: alone onstage, where she sings "I'd Rather Be Blue" to an enthusiastic audience.

overleaf, left, below: Funny Girl (Columbia, 1968). Fanny Brice (Barbra Streisand) is immediately and totally enraptured by suave gambler Nick Arnstein (Omar Sharif).

overleaf, right: Funny Girl (Columbia, 1968). Portrait of instant stardom: in an electrifying final number, Barbra Streisand as Fanny Brice sings "My Man."

323

Hello, Dolly! (Fox, 1969). At the Yonkers railroad station, waiting for the train to New York City, Dolly (Barbra Streisand) leads the citizens in a rendition of "Put on Your Sunday Clothes." In the front row with Dolly (left to right): Michael Crawford, Danny Lockin, Joyce Ames, and Tommy Tune.

Hello, Dolly! (Fox, 1969). Mrs. Dolly Levi (Barbra Streisand) is welcomed back to the Harmonia Gardens by devoted waiters. The stage Dollys had all received an equally warm reception from the staff. Streisand's young widow, however, would seem to have had a more intimate relationship with the waiters than the others, except that, judging by appearances, she would only have been a child at the time.

young clerks to an "adventure" in New York, then opens up into a large-scale song and dance as a joyful crowd congregates. The amusing "Elegance" is attractively staged and agreeably performed, as is the principal ballad, "It Only Takes a Moment," although the song itself, with its ersatz-Hammerstein lyrics on the swiftness of Cupid's arrow, is mediocre.

Naturally, Barbra Streisand is given the major share of the score, which she sings well under the circumstances. In "Before the Parade Passes By," she makes an effective affirmation of her return to the world of the living. The song leads to the film's most lavish production number, a gargantuan parade down a reconstructed Fourteenth Street of 1890. The number is stupendous in its scope and bewildering in its pointlessness. Streisand's big number, of course, is "Hello, Dolly," which she renders cheerfully if much more seductively than Carol Channing, who played it on a more appropriate note of warmth and friendliness. At one point Streisand is joined by bandleader Louis Armstrong, who had made a popular recording of the song in 1964.

The need for star insurance damaged not only Hello, Dolly! but also a musical released in the same year: the film version of the Neil Simon–Cy Coleman–Dorothy Fields stage musical Sweet Charity, very loosely adapted from Federico Fellini's Nights of Cabiria. The musical play had drawn most of its success from a wonderful performance by Gwen Verdon in the title role of a gallant, put-upon taxi dancer (a prostitute in Fellini's movie). For the film version, Shirley MacLaine was cast in the lead, but in no way was she able to duplicate the eccentric charm and seasoned dancing ability of the original star.

As in other elephantine musicals of the period, Sweet Charity was long, lavish, and noisy, but there was an added ingredient: Bob Fosse, who had staged the Broadway edition, was assigned to repeat the job on screen. An imaginative director nervously in search of a style (it was his debut as a film director), he veered out of control, juxtaposing lavish production numbers filmed against real New York locations with plainly theatrical numbers edited to a fare-thee-well and overrun with photographic gimmickry. The result was further proof that in the musical film, too much can be far worse than not enough.

Amid all the musical salutes to past American life, there were some without stage origins. The most successful was Ross Hunter's entertaining but overlong musical spoof, Thoroughly Modern Millie (1967). Set in Hollywood's traditional idea of the Roaring Twenties, in which "wild" flappers bobbed their hair, raised their hemlines, and danced incessantly to a jazz beat, the movie starred Julie Andrews as the determinedly "modern" Millie of 1922 ("Now's the time for fun—especially for the new woman"), who falls head over heels in love with her handsome boss (John Gavin), but finally settles for her faithful but irresponsible boyfriend, Jimmy (James Fox). On her way to happiness—her boyfriend turns out to be a millionaire, of course—Millie gets involved with Dorothy (Mary Tyler Moore), a demure and not-too-bright rich girl; a flamboyant wealthy widow named Muzzy Van Hassmere (Carol Channing); and Mrs. Meers (Beatrice Lillie), manager of Miss Priscilla's Home for Young Women, who turns out to be running a white slave ring.

All the harebrained giddiness of the plot was merely an

Thoroughly Modern Millie *(Universal, 1967). Julie Andrews in the title role, modeling clothes that range from modest to flapperish.*

excuse for taking broad swipes at the conventions of twenties movies, as well as for a number of enjoyable musical numbers. The screenplay by Richard Morris spoofs the exclamatory titles, the instant emotional reactions—Millie is consumed with love the very second she sets eyes on her boss—and the photographic gimmicks that were part of many silent flickers in the twenties. Until the last reel, when the players are caught up in a long and frantic slapstick chase, there is considerable fun in the madcap jazz parties given by Channing's Muzzy on ritzy Long Island and in Millie's single-minded pursuit of the perfectly named Trevor Graydon.

The pleasing musical numbers in *Thoroughly Modern Millie* combine popular standards of the past with twenties-like songs written by Sammy Cahn and Jimmy Van Heusen. Before the credits, Andrews, on her way to Miss Priscilla's hotel, sings the title song as she changes her appearance to match the hedonistic mood of the day. There are the requisite dance numbers—Jimmy teaches Millie how to do the latest dance craze, the ''Tapioca,'' and at a Jewish wedding where Millie has been hired to sing (''Sing, L'Chaim!''), the guests participate in a diverting dance which has absolutely nothing to do with the rest of the film. We also get the expected bursts of song when love strikes: for example, when Trevor spies Dorothy, we hear the romantic strains of Victor Herbert's ''Ah, Sweet Mystery of Life.''

Carol Channing, one of the handful of stage performers who may be too large for the screen to contain—Ethel Merman and Zero Mostel are others—is given two numbers styled to her unique voice and delivery. In ''Jazz Baby,'' staged at her Long Island mansion, she bellows a chorus of the song, plays the trumpet and the tambourine, and dances on top of a xylophone, all with infectious good cheer. Later, at a vaudeville show she is sponsoring for the Milk Fund, this inimitable screwball is fired from a cannon as she sings ''Do It Again.''

If life was depicted as roseate in the period musicals of the sixties, the concerns of the musical films actually set in the sixties were hardly less frivolous. *Bells Are Ringing* (1960), for example, posed the burning question of whether an operator for an answering service could snare the owner of the disembodied voice she had heard on her telephone. Vincente Minnelli's last musical film until *On a Clear Day You Can See Forever* in 1970, it proved to be an uninspired effort with only one great virtue, in the person of Judy Holliday. Written for her by friends Betty Comden and Adolph Green, with music by Jule Styne, the stage version had prospered largely on the strength of her appeal, which was considerable. As the lovelorn telephone operator, she displayed all the warmth, charm, and comic astuteness that had made her a popular actress since *Born Yesterday*. In the film version—her first movie in three years—she was completely endearing, whether doing an easy song and dance in the park to ''Just in Time'' with her new boyfriend (Dean Martin), mourning the end of a love affair in ''The Party's Over,'' or brassily proclaiming ''I'm Going Back'' (to work at the Bonjour Tristesse Brassiere Company) after all seems lost. But she was handicapped by a weak screenplay, a rather coarse and seemingly bored leading man in Dean Martin, a merely average score, and curiously disinterested direction by Vincente Minnelli.

With no star such as Judy Holliday to spark indifferent

Bye Bye Birdie (Columbia, 1963). Ann-Margret was undeniably sexy but not very convincing as an ardent teenage fan selected to give rock singer Conrad Birdie his parting kiss on television before he leaves for the army.

Sweet Charity *(Universal, 1969). Shirley MacLaine, in the title role, proclaims "I'm a Brass Band" in this filmization of the stage musical.*

Bells Are Ringing *(MGM, 1960). Judy Holliday and Doria Avila dance to "Mu-Cha-Cha" on a patio. This was Holliday's first film in three years and also, sadly, her last. An expert and lovable actress, she could not lift this musical above mediocrity, but her warmth and humanity shone through every moment on screen.*

material into life, only modest entertainment could be found in Universal's film version of Rodgers and Hammerstein's 1958 stage musical *Flower Drum Song* (1961). Nor could much enjoyment be found in *Bye Bye Birdie* (1963). The film retained some of the vitality of the long-running Broadway musical, including such buoyant tunes as "Kids" and "The Telephone Hour." But its screenplay, concerning hip-swiveling crooner Conrad Birdie's invasion of an Ohio town, was more frantic than funny, its jabs at Presley-like singers and the idiocies of television were perishable even then, and it coarsened the original material by having Ann-Margret play Birdie's most adoring teenage fan in the manner of a brashly seductive stripper. Dick Van Dyke, reprising his stage role, and Janet Leigh as his long-suffering girlfriend headed the adult contingent with only fleeting success. Director George Sidney at least kept the heavy traffic moving, and the film was popular at the box office.

How to Succeed in Business Without Really Trying (1967) was a fairly literal transcription of the musical comedy that had enjoyed a run of over 1,400 performances in 1961. The stage musical had many virtues: an amusing book by Abe Burrows, Jack Weinstock, and Willie Gilbert, suggested by Shepherd Mead's popular satirical book on the sneaky ways of getting ahead in the business world, a novel setting for a musical, a clever if not very tuneful score by Frank Loesser, and two first-rate comedy performances by Robert Morse as the upward-rising J. Pierpont Finch and Rudy Vallee as his addled boss, J. B. Biggley. Directed by David Swift, who also wrote the screenplay, the film version virtually duplicated the play, casting Morse and Vallee in the leading roles, and repeating the farcical adventures of Finch as he manipulates his way to the top ranks of World Wide Wickets Co., Inc.

As a record of the stage show, *How to Succeed* succeeds very well indeed. Its lightly malicious portraits of business types—the schemer, the sycophant, the compliant "company man," the romance-minded secretary—hardly cut deep enough to draw blood, but the characters are amusing. Frank Loesser's bright lyrics give them the chance to express their viewpoints in song: Sammy Smith, repeating his stage role of Mr. Twimble, belts out his unwavering obeisance to World Wide Wickets in "The Company Way"; Robert Morse, a wicked mind behind that boyish grin, sings a hymn of self-esteem to a mirror in "I Believe in You"; Morse and Rudy Vallee share a parody of rah-rah college songs in "Grand Old Ivy"; and the entire company explodes in a sly tribute to "The Brotherhood of Man."

Finian's Rainbow (1968) went back the furthest for its stage source. For many years, producers had contemplated a film version of the "Yip" Harburg–Fred Saidy–Burton Lane musical play (1947) that combined hearty portions of Irish whimsy with dollops of what used to be called "social significance." For reasons that remain inexplicable, it was decided that audiences of the late sixties would appreciate a story that remained stubbornly fixed in its original time, and a score that had become too familiar with repetition. The movie's chance of success was not brightened with a director (Francis Ford Coppola) who had never worked on a musical film and a cast which—with the exception of its star—was not very well known to American audiences.

Despite the warming presence of Fred Astaire, despite some Harburg-Lane songs that retain a measure of enchantment,

Flower Drum Song (Universal, 1961). Juanita Hall and Jack Soo step out in a Charleston to Rodgers and Hammerstein's "Chop Suey," while old-world Chinaman Benson Fong (right) expresses disapproval. Behind the colorful setting of San Francisco's Chinatown and the novelty of a largely Oriental cast, there was a conventional story about the clash between old-world and modern values of father and son, a musical score not up to the team's best, and a condescending attitude toward Chinese-American people.

How to Succeed in Business Without Really Trying *(United Artists, 1967). Sammy Smith and Robert Morse lead the employees of the World Wide Wickets Company in an exuberant performance of "The Brotherhood of Man." Morse played the ambitious young J. Pierpont Finch, who draws on the weapons of flattery and fraud to climb up the ladder of success. Eventually, and perhaps inevitably, he becomes chairman of the board.*

Finian's Rainbow is one of the most maladroit of sixties musicals. Its basic concept of an old Irishman, Finian McLonergan (Astaire), who, with his daughter (Petula Clark), comes to the mythical state of Missitucky carrying the pot of gold he has stolen from the leprechauns, can still pass muster. There is even some amusement in the sprightly leprechaun who follows the old man to America to recover the gold—a role played memorably on the stage by David Wayne but handled here with oppressive quaintness by Tommy Steele. However, once the plot thickens with a heavily dated and even questionable spoof of racial bigotry—a Southern senator turns black, a bright young black assumes an Uncle Tom pose—the movie begins to resemble a dust-laden musical that unaccountably escaped from the vaults after being kept from view for two decades.

Even worse than the mossy satire is the production. Poorly synchronized singing voices emerge bewilderingly from all parts of the screen. Although some of the ensemble dances are staged against attractive location settings, they still seem joyless and mechanical. The familiar songs—"How Are Things in Glocca Morra?," "Something Sort of Grandish," "Look to the Rainbow" —are performed competently (Yarburg's offbeat lyrics, with words like "animules" and "Eisenhowrish" are clever—up to a point), but their spirit is weakened by the dejected air that somehow hangs over the entire enterprise.

Although he looks haggard, Fred Astaire gives the movie its single note of distinction. He dances very little, but it hardly matters. His very presence gives the film fleeting moments of the lighter-than-air feeling it strives for so desperately. At the very end, when he waves goodbye as he sets out on a new journey alone, we sense that he is also bidding farewell to his dancing shoes, and to the dapper song-and-dance man of nearly four decades. The moment may not be poignant—Astaire never allowed tears of sentiment to dampen his art—but it makes a generally wretched film fade out with a glow.

The decade had produced some meritorious musicals adapted from the stage, but far too many failed to live up to their sources. The greatest of those that succeeded was also one of the first. When *West Side Story* opened in September, 1957, it stunned theater audiences with its dramatic story—the tragic romance of Shakespeare's *Romeo and Juliet* transposed to the violence-ridden slums of Manhattan's West Side—its electrifying score by Leonard Bernstein and Stephen Sondheim, and its brilliant choreography and staging by Jerome Robbins. The extremely laudatory reviews, and the excitement generated at every performance, guaranteed a long run for *West Side Story*.

Officially codirected by Robert Wise and Jerome Robbins (Robbins actually left early in the filming after choreographing all but two of the dance numbers), the 1961 film version was received with equal enthusiasm. (It won ten Academy Awards, including one as best picture of the year.) There was praise for Ernest Lehman's screenplay, for most if not all of the performances, and for Robert Wise's handling of the dramatic content, but the highest acclaim was reserved for Jerome Robbins's dances. His choreography infused the film with a driving excitement that carried over into the nondance portions, giving them an almost palpable tension, a nervous rhythm that crackled with energy. More than any other element in the movie, the dances captured the exhilaration and ferocity of life in the streets.

The opening of *West Side Story* is justly famous. As the overture plays, an abstract design on the screen changes color and becomes a breathtaking aerial view of Manhattan. The camera finally swoops down to a deserted slum street where members of the gang known as the Jets appear, charged with aggressive energy. When their coiled tension erupts into dance, we feel uneasy at first, wondering if the delicate balance between realism and fantasy can be sustained for two hours. (Why are these tough boys engaging in ballet steps on a New York street?) But the uneasiness disappears even as the first choreographed fight takes place between the "American" Jets and their hated Puerto Rican rivals, the Sharks. We accept it partly because the dancing has such athletic vigor, and partly because so much of the action outside the dancing has the same pulsating rhythm and movement.

West Side Story moves swiftly into its story, which parallels (a little too schematically, perhaps) the tale of Shakespeare's star-crossed lovers: Tony (Richard Beymer), the sensitive, reluctant member of the Jets, and Maria (Natalie Wood), the demure sister of the Sharks' leader Bernardo (George Chakiris). On the sidelines, sharing and participating in the inevitable tragedy, are Anita (Rita Moreno), Bernardo's hot-blooded girlfriend, and Riff (Russ Tamblyn), leader of the Jets. The plot moves inexorably to its climax: while Tony and Maria declare their love for each other, a gang rumble is set up which results in the deaths of Riff and Bernardo. Hiding in a cellar, Tony comes to believe that Maria has also been killed, and he welcomes his own death. When he learns the truth, it is too late. As he rushes joyfully to embrace Maria, he is shot and dies in her arms.

This dolorous story now has a curiously archaic air that makes *West Side Story* seem like a period piece. Street gangs may not be obsolete, but their preening manner and sneering attitudes in the movie—at least until the violence intrudes—make them resemble the Bowery Boys out for mischief. The glories of the film still reside in the score and the dancing. The Bernstein-Sondheim songs range from jazzy and feverish ("Cool") to lyrical ("Maria," "Tonight") to comical ("Gee, Officer Krupke"), and they are all richly evocative of the film's moods and characters. Before their lives turn bleak, Tony and Maria express their elation in soaring music, Tony with his hopeful, striving "Something's Coming," Maria with her entrancing "I Feel Pretty," accompanied by Anita and her teasing friends. Their love duet of "Tonight," the equivalent of the balcony scene in *Romeo and Juliet,* is surpassed only by their duet in the bridal shop in which Maria works, where they join in the beautiful, moving "One Hand, One Heart" as they exchange their private vows.

West Side Story is surely the finest dance musical since *Seven Brides for Seven Brothers.* Reprised from the stage version, the principal dance numbers remain exciting set pieces: the "challenge" rooftop dance of the Puerto Rican boys and girls between choruses of the biting, funny "America"; the volatile dance in the school gymnasium; the choreographed frenzy and terror of the gang fight that kills Bernardo and Riff. But the film also has many smaller moments in which feelings are expressed

Finian's Rainbow *(Warners, 1968). Fred Astaire does a brief solo, one of the few modest dances he performs in the film.*

in dance: the propulsive movement of Riff and the Jets as contrasted with the more sinuous movement of Bernardo and the Sharks, or the enchanting little dance that Maria does alone on the roof just before she learns that Tony has killed her brother. It all succeeds because Robert Wise and Jerome Robbins deal with the material in cinematic fashion. Their vast skill allows us to accept, after a faintly unsettling start, the sight of streetwise toughs dancing like Nureyev. And Leonard Bernstein's music carries us from acceptance to elation.

The performances in *West Side Story* are generally first-rate. Natalie Wood makes a lovely and appealing Maria (her voice was dubbed by Marni Nixon), and she is touching in her devotion to Tony, even after he has killed Bernardo. Her scream of "Don't you touch him!" to the policeman who has come to remove Tony's body is one of the film's most powerful moments. Rita Moreno, who received an Oscar as best supporting actress, is forceful as Anita, singing and dancing with lusty vigor, and George Chakiris, who was named best supporting actor, plays Bernardo convincingly. Only Richard Beymer (dubbed by Jimmy Bryant) is less than adequate as Tony, much too bland and vacuous for the role.

West Side Story is the decade's finest musical stage adaptation because it took all the elements of the Broadway version—a downbeat dramatic story, a stirring score, and inventive dances—and merged them in cinematic terms. Without slavishly following the original, without altering the material to accommodate a star, the film creates its own world, a few necessary steps away from reality but never so stylized that the theatrical effects intrude on the emotional impact. Unlike many other musicals of the sixties, it never falls prey to treating the property as a legend or an institution that must be handled reverently. It soars on its own wings, and it soars high. Not even the mustiness of its book can keep it from being numbered among the great film musicals.

In addition to the stage-adapted musicals on both past and contemporary American life, the sixties saw a cluster of musical films set in England. On the whole, the American theater has always been highly responsive to imported British plays, but British musicals do not weather the ocean voyage very well. It has, however, occasionally looked with favor on American-made musicals that captured the charm and elegance—or the quaint, picturesque ways—of an idealized Great Britain. The most successful of these musicals eventually found their way to films.

Eight years after its first stage production, *My Fair Lady* (1964) came to the screen. The Alan Jay Lerner–Frederick Loewe musical version of Bernard Shaw's *Pygmalion* had received a sensational reception on its opening in March of 1956, acclaimed for its literate book out of Shaw, the wit and melodic sweep of its score, and the sumptuous production designed by Oliver Smith. Julie Andrews was radiant and touching as the Cockney flower girl Eliza Doolittle, skillfully changing from a shrill drab to a proud and elegant woman. As Professor Henry Higgins, the peevish, incorrigible linguist who, on a bet, converts Eliza into a lady, Rex Harrison was ideally cast, making his own transformation from supercilious pedant to a man unaccountably in love entirely credible. The musical enjoyed a record run of 2,717 performances.

West Side Story *(United Artists, 1961). In the moving climax, Maria (Natalie Wood) mourns over the dead body of Tony (Richard Beymer), killed after a fatal rumble.*

opposite: West Side Story *(United Artists, 1961). Gang toughs doing ballet steps down a New York slum street? Yes, and brilliantly—as demonstrated by the "Sharks," led by George Chakiris (above), and by the "Jets," led by Russ Tamblyn (below).*

335

right: My Fair Lady *(Warners, 1964). Audrey Hepburn as flower girl Eliza Doolittle, before her transformation into the "fair lady."*

opposite: My Fair Lady *(Warners, 1964). Audrey Hepburn at her most ravishing, as Eliza Doolittle.*

below: My Fair Lady *(Warners, 1964). Eliza Doolittle (Audrey Hepburn) speaks her first complete sentence in impeccable English, delighting her teacher Henry Higgins (Rex Harrison), Higgins's friend Colonel Pickering (Wilfrid Hyde-White), and herself. Their jubilant song, "The Rain in Spain," is one of the film's glorious highlights.*

The credits for the film version certainly augured well. With Rex Harrison repeating his role of Henry Higgins and Stanley Holloway again playing Eliza's disreputable father, the refined and the raffish elements in the story were certain to be well presented and contrasted. The role of Eliza Doolittle went not to Julie Andrews but to Audrey Hepburn, a certified box-office attraction whose regal bearing and cultured voice were clearly more appropriate for the post-Higgins lady than the pre-Higgins Cockney girl. The film's direction was entrusted to George Cukor, whose impeccable taste and unobtrusive skill had enhanced many films since the early days of sound.

Happily, it turned out that the treasures of *My Fair Lady* were not tarnished on their way to film. From first frame to last, the film is gorgeous to behold, with Cecil Beaton's costumes and sets (he had created only the costumes for the stage) richly evoking the Edwardian era as it might have looked had a master designer such as Beaton been in charge. Carefully following the stage version, the film begins on a rainy evening in Covent Garden, where Henry Higgins, on his constant search for British dialects, confronts the "deliciously low" Eliza Doolittle for the first time. In the best musical tradition, their first songs reveal their characters: "Wouldn't It Be Lovely?" expresses Eliza's untutored ways and her idle dreams, while in "Why Can't the English" Higgins displays his testy, intolerant, and snobbish nature. Yet he is a man who takes great pains to conceal a streak of romanticism.

Lerner's Shavian dialogue and witty, perceptive lyrics blend delightfully with Loewe's entrancing music, as the story moves from Higgins's bet with Colonel Pickering (Wilfrid Hyde-White) that he can transform Eliza into a reasonably articulate woman who could be passed off at a party as a duchess to the grueling process of transformation. The text has a style and a substance that we expect, considering the original source, but the songs are extraordinary in their ability to enrich our knowledge of the characters. Higgins's early song "An Ordinary Man" is more eloquent than any number of dialogue exchanges in evoking his feelings of vast superiority and his contempt for those disruptive creatures of the female sex. Alfred Doolittle's "With a Little Bit of Luck" is not only a rousing production number but a perfect portrait of this amiable scoundrel. The music is also a logical extension of the characters' feelings. When Eliza finally learns to say one complete sentence correctly, the elation felt by Higgins, Pickering, and Eliza simply cannot be contained and leads to one of the triumphant sequences in musical history: their joyful performance of "The Rain in Spain." Unlike the score of Cole Porter's *Kiss Me, Kate,* for example, this is theater music that works on the screen not only because it is entirely embedded in character but also because it does not need to continually call attention to its theatricality or cleverness.

My Fair Lady moves into high gear as the new Eliza makes her rather shaky debut. She meets Higgins's mother (the impeccable Gladys Cooper), attends the Ascot races (a stunningly designed sequence in black and white), and even stirs some amorous interest in one Freddie Eynsford-Hill (Jeremy Brett), who gets to sing one of the best-known songs in the score, "On the Street Where You Live." The climax comes at the Embassy ball, where Eliza, now the perfect product of Henry Higgins,

enchants everyone with her beauty and her slightly odd manner of speaking. Henry and Pickering are ecstatic ("You Did It!"), but Eliza is hurt and angry at being ignored. She is no longer a part of any world: not assured enough for high society, too well-bred and knowing for her old slum friends.

In the closing scenes, the relationship between Higgins and Eliza not only takes on the subtle coloration supplied by Shaw but is conveyed beautifully in the Lerner and Loewe songs. Baffled by Eliza's attitude, Higgins sings a querulous "Why Can't a Woman," wondering why women cannot have the "marvelous" qualities of men. Eliza treats him with disdain, claiming in song ("Without You") that he is no longer necessary in her life. But their ties are real, and they obviously go deeper than the teacher-pupil relationship. In one of the loveliest songs in the score, Higgins sings "I've Grown Accustomed to Her Face," recognizing in his own myopic way that Eliza is a presence he cannot do without.

My Fair Lady is so clearly a model of the musical genre, so perfectly wrought in all its elements, that the question must be addressed as to why it cannot be numbered among the handful of truly outstanding film musicals. It may be that in being brought to the screen with such reverence and exquisite attention to detail, the film acquires the faint odor of embalming. It has great style and beauty, but it lacks a heartbeat. Perhaps some cinematic flourishes, a touch of cinematic daring from a director such as Vincente Minnelli, might have removed the slightly waxen pallor that covers this production of *My Fair Lady*.

The film version of another stage musical by Lerner and Loewe was released in 1967. *Camelot*, based on T. H. White's *The Once and Future King*, had aroused high expectations in December, 1960, as the first musical by the team since *My Fair Lady*. Despite the high-powered cast headed by Richard Burton and Julie Andrews, a fine score, and an impressively mounted production, it received disappointing reviews. When it was finally made into a movie, its chances of success were even less likely. The moviegoer's taste for large-scale musicals had abated, and one that dealt with King Arthur, his Queen Guenevere, and his Knights of the Round Table would not be inclined to reverse that trend. In addition, the stars of the stage version were replaced by Richard Harris and Vanessa Redgrave, two extremely capable actors, but far from box-office lures. To make matters worse, the direction was assigned to Joshua Logan, who had shown with *South Pacific* that the musical film was not his forte.

Unfortunately, the film failed to rise above its handicaps. Produced with an extraordinarily lavish hand, it aspired to re-create the magical kingdom of King Arthur's Camelot, a perfect world of chivalry and gallantry brought to ruin by an illicit love affair. There is some amusement in the early scenes, in which daily life in Arthur's court is lightly spoofed, and some poignancy in the failed dreams of Arthur and in his anguished efforts to come to terms with Guenevere's romance with his knight Launcelot. ("They answer me with pain and torment. They have betrayed me in their hearts.") But the gargantuan sets, too massive for the delicacy and grace of the central theme, and the solemn turgidity of many scenes conspire to make *Camelot* heavy going indeed.

Camelot *(Warners, 1967). Framed by over a thousand flickering candles, King Arthur (Richard Harris) takes Guenevere (Vanessa Redgrave) as his queen. The film's sets were breathtaking, and much of the music was lovely, but Joshua Logan's cumbersome direction kept the production moving at a pace that even a tired snail might surpass. Nor was there much help in Richard Harris's performance as Arthur, played almost entirely in a hoarse whisper and with a disconcerting touch of effeminacy.*

opposite: My Fair Lady *(Warners, 1964). Audrey Hepburn as "Lady" Eliza poses in a gown designed for her by Cecil Beaton.*

The failure is all the more lamentable because *Camelot* has many laudable features. Although the pageantry overpowers what is fundamentally an ordinary triangular situation (jealous husband, cheating wife, remorseful lover), there is more thought and substance in the narrative than usual, especially in its portrait of the troubled idealist who resists satisfying conventional demands for revenge. When this grandiose film is reduced to human scale, it even manages some truly moving moments, as in the final parting of Arthur and Guenevere, and in Arthur's last scene, when he orders the boy on the battlefield to return home and perpetuate the dream of Camelot.

The Lerner and Loewe songs are frequently beautiful. (Unfortunately, they were filmed with oppressive close-ups that force viewers to peer down the singers' throats.) "What Do Simple Folks Do?" is an amusing reflection by Arthur and Guenevere on the daily lives of people without royal responsibilities. In "Then You May Take Me to the Fair," Guenevere sets one knight after another against Launcelot in an attempt to deflate his sizable ego. Frederick Loewe composed some of his most bewitching melodies for *Camelot,* especially "How to Handle a Woman," Arthur's perplexed musing on ways of dealing with the enigma called woman, and the title song, a charming evocation of a perfect society that never really existed.

On a few occasions, British musicals that had scored great success in their homeland, and then repeated that success on Broadway, were ultimately adapted to the screen. The most popular of such musicals was *Oliver!,* Lionel Bart's version of Charles Dickens's novel *Oliver Twist.* Both the London and New York productions had enjoyed long runs, with audiences delighting in its clever if conventional musical score, lavish settings of early nineteenth-century London, and bright ensemble singing and dancing. Except for hardcore devotees of Dickens, who were irritated by the scrubbed and sanitized view of the London slums, theatergoers were diverted by the melodramatic tale of a resilient poorhouse orphan's adventures.

The 1968 film version veered even further from Dickens, creating a nineteenth-century London in which the teeming slum streets bustle with noise and activity but with little real threat of violence, and the upper-class streets are models of prettiness and order. In this never-never land, Mr. Bumble's Home for Paupers and Orphans resembles a modest dormitory for fresh-faced tykes, and Fagin and his gang of boy thieves seem not too far removed from Father Flanagan and Boys Town. Yet the sets and the costumes are so dazzling that only a churlish viewer could object to the artifice, or resent the old-style film magic it generates.

The expertise that went into the creation of *Oliver!* extends to Lionel Bart's musical score, which is jaunty, colorful, and slickly professional in the best "show biz" tradition. The weakest songs are those that work most shamelessly to evoke emotion in an audience: the wince-inducing "Where Is Love?," sung by Oliver, or the ill-fated Nancy's "As Long as He Needs Me," which had been played and sung so many times, even before the stage production, that it already seemed like a tired old standard. Much better are the raffish songs by Fagin (Ron Moody): his professional advice to Oliver, "You've Got to Pick a Pocket or Two," or "Reviewing the Situation," in which he decides, after some speculation, to keep to his thieving ways.

Oliver! *(Columbia, 1968). Orphan Oliver (Mark Lester) is forced to join the gang of thieving boys organized by the wily Fagin (Ron Moody).*

opposite: Camelot *(Warners, 1967). Queen Guenevere (Vanessa Redgrave) and the boisterous men and women of King Arthur's court sing "The Lusty Month of May," with the emphasis on "lusty."*

© Walt Disney Productions

Mary Poppins *(Disney, 1964)*. Bert (Dick Van Dyke) and Mary Poppins (Julie Andrews) greet their animated forest friends in the "Jolly Holiday" sequence.

The production numbers in *Oliver!* have the requisite sweep and color. The largest, to the tune of "Consider Yourself at Home," is Oliver's introduction to London, bringing out scores of residents for a rousing welcome. On the glorious set of Mr. Brownlow's block, street vendors, followed by schoolgirls in yellow skirts, blue-coated schoolboys, and marching soldiers, greet a sparkling morning by singing "Who Will Buy?" For Carol Reed, responsible for such memorable films as *The Stars Look Down, Odd Man Out,* and *The Third Man, Oliver!* represented a first attempt at a musical. In its preordained, tried-and-true fashion, the film offered little chance for him to demonstrate his well-developed directorial skills. Yet it was extremely popular, winning the Academy Award as best picture of the year, along with four other awards, including a best director Oscar for Reed.

Among the musical films of the sixties set in England, only one film without stage origins truly succeeded. This was the enchanting musical fantasy *Mary Poppins,* released by the Walt Disney studio in 1964. Based on the popular children's stories by P. L. Travers concerning a sensible but magical English nanny, the movie proved to be one of the most popular of the decade, one that pleased not only children but also adults whose imaginations had not yet congealed with age. It was also the very model of what a musical fantasy could be when informed by the creativity and technical skills of dedicated professionals. The exquisite sets of Edwardian London, precisely detailed but also properly idealized; the ravishing costumes; Bill Walsh and Don Da Gradi's diverting screenplay from the Travers stories; the score by Richard and Robert Sherman (by far the best of too many bland scores by this composing team of two brothers); and the delightful performances of a cast headed by Julie Andrews and Dick Van Dyke—all these factors contributed to the durable quality of the film, which was directed by Robert Stevenson.

Mary Poppins takes us to 1910 London, where Bert (Dick Van Dyke), a street merchant of many talents—he is a one-man band, poet, and sidewalk artist—introduces us to the neighborhood where financier Henry Banks (David Tomlinson) lives with his wife (Glynis Johns), a militant suffragette, and his two small children, Jane and Michael (Karen Dotrice and Matthew Garber). When Mr. Banks advertises for a new nanny for the children, Mary Poppins (Julie Andrews) enters the scene, flying in on her umbrella and crisply, efficiently taking charge. ("I am never cross. I have rosy cheeks. I am kind but extremely firm." In fact, she is "practically perfect in every way.") Soon her special magic envelops the awed children as she takes them on a series of marvelous adventures, accompanied by Mary's old friend Bert. Only a disastrous visit to their father's bank spoils the children's euphoria in the care of Mary Poppins. Trouble develops briefly when Mr. Banks's job is jeopardized, but all is resolved happily, of course. However, Mary must leave the Banks family and move on to help others in her unique fashion. We last see her flying across London on her umbrella.

From first to last, *Mary Poppins* combines captivating special effects with imaginative musical numbers. Before Mary arrives, all the grim-looking nannies waiting outside the Banks house to be interviewed are suddenly borne away into the air, clutching their open umbrellas. When Mary appears, she slides *up* the banister, pulls all sorts of unlikely objects out of her small carpetbag, and uses her magical gifts to help the children tidy up their room. Mary and the children join Uncle Albert (Ed Wynn), who floats upward whenever he laughs ("I Love to Laugh"), in a midair tea party. And, entering into one of Bert's sidewalk pictures for a "Jolly Holiday," they float across a stream on the shells of animated turtles, ride on an animated carrousel, and join a fox hunt (the fox has an Irish brogue). The combination of animation and reality, which Disney had used before in other films, was never better realized than in this sequence.

No other Disney musical has ever had a more delightful score than *Mary Poppins*. (It won Academy Awards for best original musical score and best song—"Chim Chim Cheree.") Only rarely does the sentiment become a bit thick, and most of the songs are clever, pointed, and infectious. They are also beautifully presented. As Mary sings "Feed the Birds" while the old Bird Woman (Jane Darwell in her last role) is surrounded by her winged charges on the steps of St. Paul's Cathedral, mawkishness is avoided by images of surpassing beauty and tenderness. On her animated holiday with the children, Mary sings the tongue-twisting "Supercalifragilisticexpialidocious," which is reprised by comical animated figures, including a madcap band. Toward the film's end, when a transformed Henry Banks giddily joins his children for a session of kite-flying ("Let's Go Fly a Kite"), the sight of the colorful kites in midair lifts the heart. And the song and dance of the chimney sweeps in "Step in Time" is surely one of the best numbers in the history of film musicals. Observed and sometimes joined by Bert and the children in London's fantastic night world, the sweeps come out of the chimneys and dance a wild Irish jig, do some fancy steps atop the chimneys, and walk across the roof railing as if it were a tightrope. After the sweeps disperse, the number closes with an eloquent shot of the quiet, deserted street.

Apart from its clever, never overly ambitious special effects, its perfectly tuned performances and production, *Mary Poppins* succeeds because, like the best fantasy films, musical or otherwise, it still keeps at least one foot firmly rooted in reality. When Mary is not taking her charges on flights of fancy, the Edwardian London settings have a genuine if necessarily romanticized look about them. (No squalid slums here.) The screenplay touches lightly and satirically on such sober matters as the suffrage movement, banking, and British rectitude. And most of all we have Mary Poppins herself who, although given to a fair amount of hocus-pocus, is still a nanny—eminently sensible, efficient, and even realistic in her way: "Practically perfect people never allow sentiment to muddle their thinking." Like *The Wizard of Oz, Mary Poppins* recognizes that every Oz must have its Kansas.

The success of *Mary Poppins* guaranteed that other films would venture into musical fantasy based on favorite children's stories, but the few that followed were wretched indeed. In addition to surprisingly shoddy special effects, instantly forgettable scores, and unimaginative screenplays, they failed to add the touch of satire, wit, or plain common sense that fantasy demanded. In 1967, Fox adapted Hugh Lofting's perennially popular stories of *Doctor Dolittle,* about the eccentric little veterinarian who could converse with animals, into a flat-footed, overproduced musical film. Rex Harrison, looking nothing like the good doctor in the

Mary Poppins *(Disney, 1964). Mary Poppins (Julie Andrews) rises airily out of the Banks chimney, to the delight of her young charges (Karen Dotrice and Matthew Garber).*

© Walt Disney Productions

right: Can-Can *(Fox, 1960). Judge Philippe Forrestier (Louis Jourdan) talks with lawyer François Durnais (Frank Sinatra), while some of the "can-can" girls listen in. Second girl from the left: Juliet Prowse.*

illustrations of the *Dolittle* books, made a game effort to play the title role, talk-singing the nondescript tunes in his Henry Higgins manner. The Leslie Bricusse screenplay, under Richard Fleischer's direction, took Dolittle and his friends on a series of whimsical adventures, but the fantasy creations—the double-ended Pushmi-Pullyu, the Great Pink Sea Snail, the Giant Luna Moth—were all unconvincing. Even worse was the 1968 production of *Chitty Chitty Bang Bang,* an oppressive and dull musical fantasy derived from Ian Fleming's story about a magical car. As in *Doctor Dolittle,* the special effects were clumsily executed, and the score by the Sherman brothers was nowhere in a league with their score for *Mary Poppins.*

Several British-based musicals of the sixties did not rely on fantasy, but they were hardly more successful than those that did. By 1968, the popularity of Julie Andrews was beginning to wane —viewers were becoming a bit weary of her cool, crisp style and cool, crisp voice—and her film on the life and career of actress Gertrude Lawrence, entitled *Star!,* was poorly reviewed and failed at the box office. The Andrews personality, wholesome, friendly, and simply nice, was at variance with the grasping, ambitious Gertrude Lawrence portrayed in the screenplay. There were a number of excellent songs by such composers as Cole Porter, Noël Coward, and Kurt Weill, some well-staged production numbers, and an excerpt from Coward's *Private Lives,* but the film was much too long and not very exhilarating.

Amid all this Anglophilic musical activity, the chic and debonair style of England's neighbor France, which had brought vitality to such musicals as *Funny Face, Gigi,* and *Les Girls,* was virtually ignored, and when it turned up only once at the start of the decade, the movie obviously came from the backlots of Hollywood rather than the streets of Paris. This was Fox's 1960 film version of the Cole Porter–Abe Burrows musical play *Can-Can,* a feeble and obvious attempt to match the wit and high professional gloss of MGM's *Gigi.* The cast even included Maurice Chevalier, still enjoying the quiet pleasures of old age as a tolerant judge named Paul Barriere, and Louis Jourdan, cast here as an upright young judge named Philippe Forrestier. After Judge Forrestier becomes amorously involved with the café owner Simone Pistache (Shirley MacLaine), and legally involved with her shifty lawyer boyfriend (Frank Sinatra), he is no longer the same man.

Can-Can is a musical film that virtually embodies the reasons for the decline of the genre in the sixties. Except for its appropriately gaudy costumes and for the exuberant performance by dancer Juliet Prowse as a cancan girl, the musical is without joy or genuine style under Walter Lang's unfocused direction, the Cole Porter score reveals the composer at his most ersatz Parisian ("Maidens Typical of France," "C'est Magnifique," "Montmartre," and "I Love Paris")—wisely, a few good old Porter standards were added to the original score—and two of the central roles are grotesquely miscast: Sinatra, who seems to have arrived in Paris by way of New Jersey, creates no discernible or even vaguely likable character in François. MacLaine does well in the musical portions, but her Pistache is simply shrill and unappealing. Maurice Chevalier and Louis Jourdan work hard at injecting some life into the dull proceedings, Chevalier with his trademarked shrugged-shoulders, *laissez faire* attitude toward life

The Sound of Music *(Fox, 1965). Maria (Julie Andrews) enjoys a picnic in the Austrian Alps with the Von Trapp children. The breathtaking scenery was one of the film's decided assets.*

opposite, below: Star! *(Fox, 1968). In a production number, Julie Andrews, as stage star Gertrude Lawrence, relates the sad saga of "Jenny," the girl who "*would *make up her mind." Although she was not the ideal choice for the role, her rendition of "Jenny" was an improvement over Ginger Rogers's version nearly a quarter-century earlier in* Lady in the Dark.

above: Doctor Dolittle *(Fox, 1967). The eminent doctor (Rex Harrison), astride a giraffe. Harrison played the role in the manner of a benign Henry Higgins, which was acceptable although not very faithful to the Hugh Lofting stories. But the production was defeated by awkward special effects, sluggish pacing, and an indifferent score in which the best song was "When I Look into Your Eyes," which Harrison sings to the lovelorn Sophie the Seal.*

top: Goodbye, Mr. Chips *(MGM, 1969). Teacher Arthur Chipping (Peter O'Toole) introduces his new wife (Petula Clark) to his school. This musical remake of the popular 1939 film based on James Hilton's novel offered a sensitive, moving performance by O'Toole as "Mr. Chips." But the Terence Rattigan screenplay was tedious, and Leslie Bricusse's score of twelve vapid songs was a handicap the film failed to surmount. The movie marked the debut of Herbert Ross as a film director.*

and love, expressed in such songs as "Live and Let Live" and "Just One of Those Things," and Jourdan with the Gallic charm he displayed so prominently in *Gigi*. For all their efforts, however, *Can-Can* emerges as a flat soufflé.

If *West Side Story* was the best musical film of the sixties, then *The Sound of Music* (1965), adapted from the long-running Broadway musical play about Maria Von Trapp and her singing family, was certainly the most popular. Its success was a foregone conclusion. How could it possibly miss, with a story that included the right amount of family sentiment (the Von Trapp children never quarrel among themselves), religion (in the Hollywood tradition of serene, benign nuns), romance (actually two romances, one adult, one adolescent), and anti-Nazi feeling (Captain Von Trapp refuses to surrender to the Nazi invaders)—and with director Robert Wise knowingly mixing the dosages together as prescribed? The packaging of *The Sound of Music* is perfect, but it hides an antiquated story whose characters are cardboard figures more suitable to the conventions of operetta in the early twenties than to a musical film of the mid-sixties. To applaud its quaint, old-fashioned ways is to ignore all that has taken place in the theater or films over the years.

The Sound of Music does have a justifiably famous opening: the camera sweeps over the Austrian Alps to catch Julie Andrews, as mischievous, warmhearted Maria, exultantly singing the title song as she rushes through the bright green valley. It is an exhilarating moment that the film never really matches again, but there is plenty left in the two remaining hours to please the legions of devotees. Once a viewer can force himself beyond the bogus sentiment of "a lark who is learning to pray," or the usual Hammerstein uplift in "Climb Ev'ry Mountain," there are unquestionably some enjoyable songs and musical numbers in *The Sound of Music*. When the eldest Von Trapp daughter (Charmian Carr) meets her shy beau (Daniel Truhitte) in the family garden, he sings "Sixteen Going on Seventeen" to her, and they do a charming little dance around the gazebo. Maria's music lesson to the children, "Do-Re-Mi," is beautifully staged, set over several days as they gambol in and around Salzburg, changing their clothing through camera wizardry. Perhaps the best of the songs is the simplest: "Edelweiss," with a tender lyric and poignant melody that make a fitting last song for Rodgers and Hammerstein.

Another of the film's virtues is Julie Andrews's performance as Maria Von Trapp. Though her no-nonsense British manner and crystal-clear voice went out of fashion in the seventies, she was a valuable asset to the films in which she appeared. In *Mary Poppins*, she kept the whimsy under control with her straightforward approach. In *The Sound of Music,* she cuts through the thick sentiment with her own sharply honed blade of authority and self-confidence, implying that at least *she* will get through all the high corn without damaging her self-esteem. It works to offset the tight-lipped stodginess of Christopher Plummer as Captain Von Trapp, the "adorable" posturings of the children, and the artificial airs of Eleanor Parker as a haughty baroness.

In the seventies, the production of musical films dwindled even more than it had in the sixties. Costs remained high, but despite huge expenditures, audiences seemed to be less responsive than ever to the genre. Despite the popularity of *That's Entertainment* (1974), MGM's compilation of clips from their old musical films, moviegoers favored the awesome special effects of "disaster" films such as *The Towering Inferno* and *The Poseidon Adventure,* or the wrenching violence of such movies as *The Godfather* and *The French Connection.* At any rate, the major musical stars of other years had either died or gone into semiretirement, leaving the field to such talented but nonmusical performers as Lucille Ball and Burt Reynolds. Only Barbra Streisand and, to a lesser extent, Liza Minnelli were on hand to fill the musical void.

Film adaptations of successful or reasonably successful stage musicals continued to appear, and the first one of the decade starred Barbra Streisand. The Burton Lane–Alan Jay Lerner musical *On a Clear Day You Can See Forever* had opened on Broadway in the fall of 1965, but it had run for a disappointing eight months. The critics generally praised its inventive and melodic score but were not pleased with the book, which dealt with a girl endowed with extrasensory perception whose psychiatrist discovers that she had a previous life in the eighteenth century. Complications ensue when he finds himself falling in love with the girl's eighteenth-century manifestation. The 1970 film version, remodeled for Streisand, retained six songs from the stage play, added several new songs, and altered a number of the plot elements.

To portray the befuddled, chain-smoking heroine, Daisy Gamble, who can make flowers grow by simply talking to them, Streisand fell back on her familiar eccentric and emphatic style. The film begins promisingly with a precredit sequence in which Daisy sings to the flowers on the roof of her rooming house ("Hurry! It's Lovely Up Here!"), causing the geraniums, peonies, and other flora to bloom at the sound of her voice. The unusual central concept—a romantic triangle with only two participants—is developed with some amusement in Lerner's screenplay. The story, however, grows wearisome and static after a while, and the odd romantic situation is not helped by the uneasy performance of French star Yves Montand as the psychiatrist.

When Daisy Gamble reverts to Melinda Tentrees, her eighteenth-century double, *On a Clear Day* becomes quite a different film. Placed in opulent settings, and wearing lavish gowns designed by Cecil Beaton, Streisand plays the clever, opportunistic Melinda with a delicious sense of parody, stretching her mock-English accent to its absolute limit. The scene in which she falls in love with Robert Tentrees (John Richardson) at an extravagant dinner party in Brighton's Royal Pavilion is the highlight of the several flashbacks. Bewitchingly photographed by Harry Stradling, she sings "Love with All the Trimmings" (new to the score) with lascivious delight.

The film contains some attractive music, notably the title song, the lyrical "He Isn't You," and "Come Back to Me," sung by Montand from the top of the Pan Am Building in New York City. The movie also has the benefit of its director, Vincente Minnelli. His first musical since *Bells Are Ringing* in 1960, the film lacks the balanced, unified feeling of his best work, with too many scenes that seem disconnected from the

above: On a Clear Day You Can See Forever *(Paramount, 1970). Transported back to the eighteenth century by hypnosis, Daisy Gamble (Barbra Streisand) assumes her identity in a previous life, a mischievous girl named Melinda. Melinda meets, falls in love with, and marries Robert Tentrees (John Richardson).*

top: On a Clear Day You Can See Forever *(Paramount, 1970). Teacher-psychiatrist Marc Chabot (Yves Montand) discovers that, besides his intended subject, he has inadvertently hypnotized another of his students, Daisy Gamble (Barbra Streisand), who has extrasensory powers. Montand's considerable Gallic charm was wasted on a role that required him to do little more than act bewildered by Streisand's double identity.*

Mame *(Warners, 1974). Lucille Ball as Auntie Mame, with her young nephew Patrick (Kirby Furlong). Misguidedly cast as the irrepressible, indestructible lady of print, stage, and screen, Ball worked gamely, handling the slapstick portions with ease and croaking out the merely average songs. But she was not an actress who could carry a musical comedy on her shoulders, and her performance mostly conveyed a sense of desperation rather than high spirits.*

rest of the movie (especially the curiously truncated scenes with Jack Nicholson, playing Streisand's stepbrother). Although the movie certainly takes its time—it is too long at 143 minutes—there is still a sense of something missing, a lack of substance in Daisy Gamble's present-day life that would serve to point up her earlier life as Melinda Tentrees. But Minnelli's sense of design and color has clearly not deserted him; it is especially evident in the brilliant, predominantly red and gold décor of the eighteenth-century sequences.

With a few conspicuous exceptions, other stage adaptations in the first half of the seventies proved unrewarding. They suffered from miscasting, unsuitable themes, cumbersome productions, and often heavy-handed direction. Jack Warner's film version of the 1969 Sherman Edwards–Peter Stone Broadway success *1776* (1972) failed for an odd reason: by remaining entirely faithful to the stage version, it magnified all of the play's glaring faults. In the theater, *1776* had received mostly glowing notices for its unusual subject matter—the stormy but historic meeting of the Second Continental Congress and its adoption of the Declaration of Independence—and for its persuasive performances and frequently enjoyable music. Once it was on screen, however, the praise seemed unaccountable.

As a conventional play or film, *1776* may have made a well-staged history lesson, although, since everyone knows the ending, one lacking in suspense. The central roles, especially William Daniels as the cantankerous John Adams, are well played, and many of the lines are appropriately clever, amusing, or faintly stirring. Peter Hunt repeated his stage direction unobtrusively. But then there is the music, and it just about ruins the film, vulgarizing and trivializing American history to a painful degree. The score is either preposterous—as when the leaders of the cause for independence squabble in song over who should write the Declaration—or embarrassing—as when Thomas Jefferson's wife Martha (Blythe Danner), after a long bedroom interlude with her husband has inspired him to write the document, sings about his "musical" ability in "He Plays the Violin," while Adams and Benjamin Franklin (Howard da Silva, repeating his stage performance) scamper around her.

Another adaptation, released in the same year as *1776,* proved to be a severe disappointment. In 1965, the musical *Man of La Mancha* had been one of the theater season's biggest hits. Derived by Dale Wasserman, Mitch Leigh, and Joe Darion from Cervantes's classic story of the mad old "knight" Don Quixote and his quest for honor and adventure, the musical had received mostly admiring reviews—there were some strong dissenters—and it enjoyed a run of nearly six years. The key song in the score, "The Impossible Dream," was performed so frequently by singers needing a guaranteed showstopper that it became as ubiquitous as had "Sonny Boy" almost four decades earlier.

Directed by Arthur Hiller and filmed largely in Spain amid appropriately stark settings, the film version of *Man of La Mancha* made the familiar—and in this case, fatal—mistake of treating the original property with the reverence and awe due a sacred relic rather than a commercial venture. Solemn, heavy, and oppressive, it began, as the stage play had, with a lengthy prologue showing Cervantes (Peter O'Toole) brought to trial by his fellow prisoners and called upon to defend himself with an entertainment or a charade. He tells of an old man who brooded too long on "man's murderous ways" and decided to become Don Quixote (also O'Toole), a knight errant sallying forth with his faithful squire Sancho Panza (James Coco) to right all the wrongs in the world.

The film centers on the Don's adventures at an inn he mistakes for a castle, where he fights to defend the honor of Aldonza (Sophia Loren), the inn's bitter, abused scullery maid whom his mind transforms into the beloved, idealized Dulcinea. Reality intrudes when a scheming doctor forces the old man to see himself for what he is, "an aging fool! . . . A madman dressed for a masquerade." Before he dies, he rises for one last time and, encouraged by a now-believing Aldonza, he sings the inspiring words of his creed as the "Man of La Mancha."

The film, on the whole, was treated savagely by the critics. In truth it was a ponderous transcription of the play, with little or no cinematic movement or inventiveness. Its main problem was that its central theme had become an irritating bromide by 1972. The concept that only the mad are truly sane ("Too much sanity may be madness") was by now overly familiar, having been advanced in the theater and films for years. The film also perpetrated an auxiliary platitude that illusion is preferable to reality, that we should see life not as it is, but as it should be.

Nevertheless, the movie has merits that were ignored in the general condemnation. As Don Quixote, Peter O'Toole gives one of his best performances. He is especially affecting in his last scenes, in which he has the fragility of a dry leaf about to crumble. Sophia Loren is convincing as Aldonza-Dulcinea, although she should not have been allowed to use her own singing voice. The score contains a number of lushly beautiful songs, notably "Dulcinea," with which Don Quixote serenades his lady fair; "The Barber's Song (Golden Helmet)," in which he mistakes a barber's shaving basin for a helmet; and "Knight of the Woeful Countenance," with which the innkeeper dubs Don Quixote as a knight.

Of the few stage adaptations released in the first half of the seventies that could be safely placed in the great tradition of film musicals, one was the 1971 version of the long-running *Fiddler on the Roof*. The stage production had opened in September of 1964 to wide acclaim. There were some grumblings about the unwarranted "Broadway" touches, but the musical, adapted from Sholom Aleichem's stories, was admired for its moving book by Joseph Stein, its richly melodic score by Jerry Bock and Sheldon Harnick, and its vigorous staging and choreography by Jerome Robbins. Zero Mostel won special praise for his pungent, outsize performance as Tevye, the beleaguered milkman who lives with his family in an impoverished Russian village at the turn of the century.

The film of *Fiddler on the Roof*, with Israeli actor Topol as Tevye, also proved to be a splendid achievement: a powerful, deeply affecting, and piercingly beautiful re-creation of a long-vanished world. As a musical fable, its view may be rose-colored (there is little sense of true poverty in the village's spotlessly gleaming homes, and even the pogrom, although harshly depicted, mutes the violence that actually occurred), but *Fiddler on the Roof* is an incomparable portrait of the traditions that bind together a family and a community, and the inexorable steps by which they are severed.

"Tradition" is more than just the precredit musical number that introduces the principal characters and the residents of Anatevka: it is the solid center of the film. Yet one by one, the traditions that Tevye and his people have cherished and lived by are broken during the course of the film, as marriages are no longer arranged by the "poppa," as men and women dance together in a public place, and—most grievous of all—as children marry out of their faith. The shattering of these traditions becomes even more intolerable to Tevye in the shadow of the dreaded pogrom.

Until the pogrom occurs, *Fiddler on the Roof* establishes the serene but meager life of Anatevka in a series of well-staged musical numbers. Longing for husbands, provided they are the men of their dreams, Tevye's daughters sing "Matchmaker, Matchmaker" as they go about their daily tasks. Tevye sings "If I Were a Rich Man" in his barn, waving his arms and legs in an exuberant dance as he contemplates a life of wealth. Especially moving is the exquisite scene of the "Sabbath Prayer," in which a montage of hands blessing the Sabbath candles creates, more effectively than any dialogue, a sense of the close ties of the Jewish community.

Glowingly photographed, scene after scene offers moments of heart-stopping beauty or wrenching power. Expressing their love for each other, tailor Motel (Leonard Frey, in an especially fine performance) and Tevye's daughter Tzeitel (Rosalind Harris) race through the sun-dappled woods as he sings "Miracle of Miracles." To convince wife Golde (Norma Crane) that Tzeitel must marry Motel, Tevye tells her of his terrifying dream, which is brilliantly enacted in a scene that evokes the awe and dread his people feel when they are confronted by the restless spirits of their beloved dead. The wedding of Motel and Tzeitel is one of the great musical sequences: after a candlelight march to the synagogue, the ceremony takes place to the song "Sunrise, Sunset" (another example of a lovely song unfortunately diminished by overexposure). Skillfully edited into a mosaic of moods, the scene catches the expression of mingled tenderness and sadness on the faces of Tevye and Golde, the elation of the guests, and the shy, hopeful faces of the bride and groom.

The rest of the film takes on a darker tone as forces conspire to oppress not only Tevye's family but also the Jewish community in Anatevka. Now married to the revolutionary student Perchik (Michael Glaser), Tevye's Hodel must leave her home to travel to Siberia, where Perchik has been imprisoned. Her parting from Tevye at the railroad station, to the song "Far from the Home I Love," is inexpressibly touching. Also eloquent is Tevye's furious, then grieving reaction to the love his daughter Chava feels for the young Christian townsman Fietka. This time he is adamant ("Chava is dead to us!"), but his loving memories of the child, seen as he sings the poignant "Chavaleh," negate his bitterness. When the Jews are finally forced to leave Anatevka, they join in a bittersweet tribute to the town ("I belong in Anatevka/ Tumble down, workaday Anatevka/ Dear little village, little town of mine"). The film ends as it began: with a view of the town's indomitable fiddler, again perched precariously on a rooftop.

Fiddler on the Roof *(United Artists, 1971).*
Tevye (Topol), his family, and his daughters'
suitors assemble for the lighting of the
Sabbath candles. One of the film's loveliest
and most poignant sequences, it expressed the
religious feeling and sense of ritual that bound
together the impoverished Jewish people of
Anatevka.

Fiddler on the Roof *(United Artists, 1971).*
The dream sequence in which the deceased wife
of Lazar Wolf the butcher rises out of her
grave to protest Lazar's planned marriage to
Tzeitel. The sequence is a splendid evocation
of Old World superstition concerning the
restless spirits of the beloved dead and their
link to the present.

Under Norman Jewison's direction, the cast performs with a genuine feeling for the material. With his raspy voice, virile appearance, and alternating expressions of compassion and implacability, Topol, although only thirty-five, is a magnificent Tevye. Norma Crane is acceptable as Golde, but Tevye's daughters are played with the right mixture of vulnerability and firmness. Rosalind Harris makes her plain Tzeitel somehow beautiful, and Neva Small is both radiant and pathetic as Chava.

Some of the reviews of *Fiddler on the Roof* complained that in opening up the play, the producers had drained the life from it, creating yet another congealed version of a Broadway success. In this case, the charge seems unwarranted. Filmed largely on location in and around Zagreb, Yugoslavia, the movie does not merely expand the stage settings to impress movie audiences, but uses the actual backgrounds to cinematic advantage, stylizing them slightly to convey the sense of a cheerful, then darkening fable. Also, the film abounds in striking cinematic touches, particularly the indelible moments of parting—the displaced Jews floating on a raft taking them away from their beloved village, or Tevye and the remnants of his family marching down the dusty road. With its strongly emotional songs that grow out of the characters' feelings, a richly textured central performance, and a filmic sense that never becomes self-conscious or intrusive, *Fiddler on the Roof* works equally well as, if not better than, it did on the stage.

The following year brought the release of the film adaptation of *Cabaret* (1972), certainly the most unusual and arguably the greatest musical film of the seventies. The story of Sally Bowles and her ''divinely decadent'' life in Berlin of the early thirties had gone through a number of versions before reaching the screen as *Cabaret.* In 1951, John van Druten had adapted Christopher Isherwood's ''Berlin Stories'' into the play *I Am a Camera,* in which Julie Harris played the giddy and amoral Sally; she then repeated the performance in a British-made film of the same title in 1955. Sally's bemused vis-à-vis in the story was Christopher Isherwood himself, objectively watching the birth pangs of the Nazi monster as he shares in Sally's adventures and misadventures. In 1966, the material was reshaped for the Joe Masteroff–John Kander–Fred Ebb musical play *Cabaret,* under Harold Prince's direction. The emphasis was shifted from Sally Bowles to the cabaret in which she performed, a microcosm of the pleasure-seeking, corrupt world just outside the door. Sally was still present, and Christopher Isherwood became an equally detached observer named Clifford Bradshaw. But the dominant figure of the musical was the leering, painted Master of Ceremonies of the cabaret, simultaneously mocking and pandering to the audience, and brilliantly realized by Joel Grey.

His demonic presence—and Joel Grey's performance—were retained for the film, but in most respects this *Cabaret* was a virtually new creation, forged by director Bob Fosse out of some of the familiar elements of past versions into a dazzling amalgam of music, drama, and social commentary. *I Am a Camera* had been basically a comedy concerning an observant writer's encounter with an outrageous young woman in prewar Berlin. *Cabaret,* the Broadway musical version, was a mixture of Brecht and Broadway, its harshness and cynicism softened by sentiment. But the film of *Cabaret* was entirely different: a multifaceted portrait of a hedonistic, increasingly dangerous society, in which every

brushstroke was important.

All aspects were reworked for the realization of this portrait: Jay Allen's screenplay restored Sally Bowles to proper focus as the highly mascaraed eye of the hurricane, while adding, altering, or eliminating characters. The hero was now a bisexual, insolvent graduate student named Brian Roberts; the opportunistic Fritz Wendel and his wealthy Jewish fiancée Natalia, rather coarsely drawn in *I Am a Camera,* were returned to the story and given deeper poignancy and significance; and the character of Sally and Brian's rich friend Baron Max von Heune was introduced to point up the sexual ambiguity and political unawareness of the time. The more conventional Broadway songs in the Kander-Ebb score were either deleted or relegated to the musical background, while the remaining songs took on new strength and power. The production captured the brazen and garish atmosphere of the time and place, and the cast, headed by Liza Minnelli as Sally and Michael York as Brian, perfectly embodied these people unwittingly caught up in the currents of history.

Cabaret cannot be discussed as a musical film in any conventional sense. Whereas music in a film was usually either performed as a set piece by the star (Betty Grable or Fred Astaire doing the big number on opening night) or evolved out of the mood of a character or a situation (Judy Garland pining for the boy next door), the music in *Cabaret* is only one of three major elements that remain separate in the film and then gradually and inexorably become fused into one. These elements are the music of the cabaret, the lives of the principal characters, and the world outside of their narrow domain. Like threads in a tapestry, each with its own color and texture, they form a complete picture only when woven together.

At first they are related to each other only by suggestion or implication. The film begins with an amorphous view of Berlin's Kit Kat Club in 1931, and as the view becomes clearer, we meet the club's depraved customers and its androgynous master of ceremonies. Wearing chalk-white makeup and crimson lips, he sings ''Willkommen'' as the club's girls, parodies of sexual allure with their pelvic thrusts and kohl-smeared eyes, pose suggestively or play their musical instruments. At this moment, the Kit Kat Club represents a world unconcerned with events (''Leave your troubles outside''). Sally is a citizen of this world: deliberately shocking, cheerfully promiscuous, a lost child masquerading as a woman of the world.

Away from the cabaret, Sally plays the leading role in a fantasy of her own devising. Speaking almost entirely in emotional hyperbole (her first words to Brian are ''Have you a cigarette, darling? I'm *desperate!*''), she regards herself as ''a strange and extraordinary person'' who is certain to become a famous film star. She takes Brian under her wing and introduces him to her friend Fritz Wendel (Fritz Wepper), a frank gigolo seeking English lessons so that he can do a more persuasive job of charming wealthy ladies. Everyone becomes part of her delusionary life: an unseen father who is indifferent to her (although she pretends otherwise); Natalia Landauer (Marisa Berenson), a rich Jewish woman who is feverishly courted by Fritz; and finally Baron Max von Heune (Helmut Griem), who indulges—and ultimately seduces—both Sally and Brian. At

Cabaret *(Allied Artists, 1972). Liza Minnelli in her Academy Award–winning role of the hedonistic Sally Bowles.*

first Sally's insulated life bears little relation to the events propelling Germany toward its hideous destiny.

Gradually, however, the separate aspects of the film converge on each other; skillfully woven by Fosse, the threads of the tapestry begin to form a pattern. The familiar decadence of the cabaret—the women wrestling in mud, a transvestite in the men's room—becomes more ominous: in a shocking moment of cruelty, the club owner is beaten by Nazi thugs while the beat of the music forms an ironic counterpoint. The songs of the Master of Ceremonies take on a sinister coloration: covered with coins that clank out an insistent rhythm, he and Sally sing orgiastically about the glories of money ("Money makes the world go 'round"). Accompanied by a girl in a gorilla costume, he sings "If You Could See Her (With My Eyes)," adding in a confidential whisper, "She doesn't look *Jewish* at all!" Only once does the film leave the cabaret for a musical number, and then it is for one of the film's most haunting scenes. As a handsome, sweet-voiced German boy begins to sing "Tomorrow Belongs to Me" in a beer garden, the camera pans down to the Nazi insignia on his sleeve. Soon the crowd joins in for an enthusiastic chorus, their singing ablaze with patriotic fervor. It is a sequence of terrifying beauty, made even more memorable by several quick shots of an old man, silently disapproving of the song.

At the same time that the film's music darkens, so do the lives of the characters. A dismayed Fritz, who has concealed his Jewishness from everyone, finds himself falling in love with Natalia Landauer, while she faces the first ugly evidence of anti-Semitism: the word "Juden" is smeared on the wall of her house, and her dog is killed. Cracks begin to form in the wall that Sally has built around herself: she learns that Max has no intention of making her a baroness and has also been sharing his favors with Brian; when she discovers that she is pregnant, she has an abortion, which angers Brian and makes him turn brutal toward her. While Max dismisses the Nazis as "stupid hooligans," Brian becomes increasingly repelled by their activities. (A Jewish vendor is murdered, and we see his bloody body covered with his prayer shawl.) Defying Nazi thugs in the street, Brian is badly beaten and is taken to the hospital.

Recognizing her selfish, inconsiderate ways, Sally acknowledges that she could never make a life with Brian in England. They part—Brian leaves Berlin—and Sally, entirely a creature of the cabaret, sings the title song in a number of stunning effectiveness. The song sums up the film's sardonic view of a society mindlessly and even brazenly laughing as the grave beckons ("Life is a cabaret, old chum"). When the Master of Ceremonies tells us once again that "life is beautiful" and the Kit Kat Girls break into a reprise of "Willkommen," the irony is devastating. The final shot of the Nazis in the audience, seen as through a prism, reinforces the irony and turns the cabaret into a gaudy charnel house.

As Sally, Liza Minnelli gives an electrifying performance that makes good use of her quicksilver style and nervous mannerisms. It is a bravura role, of course—she is required to go from a flamboyant playgirl proclaiming that "certain cigarettes make me go wildly sensual" to a poignant waif sobbing "Maybe I am just nothing!"—but she manages the changes of mood with style and sensitivity. She also sings with a dramatic eloquence that

opposite: Cabaret *(Allied Artists, 1972). Sally Bowles (Liza Minnelli), star performer at Berlin's Kit Kat Club, performs "Mein Herr" for the customers, draping herself about a chair Marlene Dietrich–style.*

inevitably reminds one of her mother at the peak of her powers. In one song, "Maybe This Time" (not in the play), she is especially reminiscent of Judy Garland, using the breathless speech and the affecting little giggle that characterized Garland in many of her singing performances. Minnelli received the Academy Award for her performance, as did Joel Grey (best supporting actor). Bob Fosse deservedly won the award as best director, and other awards went to *Cabaret* for its cinematography, sound, editing, art direction, and scoring.

The second half of the seventies saw even fewer stage adaptations than the first, and only one was a throwback to an earlier time, when a successful musical was certain to be transferred faithfully and lavishly to the screen, with most of its score and at least some of its cast intact. This was *A Little Night Music,* the Stephen Sondheim–Hugh Wheeler musical version of *Smiles of a Summer Night,* Ingmar Bergman's classic romantic comedy. The 1973 stage production had been more of a *succès d'estime* than a popular attraction, admired for its sumptuous and elegant mounting by Harold Prince and for Sondheim's extremely sophisticated score. Prince repeated his direction for the 1977 film, but the result was one of the year's disappointments, a handsome but cumbersome and doggedly stagebound musical that was reputedly mangled before its release. (It shows evidence of ruthless editing.)

Whereas *A Little Night Music* was clumsily edited, other stage-derived musical films of the late seventies were edited so hectically, presumably to match the hectic beat of their new-style music, that audiences could be expected to leave the theater afflicted with nervous twitches. A few films matched their pictorial style to the music, with dire results. *The Wiz* (1978), adapted from the long-running black stage version of *The Wizard of Oz,* was a multi-million-dollar movie in which Dorothy (singer Diana Ross), now a reclusive twenty-four-year-old Bronx schoolteacher, discovers Oz in her own backyard. Director Sidney Lumet, attempting his first musical, had sections of New York City transformed into an extraordinary display of gaudy settings, as Dorothy and her friends, Scarecrow Michael Jackson, Tinman Nipsey Russell, and Lion Ted Ross, share adventures on their way to see the Wiz (Richard Pryor). Numbers using hundreds of dancers were staged at the old World's Fair grounds, the World Trade Center, and other New York locations. Long, noisy, and almost unbearable, the film made most viewers long for Judy Garland and her traveling companions.

The film version of *Grease* (1978) also suffered from a nonstop busyness in its editing, indulging in distracting photographic gimmickry to conceal its basically hollow nature. The extremely popular stage show—the longest-running musical in theater history—had been a genial tribute to the styles, fads, and music of the fifties, as filtered through the haze of nostalgia. Nobody could claim that it even remotely approached the realm of art, but audiences responded happily to its infectious spirit and its amusing, fifties-style songs.

Directed by Randal Kleiser with only occasional cinematic style, the movie was a reasonable facsimile of the stage play, although with several significant differences. The most evident change was the tailoring of the material to the leading players, John Travolta and Olivia Newton-John. Supported by actors

A Little Night Music (New World, 1977). Diana Rigg as Countess Charlotte Malcolm, one of the women involved in the amorous complications that are unraveled on a summer evening in turn-of-the-century Sweden. Based on the Stephen Sondheim–Hugh Wheeler stage musical, which was adapted from the Ingmar Bergman film Smiles of a Summer Night, *the musical was awkwardly staged and edited, and it lacked the sophistication of the Bergman movie and the grace and elegance of the stage production.*

opposite, above, left: Cabaret *(Allied Artists, 1972). Brian Roberts (Michael York), a graduate student in prewar Berlin, shares a toast with the mercurial, promiscuous, and heedless Sally Bowles (Liza Minnelli).*

opposite, above, right: Cabaret *(Allied Artists, 1972). Shamelessly winking, leering, and braying at the audience, the Master of Ceremonies (Joel Grey) joins the Kit Kat Girls as they perform at the cabaret.*

opposite, below: Grease *(Paramount, 1978). Jeff Conaway, Olivia Newton-John, John Travolta, and Stockard Channing sing "We Go Together" in the musical's finale. Travolta, a popular television actor who achieved stardom with his galvanic performance in* Saturday Night Fever, *brought his charged sexuality to the leading role, and Australian singer Newton-John, although clearly too old for her role, was pretty and sweet-voiced as his wavering girlfriend.*

above: Jesus Christ, Superstar *(Universal, 1973). Christ (Ted Neeley) is flagellated by Roman soldiers. This musical drama with a driving rock score found its way to the screen after appearing successively as a record album and a Broadway show.*

top: Hair *(United Artists, 1979). Irreverent, defiant, and bursting with vitality, the park hippies sing the opening number, "Aquarius." Their hymn to "harmony and understanding" was an auspicious beginning for a musical that succeeded only in isolated sequences.*

(Stockard Channing, Jeff Conaway, Didi Conn) whose high school days were obviously far behind them, and by veteran performers (Sid Caesar, Eve Arden, Joan Blondell) who could add a little box-office insurance for the older set, the stars tried to make something appealing of their up-and-down romance. The songs— "Summer Nights," "Greased Lightnin'," "Hopelessly Devoted to You," "Look at Me, I'm Sandra Dee"—were clever pastiches that had little merit outside of their link to a rosy past.

The movie *Grease* holds interest only as it compares with similar musical films of other years. Obviously the film's language and blunt sexual attitudes would have sent Judy Garland into a dead faint in the Mickey-Judy films of the forties, and even Annette Funicello would have slapped Frankie Avalon's face in the fifties "beach party" movies. (Avalon, looking not much different, is featured in one of *Grease*'s more amusing numbers, "Beauty School Dropout.") But despite the movie's pretensions at being a major musical, it has no more value than any of the earlier movies. In fact, the similarities are more apparent than the differences: the overage students, the foolish, mindless musical numbers, the boy-girl complications, the total lack of interest in learning, and the noisy rumpus of rallies and dances. The older films, however, never suffered from delusions of grandeur.

Another artifact of the theater's recent past that finally became a film in the late seventies was the Gerome Ragni–James Rado–Galt MacDermot rock musical *Hair* (1979). Over a decade earlier, in 1968, *Hair* had moved to Broadway after a widely talked-about off-Broadway run, and had startled and entertained more conventional audiences with its audacious style and its driving rock music. (A rather dimly staged nude scene stirred up widespread publicity.) The musical was both a celebration of "flower power" and the pleasures of love and peace and a hippie protest against war and violence. It proved to be refreshing and surprisingly likable entertainment, and ran for over four years.

Years after the flower children had faded into history, the film version of *Hair* appeared to general acclaim. Many critics responded favorably to the still attractive, vigorous music and unabashed lyrics, to the skillful editing, and to Czech director Milos Forman's handling of a large cast of young performers. Dancer Twyla Tharp's choreography was especially praised. The slight story remained basically the same: At the height of the Vietnam War, a naïve farm boy named Claude (John Savage) comes to New York to enter the army. In Central Park, he is taken over by a band of unrestrained, life-loving hippies led by Berger (Treat Williams). He meets and falls in love with Sheila (Beverly D'Angelo), a rich girl who freely joins the park hippies. Later, Berger takes Claude's place in the army so that Claude can spend some time with Sheila. Before Claude returns, Berger is shipped overseas, and he is killed in action. His friends join in singing at his grave, and the film ends with an affecting tribute to the antiwar movement of the sixties.

There are moments of undeniable pleasure in *Hair*. The opening number, "Aquarius," in which Claude discovers the world of the park hippies, achieves sheer delight when the white horses of the park policemen prance in time with the music. The title number, vividly staged in prison, leaves no doubt that long, flowing hair represents freedom—open and untrammeled. After a day of "communion" with LSD, Claude experiences a bizarre and quite beautiful fantasy of marrying Sheila. Perhaps the film's funniest scene is built around the song "Black Boys," in which black and white girls, joined by black and white members of an army recruitment board, thumb their noses at conventional attitudes toward interracial sex. The closing scene at Berger's grave, in which swarms of young people overwhelm the rows of white crosses with their affirmative song, "Let the Sunshine In," is genuinely moving.

Still, the time lapse between the original stage production of the late sixties and the film of the late seventies creates a fatal anachronism. Where they once seemed fresh and somehow touching, the park hippies now appear to be ghosts out of their time, playing a game that has ended long before they knew it. Their joy is not only contrived and artificial, but it also has a nasty edge. Their "freedom" is a sham, depending in part on hallucinatory drugs and bought at the expense of others. Throughout the film, their behavior is supposed to be refreshingly honest and even ingratiating—yet it is actually disagreeable and even threatening. Apparently they take pleasure in badgering, humiliating, and preying on people. They cheerfully demolish a dinner party given by Sheila's parents—people who have done them no offense—and we are expected to laugh and applaud. Too often the film's targets are easy: foolish rich women, rule-bound military men, uncomprehending middle-class parents.

The movie also makes the mistake of calling for unearned emotional responses. We are asked to be moved by Berger's sacrifice in taking Claude's place in the army, but in view of Berger's strong opposition to participating in the war, this sacrifice is not only ironic, it is also unconvincing and inexplicable. (Why would Berger persist in maintaining Claude's identity—and how could the army avoid discovering its error?) This unwarranted manipulation of the audience's emotions is also evident in the musical numbers. For example, we are suddenly confronted by a young black woman (Cheryl Barnes) who is clutching the hand of her adorable little boy. She asks her husband, one of the park hippies, to return to her, and when he refuses, she sings the plaintive "Easy to Be Hard." She sings it beautifully, but how can we feel any sympathy for her plight when she has just turned up in the film, her desolation as strong as if she were a leading character we had come to know? In the musical film, if the song is not merely a staged number interrupting or irrelevant to the plot, then it springs from the character's pent-up emotions. And having met and presumably sympathized with the character, we can share his or her feeling. But here, the number leaves the viewer impressed with the performance but baffled and uninvolved.

For all of its high spirits, *Hair* is a cheerless musical trying to fill its hollow center with frenetic activity. Despite the startling beauty of some of its images and the vigor of much of its singing and dancing, it is a film cut off from its rightful time and place, a sixties concept with a seventies sensibility.

Musical adaptations from classic or perennially popular novels were variably effective in the seventies. A 1973 musicalization of Mark Twain's *Tom Sawyer,* produced by *The Reader's Digest* for the enjoyment of family audiences, was bland but pleasant enter-

above: Lost Horizon *(Columbia, 1973). The radiant Liv Ullmann, never less than sincere even under the direst circumstances, prances about Shangri-La with a group of children, singing "The World Is a Circle."*

top: Tom Sawyer *(United Artists, 1973). Jeff East as Huckleberry Finn and Johnny Whitaker as Tom enjoy their freedom in this musical version of Mark Twain's classic story.*

tainment. It was filmed on location in Arrow Rock, Missouri. Snub-nosed and freckle-faced Johnny Whitaker was well cast as Tom, and Celeste Holm as Aunt Polly, Jeff East as Huckleberry Finn, and Jodie Foster as Becky Thatcher provided good support. The untiring Sherman brothers, who also wrote the screenplay, contributed one of their better scores, including "Gratifaction," "A Man's Gotta Be What He's Born to Be," and the nicely staged title song, in which Aunt Polly, Cousin Mary, and Cousin Sidney express their divergent views of Tom's personality.

The most execrable musical adaptation of a well-known novel was Ross Hunter's 1973 production of James Hilton's *Lost Horizon*. Frank Capra's version of the novel, released in 1937, was one of that year's most popular films: an effective fantasy-adventure concerning an idealistic man (Ronald Colman) who discovers Shangri-La, a perfect world of peace and tranquility, in a remote area of Tibet. Expanded to grandiose proportions, the story now seemed fatuous and hollow, and the theme—"There's a longing for Shangri-La in everyone's heart"—the epitome of "show biz" sentimentality.

It may be unkind to dwell on this film's myriad faults, and yet it is an anthology of missteps in creating a musical fantasy. The direction by Charles Jarrott, whose only other film credits were two historical costume dramas, *Anne of the Thousand Days* and *Mary, Queen of Scots,* is devoid of imagination. The gargantuan sets—Shangri-La resembles Caesar's Palace East—overwhelm the basically fragile story. The songs by Burt Bacharach and Hal David are replete with the sappiest of sentiments concerning the perfection of the world and the rewards of friendship and family life ("Friendly Doors," "Different People," "Living Together, Growing Together"). They add little or nothing to the development of the story or the characters. Most embarrassing are the empty platitudes that the usually capable players, including Liv Ullmann, Peter Finch, Michael York, and Charles Boyer, are asked to mouth.

No entirely original musical turned up until the middle of the decade, and when one finally appeared, it was a follow-up to an earlier film. *Funny Lady* (1975), directed by Herbert Ross as a continuation of *Funny Girl,* brought Barbra Streisand back to repeat her role of comedienne-singer Fanny Brice. Essentially, it concerned Fanny's sagging career in the thirties and her involvement with impresario Billy Rose (James Caan). Whereas Fanny's romance with and marriage to gambler Nick Arnstein, in spite of its triteness, had a certain dramatic content, her relationship with Rose, at least in this movie fabrication, never seemed to get beyond a certain abrasiveness and grudging respect, and *Funny Lady* suffers accordingly. The movie traces her meeting with the brash, ambitious songwriter and promoter, their subsequent marriage, and their rocky life together as Fanny's career falters and Rose rises to the top.

Lacking in emotional force, the screenplay settles for mild banter or squabbles between Fanny and Billy. Streisand, carrying over from the earlier film, plays Fanny with ease, but Caan, without a genuine character to create, merely walks through his role. Musically, however, the film has many good moments. As usual, Streisand is at her most effective in solo performances, where the camera can concentrate on her unique mannerisms and

Funny Lady *(Columbia, 1975). Barbra Streisand as Fanny Brice performs in* Crazy Quilt, *the disastrous musical revue staged by husband-to-be Billy Rose.*

style (the tilted chin, the extravagant gestures, the nasal emphasis, the mounting intensity). She does an expressive rendition of "Am I Blue?" (the song begins with a startling close-up of her blue eyes), and she gives a sensitive reading of Billy Rose's "More than You Know" at a recording session. She also performs two numbers that are strongly reminiscent of those in *Funny Girl:* a staging of "How Lucky Can You Get" that suggests "My Man" in its acceleration from sorrow to defiance, and "Let's Hear It for Me," in which her singing as she travels by train and private plane to be with Billy has the style and aggressive tone of "Don't Rain on My Parade."

Streisand starred a year later in a new version of *A Star Is Born* (1976). The popular 1937 and 1954 versions had centered on what Hollywood liked to sentimentalize as "the heartbreak and the triumph" that existed side by side in the movie colony. But this newest edition, although it retained the basic story of two theatrical careers, one rising, one plummeting, changed the background to the frenetic world of rock music. Doubling as executive producer and composer of some of the music with Paul Williams, Streisand played Esther Hoffman, an aspiring singer who marries John Norman Howard (Kris Kristofferson), a famous rock star whose drinking is destroying his talent and his popularity. He is finally killed in a car crash, and Esther sings a tribute to him at a memorial concert.

The perils of egomania in filmmaking have seldom been demonstrated as blatantly as in this movie. Firmly in control of virtually all of the film's behind-the-scene elements—director Frank Pierson was consigned to directing traffic—Streisand also dominates almost every scene in front of the camera, even many of those in which she appears with Kris Kristofferson. Unfortunately, although she sings with her usual power and feeling, she is simply not a convincing rock star, and her overwhelming assurance from the beginning makes her early undiscovered status most unlikely. (This Esther would *insist* on stardom.) Nor does the rock scene lend itself comfortably to the basic sentimentality of the story: the ear-splitting music and the shrieking crowds all serve to undermine any emotional impact it may have had. The closing scene, in which Esther stands before a mourning audience holding an array of lighted candles, tries for the same tear-jerking effect as the famous "This is Mrs. Norman Maine" of the earlier versions, but it seems maudlin and incongruous after everything that has preceded it.

Among the original musical films of the seventies, Peter Bogdanovich's *At Long Last Love* (1975) was emphatically different, but unfortunately, it was also a disaster of notable proportions. Written, produced, and directed by Bogdanovich as another of his homages to venerable film genres, the movie was a fond recollection of the chic musical films of the thirties in which suave gentlemen, usually resembling Fred Astaire, sang and danced in Art Deco settings with elegantly gowned ladies not unlike Ginger Rogers. The songs were either romantic or sophisticated, and the mood was frivolous. It may have seemed a splendid notion to re-create a musical film of this era, adding the advantages of color and giving contemporary performers the chance to sing and dance to thirteen of Cole Porter's witty and wicked tunes.

From the idea to the execution lay many a pitfall, and

At Long Last Love tumbles headlong into almost every one of them. The film is not totally meretricious: the Porter songs, as expected, are clever, ingeniously rhymed, and occasionally bawdy in a mild way. The sets and costumes, usually variations of black against silver or white on white, are lovely, capturing the sleek, elegant, and rather arid look of the thirties musicals. The plot is properly simple, dealing with the interactions of four people: playboy Michael, playgirl Brook, actress Kitty, and Italian gigolo Johnny. They fall in and out of love, observed by servants Rodney and Elizabeth.

Then what went so terribly wrong? Unfortunately, almost everything. First there was the misguided casting of Burt Reynolds and Cybill Shepherd as Michael and Brook. An engaging comedian, Reynolds is entirely out of place as the debonair, wealthy man about town, and his usual tongue-in-cheek, insouciant manner edges the movie toward clumsy satire rather than the intended tribute to a vanished style. His attempts at singing and dancing are embarrassing. Cybill Shepherd is even worse, shrill, awkward, and amateurish in all areas of musical comedy and inept as a comedienne. The other cast members are only marginally better. The one truly refreshing note is sounded by veteran actress Mildred Natwick as Michael's frisky mother. Appearing briefly midway through the movie, she instinctively assumes the proper tone and attitude: brittle, funny, and perfectly serious about the inane things she is called upon to say.

Bogdanovich's screenplay completely lacks sparkle and charm. But perhaps his most fatal mistake was his particular selection of Cole Porter songs. Ranging from such familiar tunes as "You're the Top" and "I Get a Kick Out of You" to more esoteric numbers such as the risqué "But in the Morning, No" and "Most Gentlemen Don't Like Love," the score deliberately avoids Porter's lushly romantic music. The result is too stylized, too specialized, too "chichi" for a seventies movie audience to tolerate except in small doses.

A few other original musicals attempted to evoke the past, with equally poor results. In *New York, New York* (1977), director Martin Scorsese recalled the Big Band era of the forties in a musical drama concerning the romance and shaky marriage of a musician (Robert De Niro) and a band singer (Liza Minnelli). Much of the forties ambiance was accurately re-created, and Minnelli gave vibrant readings of some good songs, especially the title song, but De Niro's character was so harsh and unpleasant and his squabbles with Minnelli so long and depressing that the film was easily the gloomiest musical in some time. *The Buddy Holly Story* (1977), dealing with the rock star who died in a plane crash in 1959, just as his fame had peaked, was much less pretentious and much better. Holly's story curiously resembles that of Glenn Miller: defiant musician searches for his own sound, finally becomes popular, marries his loyal girlfriend, and is then killed in a crash. But the rock music was presented without apology or gimmickry (a sequence set in the Apollo Theatre in Harlem was vividly staged), and Gary Busey was excellent as Holly, making the musician a likable and understandable person.

At the end of the decade, Bob Fosse, director of *Cabaret*, created the most striking—and certainly the most controversial— original musical film to appear in many years. Audacious or

New York, New York *(United Artists, 1977). Liza Minnelli in the production number "Happy Endings," most of which was later deleted from the release print of the film.*

opposite, above: A Star Is Born *(Warners, 1976). Barbra Streisand, as rising rock star Esther Hoffman, sings for her fans.*

opposite, center: At Long Last Love *(Fox, 1975). Stepping out for a good time (theirs, not the audience's) are Duilio Del Prete, Cybill Shepherd, Burt Reynolds, and Madeline Kahn. This musical was sorely afflicted by leading players with the musical talent of a tone-deaf frog and by a screenplay with as much genuine gaiety as a sinking ship. The amusing thirties décor and witty though brittle Cole Porter songs could not save it from disaster.*

opposite, below: Bugsy Malone *(Paramount, 1976). Jodie Foster as Tallulah, the saloon "canary," in a musical spoof of thirties gangster films in which all the roles were played by children. The idea did not work: after an amusing half-hour, the film became excessively coy, oppressive, and distasteful. The stylized sets were handsome, and a few of the production numbers were diverting. But the movie was a concept that had best remained stillborn.*

The Buddy Holly Story *(Columbia, 1978). Gary Busey's driving performance as the ill-fated rock star won him an Oscar nomination as best actor.*

opposite, above: All That Jazz *(Fox, 1979). Ben Vereen as television host O'Connor Flood and Roy Scheider as Joe Gideon sing in "Bye, Bye, Life," the film's last fantasy sequence.*

opposite, below: All That Jazz *(Fox, 1979). Even at the point of death, Joe Gideon (Roy Scheider) views all of life in terms of show business, as chorus girls dance around his hospital bed.*

intimidating, dazzling or simply bewildering, depending on one's point of view, *All That Jazz* (1979) was Fosse's extravagant homage to the musical stage he loved—a love tempered by wit and irony—and an autobiographical account of one man's hectic travail in the theater, ending with the ultimate experience of his death. (Fosse, of course, survived his heart attack and is still very active in the theater and films.) His Joe Gideon (Roy Scheider), egotistical, selfish, and womanizing, but also guilt-ridden and striving for a perfection he can never achieve, perceives his entire life in terms of show business. This obsessive view is his gift, his burden, and his tragic flaw.

All That Jazz was the most cinematic musical in a very long time. In a style clearly influenced by Italian director Federico Fellini, Fosse uses the camera with bold assurance, moving from naturalistic scenes of frenzied theatrical activity to flights of fantasy, without signaling the audience when the realism ends and the fantasy begins. Viewed entirely through Joe Gideon's brilliant, disorderly mind, the world is composed of the important people in his life—his ex-wife, his present girlfriend, his young daughter, and all the slightly mad, flamboyant show people he works with, as well as figures from his past and future, most especially the ravishing young woman who represents the Angel of Death. *All That Jazz* has some painful moments, and is not easy to follow; it demands the attention that many viewers, irritated by Fosse's self-indulgence, were unwilling to give.

The film begins with a view that becomes a recurrent theme: Gideon, bleary-eyed and disheveled, beginning his day with pills, music, and the salutation "It's show time, folks!" Life and show business are one and the same: challenging and precarious. ("To be on the wire is life; the rest is waiting.") We follow him to a dance audition—and the movie's first production number, "On Broadway"—in which swarms of hopeful dancers compete in an atmosphere of dedication and fear. We begin to understand Gideon's complex nature: his feelings of guilt ("I really screwed up that marriage" "I'm a lousy father"), his futile search for perfection (he is continually editing and reediting a film resembling Fosse's *Lenny,* in which comedian Cliff Gorman keeps returning ironically to the subject of death), and his relationships with women. His ex-wife Audrey (Leland Palmer, in a role suggesting Fosse's ex-wife Gwen Verdon), a lead dancer in his current show, understands exactly what an attractive monster he is. Casually promiscuous, he is already cheating on his new girlfriend Katie (Ann Reinking). At various times we also see the beautiful young Angelique (Jessica Lange), all in white, who is waiting serenely and patiently for his demise. (Joe's mother tells her, "Ever since he was so high, he's had such a crush on you!")

Splendidly photographed by Giuseppe Rotunno, who worked with Fellini, *All That Jazz* follows Gideon through the exhausting, driving day-to-day routine. There are a few quiet moments—in one of the film's best scenes, he gives a private dance lesson to his young daughter Michelle (Erzsebet Foldi), showing a pride and a tenderness he usually conceals. But all of his energy is given to choreographing the movie's most outstanding musical number, "Take Off with Us." Brilliantly conceived, the number involves a group of dancers in sensuous choreographed movement.

Can't Stop the Music *(AFD, 1980). In a gymnasium, backed by exercising men, the Village People perform their hit recording of "Y.M.C.A." The number reflected what the* New York Times *critic referred to as "the boy-meet-boy world" of the movie.*

overleaf, above: The Jazz Singer *(AFD, 1980). Singer Jesse Robin, born Rabinovitch (Neil Diamond), performs for an enthusiastic audience.*

overleaf, below: Pennies from Heaven *(MGM, 1981). Steve Martin and Bernadette Peters play ill-starred lovers in Chicago during the Depression years. Inspired by the British television production of the same name, the musical concerns a group of people who escape the misery and disappointment of their lives by fantasizing to the melodies and lyrics of the popular songs of the day. In an unusual concept, their voices are synchronized to actual recordings by Bing Crosby, Rudy Vallee, and many others.*

opposite: The Rose *(Fox, 1979). Bette Midler belts out a song as the doomed and driven rock singer called "The Rose," modeled after the late Janis Joplin.*

Inevitably, the strain tells, and Gideon has a heart attack. Confined to a hospital bed, he is irrepressibly theatrical as always, even after a serious heart operation. The hospital itself becomes a gigantic stage on which he creates hallucinatory musical numbers that relate to his plight, built around such songs as "There'll Be Some Changes Made" and "Who's Sorry Now?" As death grows near, he leaves his bed and wanders through the hospital, going into the autopsy room and into a ward where he embraces a dying old woman in an ineffably touching moment. The film closes with a truly imaginative musical number: in his "final appearance on this earth," Joe Gideon joins family and friends in a rousing "Bye, Bye, Life," led by the fatuous, painfully "sincere" television master of ceremonies (Ben Vereen) who has turned up periodically in Gideon's mind. This time Gideon's showstopper is also a heart-stopper.

All That Jazz has flaws: the operation scene is unnecessarily graphic, some of the aspects of the plot are less than fresh, a few scenes overstress their point or go on too long, and occasionally the irony is obvious and heavy-handed. (For example, shots of Gideon's operation alternate with a scene of his backers discussing the refinancing of the show without him.) It is also true that Gideon's coldness makes us care less than we should about his fate, although lovability is not necessarily a requirement for a hero in a musical. But no musical since *Cabaret* has worked so assiduously to weld all the elements of a musical film (or more accurately a drama with music) into a single entity that could only be done on the screen: a personal statement that could be dismissed or even mocked but that could not be ignored.

Other musical films at the close of the seventies and the start of the eighties offered little evidence that the genre was about to undergo a rebirth. Several musicals recalled films of earlier years, but added the contemporary bluntness and raunchiness, as well as the glitter and flash, that seemed to find favor with audiences. *The Rose* (1979), suggested by the short, frenzied life of rock singer Janis Joplin, was reminiscent of the tormented-singer musical dramas of the fifties (*I'll Cry Tomorrow, Love Me or Leave Me*), but the driving music, the harsh language, and a no-holds-barred performance by Bette Midler as Rose brought it squarely into more recent times. *The Blues Brothers* (1980), an extravagant farce with "Saturday Night Live" alumni John Belushi and Dan Aykroyd, had its roots in the sort of slapdash musical farce turned out by Paramount in the thirties. *Fame* (1980), with its view of aspiring young performers, had a distant relative in the Mickey-Judy musicals. However, its musical numbers, although vividly staged, seemed curiously detached from the rest of the film. *Can't Stop the Music* (1980), directed by comedienne Nancy Walker, was an admitted throwback to musical films of the forties, but its style, attitude, and sensibility were clearly locked into the eighties.

A musical fantasy entitled *Xanadu* (1980) only confirmed once again that the form is difficult to carry off successfully. A misguided attempt to merge the past (ethereal fantasy, Gene Kelly) with the present (roller derbies, disco music), *Xanadu* starred Olivia Newton-John as a muse who comes to earth to help a struggling artist (Michael Beck). The film's music was popular for a time, but the foolish screenplay, ugly settings and costumes, and unfocused direction doomed the enterprise to quick extinction. Kelly sang and danced a little, but his presence was merely a sop to the older generation.

Undoubtedly the musical film most appropriate for bringing this chronicle full circle is the 1980 remake of *The Jazz Singer*. On an October evening in 1927, the original version of Samson Raphaelson's sentimental tale of filial betrayal and redemption had entered the annals of film history, the first feature-length movie to use audible dialogue. In the title role, Al Jolson had electrified the audience with his songs. In 1953, comedian Danny Thomas starred in a dated but respectable version.

By 1980, however, the moss that had formed around the story of the implacable Old World cantor and his defiant New World son could easily blanket a forest. There seemed to be no justification for a third edition, a fact that apparently never daunted the producers. With popular singer Neil Diamond as "jazz singer" (actually rock star) Jesse Robin, born Rabinovitch, and Laurence Olivier as his heartbroken father, the new film tried to recapture the emotional aura of the original. But the attitudes of the eighties are so drastically, so irretrievably different from those of half a century earlier that the film made as little sense as its title. Complete with exclamatory dialogue, tears, and embraces, many key scenes verged perilously on the laughable. (One major change turned Jessie's hand-wringing mother into a whining wife.)

Diamond's songs, frequently inserted into all the hard-breathing histrionics, were, on the whole, effectively rendered in his raspy voice, but his performance was so bland and devoid of genuine feeling that any possible audience sympathy was quickly dissipated. In contrast, Laurence Olivier delivered yet another of his now-standard mittel-European impressions complete with quivering body, extravagant gestures, and as many inflections in each sentence as he could possibly manage. Only Lucie Arnaz, in the obligatory role of Jesse's friend and lover, gave a likable and believable performance.

The immediate years ahead do not promise a resurgence of the musical genre. There will be occasional musical films with a contemporary beat, as well as a few adaptations of such stage successes as *Annie* and *A Chorus Line*. Yet, although the Hollywood musical may be dormant, it is far from moribund. The impulses that cause otherwise rational people to raise their voices in song, to lift their feet in dance—a newly discovered love, a spring morning, or a longing too deep to be borne in silence—could never be dismissed permanently from the screen. In spite of spiraling costs, or the lack of superior musical talent, or the evident preference of current movie audiences for a different sort of fare, the musical film will survive into the eighties and beyond.

Today, an acceptable musical film may be like a bright gold coin amid a barrel of worn copper pennies. Yet the treasure trove of Hollywood musicals from the past remains a glowing gift every generation can inherit. The great musical films have become embedded in the consciousness of everyone who values their beauty, their talent, their perennial capacity to lift the heart. By now they have moved beyond memory, beyond nostalgia, to carry us aloft forever on wings of song.

SELECTED BIBLIOGRAPHY

Anderton, Barbie. *Sonny Boy: The World of Al Jolson*. London: Jupiter Books, 1975.

Astaire, Fred. *Steps in Time*. New York: Harper & Brothers, 1959.

Basinger, Jeanine. *Shirley Temple*. New York: Pyramid Publications, 1975.

———. *Gene Kelly*. New York: Pyramid Publications, 1976.

Beckerman, Bernard, and Siegman, Howard, eds. *On Stage: Selected Theater Reviews from "The New York Times," 1920–1970*. New York: Arno Press/Quadrangle Books, 1973.

Burton, Jack. *The Blue Book of Hollywood Musicals*. Watkins Glen, N.Y.: Century House, 1953.

Comden, Betty, and Green, Adolph. *"Singin' in the Rain": Story and Screenplay*. New York: Viking Press, 1972.

———. "How the Kids Made Musical History." *Saturday Review*, April 22, 1972.

Croce, Arlene. *The Fred Astaire & Ginger Rogers Book*. New York: Outerbridge & Lazard, 1972.

Crowther, Bosley. *The Lion's Share*. New York: E. P. Dutton & Company, 1957.

Dickens, Homer. *The Films of Ginger Rogers*. Secaucus, N.J.: The Citadel Press, 1975.

Eames, John Douglas. *The MGM Story*. London: Octopus Books, 1975.

Fordin, Hugh. *The World of Entertainment*. Garden City, N.Y.: Doubleday & Company, 1975.

Frank, Gerold. *Judy*. New York: Harper & Row, 1975.

Geduld, Harry M. *The Birth of the Talkies*. Bloomington: Indiana University Press, 1975.

Gottfried, Martin. *Broadway Musicals*. New York: Harry N. Abrams, 1979.

Green, Stanley, and Goldblatt, Burt. *Starring Fred Astaire*. New York: Dodd, Mead and Company, 1973.

Gussow, Mel. *Don't Say Yes Until I Finish Talking: A Biography of Darryl F. Zanuck*. Garden City, N.Y.: Doubleday and Company, 1971.

Harvey, Stephen. *Fred Astaire*. New York: Pyramid Publications, 1975.

Higham, Charles. *Warner Brothers*. New York: Charles Scribner's Sons, 1975.

Hirschhorn, Clive. *Gene Kelly*. Chicago: Henry Regnery Company, 1975.

Honeycutt, Kirk. "Dancing on Film and Strolling Down

Top Hat (RKO, 1935). A prime example of the B.W.S. (Big White Set) that figured importantly in Astaire-Rogers musicals.

Memory Lane" (interview with Gene Kelly). *New York Times*, June 1, 1980.

Hotchner, A. E. *Doris Day: Her Own Story*. New York: William Morrow and Company, 1976.

Juneau, James. *Judy Garland*. New York: Pyramid Publications, 1974.

Knox, Donald. *The Magic Factory: How MGM Made "An American in Paris."* New York: Praeger Publishers, 1973.

Kobal, John. *Gotta Sing, Gotta Dance: A Pictorial History of Film Musicals*. London: The Hamlyn Publishing Group, 1970.

Kreuger, Miles. *The Movie Musical from Vitaphone to 42nd Street*. New York: Dover Publications, 1975.

———. *"Show Boat": The Story of a Classic American Musical*. New York: Oxford University Press, 1977.

Marx, Arthur. *Goldwyn: A Biography of the Man Behind the Myth*. New York: W. W. Norton & Company, 1976.

McClelland, Doug. *Susan Hayward: The Divine Bitch*. New York: Pinnacle Books, 1972.

McGilligan, Patrick. *Ginger Rogers*. New York: Pyramid Publications, 1975.

McVay, Douglas. *The Musical Film*. New York: A. S. Barnes & Co.: London: A. Zwimmer, 1967.

Milne, Tom. *Mamoulian*. Bloomington: Indiana University Press, 1970.

Minnelli, Vincente (with Hector Arce). *I Remember It Well*. Garden City, N.Y.: Doubleday and Company, 1974.

Moshier, W. Franklin. *The Alice Faye Movie Book*. New York: A & W Visual Library, 1974.

Parish, James Robert. *Hollywood's Great Love Teams*. New Rochelle, N.Y.: Arlington House, 1974.

———. *The Jeanette MacDonald Story*. New York: Mason/Charter, 1976.

Peary, Gerald. *Rita Hayworth*. New York: Pyramid Publications, 1975.

Pike, Bob, and Martin, Dave. *The Genius of Busby Berkeley*. Reseda, Calif.: CFS Books, 1973.

Ringgold, Gene, and Bodeen, De Witt. *Chevalier: The Films and Career of Maurice Chevalier*. Secaucus, N.J.: The Citadel Press, 1973.

Rooney, Mickey. *i.e.: The Autobiography of Mickey Rooney*. New York: G. P. Putnam's Sons, 1965.

Schickel, Richard. *The Men Who Made the Movies*. New York: Atheneum, 1975.

Sennett, Ted. *Warner Brothers Presents*. New Rochelle, N.Y.: Arlington House, 1971.

Springer, John. *All Talking! All Singing! All Dancing!: A Pictorial History of the Movie Musical*. New York: The Citadel Press, 1966.

Stern, Lee Edward. *The Movie Musical*. New York: Pyramid Publications, 1974.

———. *Jeanette MacDonald*. New York: Pyramid Publications, 1977.

Taylor, John Russell, and Jackson, Arthur. *The Hollywood Musical*. New York: McGraw-Hill Book Company, 1971.

Thomas, Bob. *King Cohn*. New York: G. P. Putnam's Sons, 1967.

Thomas, Lawrence B. *The MGM Years*. New York: Columbia House, 1972.

Thomas, Tony, and Terry, Jim (with Busby Berkeley). *The Busby Berkeley Book*. New York: A & W Visual Library, 1973.

Walker, Alexander. *The Shattered Silents: How the Talkies Came to Stay*. New York: William Morrow and Company, 1979.

Weinberg, Herman G. *The Lubitsch Touch: A Critical Study*. New York: E. P. Dutton & Co., 1968.

SELECTED FILMOGRAPHY

The director's name follows the release date. A (c) following the release date indicates that the film is in color. Sp: Screenplay; MS: Musical Score; b/o: based on; (s): silent; (nm): nonmusical; (pt): part-talkie.

Alexander's Ragtime Band. Fox, 1938. Henry King. Sp: Kathryn Scola and Lamar Trotti. MS: Irving Berlin. Cast: Alice Faye, Tyrone Power, Don Ameche, Ethel Merman, Jack Haley, Jean Hersholt, Helen Westley.

All That Jazz. Fox, 1979 (c). Bob Fosse. Sp: Robert Alan Aurthur and Bob Fosse; MS: various writers. Cast: Roy Scheider, Ann Reinking, Leland Palmer, Jessica Lange, Cliff Gorman, Erzsebet Foldi, Ben Vereen, Deborah Geffner, Anthony Holland, Max Wright.

An American in Paris. MGM, 1951 (c). Vincente Minnelli. Sp: Alan Jay Lerner. MS: George and Ira Gershwin. Cast: Gene Kelly, Leslie Caron, Georges Guetary, Oscar Levant, Nina Foch.

Anchors Aweigh. MGM, 1945 (c). George Sidney. Sp: Isobel Lennart, b/o story by Natalie Marcin. MS: Jule Styne and Sammy Cahn. Cast: Gene Kelly, Frank Sinatra, Kathryn Grayson, Jose Iturbi, Dean Stockwell, Pamela Britton.

Annie Get Your Gun. MGM, 1950 (c). George Sidney. Sp: Sidney Sheldon, b/o the 1946 musical play. MS: Irving Berlin. Cast: Betty Hutton, Howard Keel, Louis Calhern, J. Carrol Naish, Edward Arnold, Keenen Wynn, Benay Venuta.

Anything Goes. Paramount, 1936. Lewis Milestone. Sp: b/o the 1934 musical play. MS: Cole Porter; additional songs by Leo Robin and Richard Whiting. Cast: Bing Crosby, Ida Lupino, Ethel Merman, Charles Ruggles, Grace Bradley, Arthur Treacher. Remade in 1956.

Applause. Paramount, 1929. Rouben Mamoulian. Sp: Garrett Fort, b/o novel by Beth Brown. MS: E. Y. Harburg, Jay Gorney, Dolly Morse, and Joe Burke. Cast: Helen Morgan, Joan Peers, Fuller Mellish, Jr., Joe King.

Artists and Models. Paramount, 1937. Raoul Walsh. Sp: Walter DeLeon and Francis Martin, b/o story and adaptation by Sig Herzig, Gene Thackrey, Eve Greene, and Harlan Ware. MS: various writers. Cast: Jack Benny, Ida Lupino, Richard Arlen, Gail Patrick, Ben Blue, Judy Canova, the Yacht Club Boys, Martha Raye.

At Long Last Love. Fox, 1975 (c). Peter Bogdanovich. Sp: Peter Bogdanovich. MS: Cole Porter. Cast: Burt Reynolds, Cybill Shepherd, Madeline Kahn, Duilio Del Prete, Mildred Natwick, Eileen Brennan, John Hillerman.

Babes in Arms. MGM, 1939. Busby Berkeley. Sp: Jack McGowan and Kay Van Riper, b/o the 1937 musical play. MS: Richard Rodgers and Lorenz Hart and others. Cast: Mickey Rooney, Judy Garland, Charles Winninger, Guy Kibbee, June Preisser, Douglas McPhail.

Babes on Broadway. MGM, 1941. Busby Berkeley. Sp: Fred Finklehoffe and Elaine Ryan, b/o story by Fred Finklehoffe. MS: various writers. Cast: Mickey Rooney, Judy Garland, Fay Bainter, Virginia Weidler, Ray McDonald, Richard Quine.

The Band Wagon. MGM, 1953 (c). Vincente Minnelli. Sp: Betty Comden and Adolph Green. MS: Arthur Schwartz and Howard Dietz. Cast: Fred Astaire, Cyd Charisse, Nanette Fabray, Jack Buchanan, Oscar Levant.

The Barkleys of Broadway. MGM, 1949 (c). Charles Walters. Sp: Betty Comden and Adolph Green. MS: Harry Warren and Ira Gershwin. Cast: Fred Astaire, Ginger Rogers, Oscar Levant, Billie Burke, Gale Robbins.

Bathing Beauty. MGM, 1944 (c). George Sidney. Sp: Dorothy Kingsley, Allen Boretz, and Frank Waldman, b/o story by Kenneth Earl, M. M. Musselman, and Curtis Kenyon. MS: Johnny Green. Cast: Esther Williams, Red Skelton, Basil Rathbone, Bill Goodwin, Ethel Smith, Jean Porter, Harry James and his orchestra.

The Belle of New York. MGM, 1952 (c). Charles Walters. Sp: Robert O'Brien and Irving Elinson, b/o play by Hugh Morton. MS: Harry Warren and Johnny Mercer. Cast: Fred Astaire, Vera-Ellen, Marjorie Main, Keenan Wynn, Alice Pearce, Gale Robbins.

Bells Are Ringing. MGM, 1960 (c). Vincente Minnelli. Sp: Betty Comden and Adolph Green, b/o their 1956 musical play. MS: Jule Styne, Betty Comden, and Adolph Green. Cast: Judy Holliday, Dean Martin, Fred Clark, Eddie Foy, Jr., Jean Stapleton, Frank Gorshin.

The Benny Goodman Story. Universal-International, 1956 (c). Valentine Davies. Sp: Valentine Davies. MS: various writers. Cast: Steve Allen, Donna Reed, Berta

Gersten, Herbert Anderson, Robert F. Simon, Sammy Davis, Jr., Harry James, Lionel Hampton, Gene Krupa.

Best Foot Forward. MGM, 1943 (c). Edward Buzzell. Sp: Irving Brecher and Fred Finklehoffe, b/o the 1941 musical play. MS: Hugh Martin and Ralph Blane. Cast: Lucille Ball, William Gaxton, Virginia Weidler, Tommy Dix, Nancy Walker, June Allyson, Gloria De Haven.

The Big Broadcast. Paramount, 1932. Frank Tuttle. Sp: George Marion, Jr., b/o play by William Ford Manley. MS: various writers. Cast: Bing Crosby, Stuart Erwin, Leila Hyams, Sharon Lynn, George Burns, Gracie Allen, Kate Smith, the Boswell Sisters, Arthur Tracy.

The Big Broadcast of 1937. Paramount, 1936. Mitchell Leisen. Sp: Walter DeLeon and Francis Martin, b/o story by Erwin Gelsey, Arthur Kober, and Barry Trivers. MS: Ralph Rainger and Leo Robin. Cast: Jack Benny, George Burns, Gracie Allen, Shirley Ross, Martha Raye, Ray Milland, Bob Burns, Benny Fields, Leopold Stokowski.

The Big Broadcast of 1938. Paramount, 1938. Mitchell Leisen. Sp: Walter DeLeon, Francis Martin, and Ken Englund, b/o story by Frederick Hazlitt Brennan. MS: Ralph Rainger and Leo Robin. Cast: W. C. Fields, Martha Raye, Bob Hope, Dorothy Lamour, Shirley Ross, Ben Blue, Kirsten Flagstad.

Billy Rose's Diamond Horseshoe. Fox, 1945 (c). George Seaton. Sp: George Seaton, b/o play by Kenyon Nicholson. MS: Harry Warren and Mack Gordon. Cast: Betty Grable, Dick Haymes, William Gaxton, Phil Silvers, Beatrice Kay, Margaret Dumont. Previously filmed in 1928 as *The Barker* (pt).

Billy Rose's Jumbo. MGM, 1962 (c). Charles Walters. Sp: Sidney Sheldon, b/o the 1935 musical play *Jumbo*. MS: Richard Rodgers and Lorenz Hart. Cast: Doris Day, Stephen Boyd, Jimmy Durante, Martha Raye, Dean Jagger, Joseph Waring, Lynn Wood.

Birth of the Blues. Paramount, 1941. Victor Schertzinger. Sp: Harry Tugend and Walter DeLeon, b/o story by Harry Tugend. MS: various writers. Cast: Bing Crosby, Mary Martin, Brian Donlevy, Carolyn Lee, Eddie ("Rochester") Anderson, Jack Teagarden, J. Carrol Naish, Warren Hymer.

Bitter Sweet. MGM, 1940 (c). W. S. Van Dyke II. Sp: Lesser Samuels, b/o the 1929 operetta. MS: Noël Coward. Cast: Jeanette MacDonald, Nelson Eddy, George Sanders, Ian Hunter, Felix Bressart, Edward Ashley, Lynne Carver. Previously filmed in 1933.

Blue Skies. Paramount, 1946 (c). Stuart Heisler. Sp: Arthur Sheekman, adapted by Allan Scott, and b/o idea by Irving Berlin. MS: Irving Berlin. Cast: Bing Crosby, Fred Astaire, Joan Caulfield, Billy DeWolfe, Olga San Juan, Mikhail Rasumny.

Born to Dance. MGM, 1936. Roy Del Ruth. Sp: Sid Silvers and Jack McGowan. MS: Cole Porter. Cast: Eleanor Powell, James Stewart, Virginia Bruce, Buddy Ebsen, Una Merkel, Frances Langford.

Broadway Gondolier. Warners, 1935. Lloyd Bacon. Sp: Warren Duff and Sig Herzig, b/o story by Sig Herzig, E. Y. Harburg, and Hans Kraly. MS: Harry Warren and Al Dubin. Cast: Dick Powell, Joan Blondell, Adolphe Menjou, the Mills Brothers, Louise Fazenda, Hobart Cavanaugh.

Brigadoon. MGM, 1954 (c). Vincente Minnelli. Sp: Alan Jay Lerner, b/o his 1947 musical play. MS: Frederick Loewe and Alan Jay Lerner. Cast: Gene Kelly, Cyd Charisse, Van Johnson, Elaine Stewart, Barry Jones, Hugh Laing.

The Broadway Melody. MGM, 1929. Harry Beaumont. Sp: Sarah Y. Mason, Norman Houston, and James Gleason, b/o story by Edmund Goulding. MS: Nacio Herb Brown and Arthur Freed. Cast: Charles King, Bessie Love, Anita Page, Jed Prouty, Edward Dillon. Sequence in color.

Broadway Melody of 1936. MGM, 1935. Roy Del Ruth. Sp: Jack McGowan and Sid Silvers, b/o story by Moss Hart. MS: Nacio Herb Brown and Arthur Freed. Cast: Jack Benny, Eleanor Powell, Robert Taylor, Una Merkel, Sid Silvers, Buddy Ebsen, June Knight, Vilma Ebsen.

Broadway Melody of 1938. MGM, 1937. Roy Del Ruth. Sp: Jack McGowan, b/o story by Jack McGowan and Sid Silvers. MS: Nacio Herb Brown and Arthur Freed. Cast: Robert Taylor, Eleanor Powell, George Murphy, Binnie Barnes, Sophie Tucker, Judy Garland, Buddy Ebsen, Willie Howard.

Broadway Melody of 1940. MGM, 1940. Norman Taurog. Sp: Leon Gordon and George Oppenheimer, b/o story by Jack McGowan and Dore Schary. MS: Cole Porter. Cast: Fred Astaire, Eleanor Powell, George Murphy, Frank Morgan, Ian Hunter, Florence Rice.

Broadway Rhythm. MGM, 1944 (c). Roy Del Ruth. Sp: Dorothy Kingsley and Harry Clork, b/o story by Jack McGowan and musical play by Jerome Kern and Oscar Hammerstein II. MS: various writers. Cast: George Murphy, Ginny Simms, Charles Winninger, Gloria De Haven, Nancy Walker, Lena Horne.

The Buddy Holly Story. Columbia, 1978 (c). Steve Rash. Sp: Robert Gittler, b/o story by Steve Rash and Fred Bauer. MS: Buddy Holly. Cast: Gary Busey, Don Stroud, Charles Martin Smith, Maria Richwine, Bill Jordan, Conrad Janis.

Bye Bye Birdie. Columbia, 1963 (c). George Sidney. Sp: Irving Brecher, b/o the 1960 musical play. MS: Charles Strouse and Lee Adams. Cast: Dick Van Dyke, Janet Leigh, Ann-Margret, Paul Lynde, Maureen Stapleton, Bobby Rydell, Jesse Pearson.

By the Light of the Silvery Moon. Warners, 1953 (c). David Butler. Sp: Robert O'Brien and Irving Elinson, b/o stories by Booth Tarkington. MS: various writers. Cast: Doris Day, Gordon MacRae, Rosemary DeCamp, Leon Ames, Billy Gray, Mary Wickes, Russell Arms.

Cabaret. Allied Artists, 1972 (c). Bob Fosse. Sp: Jay Allen, b/o the 1966 musical play, which was adapted from John Van Druten's play *I Am a Camera* (filmed in 1955) and Christopher Isherwood's novel *Goodbye to Berlin*. MS: John Kander and Fred Ebb. Cast: Liza Minnelli, Michael York, Joel Grey, Helmut Griem, Marisa Berenson, Fritz Wepper.

Cabin in the Sky. MGM, 1943. Vincente Minnelli. Sp: Joseph Schrank, b/o the 1940 musical play. MS: Vernon Duke and John Latouche; additional songs by Harold Arlen and E. Y. Harburg. Cast: Ethel Waters, Eddie ("Rochester") Anderson, Lena Horne, John W. ("Bubbles") Sublett, Rex Ingram, Kenneth Spencer.

Calamity Jane. Warners, 1953 (c). David Butler. Sp: James O'Hanlon. MS: Sammy Fain and Paul Francis Webster. Cast: Doris Day, Howard Keel, Allyn McLerie, Phil Carey, Dick Wesson, Paul Harvey, Gail Robbins.

Call Me Madam. Fox, 1953 (c). Walter Lang. Sp: Arthur Sheekman, b/o the 1950 musical play. MS: Irving Berlin. Cast: Ethel Merman, George Sanders, Donald O'Connor, Vera-Ellen, Billy De Wolfe, Helmut Dantine, Walter Slezak.

Camelot. Warners, 1967 (c). Joshua Logan. Sp: Alan Jay Lerner, b/o the 1960 musical play. MS: Frederick Loewe and Alan Jay Lerner. Cast: Richard Harris, Vanessa Redgrave, Franco Nero, David Hemmings, Lionel Jeffries, Laurence Naismith, Pierre Olaf, Estelle Winwood.

Can-Can. Fox, 1960 (c). Walter Lang. Sp: Dorothy Kingsley and Charles Lederer, b/o the 1953 musical play. MS: Cole Porter. Cast: Frank Sinatra, Shirley MacLaine, Maurice Chevalier, Louis Jourdan, Juliet Prowse, Marcel Dalio, Leon Belasco.

Captain January. Fox, 1936. David Butler. Sp: Sam Hellman, Gladys Lehman, and Harry Tugend, b/o novel by Laura E. Richards. MS: Jack Yellen and Lew Pollack. Cast: Shirley Temple, Guy Kibbee, Slim Summerville, June Lang, Buddy Ebsen, Sara Haden, Jane Darwell. Previously filmed in 1924 (s).

Carefree. RKO, 1938. Mark Sandrich. Sp: Allan Scott and Ernest Pagano, b/o story by Dudley Nichols and Hagar Wilde. MS: Irving Berlin. Cast: Fred Astaire, Ginger Rogers, Ralph Bellamy, Luella Gear, Jack Carson.

Carmen Jones. Fox, 1954 (c). Otto Preminger. Sp: Harry Kleiner, b/o the 1943 musical play. MS: Georges Bizet and Oscar Hammerstein II. Cast: Harry Belafonte, Dorothy Dandridge, Olga James, Pearl Bailey, Diahann Carroll, Roy Glenn.

Carousel. Fox, 1956 (c). Henry King. Sp: Phoebe and Henry Ephron, b/o the 1945 musical play, which was adapted from Ferenc Molnár's play *Liliom* (filmed in 1930). MS: Richard Rodgers and Oscar Hammerstein II. Cast: Gordon MacRae, Shirley Jones, Cameron Mitchell, Barbara Ruick, Claramae Turner, Robert Rounseville, Gene Lockhart.

Centennial Summer. Fox, 1946 (c). Otto Preminger. Sp: Michael Kanin, b/o novel by Albert E. Idell. MS: Jerome Kern, Oscar Hammerstein II, Leo Robin, and Johnny Mercer. Cast: Jeanne Crain, Cornel Wilde, Linda Darnell, Walter Brennan, Constance Bennett, Dorothy Gish.

Chitty Chitty Bang Bang. United Artists, 1968 (c). Ken Hughes. Sp: Roald Dahl and Ken Hughes, b/o novel by Ian Fleming. MS: Richard M. and Robert S. Sherman. Cast: Dick Van Dyke, Sally Ann Howes, Lionel Jeffries, Gert Frobe, Heather Ripley, Adrian Hall, Benny Hill.

College Humor. Paramount, 1933. Wesley Ruggles. Sp: Claude Binyon and Frank Butler, b/o story by Dean Fales. MS: Sam Coslow and Arthur Johnston. Cast: Bing Crosby, Jack Oakie, Richard Arlen, Mary Carlisle, Mary Kornman, George Burns, Gracie Allen.

Coney Island. Fox, 1943 (c). Walter Lang. Sp: George Seaton. MS: Ralph Rainger and Leo Robin. Cast: Betty Grable, George Montgomery, Cesar Romero, Charles Winninger, Phil Silvers, Paul Hurst. Remade in 1950 as *Wabash Avenue*.

A Connecticut Yankee in King Arthur's Court. Paramount, 1949 (c). Tay Garnett. Sp: b/o novel by Mark Twain, filmed in 1921 (s) and 1931 (nm). MS: Jimmy Van Heusen and Johnny Burke. Cast: Bing Crosby, William Bendix, Sir Cedric Hardwicke, Rhonda Fleming, Murvyn Vye, Virginia Field.

Cover Girl. Columbia, 1944 (c). Charles Vidor. Sp: Virginia Van Upp. MS: Jerome Kern and Ira Gershwin. Cast: Rita Hayworth, Gene Kelly, Phil Silvers, Eve Arden, Otto Kruger, Lee Bowman.

The Cuban Love Song. MGM, 1931. W. S. Van Dyke II. Sp: John Lynch, b/o story by G. Gardner Sullivan and Bess Meredyth. MS: Jimmy McHugh and Dorothy Fields. Cast: Lawrence Tibbett, Lupe Velez, Jimmy Durante, Karen Morley, Louise Fazenda, Hale Hamilton.

Curly Top. Fox, 1935. Irving Cummings. Sp: Patterson McNutt and Arthur Beckhard. MS: Ray Henderson, Ted Koehler, Edward Heyman, and Irving Caesar. Cast: Shirley Temple, John Boles, Rochelle Hudson, Jane Darwell, Arthur Treacher, Rafaela Ottiano.

Daddy Long Legs. Fox, 1955 (c). Jean Negulesco. Sp: Phoebe and Henry Ephron, b/o novel by Jean Webster. MS: Johnny Mercer. Cast: Fred Astaire, Leslie Caron, Thelma Ritter, Terry Moore, Fred Clark, Larry Keating, Charlotte Austin. Previously filmed in 1919 (s) and 1931 (nm).

Dames. Warners, 1934. Ray Enright and Busby Berkeley. Sp: Robert Lord and Delmer Daves. MS: Harry Warren, Al Dubin, and others. Cast: Dick Powell, Ruby Keeler, Joan Blondell, ZaSu Pitts, Guy Kibbee, Hugh Herbert, Arthur Vinton.

Damn Yankees. Warners, 1958 (c). George Abbott and Stanley Donen. Sp: George Abbott, b/o the 1955 musical play, which was adapted from novel by Douglass Wallop. MS: Richard Adler and Jerry Ross. Cast: Tab Hunter, Gwen Verdon, Ray Walston, Shannon Bolin, Nathaniel Frey, Jimmie Komack, Jean Stapleton.

A Damsel in Distress. RKO, 1937. George Stevens. Sp: P. G. Wodehouse, S. K. Lauren, and Ernest Pagano, b/o book by P. G. Wodehouse. MS: George and Ira Gershwin. Cast: Fred Astaire, Joan Fontaine, George Burns, Gracie Allen, Reginald Gardiner, Constance Collier, Montagu Love.

Dancing Lady. MGM, 1933. Robert Z. Leonard. Sp: Allen Rivkin and P. J. Wolfson, b/o novel by James Warner Bellah. MS: Nacio Herb Brown and Arthur Freed. Cast: Joan Crawford, Clark Gable, Franchot Tone, Fred Astaire, Robert Benchley, Nelson Eddy, May Robson.

A Date with Judy. MGM, 1948 (c). Richard Thorpe. Sp: Dorothy Cooper and Dorothy Kingsley, b/o characters created by Aleen Leslie. MS: various writers. Cast: Wallace Beery, Jane Powell, Elizabeth Taylor, Carmen Miranda, Robert Stack, Xavier Cugat and his orchestra.

Deep in My Heart. MGM, 1954 (c). Stanley Donen. Sp: Leonard Spigelgass, b/o book by Elliott Arnold. MS: Sigmund Romberg and various lyricists. Cast: Jose Ferrer, Merle Oberon, Helen Traubel, Doe Avedon, Walter Pidgeon, Paul Henreid, and guest stars Gene Kelly, Ann Miller, Howard Keel, Cyd Charisse, Jane Powell, Tony Martin.

The Desert Song. Warners, 1929. Roy Del Ruth. Sp: Harvey Gates, b/o the 1926 musical play. MS: Sigmund Romberg and Oscar Hammerstein II. Cast: John Boles, Carlotta King, Louise Fazenda, Johnny Arthur, Edward Martindel, Myrna Loy. Remade in 1943 and 1953. Some sequences in color.

Doctor Dolittle. Fox, 1967 (c). Richard Fleischer. Sp: Leslie Bricusse, b/o stories by Hugh Lofting. MS: Leslie Bricusse. Cast: Rex Harrison, Samantha Eggar, Anthony Newley, William Dix, Richard Attenborough, Peter Bull, Portia Nelson.

Doctor Rhythm. Paramount, 1938. Frank Tuttle. Sp: Jo Swerling and Richard Connell, b/o story by O. Henry. MS: James V. Monaco and Johnny Burke. Cast: Bing Crosby, Beatrice Lillie, Mary Carlisle, Andy Devine, Rufe Davis, Laura Hope Crews, Sterling Holloway.

The Dolly Sisters. Fox, 1945 (c). Irving Cummings.

Sp: John Larkin and Marian Spitzer. MS: James Monaco and Mack Gordon. Cast: Betty Grable, John Payne, June Haver, S. Z. Sakall, Reginald Gardiner, Frank Latimore, Gene Sheldon.

Down Argentine Way. Fox, 1940 (c). Irving Cummings. Sp: Karl Tunberg and Darrell Ware, b/o story by Rian James and Ralph Spence. MS: Harry Warren and Mack Gordon. Cast: Betty Grable, Don Ameche, Carmen Miranda, Charlotte Greenwood, J. Carrol Naish, Henry Stephenson.

Down to Earth. Columbia, 1947 (c). Alexander Hall. Sp: Edwin Blum and Don Hartman. MS: Allan Roberts and Doris Fisher. Cast: Rita Hayworth, Larry Parks, Marc Platt, Roland Culver, James Gleason, Edward Everett Horton.

Du Barry Was a Lady. MGM, 1943 (c). Roy Del Ruth. Sp: Irving Brecher, adapted by Nancy Hamilton, and b/o the 1939 musical play. MS: Cole Porter and various writers. Cast: Red Skelton, Lucille Ball, Gene Kelly, Virginia O'Brien, Rags Ragland, Zero Mostel.

Easter Parade. MGM, 1948 (c). Charles Walters. Sp: Sidney Sheldon, Frances Goodrich, and Albert Hackett, b/o story by Goodrich and Hackett. MS: Irving Berlin. Cast: Fred Astaire, Judy Garland, Peter Lawford, Ann Miller, Keenan Wynn.

Easy to Love. MGM, 1953 (c). Charles Walters. Sp: Laslo Vadnay and William Roberts. MS: various writers. Cast: Esther Williams, Van Johnson, Tony Martin, John Bromfield, Edna Skinner, King Donovan, Carroll Baker.

The Eddy Duchin Story. Columbia, 1956 (c). George Sidney. Sp: Samuel Taylor, b/o story by Leo Katcher. MS: various writers. Cast: Tyrone Power, Kim Novak, Victoria Shaw, James Whitmore, Rex Thompson, Shepperd Strudwick, Frieda Inescort.

The Emperor Waltz. Paramount, 1948 (c). Billy Wilder. Sp: Charles Brackett and Billy Wilder. MS: various writers. Cast: Bing Crosby, Joan Fontaine, Roland Culver, Lucile Watson, Richard Haydn, Harold Vermilyea.

Fiddler on the Roof. United Artists, 1971 (c). Norman Jewison. Sp: Joseph Stein, b/o his 1964 musical play. MS: Jerry Bock and Sheldon Harnick. Cast: Topol, Norma Crane, Leonard Frey, Molly Picon, Paul Mann, Rosalind Harris, Neva Small, Michael Glaser.

Finian's Rainbow. Warners, 1968 (c). Francis Ford Coppola. Sp: E. Y. Harburg and Fred Saidy, b/o their 1947 musical play. MS: Burton Lane and E. Y. Harburg. Cast: Fred Astaire, Petula Clark, Tommy Steele, Don Francks, Keenan Wynn, Al Freeman, Jr.

The Firefly. MGM, 1937. Robert Z. Leonard. Sp: Frances Goodrich and Albert Hackett, b/o the 1912 musical play. MS: Rudolf Friml and Otto Harbach. Cast: Jeanette MacDonald, Allan Jones, Warren William, Billy Gilbert, Henry Daniell, Douglass Dumbrille.

The Fleet's In. Paramount, 1942. Victor Schertzinger. Sp: Walter DeLeon, Sid Silvers, and Ralph Spence, b/o story by Monte Brice and play by Kenyon Nicholson and Charles Robinson. MS: Victor Schertzinger and Johnny Mercer. Cast: Dorothy Lamour, William Holden, Betty Hutton, Eddie Bracken, Gil Lamb, Cass Daley, Jimmy Dorsey and his band. Previously filmed in 1936 as *Lady, Be Careful* (nm) and remade in 1952 as *Sailor Beware* (nm).

Flirtation Walk. Warners, 1934. Frank Borzage. Sp: Delmer Daves, b/o story by Delmer Daves and Lou Edelman. MS: Allie Wrubel and Mort Dixon. Cast: Dick Powell, Ruby Keeler, Pat O'Brien, Ross Alexander, Glen Boles, John Eldredge, Henry O'Neill, Guinn Williams.

Flower Drum Song. Universal-International, 1961 (c). Henry Koster. Sp: Joseph Fields, b/o the 1958 musical play. MS: Richard Rodgers and Oscar Hammerstein II. Cast: Nancy Kwan, James Shigeta, Miyoshi Umeki, Juanita Hall, Benson Fong, Jack Soo, Victor Sen Yung.

Flying Down to Rio. RKO, 1933. Thornton Freeland. Sp: Lou Brock. MS: Vincent Youmans, Gus Kahn, and Edward Eliscu. Cast: Gene Raymond, Dolores Del Rio, Fred Astaire, Ginger Rogers, Raoul Roulien.

Folies Bergère. Twentieth Century, 1935. Roy Del Ruth. Sp: Bess Meredyth and Hal Long, b/o play by Rudolph Lothar and Hans Adler. MS: Jack Meskill and Jack Stern. Cast: Maurice Chevalier, Merle Oberon, Ann Sothern, Eric Blore, Ferdinand Munier, Walter Byron. Remade in 1941 as *That Night in Rio* and in 1951 as *On the Riviera*.

Follow the Fleet. RKO, 1936. Mark Sandrich. Sp: Dwight Taylor and Allan Scott, b/o a play by Hubert Osborne. MS: Irving Berlin. Cast: Fred Astaire, Ginger Rogers, Harriet Hilliard, Randolph Scott, Astrid Allwyn. Previously filmed in 1925 as *Shore Leave* (s) and in 1930 as *Hit the Deck* and remade in 1955 as *Hit the Deck*.

Footlight Parade. Warners, 1933. Lloyd Bacon. Musical numbers directed by Busby Berkeley. Sp: Manuel Seff and James Seymour. MS: Sammy Fain, Irving Kahal, Harry Warren, and Al Dubin. Cast: James Cagney, Joan Blondell, Ruby Keeler, Dick Powell, Guy Kibbee, Ruth Donnelly, Frank McHugh.

For Me and My Gal. MGM, 1942. Busby Berkeley. Sp: Richard Sherman, Sid Silvers, and Fred Finklehoffe, b/o story by Howard Emmett Rogers. MS: various writers. Cast: Judy Garland, Gene Kelly, George Murphy, Marta Eggerth, Ben Blue, Keenan Wynn.

42nd Street. Warners, 1933. Lloyd Bacon. Musical numbers directed by Busby Berkeley. Sp: Rian James and James Seymour, b/o story by Bradford Ropes. MS: Harry Warren and Al Dubin. Cast: Warner Baxter, Dick Powell, Ruby Keeler, Bebe Daniels, Ginger Rogers, George Brent, Una Merkel, George E. Stone.

Funny Face. Paramount, 1957 (c). Stanley Donen. Sp: Leonard Gershe. MS: George and Ira Gershwin, plus Roger Edens and Leonard Gershe. Cast: Fred Astaire, Audrey Hepburn, Kay Thompson, Michel Auclair, Robert Flemyng.

Funny Girl. Columbia, 1968 (c). William Wyler. Sp: Isobel Lennart, b/o the 1964 musical play. MS: Jule Styne and Bob Merrill. Cast: Barbra Streisand, Omar Sharif, Kay Medford, Anne Francis, Walter Pidgeon, Lee Allen, Mae Questel, Gerald Mohr.

Funny Lady. Columbia, 1975 (c). Herbert Ross. Sp: Jay Presson Allen and Arnold Schulman, b/o story by Arnold Schulman. MS: John Kander and Fred Ebb. Cast: Barbra Streisand, James Caan, Omar Sharif, Roddy McDowell, Ben Vereen, Carole Wells.

A Funny Thing Happened on the Way to the Forum. United Artists, 1966 (c). Richard Lester. Sp: Melvin Frank and Michael Pertwee, b/o the 1962 musical play. MS: Stephen Sondheim. Cast: Zero Mostel, Jack Gilford, Michael Crawford, Buster Keaton, Phil Silvers, Michael Hordern, Patricia Jessel, Annette Andre.

The Gang's All Here. Fox, 1943 (c). Busby Berkeley. Sp: Walter Bullock, b/o story by Nancy Winter, George Root, Jr., and Tom Bridges. MS: Harry Warren and Leo Robin. Cast: Alice Faye, Carmen Miranda, James Ellison, Charlotte Greenwood, Eugene Pallette, Benny Goodman and his orchestra.

The Gay Desperado. United Artists, 1936. Rouben Mamoulian. Sp: Wallace Smith, b/o story by Leo Birinski. MS: Holt Marvell, George Posford, and Miguel Sandoval. Cast: Nino Martini, Ida Lupino, Leo Carrillo, Harold Huber, James Blakeley, Mischa Auer, Stanley Fields.

The Gay Divorcee. RKO, 1934. Mark Sandrich. Sp: George Marion, Jr., Edward Kaufman, and Dorothy Yost, b/o the 1932 musical play *Gay Divorce*. MS: Cole Porter, Mack Gordon, Harry Revel, Con Conrad, and Herb Magidson. Cast: Fred Astaire, Ginger Rogers, Edward Everett Horton, Alice Brady, Eric Blore, Erik Rhodes.

Gentlemen Prefer Blondes. Fox, 1953 (c). Howard Hawks. Sp: Charles Lederer, b/o the 1949 musical play and novel by Anita Loos. MS: Jule Styne and Leo Robin. Cast: Marilyn Monroe, Jane Russell, Charles Coburn, Elliott Reid, Tommy Noonan, George Winslow. Previously filmed in 1928 (s).

George White's Scandals. Fox, 1934. George White, Thornton Freeland, and Harry Lachman. Sp: Jack Yellen, b/o story by George White. MS: Ray Henderson, Jack Yellen, and Irving Caesar. Cast: Rudy Vallee, Jimmy Durante, Alice Faye, Adrienne Ames, Gregory Ratoff, Dixie Dunbar, Cliff Edwards.

George White's 1935 Scandals. Fox, 1935. George White. Sp: Jack Yellen and Patterson McNutt. MS: Jack Yellen, Cliff Friend, and Joseph Meyer. Cast: Alice Faye, James Dunn, Ned Sparks, Lyda Roberti, Cliff Edwards, Arline Judge, Eleanor Powell.

Gigi. MGM, 1958 (c). Vincente Minnelli. Sp: Alan Jay Lerner, b/o novel by Colette. MS: Frederick Loewe and Alan Jay Lerner. Cast: Leslie Caron, Maurice Chevalier, Louis Jourdan, Hermione Gingold, Eva Gabor, Isabel Jeans, Jacques Bergerac. Previously filmed in 1948 (nm).

Girl Crazy. MGM, 1943. Norman Taurog. Musical numbers directed by Busby Berkeley. Sp: Fred Finklehoffe, b/o the 1930 musical play. MS: George and Ira Gershwin. Cast: Mickey Rooney, Judy Garland, Gil Stratton, Nancy Walker, Rags Ragland, June Allyson, Tommy Dorsey and his orchestra. Previously filmed in 1932 and remade in 1965 as *When the Boys Meet the Girls*.

The Girl of the Golden West. MGM, 1938. Robert Z. Leonard. Sp: Isabel Dawn and Boyce DeGaw, b/o 1905 play by David Belasco. MS: Sigmund Romberg and Gus Kahn. Cast: Jeanette MacDonald, Nelson Eddy, Walter Pidgeon, Leo Carrillo, Buddy Ebsen, Leonard Penn. Previously filmed in 1923 (s) and 1930 (nm).

The Glass Slipper. MGM, 1955 (c). Charles Walters. Sp: Helen Deutsch. MS: Bronislau Kaper and Helen Deutsch. Cast: Leslie Caron, Michael Wilding, Keenan Wynn, Estelle Winwood, Elsa Lanchester, Barry Jones, Amanda Blake.

Glorifying the American Girl. Paramount, 1930. Millard Webb. Sp: Joseph Patrick McEvoy, b/o his story. MS: various writers. Cast: Mary Eaton, Edward Crandall, Dan Healy, Eddie Cantor, Helen Morgan, Rudy Vallee. With color sequences.

The Glenn Miller Story. Universal, 1954 (c). Anthony Mann. Sp: Valentine Davies and Oscar Brodney. MS: various writers. Cast: James Stewart, June Allyson, Charles Drake, George Tobias, Henry Morgan, Marion Ross, Phil Harris.

Go into Your Dance. Warners, 1935. Archie Mayo. Sp: Earl Baldwin, b/o novel by Bradford Ropes. MS: Harry Warren and Al Dubin. Cast: Al Jolson, Ruby Keeler, Glenda Farrell, Helen Morgan, Patsy Kelly, Phil Regan, Sharon Lynn.

The Gold Diggers of Broadway. Warners, 1929 (c). Roy Del Ruth. Sp: Robert Lord, b/o play by Avery Hopwood. MS: Joe Burke and Al Dubin. Cast: Nancy Welford, Conway Tearle, Winnie Lightner, Ann Pennington, Lilyan Tashman, Nick Lucas. Previously filmed in 1923 (s) and remade in 1933 as *Gold Diggers of 1933*.

Gold Diggers of 1933. Warners, 1933. Mervyn LeRoy. Musical numbers directed by Busby Berkeley. Sp: Erwin Gelsey and James Seymour, b/o play by Avery Hopwood. MS: Harry Warren and Al Dubin. Cast: Dick Powell, Joan Blondell, Ruby Keeler, Warren William, Guy Kibbee, Aline MacMahon, Ginger Rogers. Previously filmed in 1923 as *The Gold Diggers* (s) and in 1929 as *The Gold Diggers of Broadway*.

Gold Diggers of 1935. Warners, 1935. Busby Berkeley. Sp: Manuel Seff and Peter Milne, b/o story by Robert Lord and Peter Milne. MS: Harry Warren and Al Dubin. Cast: Dick Powell, Adolphe Menjou, Alice Brady, Gloria Stuart, Glenda Farrell, Hugh Herbert, Frank McHugh, Wini Shaw.

Gold Diggers of 1937. Warners, 1936. Lloyd Bacon. Musical numbers directed by Busby Berkeley. Sp: Warren Duff, b/o play by Richard Maibaum, Michael Wallace, and George Haight. MS: Harry Warren and Al Dubin, and Harold Arlen and E. Y. Harburg. Cast: Dick Powell, Joan Blondell, Victor Moore, Glenda Farrell, Lee Dixon, Osgood Perkins, Rosalind Marquis.

The Goldwyn Follies. A Samuel Goldwyn Production, released by United Artists, 1938 (c). George Marshall. Sp: Ben Hecht, b/o his story. MS: George and Ira Gershwin and others. Cast: Adolphe Menjou, Vera Zorina, Andrea Leeds, Kenny Baker, Edgar Bergen and Charlie McCarthy, the Ritz Brothers, Bobby Clark, Ella Logan.

Good News. MGM, 1948 (c). Charles Walters. Sp: Betty Comden and Adolph Green, b/o the 1927 musical play. MS: B. G. DeSylva, Lew Brown, and Ray Henderson and others. Cast: June Allyson, Peter Lawford, Patricia Marshall, Joan McCracken, Mel Torme. Previously filmed in 1930.

Grease. Paramount, 1978 (c). Randal Kleiser. Sp: Bronte Woodard, b/o the 1972 musical play. MS: Jim Jacobs and Warren Casey. Cast: John Travolta, Olivia Newton-John, Stockard Channing, Jeff Conaway, Didi Conn, Jamie Donnelly, Eve Arden, Frankie Avalon, Joan Blondell, Sid Caesar, Alice Ghostley, Dody Goodman.

The Great American Broadcast. Fox, 1941. Archie Mayo. Sp: Don Ettlinger, Edwin Blum, Robert Ellis, and Helen Logan. MS: Harry Warren and Mack Gordon. Cast: Alice Faye, John Payne, Jack Oakie, Cesar Romero, the Four Ink Spots, the Nicholas Brothers.

The Great Caruso. MGM, 1951 (c). Richard Thorpe. Sp: Sonya Levien and William Ludwig, b/o book by Dorothy Caruso. MS: various writers. Cast: Mario Lanza, Ann Blyth, Dorothy Kirsten, Jarmila Novotna, Carl Benton Reid.

The Great Victor Herbert. Paramount, 1939. Andrew L. Stone. Sp: Russel Crouse and Robert Lively, b/o story by Robert Lively and Andrew L. Stone. MS: Victor Herbert and various lyricists. Cast: Mary Martin, Allan Jones, Walter Connolly, Susanna Foster, Lee Bowman, Judith

Barrett, Jerome Cowan.

The Great Waltz. MGM, 1938. Julien Duvivier. Sp: Samuel Hoffenstein and Walter Reisch, b/o story by Gottfried Reinhardt. MS: Johann Strauss the Younger and Oscar Hammerstein II. Cast: Luise Rainer, Fernand Gravet, Miliza Korjus, Hugh Herbert, Lionel Atwill, Curt Bois, Leonid Kinskey. Remade in 1972.

The Great Ziegfeld. MGM, 1936. Robert Z. Leonard. Sp: William Anthony McGuire. MS: Walter Donaldson and Harold Adamson. Cast: William Powell, Myrna Loy, Luise Rainer, Virginia Bruce, Frank Morgan, Ray Bolger, Nat Pendleton.

Guys and Dolls. A Samuel Goldwyn Production, released by MGM, 1955 (c). Joseph L. Mankiewicz. Sp: Joseph L. Mankiewicz, b/o the 1950 musical play. MS: Frank Loesser. Cast: Marlon Brando, Frank Sinatra, Jean Simmons, Vivian Blaine, Stubby Kaye, Robert Keith, B. S. Pully, Sheldon Leonard.

Gypsy. Warners, 1962 (c). Mervyn LeRoy. Sp: Leonard Spigelgass, b/o the 1959 musical play. MS: Jule Styne and Stephen Sondheim. Cast: Rosalind Russell, Natalie Wood, Karl Malden, Paul Wallace, Betty Bruce, Diane Pace, Faith Dane, Roxanne Arlen.

Hair. United Artists, 1979 (c). Milos Forman. Sp: Michael Weller, b/o the 1968 musical play. MS: Galt MacDermot, Gerome Ragni, and James Rado. Cast: John Savage, Treat Williams, Beverly D'Angelo, Annie Golden, Cheryl Barnes, Dorsey Wright, Nicholas Ray, Charlotte Rae.

Hallelujah! MGM, 1929. King Vidor. Sp: Wanda Tuchock and Ransom Rideout. MS: Irving Berlin, spirituals, and traditional songs. Cast: Daniel Haynes, Nina Mae McKinney, William Fountaine, Fannie Belle de Knight.

Hallelujah, I'm a Bum. United Artists, 1933. Lewis Milestone. Sp: S. N. Behrman, b/o story by Ben Hecht. MS: Richard Rodgers and Lorenz Hart. Cast: Al Jolson, Madge Evans, Frank Morgan, Harry Langdon, Chester Conklin, Tammany Young, Tyler Brooke.

Happy Days. Fox, 1930. Benjamin Stoloff. Sp: Edwin Burke, b/o story by Sidney Lanfield, MS: various writers. Cast: Janet Gaynor, Will Rogers, Charles Farrell, Warner Baxter, Victor McLaglen, Edmund Lowe, Dixie Lee, Ann Pennington, Alice White, El Brendel.

The Harvey Girls. MGM, 1946 (c). George Sidney. Sp: Edmund Beloin, Nathaniel Curtis, Harry Crane, James O'Hanlon, and Samson Raphaelson, b/o book by Samuel Hopkins Adams. MS: Harry Warren and Johnny Mercer. Cast: Judy Garland, John Hodiak, Angela Lansbury, Marjorie Main, Virginia O'Brien, Cyd Charisse, Ray Bolger, Kenny Baker.

Hello, Dolly! Fox, 1969 (c). Gene Kelly. Sp: Ernest Lehman, b/o the 1964 musical play, which was adapted from Thornton Wilder's play *The Matchmaker*, filmed in 1958. MS: Jerry Herman. Cast: Barbra Streisand, Walter Matthau, Michael Crawford, Tommy Tune, Marianne MacAndrew, E. J. Peaker, Louis Armstrong.

Hello, Frisco, Hello. Fox, 1943 (c). Bruce Humberstone. Sp: Robert Ellis, Helen Logan, and Richard Macaulay. MS: Harry Warren and Mack Gordon. Cast: Alice Faye, John Payne, Jack Oakie, Lynn Bari, Laird Cregar, June Havoc, Ward Bond.

Here Comes the Groom. Paramount, 1951. Frank Capra. Sp: Virginia Van Upp, Liam O' Brien, and Myles Connelly, b/o story by Robert Riskin and Liam O'Brien. MS: Ray Evans and Jay Livingston, Hoagy Carmichael and Johnny Mercer. Cast: Bing Crosby, Jane Wyman, Franchot Tone, Alexis Smith, James Barton.

High Society. MGM, 1956 (c). Charles Walters. Sp: John Patrick, b/o play by Philip Barry. MS: Cole Porter. Cast: Bing Crosby, Grace Kelly, Frank Sinatra, Celeste Holm, John Lund, Louis Calhern, Sidney Blackmer, Margalo Gillmore, Louis Armstrong. A musical remake of *The Philadelphia Story* (1940).

High, Wide and Handsome. Paramount, 1937. Rouben Mamoulian. Sp: Oscar Hammerstein II, b/o his story. MS: Jerome Kern and Oscar Hammerstein II. Cast: Irene Dunne, Randolph Scott, Dorothy Lamour, Raymond Walburn, Charles Bickford, Elizabeth Patterson, William Frawley, Akim Tamiroff.

Hit the Deck. MGM, 1955 (c). Roy Howland. Sp: Sonya Levien and William Ludwig, b/o the 1927 musical play and the play by Hubert Osborne. MS: Vincent Youmans and various lyricists. Cast: Jane Powell, Debbie Reynolds, Vic Damone, Ann Miller, Walter Pidgeon, Tony Martin, Russ Tamblyn, Gene Raymond, Kay Armen.

Previously filmed in 1925 as *Shore Leave* (s), in 1930 as *Hit the Deck*, and in 1936 as *Follow the Fleet*.

Hitting a New High. RKO Radio, 1937. Raoul Walsh. Sp: Gertrude Purcell and John Twist, b/o story by Robert Harari and Maxwell Shane. MS: Harold Adamson and Jimmy McHugh. Cast: Lily Pons, Jack Oakie, Eric Blore, Edward Everett Horton, John Howard, Eduardo Ciannelli.

Holiday Inn. Paramount, 1942. Mark Sandrich. Sp: Claude Binyon, b/o idea by Irving Berlin. MS: Irving Berlin. Cast: Bing Crosby, Fred Astaire, Marjorie Reynolds, Virginia Dale, Walter Abel, Louise Beavers.

The Hollywood Revue of 1929. MGM, 1929. Charles F. Riesner. Sp: Al Boasberg and Robert E. Hopkins. MS: various writers. Cast: Jack Benny, Conrad Nagel, Joan Crawford, Marion Davies, Laurel and Hardy, Marie Dressler, Buster Keaton, Norma Shearer, John Gilbert, Bessie Love. Some sequences in color.

Honey. Paramount, 1930. Wesley Ruggles. Sp: Herman J. Mankiewicz, b/o play by Alice Duer Miller. MS: W. Franke Harling and Sam Coslow. Cast: Nancy Carroll, Stanley Smith, Lillian Roth, Skeets Gallagher, ZaSu Pitts, Mitzi Green, Jobyna Howland. Previously filmed in 1919 (s).

Honeymoon Hotel. Warners, 1937. Busby Berkeley. Sp: Jerry Wald, Maurice Leo, and Richard Macaulay, b/o story by Jerry Wald and Maurice Leo. MS: Richard Whiting and Johnny Mercer. Cast: Dick Powell, Rosemary Lane, Lola Lane, Hugh Herbert, Glenda Farrell, Ted Healy, Frances Langford, Benny Goodman and his orchestra.

Director Busby Berkeley poses with the cutout lobby display for Footlight Parade *(Warners, 1933).*

How to Succeed in Business Without Really Trying. United Artists, 1967 (c). David Swift. Sp: David Swift, b/o the 1961 musical play and book by Shepherd Mead. MS: Frank Loesser. Cast: Robert Morse, Rudy Vallee, Michele Lee, Anthony Teague, Maureen Arthur, Murray Matheson, Sammy Smith, Paul Hartman.

I'll Cry Tomorrow. MGM, 1955. Daniel Mann. Sp: Helen Deutsch and Jay Richard Kennedy, b/o book by Lillian Roth. MS: various writers. Cast: Susan Hayward, Richard Conte, Eddie Albert, Jo Van Fleet, Don Taylor, Ray Danton, Margo.

I'll See You in My Dreams. Warners, 1951. Michael Curtiz. Sp: Melville Shavelson and Jack Rose. MS: Gus Kahn and various composers. Cast: Danny Thomas, Doris Day, Frank Lovejoy, Patrice Wymore, James Gleason, Mary Wickes, Jim Backus.

I Married an Angel. MGM, 1942. W. S. Van Dyke II. Sp: Anita Loos, b/o the 1938 musical play. MS: Richard Rodgers and Lorenz Hart. Cast: Jeanette MacDonald, Nelson Eddy, Edward Everett Horton, Binnie Barnes, Reginald Owen, Douglass Dumbrille, Janis Carter, Anne Jeffreys.

Interrupted Melody. MGM, 1955 (c). Curtis Bernhardt. Sp: William Ludwig and Sonya Levien, b/o life story of Marjorie Lawrence. MS: various writers. Cast: Eleanor Parker, Glenn Ford, Roger Moore, Cecil Kellaway, Peter Leeds, Evelyn Ellis.

In the Good Old Summertime. MGM, 1949 (c).

Robert Z. Leonard. Sp: Albert Hackett, Frances Goodrich, and Ivan Tors, b/o screenplay by Samson Raphaelson and play by Miklos Lazlo. MS: various writers. Cast: Judy Garland, Van Johnson, S. Z. Sakall, Spring Byington, Buster Keaton. A musical remake of *The Shop Around the Corner* (1940).

Invitation to the Dance. MGM, 1956 (c). Gene Kelly. Ballet film conceived by Gene Kelly. MS: various composers. Cast: Gene Kelly, Igor Youskevitch, Tamara Toumanova, Diana Adams, Belita, David Kasday, Claire Sombert.

It's Always Fair Weather. MGM, 1955 (c). Gene Kelly and Stanley Donen. Sp: Betty Comden and Adolph Green. MS: André Previn, Betty Comden, and Adolph Green. Cast: Gene Kelly, Cyd Charisse, Dan Dailey, Dolores Gray, Michael Kidd, David Burns, Jay C. Flippen.

Jailhouse Rock. MGM, 1957. Richard Thorpe. Sp: Guy Trosper, b/o story by Ned Young. MS: Mike Stoller and Jerry Leiber. Cast: Elvis Presley, Judy Tyler, Mickey Shaughnessy, Vaughn Taylor, Jennifer Holden.

The Jazz Singer. Warners, 1927. Alan Crosland. Sp: Al Cohn, b/o play by Samson Raphaelson. MS: various writers. Cast: Al Jolson, Eugenie Besserer, May McAvoy, Warner Oland. Remade in 1953 and 1980.

Jesus Christ, Superstar. Universal, 1973 (c). Norman Jewison. Sp: Melvyn Bragg and Norman Jewison, b/o the 1970 rock opera. MS: Andrew Lloyd Weber and Tim Rice. Cast: Ted Neeley, Carl Anderson, Yvonne Ellman, Barry Denham, Bob Bingham, Joshua Mostel.

Jolson Sings Again. Columbia, 1949 (c). Henry Levin. Sp: Sidney Buchman. MS: various writers. Cast: Larry Parks, Barbara Hale, William Demarest, Ludwig Donath, Bill Goodwin, Tamara Shayne.

The Jolson Story. Columbia, 1946 (c). Alfred E. Green. Sp: Stephen Longstreet, adapted by Harry Chandlee and Andrew Solt. MS: various writers. Cast: Larry Parks, Evelyn Keyes, Ludwig Donath, Bill Goodwin, William Demarest, Tamara Shayne.

Just Imagine. Fox, 1930. David Butler. Sp: B. G. DeSylva, Lew Brown, and Ray Henderson. MS: B. G. DeSylva, Lew Brown, and Ray Henderson. Cast: John Garrick, Maureen O'Sullivan, El Brendel, Marjorie White, Frank Albertson, Hobart Bosworth, Mischa Auer.

The Kid from Brooklyn. A Samuel Goldwyn Production, released by RKO Radio, 1946 (c). Norman Z. McLeod. Sp: Grover Jones, Frank Butler, and Richard Connell, b/o play by Lynn Root and Harry Clork. MS: Jule Styne and Sammy Cahn. Cast: Danny Kaye, Virginia Mayo, Vera-Ellen, Steve Cochran, Walter Abel, Eve Arden. Previously filmed in 1936 as *The Milky Way* (nm).

The Kid from Spain. A Samuel Goldwyn Production, released by United Artists, 1932. Leo McCarey. Sp: William Anthony McGuire, Bert Kalmar, and Harry Ruby. MS: Harry Ruby and Bert Kalmar. Cast: Eddie Cantor, Lyda Roberti, Robert Young, Ruth Hall, John Miljan.

Kid Millions. A Samuel Goldwyn Production, released by United Artists, 1934. Roy Del Ruth. Sp: Arthur Sheekman, Nat Perrin, and Nunnally Johnson. MS: various writers. Cast: Eddie Cantor, Ann Sothern, Ethel Merman, George Murphy, Jessie Block, Eve Sully, Burton Churchill. One sequence in color.

The King and I. Fox, 1956 (c). Walter Lang. Sp: Ernest Lehman, b/o the 1951 musical play which was adapted from a book by Margaret Landon and a 1946 film, both titled *Anna and the King of Siam*. MS: Richard Rodgers and Oscar Hammerstein II. Cast: Deborah Kerr, Yul Brynner, Rita Moreno, Martin Benson, Terry Saunders.

King of Jazz. Universal, 1930 (c). John Murray Anderson. Sp: Edward T. Lowe, Jr., Harry Ruskin, and Charles MacArthur. MS: various composers. Cast: Paul Whiteman, John Boles, Laura La Plante, Jeanette Loff, Glenn Tryon, Stanley Smith, the Brox Sisters, Bing Crosby.

The King Steps Out. Columbia, 1936. Josef von Sternberg. Sp: Sidney Buchman, b/o operetta by Gustav Holm and others. MS: Fritz Kreisler and Dorothy Fields. Cast: Grace Moore, Franchot Tone, Walter Connolly, Raymond Walburn, Victor Jory, Elizabeth Risdon.

Kismet. MGM, 1955 (c). Vincente Minnelli. Sp: Charles Lederer and Luther Davis, b/o their musical play, which was adapted from play by Alexander Knoblock. MS: Robert Wright and George Forrest, derived from the music of Alexander Borodin. Cast: Howard Keel, Ann Blyth, Dolores Gray, Vic Damone, Monty Woolley, Sebastian Cabot. Previously filmed in 1930 (nm) and 1944 (nm).

Kiss Me, Kate. MGM, 1953 (c). George Sidney. Sp: Dorothy Kingsley, b/o the 1948 musical play. MS: Cole

Porter. Cast: Kathryn Grayson, Howard Keel, Ann Miller, Tommy Rall, Bob Fosse, Bobby Van, James Whitmore, Keenan Wynn.

Lady Be Good. MGM, 1941. Norman Z. McLeod. Sp: Jack McGowan, Kay Van Riper, and John McClain, b/o story by Jack McGowan. MS: George and Ira Gershwin. Cast: Eleanor Powell, Ann Sothern, Robert Young, Lionel Barrymore, Red Skelton, John Carroll, Dan Dailey.

Lady in the Dark. Paramount, 1944 (c). Mitchell Leisen. Sp: Frances Goodrich and Albert Hackett, b/o the 1941 musical play. MS: Kurt Weill and Ira Gershwin. Cast: Ginger Rogers, Ray Milland, Warner Baxter, Jon Hall, Mischa Auer, Barry Sullivan, Mary Phillips.

Les Girls. MGM, 1957 (c). George Cukor. Sp: John Patrick, b/o story by Vera Caspary. MS: Cole Porter. Cast: Gene Kelly, Mitzi Gaynor, Kay Kendall, Taina Elg, Jacques Bergerac, Leslie Phillips, Henry Daniell.

Lili. MGM, 1953 (c). Charles Walters. Sp: Helen Deutsch, b/o story by Paul Gallico. MS: Bronislau Kaper and Helen Deutsch. Cast: Leslie Caron, Mel Ferrer, Jean Pierre Aumont, Zsa Zsa Gabor, Kurt Kasznar, Amanda Blake.

Lillian Russell. Fox, 1940. Irving Cummings. Sp: William Anthony McGuire. MS: various writers. Cast: Alice Faye, Don Ameche, Henry Fonda, Edward Arnold, Warren William, Leo Carrillo, Helen Westley, Lynn Bari, Nigel Bruce.

A Little Night Music. New World Pictures, 1977 (c). Harold Prince. Sp: Hugh Wheeler, b/o his book for the 1973 musical play, which was adapted from Ingmar Bergman's 1956 film *Smiles of a Summer Night*. MS: Stephen Sondheim. Cast: Elizabeth Taylor, Diana Rigg, Len Cariou, Lesley-Anne Down, Hermione Gingold, Laurence Guitard, Christopher Guard.

Lost Horizon. Columbia, 1973 (c). Charles Jarrott. Sp: Larry Kramer, b/o novel by James Hilton. MS: Burt Bacharach and Hal David. Cast: Peter Finch, Liv Ullmann, Sally Kellerman, George Kennedy, Michael York, Olivia Hussey, John Gielgud, Bobby Van, Charles Boyer. A musical remake of the 1937 film.

Lovely to Look At. MGM, 1952 (c). Mervyn LeRoy. Sp: George Wells and Harry Ruby, b/o the 1933 musical play *Roberta*. MS: Jerome Kern and Otto Harbach. Cast: Kathryn Grayson, Red Skelton, Howard Keel, Marge Champion, Gower Champion, Ann Miller, Zsa Zsa Gabor. Previously filmed in 1935 as *Roberta*.

Love Me Forever. Columbia, 1935. Victor Schertzinger. Sp: Jo Swerling and Sidney Buchman, b/o story by Victor Schertzinger. MS: Victor Schertzinger and Gus Kahn. Cast: Grace Moore, Leo Carrillo, Michael Bartlett, Robert Allen, Spring Byington.

Love Me or Leave Me. MGM, 1955 (c). Charles Vidor. Sp: Daniel Fuchs and Isobel Lennart, b/o story by Daniel Fuchs. MS: various writers. Cast: James Cagney, Doris Day, Cameron Mitchell, Robert Keith, Tom Tully, Harry Bellaver, Richard Gaines.

Love Me Tonight. Paramount, 1932. Rouben Mamoulian. Sp: Samuel Hoffenstein, Waldemar Young, and George Marion, Jr. MS: Richard Rodgers and Lorenz Hart. Cast: Maurice Chevalier, Jeanette MacDonald, Myrna Loy, C. Aubrey Smith, Charles Ruggles, Charles Butterworth.

The Love Parade. Paramount, 1929. Ernst Lubitsch. Sp: Ernest Vajda and Guy Bolton, b/o play by Leon Xanrof and Jules Chancel. MS: Victor Schertzinger and Clifford Grey. Cast: Maurice Chevalier, Jeanette MacDonald, Lupino Lane, Lillian Roth, Edgar Norton, Lionel Belmore.

Lullaby of Broadway. Warners, 1951 (c). David Butler. Sp: Earl Baldwin. MS: various writers. Cast: Doris Day, Gene Nelson, S. Z. Sakall, Billy De Wolfe, Gladys George.

Mame. Warners, 1974 (c). Gene Saks. Sp: Paul Zindel, b/o the 1966 musical play, which was adapted from the 1958 film *Auntie Mame* and novel by Patrick Dennis. MS: Jerry Herman. Cast: Lucille Ball, Bea Arthur, Robert Preston, Jane Connell, Bruce Davison, Kirby Furlong, Doria Cook.

Mammy. Warners, 1930. Michael Curtiz. Sp: Gordon Rigby and Joseph Jackson, b/o story by Irving Berlin. MS: Irving Berlin. Cast: Al Jolson, Lois Moran, Louise Dresser, Lowell Sherman, Hobart Bosworth, Tully Marshall.

Man of La Mancha. United Artists, 1972 (c). Arthur Hiller. Sp: Dale Wasserman, b/o the 1965 musical play and the novel by Miguel de Cervantes. MS: Mitch Leigh and Joe Darion. Cast: Peter O'Toole, Sophia Loren, James Coco, Harry Andrews, John Castle, Brian Blessed,

Ian Richardson.

Mary Poppins. A Walt Disney Production, released by Buena Vista, 1964 (c). Robert Stevenson. Sp: Bill Walsh and Don Da Gradi, b/o the books by P. L. Travers. MS: Richard M. and Robert B. Sherman. Cast: Julie Andrews, Dick Van Dyke, David Tomlinson, Glynis Johns, Ed Wynn, Arthur Treacher, Karen Dotrice, Matthew Garber.

Maytime. MGM, 1937. Robert Z. Leonard. Sp: Noel Langley, b/o the 1917 musical play by Rida Johnson Young. MS: Sigmund Romberg, with special lyrics by Bob Wright and Chet Forrest. Cast: Jeanette MacDonald, Nelson Eddy, John Barrymore, Herman Bing, Tom Brown, Rafaela Ottiano.

Meet Me in St. Louis. MGM, 1944 (c). Vincente Minnelli. Sp: Fred Finklehoffe and Irving Brecher, b/o stories by Sally Benson. MS: Hugh Martin and Ralph Blane. Cast: Judy Garland, Margaret O'Brien, Mary Astor, Leon Ames, Lucille Bremer, Tom Drake, Marjorie Main, Harry Davenport, Hank Daniels, Joan Carroll.

The Merry Widow. MGM, 1934. Ernst Lubitsch. Sp: Samson Raphaelson and Ernest Vajda, b/o operetta by Victor Leon and Leon Stein. MS: Franz Lehár, with new lyrics by Lorenz Hart and Gus Kahn. Cast: Maurice Chevalier, Jeanette MacDonald, Edward Everett Horton, Una Merkel, George Barbier. Previously filmed in 1925 (s) and remade in 1952.

The Merry Widow. MGM, 1952 (c). Curtis Bernhardt. Sp: Sonya Levien and William Ludwig, b/o operetta by Victor Leon and Leon Stein. MS: Franz Lehár and Paul Francis Webster. Cast: Lana Turner, Fernando Lamas,

Choreographer Hermes Pan poses with Ginger Rogers and Fred Astaire on the set of The Story of Vernon and Irene Castle *(RKO, 1939).*

Richard Haydn, Una Merkel, Thomas Gomez, John Abbott, Marcel Dalio. Previously filmed in 1925 (s) and 1934.

Mississippi. Paramount, 1935. Edward A. Sutherland. Sp: Francis Martin and Jack Cunningham, b/o novel by Booth Tarkington. MS: Richard Rodgers and Lorenz Hart. Cast: Bing Crosby, W. C. Fields, Joan Bennett, Queenie Smith, Gail Patrick, Claude Gillingwater. Previously filmed in 1924 as *The Fighting Coward* (s).

Monte Carlo. Paramount, 1930. Ernst Lubitsch. Sp: Ernest Vajda and Vincent Lawrence, b/o a play by Hans Müller and episodes from *Monsieur Beaucaire* by Booth Tarkington. MS: Richard Whiting, Frank Harling, and Leo Robin. Cast: Jeanette MacDonald, Jack Buchanan, ZaSu Pitts, Claude Allister, Lionel Belmore.

Moon Over Miami. Fox, 1941 (c). Walter Lang. Sp: Vincent Lawrence and Brown Holmes, adapted by George Seaton and Lynn Starling from play by Stephen Powys. MS: Ralph Rainger and Leo Robin. Cast: Betty Grable, Don Ameche, Robert Cummings, Charlotte Greenwood, Carole Landis, Jack Haley. Previously filmed in 1938 as *Three Blind Mice* (nm) and remade in 1946 as *Three Little Girls in Blue*.

Mother Wore Tights. Fox, 1947 (c). Walter Lang. Sp: Lamar Trotti, b/o book by Miriam Young. MS: Josef Myrow and Mack Gordon. Cast: Betty Grable, Dan Dailey, Mona Freeman, Connie Marshall, Vanessa Brown.

Music for Millions. MGM, 1944. Henry Koster. Sp: Myles Connolly. MS: various writers. Cast: June Allyson, Margaret O'Brien, Jose Iturbi, Jimmy Durante, Marsha

Hunt, Hugh Herbert, Marie Wilson, Larry Adler.

The Music Man. Warners, 1962 (c). Morton Da Costa. Sp: Marion Hargrove, b/o the 1957 musical play. MS: Meredith Willson. Cast: Robert Preston, Shirley Jones, Paul Ford, Buddy Hackett, Hermione Gingold, Pert Kelton, Timmy Everett, Ronny Howard, Susan Luckey.

My Dream Is Yours. Warners, 1949 (c). Michael Curtiz. Sp: Harry Kurnitz and Dane Lussier. MS: Harry Warren and Ralph Freed. Cast: Jack Carson, Doris Day, Lee Bowman, Adolphe Menjou, Eve Arden, S. Z. Sakall, Selena Royle.

My Fair Lady. Warners, 1964 (c). George Cukor. Sp: Alan Jay Lerner, b/o the 1956 musical play and George Bernard Shaw's play *Pygmalion*, filmed in 1938. MS: Frederick Loewe and Alan Jay Lerner. Cast: Rex Harrison, Audrey Hepburn, Stanley Holloway, Gladys Cooper, Wilfrid Hyde-White, Theodore Bikel, Jeremy Brett.

My Gal Sal. Fox, 1942 (c). Irving Cummings. Sp: Seton I. Miller, Darrell Ware, and Karl Tunberg. MS: Ralph Rainger, Leo Robin, and Paul Dresser. Cast: Rita Hayworth, Victor Mature, Carole Landis, John Sutton, James Gleason, Phil Silvers, Walter Catlett, Mona Maris.

My Sister Eileen. Columbia, 1955 (c). Richard Quine. Sp: Blake Edwards and Richard Quine, b/o play by Joseph Fields and Jerome Chodorov. MS: Jule Styne and Leo Robin. Cast: Betty Garrett, Janet Leigh, Jack Lemmon, Bob Fosse, Kurt Kasznar, Dick York, Tommy Rall. A musical remake of the 1942 film.

Naughty Marietta. MGM, 1935. W. S. Van Dyke II. Sp: Albert Hackett, Frances Goodrich, and John Lee Mahin, b/o operetta by Victor Herbert and Rida Johnson Young. MS: Victor Herbert, with new lyrics by Gus Kahn. Cast: Nelson Eddy, Jeanette MacDonald, Frank Morgan, Elsa Lanchester, Douglass Dumbrille.

Neptune's Daughter. MGM, 1949 (c). Edward Buzzell. Sp: Dorothy Kingsley. MS: Frank Loesser. Cast: Esther Williams, Red Skelton, Ricardo Montalban, Betty Garrett, Keenan Wynn, Xavier Cugat and his orchestra.

New Moon. MGM, 1940. Robert Z. Leonard. Sp: Jacques Deval and Robert Arthur, b/o the 1928 musical play. MS: Sigmund Romberg and Oscar Hammerstein II. Cast: Jeanette MacDonald, Nelson Eddy, Mary Boland, George Zucco, H. B. Warner, Grant Mitchell, Stanley Fields. Previously filmed in 1930.

New York, New York. United Artists, 1977 (c). Martin Scorsese. Sp: Earl MacRauch and Mardik Martin, b/o story by Earl MacRauch. MS: John Kander and Fred Ebb. Cast: Liza Minnelli, Robert De Niro, Lionel Stander, Barry Primus, Mary Kay Place, Georgie Auld.

Night and Day. Warners, 1946 (c). Michael Curtiz. Sp: Charles Hoffman, Leo Townsend, and William Bowers, b/o career of Cole Porter. MS: Cole Porter. Cast: Cary Grant, Alexis Smith, Monty Woolley, Ginny Simms, Jane Wyman, Eve Arden, Mary Martin.

Oklahoma! An Arthur Hornblow Production, released by Magna Theatre Corporation, 1955 (c). Fred Zinnemann. Sp: Sonya Levien and William Ludwig, b/o the 1943 musical play. MS: Richard Rodgers and Oscar Hammerstein II. Cast: Gordon MacRae, Shirley Jones, Charlotte Greenwood, Rod Steiger, Gloria Grahame, Eddie Albert, Gene Nelson.

Oliver! Columbia, 1968 (c). Carol Reed. Sp: Vernon Harris, b/o the 1963 musical play, which was adapted from Charles Dickens's novel *Oliver Twist*, filmed in 1916 (s), 1922 (s), 1933 (nm), and 1951 (nm). MS: Lionel Bart. Cast: Ron Moody, Oliver Reed, Mark Lester, Shani Wallis, Harry Secombe, Jack Wild, Hugh Griffith, Peggy Mount.

On a Clear Day You Can See Forever. Paramount, 1970 (c). Vincente Minnelli. Sp: Alan Jay Lerner, b/o the 1965 musical play. MS: Burton Lane and Alan Jay Lerner. Cast: Barbra Streisand, Yves Montand, Larry Blyden, Bob Newhart, Jack Nicholson, Simon Oakland, John Richardson.

On an Island with You. MGM, 1948 (c). Richard Thorpe. Sp: Dorothy Kingsley, Dorothy Cooper, Charles Martin, and Hans Wilhelm, b/o story by Charles Martin and Hans Wilhelm. MS: Nacio Herb Brown and Edward Heyman. Cast: Esther Williams, Peter Lawford, Ricardo Montalban, Jimmy Durante, Cyd Charisse, Xavier Cugat and his orchestra.

One Hour with You. Paramount, 1932. Ernst Lubitsch. Sp: Samson Raphaelson. MS: Oscar Straus, Richard Whiting, and Leo Robin. Cast: Maurice Chevalier, Jeanette MacDonald, Genevieve Tobin, Charles Ruggles, Roland Young, George Barbier. A musical remake of Lubitsch's 1924 film *The Marriage Circle*.

One in a Million. Fox, 1936. Sidney Lanfield. Sp: Leonard Praskins and Mark Kelly. MS: Sidney Mitchell and Lew Pollack. Cast: Sonja Henie, Adolphe Menjou, Don Ameche, Jean Hersholt, Ned Sparks, the Ritz Brothers, Arline Judge, Dixie Dunbar, Borrah Minnevitch.

One Night of Love. Columbia, 1934. Victor Schertzinger. Sp: S. K. Lauren, b/o story by Dorothy Speare and Charles Beahan. MS: Victor Schertzinger and Gus Kahn. Cast: Grace Moore, Tullio Carminati, Lyle Talbot, Mona Barrie, Luis Alberni.

On Moonlight Bay. Warners, 1951 (c). Roy Del Ruth. Sp: Melville Shavelson and Jack Rose, b/o stories by Booth Tarkington. MS: various writers. Cast: Doris Day, Gordon MacRae, Leon Ames, Rosemary DeCamp, Billy Gray, Jack Smith.

On the Avenue. Fox, 1937. Roy Del Ruth. Sp: Gene Markey and William Conselman. MS: Irving Berlin. Cast: Dick Powell, Madeleine Carroll, Alice Faye, the Ritz Brothers, George Barbier, Alan Mowbray, Cora Witherspoon.

On the Town. MGM, 1949 (c). Stanley Donen and Gene Kelly. Sp: Betty Comden and Adolph Green, b/o their 1944 musical play. MS: Leonard Bernstein, Roger Edens, Betty Comden, and Adolph Green. Cast: Gene Kelly, Frank Sinatra, Jules Munshin, Vera-Ellen, Betty Garrett, Ann Miller, Alice Pearce.

On with the Show. Warners, 1929 (c). Alan Crosland. Sp: Robert Lord, b/o story by Humphrey Pearson. MS: Harry Akst and Grant Clarke. Cast: Betty Compson, Arthur Lake, Sally O'Neil, Joe E. Brown, Louise Fazenda, Ethel Waters, Sam Hardy.

On Your Toes. Warners, 1939. Ray Enright. Sp: Sig Herzig and Lawrence Riley, b/o the 1936 musical play. MS: Richard Rodgers and Lorenz Hart. Cast: Eddie Albert, Vera Zorina, Alan Hale, Erik Rhodes, James Gleason, Frank McHugh, Queenie Smith, Donald O'Connor.

The Opposite Sex. MGM, 1956 (c). David Miller. Fay and Michael Kanin, b/o play by Clare Boothe. MS: Nicholas Brodszky and Sammy Cahn. Cast: June Allyson, Joan Collins, Dolores Gray, Ann Sheridan, Ann Miller, Leslie Nielsen, Charlotte Greenwood, Agnes Moorehead. A musical remake of *The Women* (1939).

Orchestra Wives. Fox, 1942. Archie Mayo. Sp: Karl Tunberg and Darrell Ware, b/o story by James Prindle. MS: Harry Warren and Mack Gordon. Cast: George Montgomery, Ann Rutherford, Glenn Miller and his orchestra, Lynn Bari, Carole Landis, Cesar Romero, Virginia Gilmore, Jackie Gleason.

Paint Your Wagon. Paramount, 1969 (c). Joshua Logan. Sp: Paddy Chayefsky, b/o the 1951 musical play. MS: Frederick Loewe and Alan Jay Lerner. Cast: Lee Marvin, Clint Eastwood, Jean Seberg, Harve Presnell, Ray Walston, Tom Ligon.

The Pajama Game. Warners, 1957 (c). George Abbott and Stanley Donen. Sp: George Abbott and Richard Bissell, b/o the 1954 musical play, which was adapted from a novel by Richard Bissell. MS: Richard Adler and Jerry Ross. Cast: Doris Day, John Raitt, Carol Haney, Eddie Foy, Jr., Reta Shaw, Barbara Nichols, Thelma Pelish, Ralph Dunn.

Pal Joey. Columbia, 1957 (c). George Sidney. Sp: Dorothy Kingsley, b/o the 1940 musical play, which was adapted from stories by John O'Hara. MS: Richard Rodgers and Lorenz Hart. Cast: Frank Sinatra, Rita Hayworth, Kim Novak, Hank Henry, Barbara Nichols, Bobby Sherwood, Elizabeth Patterson.

Palmy Days. A Samuel Goldwyn Production, released by United Artists, 1931. Edward Sutherland. Sp: Eddie Cantor, Morrie Ryskind, and David Freedman. MS: various writers. Cast: Eddie Cantor, Charlotte Greenwood, George Raft, Spencer Charters, Barbara Weeks, Charles B. Middleton.

Panama Hattie. MGM, 1942. Norman Z. McLeod. Sp: Jack McGowan and Wilkie Mahoney, b/o the 1940 musical play. MS: Cole Porter and various writers. Cast: Ann Sothern, Dan Dailey, Red Skelton, Marsha Hunt, Virginia O'Brien, Rags Ragland.

Paramount on Parade. Paramount, 1930. Twelve Paramount directors. MS: various writers. Cast: Maurice Chevalier, Clara Bow, Gary Cooper, Fredric March, Kay Francis, Ruth Chatterton, Nancy Carroll, Jack Oakie, Leon Errol, Jean Arthur. Some sequences in Technicolor.

Pennies from Heaven. Columbia, 1936. Norman Z. McLeod. Sp: Jo Swerling, b/o book by Katharine Leslie Moore. MS: Arthur Johnston and Johnny Burke. Cast: Bing Crosby, Madge Evans, Edith Fellows, Donald Meek, Louis Armstrong and his orchestra, Tom Dugan.

Pigskin Parade. Fox, 1936. David Butler. Sp: Harry Tugend, Jack Yellen, and William Conselman, b/o story by Arthur Sheekman, Nat Perrin, and Mark Kelly. MS: Sidney Mitchell and Lew Pollack. Cast: Patsy Kelly, Jack Haley, Stuart Erwin, Johnny Downs, Betty Grable, Dixie Dunbar, Judy Garland, Tony Martin.

Pin Up Girl. Fox, 1944 (c). Bruce Humberstone. Sp: Robert Ellis, Helen Logan, and Earl Baldwin, b/o story by Libbie Block. MS: James Monaco and Mack Gordon. Cast: Betty Grable, Martha Raye, Joe E. Brown, John Harvey, Eugene Pallette, Dorothea Kent.

The Pirate. MGM, 1948 (c). Vincente Minnelli. Sp: Frances Goodrich and Albert Hackett, b/o play by S. N. Behrman. MS: Cole Porter. Cast: Judy Garland, Gene Kelly, Walter Slezak, Gladys Cooper, Reginald Owen, the Nicholas Brothers.

Poor Little Rich Girl. Fox, 1936. Irving Cummings. Sp: Sam Hellman, Gladys Lehman, and Harry Tugend, b/o stories by Eleanor Gates and Ralph Spence. MS: Harry Revel and Mack Gordon. Cast: Shirley Temple, Alice Faye, Jack Haley, Michael Whalen, Gloria Stuart, Sara Haden, Claude Gillingwater. Previously filmed in 1917 (s).

Porgy and Bess. A Samuel Goldwyn Production, released by Columbia, 1959 (c). Otto Preminger. Sp: N. Richard Nash, b/o on the 1935 folk opera. MS: George Gershwin, Ira Gershwin, and DuBose Heyward. Cast: Sidney Poitier, Dorothy Dandridge, Sammy Davis, Jr., Pearl Bailey, Brock Peters, Diahann Carroll.

Red Garters. Paramount, 1954 (c). George Marshall. Sp: Michael Fessier. MS: Jay Livingston and Ray Evans. Cast: Rosemary Clooney, Jack Carson, Guy Mitchell, Pat Crowley, Joanne Gilbert, Gene Barry, Cass Daley, Buddy Ebsen.

Rhapsody in Blue. Warners, 1945. Irving Rapper. Sp: Sonya Levien, Howard Koch, and Elliott Paul. MS: George and Ira Gershwin. Cast: Robert Alda, Joan Leslie, Alexis Smith, Charles Coburn, Oscar Levant, Rosemary DeCamp, Morris Carnovsky.

Rhythm on the Range. Paramount, 1936. Norman Taurog. Sp: Walter DeLeon, Francis Martin, John C. Moffitt, and Sidney Salkow, b/o story by Mervin J. Houser. MS: various writers. Cast: Bing Crosby, Frances Farmer, Bob Burns, Martha Raye, Samuel S. Hinds, Warren Hymer, Lucille Gleason. Remade in 1956 as *Pardners*.

Rio Rita. RKO, 1929. Luther Reed. Sp: Luther Reed and Russell Mack, b/o the 1927 musical play. MS: Harry Tierney and Joseph McCarthy. Cast: Bebe Daniels, John Boles, Bert Wheeler, Robert Woolsey, Don Alvarado, Dorothy Lee, Georges Renavent. With color sequences. Remade in 1942.

Roberta. RKO, 1935. William A. Seiter. Sp: Jane Murfin, Sam Mintz, and Allan Scott, b/o the 1933 musical play. MS: Jerome Kern, Otto Harbach, Dorothy Fields, and Jimmy McHugh. Cast: Fred Astaire, Ginger Rogers, Irene Dunne, Randolph Scott, Helen Westley. Remade in 1952 as *Lovely to Look At*.

Roman Scandals. A Samuel Goldwyn Production, released by United Artists, 1933. Frank Tuttle. Sp: George S. Kaufman and Robert E. Sherwood. MS: Harry Warren, Al Dubin, and L. Wolfe Gilbert. Cast: Eddie Cantor, Ruth Etting, Gloria Stuart, David Manners, Verree Teasdale, Edward Arnold, Alan Mowbray.

Rosalie. MGM, 1937. W. S. Van Dyke II. Sp: William Anthony McGuire, b/o the 1928 musical play. MS: Cole Porter. Cast: Eleanor Powell, Nelson Eddy, Frank Morgan, Ray Bolger, Edna May Oliver, Ilona Massey, Billy Gilbert, Reginald Owen.

The Rose. Fox, 1979 (c). Mark Rydell. Sp: Bill Kerby and Bo Goldman, b/o story by Bill Kerby. MS: various writers. Cast: Bette Midler, Alan Bates, Frederic Forrest, Harry Dean Stanton, Barry Primus, David Keith, Sandra McCabe, Will Hare.

Rose Marie. MGM, 1936. W. S. Van Dyke II. Sp: Frances Goodrich, Albert Hackett, and Alice Duer Miller, b/o the 1924 musical play. MS: Rudolf Friml, Oscar Hammerstein II, and Otto Harbach, with new music and lyrics by Herbert Stothart and Gus Kahn. Cast: Jeanette MacDonald, Nelson Eddy, James Stewart, Allan Jones, Reginald Owen. Previously filmed in 1928 (s) and remade in 1954.

Rose Marie. MGM, 1954 (c). Mervyn LeRoy. Sp: Ronald Miller and George Froeschel, b/o the 1924 musical play. MS: Rudolf Friml, Oscar Hammerstein II, and Otto Harbach. Cast: Ann Blyth, Howard Keel, Fernando Lamas, Bert Lahr, Marjorie Main, Joan Taylor. Previously filmed in

1928 (s) and 1936.

Rose of Washington Square. Fox, 1939. Gregory Ratoff. Sp: Nunnally Johnson, b/o story by John Larkin and Jerry Horwitz. MS: various writers. Cast: Alice Faye, Tyrone Power, Al Jolson, William Frawley, Joyce Compton, Hobart Cavanaugh, Louis Prima.

Royal Wedding. MGM, 1951 (c). Stanley Donen. Sp: Alan Jay Lerner. MS: Burton Lane and Alan Jay Lerner. Cast: Fred Astaire, Jane Powell, Peter Lawford, Sarah Churchill, Keenan Wynn, Albert Sharpe.

Sally. Warners, 1929 (c). John Francis Dillon. Sp: Waldemar Young, b/o the 1920 musical play. MS: Jerome Kern, Guy Bolton, and Clifford Grey, plus others. Cast: Marilyn Miller, Alexander Gray, Joe E. Brown, T. Roy Barnes, Pert Kelton, Ford Sterling, Maude Turner.

Seven Brides for Seven Brothers. MGM, 1954 (c). Stanley Donen. Sp: Dorothy Kingsley, Frances Goodrich, and Albert Hackett, b/o Stephen Vincent Benét's story "The Sobbin' Women." MS: Gene de Paul and Johnny Mercer. Cast: Jane Powell, Howard Keel, Tommy Rall, Julie Newmar, Russ Tamblyn, Jeff Richards, Matt Mattox.

1776. A Jack L. Warner Production, released by Columbia Pictures, 1972 (c). Peter Hunt. Sp: Peter Stone, b/o the 1969 musical play. MS: Sherman Edwards. Cast: William Daniels, Howard da Silva, Ken Howard, Blythe Danner, Donald Madden, John Cullum.

Shall We Dance. RKO, 1937. Mark Sandrich. Sp: Allan Scott and Ernest Pagano, b/o story by Lee Loeb and Harold Buchman. MS: George and Ira Gershwin. Cast: Fred Astaire, Ginger Rogers, Edward Everett Horton, Eric Blore, Jerome Cowan.

She Loves Me Not. Paramount, 1934. Elliott Nugent. Sp: Benjamin Glazer, b/o novel by Edward Hope and play by Howard Lindsay. MS: Harry Revel and Mack Gordon. Cast: Bing Crosby, Miriam Hopkins, Kitty Carlisle, Edward Nugent, Henry Stephenson, Lynne Overman, Judith Allen. Remade in 1955 as *How to Be Very, Very Popular*.

The Shocking Miss Pilgrim. Fox, 1947 (c). George Seaton. Sp: George Seaton, b/o story by Ernest and Fredericka Maas. MS: George and Ira Gershwin. Cast: Betty Grable, Dick Haymes, Anne Revere, Allyn Joslyn, Gene Lockhart, Elizabeth Patterson.

Show Boat. Universal, 1936. James Whale. Sp: Oscar Hammerstein II, b/o his 1927 musical play, which was adapted from the novel by Edna Ferber. MS: Jerome Kern and Oscar Hammerstein II. Cast: Irene Dunne, Allan Jones, Helen Morgan, Paul Robeson, Charles Winninger, Helen Westley. Previously filmed in 1929 (pt) and remade in 1951.

Show Boat. MGM, 1951 (c). George Sidney. Sp: John Lee Mahin, b/o the 1927 musical play and the novel by Edna Ferber. MS: Jerome Kern and Oscar Hammerstein II. Cast: Kathryn Grayson, Howard Keel, Marge and Gower Champion, Ava Gardner, Joe E. Brown, Agnes Moorehead, William Warfield. Previously filmed in 1929 (pt) and 1936.

Show of Shows. Warners, 1929 (c). John Adolfi. MS: various writers. Cast: Frank Fay, Loretta Young, Beatrice Lillie, Douglas Fairbanks, Jr., John Barrymore, Ted Lewis and his Band, Louise Fazenda, Rin-Tin-Tin, Chester Morris, Harriette Lake (Ann Sothern), Richard Barthelmess.

Silk Stockings. MGM, 1957 (c). Rouben Mamoulian. Sp: Leonard Gershe and Leonard Spigelgass, b/o the 1955 musical play, which was adapted from the 1939 film *Ninotchka*. MS: Cole Porter. Cast: Fred Astaire, Cyd Charisse, Janis Paige, Peter Lorre, Jules Munshin, Joseph Buloff.

Sing, Baby, Sing. Fox, 1936. Sidney Lanfield. Sp: Milton Sperling, Jack Yellen, and Harry Tugend, b/o story by Milton Sperling and Jack Yellen. MS: various writers. Cast: Alice Faye, Adolphe Menjou, Gregory Ratoff, Ted Healy, Patsy Kelly, Michael Whalen, the Ritz Brothers, Dixie Dunbar, Tony Martin.

The Singing Fool. Warners, 1928. Lloyd Bacon. Sp: C. Graham Baker and Joseph Jackson. MS: B. G. DeSylva, Lew Brown, and Ray Henderson, plus others. Cast: Al Jolson, Betty Bronson, Josephine Dunn, Davey Lee, Reed Howes.

Singin' in the Rain. MGM, 1952 (c). Stanley Donen and Gene Kelly. Sp: Betty Comden and Adolph Green. MS: Nacio Herb Brown and Arthur Freed. Cast: Gene Kelly, Debbie Reynolds, Donald O'Connor, Jean Hagen, Millard Mitchell, Cyd Charisse.

Sing You Sinners. Paramount, 1938. Wesley Ruggles. Sp: Claude Binyon, b/o his story. MS: James Monaco and Johnny Burke. Cast: Bing Crosby, Fred MacMurray, Ellen Drew, Donald O'Connor, Elizabeth Patterson.

Small Town Girl. MGM, 1953 (c). Leslie Kardos. Sp: Dorothy Cooper and Dorothy Kingsley, b/o story by Dorothy Cooper. MS: Nicholas Brodszky and Leo Robin. Cast: Jane Powell, Farley Granger, Ann Miller, Bobby Van, Robert Keith, Chill Wills, S. Z. Sakall, Fay Wray.

The Smiling Lieutenant. Paramount, 1931. Ernst Lubitsch. Sp: Ernest Vajda, Samson Raphaelson, and Ernst Lubitsch, b/o operetta *A Waltz Dream* by Leopold Jacobson, Felix Dormann, and Oscar Straus, and novel by Hans Müller. MS: Oscar Straus and Clifford Grey. Cast: Maurice Chevalier, Claudette Colbert, Miriam Hopkins, George Barbier, Charles Ruggles.

A Song Is Born. A Samuel Goldwyn Production, released by RKO Radio, 1948 (c). Howard Hawks. Sp: Harry Tugend and others, b/o story by Thomas Monroe and Billy Wilder. MS: Don Raye and Gene De Paul. Cast: Danny Kaye, Virginia Mayo, Benny Goodman, Hugh Herbert, Steve Cochran, Felix Bressart. A musical remake of *Ball of Fire* (1942).

The Sound of Music. Fox, 1965 (c). Robert Wise. Sp: Ernest Lehman, b/o the 1959 musical play. MS: Richard Rodgers and Oscar Hammerstein II. Cast: Julie Andrews, Christopher Plummer, Eleanor Parker, Richard Haydn, Peggy Wood.

South Pacific. Fox, 1958 (c). Joshua Logan. Sp: Paul Osborn, b/o the 1949 musical play. MS: Richard Rodgers and Oscar Hammerstein II. Cast: Mitzi Gaynor, Rossano Brazzi, Ray Walston, John Kerr, France Nuyen, Juanita Hall, Russ Brown, Jack Mullaney.

Springtime in the Rockies. Fox, 1942 (c). Irving Cummings. Sp: Walter Bullock and Ken Englund, b/o story by Philip Wylie. MS: Harry Warren and Mack Gordon. Cast: Betty Grable, John Payne, Carmen Miranda, Cesar Romero, Charlotte Greenwood, Edward Everett Horton, Harry James and his orchestra. Previously filmed in 1937 as *Second Honeymoon* (nm).

Stand Up and Cheer. Fox, 1934. Hamilton MacFadden. Sp: Ralph Spence, b/o story outline by Will Rogers and Philip Klein. MS: Lew Brown and Jay Gorney. Cast: Warner Baxter, Madge Evans, James Dunn, Shirley Temple, Sylvia Froos, John Boles, Arthur Byron, Aunt Jemima, Nick (Dick) Foran.

Star! Fox, 1968 (c). Robert Wise. Sp: William Fairchild. MS: various writers. Cast: Julie Andrews, Richard Crenna, Michael Craig, Daniel Massey, Robert Reed, Bruce Forsyth, Beryl Reid.

A Star Is Born. Warners, 1954 (c). George Cukor. Sp: Moss Hart, b/o the 1937 screenplay by Dorothy Parker, Alan Campbell, and Robert Carson. MS: Harold Arlen and Ira Gershwin, others. Cast: Judy Garland, James Mason, Jack Carson, Charles Bickford, Tommy Noonan. A musical remake of the 1937 film; remade in 1976.

A Star Is Born. Warners, 1976 (c). Frank Pierson. Sp: John Gregory Dunne, Joan Didion, and Frank Pierson. MS: Paul Williams, Barbra Streisand, and others. Cast: Barbra Streisand, Kris Kristofferson, Paul Mazursky, Gary Busey, Oliver Clark, Marta Heflin. Previously filmed in 1937 (nm) and 1954.

Star-Spangled Rhythm. Paramount, 1942. George Marshall. Sp: Harry Tugend. MS: Harold Arlen and Johnny Mercer. Cast: Betty Hutton, Victor Moore, Eddie Bracken, Walter Abel, Anne Revere, Gil Lamb, and guest stars Bing Crosby, Bob Hope, Fred MacMurray, Dorothy Lamour, Mary Martin, Vera Zorina, Dick Powell, others.

State Fair. Fox, 1945 (c). Walter Lang. Sp: Sonya Levien, Paul Green, and Oscar Hammerstein II, b/o novel by Philip Stong. MS: Richard Rodgers and Oscar Hammerstein II. Cast: Jeanne Crain, Dana Andrews, Dick Haymes, Vivian Blaine, Charles Winninger, Fay Bainter. Previously filmed in 1933 (nm) and remade in 1962.

Stormy Weather. Fox, 1943. Andrew Stone. Sp: Frederick Jackson and Ted Koehler, b/o story by Jerry Horwin and Seymour R. Robinson. MS: various writers. Cast: Bill Robinson, Lena Horne, Cab Calloway and his band, Fats Waller, Katherine Dunham and her troupe, Ada Brown.

The Story of Vernon and Irene Castle. RKO, 1939. H. C. Potter. Sp: Richard Sherman, Oscar Hammerstein II, and Dorothy Yost, b/o story by Irene Castle. MS: various writers. Cast: Fred Astaire, Ginger Rogers, Edna May Oliver, Walter Brennan, Lew Fields.

Strike Up the Band. MGM, 1940. Busby Berkeley. Sp: John Monks, Jr., and Fred Finklehoffe. MS: George and Ira Gershwin, Arthur Freed, and Roger Edens. Cast: Mickey Rooney, Judy Garland, Paul Whiteman, June

Preisser, William Tracy, Larry Nunn.

The Student Prince. MGM, 1954 (c). Richard Thorpe. Sp: William Ludwig and Sonya Levien, b/o the 1924 operetta. MS: Sigmund Romberg, Nicholas Brodszky, and Paul Francis Webster. Cast: Edmund Purdom (with the singing voice of Mario Lanza), Ann Blyth, John Ericson, Louis Calhern, Edmund Gwenn, S. Z. Sakall, Betta St. John.

Summer Holiday. MGM, 1948 (c). Rouben Mamoulian. Sp: Frances Goodrich and Albert Hackett, b/o Eugene O'Neill's play *Ah, Wilderness*, filmed in 1935. MS: Harry Warren and Ralph Blane. Cast: Mickey Rooney, Walter Huston, Gloria De Haven, Agnes Moorehead, Frank Morgan, Marilyn Maxwell, Jackie ("Butch") Jenkins.

Summer Stock. MGM, 1950 (c). Charles Walters. Sp: George Wells and Sy Gomberg. MS: Harry Warren and Mack Gordon. Cast: Gene Kelly, Judy Garland, Gloria De Haven, Eddie Bracken, Phil Silvers, Hans Conried.

Sunny Side Up. Fox, 1929. David Butler. Sp: B. G. DeSylva, Lew Brown, and Ray Henderson. MS: B.G. De Sylva, Lew Brown, and Ray Henderson. Cast: Janet Gaynor, Charles Farrell, El Brendel, Frank Albertson, Sharon Lynn, Mary Forbes, Marjorie White, Alan Paull.

Sun Valley Serenade. Fox, 1941. Bruce Humberstone. Sp: Robert Ellis and Helen Logan, b/o story by Art Arthur and Robert Harari. MS: Harry Warren and Mack Gordon. Cast: Sonja Henie, John Payne, Glenn Miller, Milton Berle, Lynn Bari, Joan Davis, the Nicholas Brothers.

Sweet Adeline. Warners, 1935. Mervyn LeRoy. Sp: Erwin S. Gelsey, b/o the 1929 musical play. MS: Jerome Kern and Oscar Hammerstein II. Cast: Irene Dunne, Donald Woods, Hugh Herbert, Ned Sparks, Joseph Cawthorn, Wini Shaw, Louis Calhern.

Sweet Charity. Universal, 1969 (c). Bob Fosse. Sp: Peter Stone, b/o the 1966 musical play, which was adapted from Federico Fellini's 1957 film *Nights of Cabiria*. MS: Cy Coleman and Dorothy Fields. Cast: Shirley MacLaine, John McMartin, Ricardo Montalban, Sammy Davis, Jr., Chita Rivera, Paula Kelly, Stubby Kaye.

Sweethearts. MGM, 1938 (c). W. S. Van Dyke II. Sp: Dorothy Parker and Alan Campbell. MS: Victor Herbert, Bob Wright, and Chet Forrest. Cast: Jeanette MacDonald, Nelson Eddy, Frank Morgan, Ray Bolger, Florence Rice, Mischa Auer, Herman Bing, Reginald Gardiner.

Sweetie. Paramount, 1929. Frank Tuttle. Sp: George Marion, Jr., and Lloyd Corrigan. MS: Richard Whiting and George Marion, Jr. Cast: Nancy Carroll, Helen Kane, Stanley Smith, Jack Oakie, Stuart Erwin, Wallace MacDonald.

Sweet Rosie O'Grady. Fox, 1943 (c). Irving Cummings. Sp: Ken Englund, b/o stories by William R. Lipman, Frederick Stephani, and Edward Van Every. MS: Harry Warren and Mack Gordon. Cast: Betty Grable, Robert Young, Adolphe Menjou, Reginald Gardiner, Virginia Grey, Phil Regan. Previously filmed in 1937 as *Love Is News* (nm) and remade in 1948 as *That Wonderful Urge* (nm).

Swing Time. RKO, 1936. George Stevens. Sp: Howard Lindsay and Allan Scott, b/o story by Erwin Gelsey. MS: Jerome Kern and Dorothy Fields. Cast: Fred Astaire, Ginger Rogers, Victor Moore, Helen Broderick, Eric Blore, Betty Furness.

Take Me Out to the Ball Game. MGM, 1949 (c). Busby Berkeley. Sp: Harry Tugend and George Wells, b/o story by Gene Kelly and Stanley Donen. MS: Roger Edens, Betty Comden, and Adolph Green. Cast: Gene Kelly, Esther Williams, Frank Sinatra, Betty Garrett, Jules Munshin, Edward Arnold.

Tea for Two. Warners, 1950 (c). David Butler. Sp: Harry Clork, suggested by the 1925 musical play *No, No, Nanette*. MS: Vincent Youmans and various writers. Cast: Doris Day, Gordon MacRae, Gene Nelson, Eve Arden, Billy De Wolfe, S. Z. Sakall. Previously filmed in 1930 and 1940 as *No, No, Nanette*.

Thanks a Million. Fox, 1935. Roy Del Ruth. Sp: Nunnally Johnson, b/o story by Melville Crossman. MS: Arthur Johnston and Gus Kahn. Cast: Dick Powell, Ann Dvorak, Fred Allen, Patsy Kelly, Raymond Walburn, Benny Baker. Remade in 1946 as *If I'm Lucky*.

Thank Your Lucky Stars. Warners, 1943. David Butler. Sp: Norman Panama, Melvin Frank, and James V. Kern, b/o story by Everett Freeman and Arthur Schwartz. MS: Frank Loesser and Arthur Schwartz. Cast: Eddie Cantor, Dennis Morgan, Joan Leslie, Edward Everett Horton, and guest stars Bette Davis, Errol Flynn, John Garfield, Ann Sheridan, Humphrey Bogart, others.

That Night in Rio. Fox, 1941 (c). Irving Cummings. Sp: George Seaton, Bess Meredyth, and Hal Long, b/o play by Rudolph Lothar and Hans Adler. MS: Harry Warren and Mack Gordon. Cast: Alice Faye, Don Ameche, Carmen Miranda, S. Z. Sakall, J. Carrol Naish, Curt Bois, Leonid Kinskey. Previously filmed in 1935 as *Folies Bergère* and remade in 1951 as *On the Riviera*.

There's No Business like Show Business. Fox, 1954 (c). Walter Lang. Sp: Henry and Phoebe Ephron, b/o story by Lamar Trotti. MS: Irving Berlin. Cast: Ethel Merman, Dan Dailey, Mitzi Gaynor, Marilyn Monroe, Donald O'Connor, Johnnie Ray.

This Is the Army. Warners, 1943 (c). Michael Curtiz. Sp: Casey Robinson and Claude Binyon, b/o the 1942 musical play. MS: Irving Berlin. Cast: George Murphy, Ronald Reagan, Joan Leslie, George Tobias, Kate Smith, Frances Langford, Joe Louis, Gertrude Niesen, Charles Butterworth, Irving Berlin.

Thoroughly Modern Millie. Universal, 1967 (c). George Roy Hill. Sp: Richard Morris. MS: Jimmy Van Heusen and Sammy Cahn. Cast: Julie Andrews, Mary Tyler Moore, Carol Channing, James Fox, Beatrice Lillie, John Gavin, Jack Soo, Pat Morita.

Thousands Cheer. MGM, 1943 (c). George Sidney. Sp: Paul Jarrico and Richard Collins. MS: various writers. Cast: Kathryn Grayson, Gene Kelly, Mary Astor, John Boles, and with guest stars Judy Garland, Red Skelton, Eleanor Powell, Ann Sothern, Lucille Ball, Lena Horne, June Allyson, Jose Iturbi, and others.

Three Little Girls in Blue. Fox, 1946 (c). Bruce Humberstone. Sp: Valentine Davies, Brown Holmes, Lynn Starling, Robert Ellis, and Helen Logan, b/o play by Stephen Powys. MS: Josef Myrow and Mack Gordon. Cast: June Haver, Vivian Blaine, Vera-Ellen, George Montgomery, Celeste Holm. Previously filmed in 1938 as *Three Blind Mice* (nm) and in 1941 as *Moon over Miami*.

Three Little Words. MGM, 1950 (c). Richard Thorpe. Sp: George Wells. MS: Harry Ruby and Bert Kalmar. Cast: Fred Astaire, Vera-Ellen, Red Skelton, Arlene Dahl, Debbie Reynolds, Gloria De Haven.

Till the Clouds Roll By. MGM, 1946 (c). Richard Whorf. Sp: Myles Connolly and Jean Holloway, b/o story by Guy Bolton. MS: Jerome Kern and various lyricists. Cast: Robert Walker, Judy Garland, Lucille Bremer, Van Heflin, Dorothy Patrick, June Allyson, Lena Horne, Kathryn Grayson, Frank Sinatra, Van Johnson.

The Toast of New Orleans. MGM, 1950 (c). Norman Taurog. Sp: Sy Gomberg and George Wells. MS: Nicholas Brodszky and Sammy Cahn. Cast: Mario Lanza, Kathryn Grayson, David Niven, J. Carrol Naish, James Mitchell.

Tom Sawyer. A Readers Digest Production, released by United Artists, 1973 (c). Don Taylor. Sp: Robert B. and Richard M. Sherman, b/o the novel by Mark Twain, previously filmed in 1930 (nm) and 1938 (nm). MS: Robert B. and Richard M. Sherman. Cast: Johnny Whitaker, Celeste Holm, Warren Oates, Jodie Foster, Jeff East, Lucille Brown.

Tonight and Every Night. Columbia, 1945 (c). Victor Saville. Sp: Lesser Samuels and Abem Finkel, b/o play by Lesley Storm. MS: Jule Styne and Sammy Cahn. Cast: Rita Hayworth, Janet Blair, Lee Bowman, Marc Platt, Leslie Brooks, Florence Bates.

Too Many Girls. RKO Radio, 1940. George Abbott. Sp: John Twist, b/o the 1939 musical play. MS: Richard Rodgers and Lorenz Hart. Cast: Lucille Ball, Richard Carlson, Ann Miller, Eddie Bracken, Frances Langford, Desi Arnaz, Hal LeRoy.

Top Hat. RKO, 1935. Mark Sandrich. Sp: Dwight Taylor and Allan Scott. MS: Irving Berlin. Cast: Fred Astaire, Ginger Rogers, Edward Everett Horton, Helen Broderick, Eric Blore, Erik Rhodes.

Two Girls and a Sailor. MGM, 1944. Richard Thorpe. Sp: Richard Connell and Gladys Lehman. MS: various writers. Cast: June Allyson, Van Johnson, Gloria De Haven, Jimmy Durante, Tom Drake, and guest stars Jose Iturbi, Gracie Allen, Virginia O'Brien, Lena Horne, Xavier Cugat and Harry James and their orchestras.

The Unsinkable Molly Brown. MGM, 1964 (c). Charles Walters. Sp: Helen Deutsch, b/o the 1960 musical play. MS: Meredith Willson. Cast: Debbie Reynolds, Harve Presnell, Ed Begley, Audrey Christie, Jack Kruschen, Hermione Baddeley, Martita Hunt.

Up in Arms. A Samuel Goldwyn Production, released by RKO Radio, 1944 (c). Elliott Nugent. Sp: Don Hartman, Allen Boretz, and Robert Pirosh, b/o play by Owen Davis.

MS: Harold Arlen and Ted Koehler. Cast: Danny Kaye, Dinah Shore, Dana Andrews, Constance Dowling, Louis Calhern, George Mathews. Previously filmed in 1926 as *The Nervous Wreck* (s) and in 1930 as *Whoopee*.

Week-End in Havana. Fox, 1941 (c). Walter Lang. Sp: Karl Tunberg and Darrell Ware. MS: Harry Warren, James Monaco, and Mack Gordon. Cast: Alice Faye, John Payne, Carmen Miranda, Cesar Romero, Cobina Wright, Jr., George Barbier.

We're Not Dressing. Paramount, 1934. Norman Taurog. Sp: Horace Jackson, Francis Martin, and George Marion, Jr., b/o story by Benjamin Glazer. MS: Harry Revel and Mack Gordon. Cast: Bing Crosby, Carole Lombard, George Burns, Gracie Allen, Ethel Merman, Leon Errol, Ray Milland.

West Side Story. United Artists, 1961 (c). Robert Wise and Jerome Robbins. Sp: Ernest Lehman, b/o the 1957 musical play. MS: Leonard Bernstein and Stephen Sondheim. Cast: Natalie Wood, Richard Beymer, Rita Moreno, George Chakiris, Russ Tamblyn, Tucker Smith, Tony Mordente, Ned Glass, Simon Oakland.

When My Baby Smiles at Me. Fox, 1948 (c). Walter Lang. Sp: Lamar Trotti, b/o play *Burlesque* by George Manker Watters and Arthur Hopkins. MS: Joseph Myrow and Mack Gordon. Cast: Betty Grable, Dan Dailey, Jack Oakie, June Havoc, Jean Wallace, Richard Arlen. Previously filmed in 1929 as *The Dance of Life* and in 1937 as *Swing High, Swing Low*.

Where's Charley? Warners, 1952 (c). David Butler. Sp: John Monks, Jr., b/o the 1948 musical play, which was adapted from Brandon Thomas's play *Charley's Aunt*, filmed in 1925 (s), 1930 (nm), and 1941 (nm). MS: Frank Loesser. Cast: Ray Bolger, Allyn McLerie, Robert Shackleton, Mary Germaine, Horace Cooper.

White Christmas. Paramount, 1954 (c). Michael Curtiz. Sp: Norman Panama, Melvin Frank, and Norman Krasna. MS: Irving Berlin. Cast: Bing Crosby, Danny Kaye, Rosemary Clooney, Vera-Ellen, Dean Jagger, Mary Wickes.

Whoopee. A Samuel Goldwyn Production, released by United Artists, 1930 (c). Thornton Freeland. Sp: William

Conselman, b/o the 1928 musical play and play by Owen Davis. MS: Walter Donaldson and Gus Kahn. Cast: Eddie Cantor, Eleanor Hunt, Paul Gregory, Ethel Shutta, Betty Grable. Previously filmed in 1926 (s) and remade in 1944 as *Up in Arms*.

Willy Wonka and the Chocolate Factory. Paramount, 1971 (c). Mel Stuart. Sp: Roald Dahl, b/o his story. MS: Leslie Bricusse and Anthony Newley. Cast: Gene Wilder, Jack Albertson, Peter Ostrum, Denise Nickerson, Roy Kinnear.

With a Song in My Heart. Fox, 1952 (c). Walter Lang. Sp: Lamar Trotti. MS: various writers. Cast: Susan Hayward, Rory Calhoun, David Wayne, Thelma Ritter, Robert Wagner, Helen Westcott, Una Merkel.

The Wiz. Universal, 1978 (c). Sidney Lumet. Sp: Joel Schumacher, b/o the 1976 musical play. MS: Charlie Smalls. Cast: Diana Ross, Ted Ross, Michael Jackson, Nipsey Russell, Mabel King, Richard Pryor, Theresa Merritt, Thelma Carpenter, Lena Horne.

The Wizard of Oz. MGM, 1939 (c). Victor Fleming. Sp: Florence Ryerson, Noel Langley, and Edgar Allan Woolf, b/o stories by L. Frank Baum. MS: Harold Arlen and E. Y. Harburg. Cast: Judy Garland, Bert Lahr, Ray Bolger, Jack Haley, Frank Morgan, Margaret Hamilton, Billie Burke. Previously filmed in 1910 (s) and 1925 (s).

Wonder Bar. Warners, 1934. Lloyd Bacon. Sp: Earl Baldwin, b/o play by Geza Herczeg, Karl Farkas, and Robert Katscher. MS: Harry Warren and Al Dubin. Cast: Al Jolson, Kay Francis, Dolores Del Rio, Dick Powell, Hal LeRoy, Guy Kibbee, Ruth Donnelly, Hugh Herbert, Louise Fazenda.

Words and Music. MGM, 1948 (c). Norman Taurog. Sp: Fred Finklehoffe, b/o story by Guy Bolton. MS: Richard Rodgers and Lorenz Hart. Cast: Mickey Rooney, Tom Drake, Janet Leigh, Betty Garrett, Perry Como, Ann Sothern, Judy Garland, June Allyson, Gene Kelly, Vera-Ellen, Cyd Charisse, Lena Horne.

Yankee Doodle Dandy. Warners, 1942. Michael Curtiz. Sp: Robert Buckner and Edmund Joseph. MS: George M. Cohan. Cast: James Cagney, Walter Huston,

Joan Leslie, Rosemary DeCamp, Jeanne Cagney, Irene Manning.

Yolanda and the Thief. MGM, 1945 (c). Vincente Minnelli. Sp: Irving Brecher, b/o story by Jacques Thery and Ludwig Bemelmans. MS: Harry Warren and Arthur Freed. Cast: Fred Astaire, Lucille Bremer, Frank Morgan, Mildred Natwick, Leon Ames, Mary Nash.

You Can't Have Everything. Fox, 1937. Norman Taurog. Sp: Harry Tugend, Jack Yellen, and Karl Tunberg, b/o story by Gregory Ratoff. MS: Harry Revel and Mack Gordon. Cast: Alice Faye, Don Ameche, the Ritz Brothers, Charles Winninger, Louise Hovick (Gypsy Rose Lee), Rubinoff, Tony Martin.

You'll Never Get Rich. Columbia, 1941. Sidney Lanfield. Sp: Michael Fessier and Ernest Pagano. MS: Cole Porter. Cast: Fred Astaire, Rita Hayworth, John Hubbard, Robert Benchley, Osa Massen, Frieda Inescort.

Young at Heart. Warners, 1954 (c). Gordon Douglas. Sp: Julius J. Epstein and Lenore Coffee, b/o story by Fannie Hurst. MS: various writers. Cast: Doris Day, Frank Sinatra, Ethel Barrymore, Gig Young, Robert Keith, Elisabeth Fraser, Dorothy Malone, Alan Hale. A musical remake of *Four Daughters* (1938).

You Were Never Lovelier. Columbia, 1942. William A. Seiter. Sp: Michael Fessier, Ernest Pagano, and Delmer Daves, b/o story by Carlos Olivari and Sixto Pondal Rios. MS: Jerome Kern and Johnny Mercer. Cast: Fred Astaire, Rita Hayworth, Adolphe Menjou, Xavier Cugat, Leslie Brooks, Adele Mara, Isobel Elsom, Larry Parks.

Ziegfeld Follies. MGM, 1946 (c). George Sidney, Robert Lewis, Lemuel Ayres, and Vincente Minnelli. Sp and MS: various writers. Cast: Judy Garland, Gene Kelly, Fred Astaire, Lena Horne, Esther Williams, William Powell, Lucille Ball, and many other MGM stars.

Ziegfeld Girl. MGM, 1941. Robert Z. Leonard. Sp: Marguerite Roberts and Sonya Levien, b/o story by William Anthony McGuire. MS: various writers. Cast: Lana Turner, James Stewart, Hedy Lamarr, Judy Garland, Tony Martin, Ian Hunter, Jackie Cooper, Philip Dorn, Edward Everett Horton, Eve Arden, Dan Dailey.

FILM PROPERTIES OF:

CBS Theatrical Films

My Fair Lady, *1964*

Columbia Pictures

The Buddy Holly Story, *1978*
Bye Bye Birdie, *1963*
Cover Girl, *1944*
Down to Earth, *1947*
The Eddy Duchin Story, *1956*
Funny Girl, *1968*
Funny Lady, *1975*
The Jolson Story, *1946*
The King Steps Out, *1936*
Lost Horizon, *1973*
Love Me Forever, *1935*
My Sister Eileen, *1955*
Oliver!, *1968*
One Night of Love, *1934*
Pal Joey, *1957*
Pennies from Heaven, *1936*
Tonight and Every Night, *1945*
You'll Never Get Rich, *1941*
You Were Never Lovelier, *1942*

EMI Films, Inc.

Can't Stop the Music, *1980*
The Jazz Singer, *1980*

Hope Enterprises, Inc.

The Seven Little Foys, *1955*

Lorimar and ABC

Cabaret, *1972*

Metro-Goldwyn-Mayer Film Co.

An American in Paris, *1951*
Anchors Aweigh, *1945*
Annie Get Your Gun, *1950*

Betty Grable as the sassy heroine of Coney Island *(Fox, 1943).*

Babes in Arms, *1939*
Babes on Broadway, *1941*
The Band Wagon, *1953*
The Barkleys of Broadway, *1949*
Bathing Beauty, *1944*
The Belle of New York, *1952*
Bells Are Ringing, *1960*
Best Foot Forward, *1943*
Billy Rose's Jumbo, *1962*
Bitter Sweet, *1940*
Born to Dance, *1936*
Brigadoon, *1954*
The Broadway Melody, *1929*
Broadway Melody of 1936, *1935*
Broadway Melody of 1938, *1937*

Broadway Melody of 1940, *1940*
Cabin in the Sky, *1943*
Dancing Lady, *1933*
A Date with Judy, *1948*
Deep in My Heart, *1954*
Du Barry Was a Lady, *1943*
Easter Parade, *1948*
The Firefly, *1937*
For Me and My Gal, *1942*
Gigi, *1958*
Girl Crazy, *1943*
The Girl of the Golden West, *1938*
The Glass Slipper, *1955*
Goodbye, Mr. Chips, *1969*
Good News, *1930*

Good News, *1947*
The Great Caruso, *1951*
The Great Waltz, *1938*
The Great Ziegfeld, *1936*
Hallelujah!, *1929*
The Harvey Girls, *1946*
High Society, *1956*
The Hollywood Revue of 1929
I'll Cry Tomorrow, *1955*
I Married an Angel, *1942*
Interrupted Melody, *1955*
In the Good Old Summertime, *1949*
Invitation to the Dance, *1956*
It's Always Fair Weather, *1955*
Jailhouse Rock, *1957*
Kismet, *1955*
Kiss Me, Kate, *1953*
Lady Be Good, *1941*
Les Girls, *1957*
Lili, *1953*
Love Me or Leave Me, *1955*
Maytime, *1937*
Meet Me in St. Louis, *1944*
The Merry Widow, *1934*
The Merry Widow, *1952*
Naughty Marietta, *1935*
Neptune's Daughter, *1949*
New Moon, *1940*
On the Town, *1949*
The Opposite Sex, *1956*
Pennies from Heaven, *1981*
The Pirate, *1948*
Roberta, *1935*
Rosalie, *1937*
Rose Marie, *1936*
Rose Marie, *1954*
Royal Wedding, *1951*
Seven Brides for Seven Brothers, *1954*

Show Boat, *1951*
Silk Stockings, *1957*
Singin' in the Rain, *1952*
Small Town Girl, *1953*
Strike Up the Band, *1940*
The Student Prince, *1954*
Summer Holiday, *1948*
Summer Stock, *1950*
Sweethearts, *1938*
Take Me Out to the Ball Game, *1949*
Texas Carnival, *1951*
That Midnight Kiss, *1949*
Thousands Cheer, *1943*
Three Little Words, *1950*
Till the Clouds Roll By, *1946*
Two Weeks with Love, *1950*
The Unsinkable Molly Brown, *1964*
The Wizard of Oz, *1939*
Words and Music, *1948*
Yolanda and the Thief, *1945*
Ziegfeld Follies, *1946*
Ziegfeld Girl, *1941*

Paramount Pictures Corporation

Bugsy Malone, *1976*
Funny Face, *1957*
Grease, *1978*
Honey, *1930*
On a Clear Day You Can See Forever, *1970*
Red Garters, *1954*
Sing You Sinners, *1938*
White Christmas, *1954*

RKO General Pictures

Carefree, *1938*
A Damsel in Distress, *1937*
Flying Down to Rio, *1933*
Follow the Fleet, *1936*
The Gay Divorcee, *1934*
Hitting a New High, *1937*
Shall We Dance, *1937*
The Story of Vernon and Irene Castle, *1939*
Swing Time, *1936*
Top Hat, *1935*

Rodgers and Hammerstein

Oklahoma!, *1955*

Sascha-Film Gesellschaft M.B.H. and New World Pictures Inc.

A Little Night Music, *1977*

Twentieth Century-Fox Film Corporation

Alexander's Ragtime Band, *1938*
All That Jazz, *1979*
At Long Last Love, *1975*
Billy Rose's Diamond Horseshoe, *1945*
Can-Can, *1960*
Captain January, *1936*

Cover and an inside page from a book of paper dolls for Holiday Inn *(Paramount, 1942).*

Carousel, *1956*
Coney Island, *1943*
Daddy Long Legs, *1955*
Delicious, *1931*
Doctor Dolittle, *1967*
The Dolly Sisters, *1945*
Down Argentine Way, *1940*
Folies Bergère, *1935*
The Gang's All Here, *1943*
Gentlemen Prefer Blondes, *1953*
George White's Scandals, *1934*
George White's 1935 Scandals, *1935*
Happy Days, *1930*
Hello, Dolly!, *1969*
Hello, Frisco, Hello, *1943*
Just Imagine, *1930*
The King and I, *1956*
Lillian Russell, *1940*
The Littlest Rebel, *1935*
Mother Wore Tights, *1947*
My Gal Sal, *1942*
One in a Million, *1936*
On the Avenue, *1937*
On the Riviera, *1951*
Pin Up Girl, *1944*
Rebecca of Sunnybrook Farm, *1938*
The Rose, *1979*
Rose of Washington Square, *1939*
The Shocking Miss Pilgrim, *1947*
The Sound of Music, *1965*
South Pacific, *1958*
Springtime in the Rockies, *1942*
Stand Up and Cheer, *1934*
Star!, *1968*
State Fair, *1945*
Sunny Side Up, *1929*
Sweet Rosie O'Grady, *1943*
That Night in Rio, *1941*
There's No Business like Show Business, *1954*

Three Little Girls in Blue, *1946*
Tin Pan Alley, *1940*
Wabash Avenue, *1950*
Week-End in Havana, *1941*
When My Baby Smiles at Me, *1948*
Where Do We Go from Here?, *1945*
With a Song in My Heart, *1952*
You Can't Have Everything, *1937*

United Artists Corporation

Broadway Gondolier, *1935*
Dames, *1934*
The Desert Song, *1929*
Fashions of 1934
Fiddler on the Roof, *1971*
Flirtation Walk, *1934*
Footlight Parade, *1933*
42nd Street, *1933*
Go into Your Dance, *1935*
The Gold Diggers of Broadway, *1929*
Gold Diggers of 1933
Gold Diggers of 1935
Gold Diggers of 1937
Hair, *1979*
Hearts Divided, *1936*
How to Succeed in Business Without Really Trying, *1967*
The Jazz Singer, *1927*
Mammy, *1930*
New York, New York, *1977*
Night and Day, *1946*
On with the Show, *1929*
Ready, Willing and Able, *1937*
Rhapsody in Blue, *1945*
Sally, *1929*
Shine on Harvest Moon, *1944*
Show of Shows, *1929*
The Singing Fool, *1928*
Thank Your Lucky Stars, *1943*

Tom Sawyer, *1973*
West Side Story, *1961*
Wonder Bar, *1934*
Yankee Doodle Dandy, *1942*

Universal Pictures

Anything Goes, *1936*
Applause, *1929*
Artists and Models, *1937*
The Big Broadcast of 1938
College Swing, *1938*
Collegiate, *1935*
The Fleet's In, *1942*
Flower Drum Song, *1961*
The Glenn Miller Story, *1954*
High, Wide and Handsome, *1937*
Holiday Inn, *1942*
Jesus Christ, Superstar, *1973*
King of Jazz, *1930*
Lady in the Dark, *1944*
Love Me Tonight, *1932*
The Love Parade, *1929*
Mississippi, *1935*
Monte Carlo, *1930*
One Hour with You, *1932*
One Hundred Men and a Girl, *1937*
Paramount on Parade, *1930*
Rhythm on the Range, *1936*
She Loves Me Not, *1934*
Show Boat, *1936*
The Smiling Lieutenant, *1931*
Star-Spangled Rhythm, *1942*
Sweet Charity, *1969*
Sweetie, *1929*
Thoroughly Modern Millie, *1967*
The Vagabond King, *1930*
We're Not Dressing, *1934*

Walt Disney Productions

Bedknobs and Broomsticks, *1971*
Mary Poppins, *1964*

Warner Bros. Inc.

By the Light of the Silvery Moon, *1953*
Calamity Jane, *1953*
Camelot, *1967*
Damn Yankees, *1958*
The Eddie Cantor Story, *1953*
Finian's Rainbow, *1968*
Gypsy, *1962*
The Jazz Singer, *1953*
Mame, *1974*
The Music Man, *1962*
On Moonlight Bay, *1951*
The Pajama Game, *1957*
Rio Rita, *1929*
A Star Is Born, *1954*
A Star Is Born, *1976*
This Is the Army, *1943*
Where's Charley?, *1952*
Young at Heart, *1954*

FILM COPYRIGHTS

1	From the MGM release: *The Hollywood Revue of 1929*	© 1929 Metro-Goldwyn-Mayer Distributing Corporation. Renewed 1957 Loew's Inc.	17	From the MGM release: *Easter Parade*, 1948	© 1948 Loew's Inc. Renewed 1975 Metro-Goldwyn-Mayer Inc.		Pictures, Inc. Renewed 1957 Warner Bros. Pictures, Inc. All rights reserved. Released through United Artists Television.
2–3	*Gold Diggers of 1935*	Copyright © 1935 First National Pictures, Inc. Renewed 1962 United Artists Associated, Inc. All rights reserved.	18–19	*The King and I*, 1956	© 1956 Twentieth Century-Fox Film Corporation		
			20–21	*Carousel*, 1956	© 1956 Twentieth Century-Fox Film Corporation	33	*Mammy*, 1930	Copyright © 1930 Warner Bros. Pictures, Inc. Renewed 1957 Associated Artists Productions Corp. All rights reserved. Released through United Artists Television.
4–5	*Top Hat*, 1935	Courtesy RKO General Pictures	22–23	*Mary Poppins*, 1964	© 1964 Walt Disney Productions		
7	*Rebecca of Sunnybrook Farm*, 1938	© 1938 Twentieth Century-Fox Film Corporation	24–25	*Hello, Dolly!*, 1969	© Chenault Productions, Inc. and Twentieth Century-Fox Film Corporation	35	*Sally*, 1929	Copyright © 1929 First National Pictures, Inc. Renewed 1957 Warner Bros. Pictures, Inc. All rights reserved. Released through United Artists Corp.
8–9	From the MGM release: *Naughty Marietta*, 1935	© 1935, 1962 Metro-Goldwyn-Mayer Inc.	26–27	*Cabaret*, 1972	Courtesy Lorimar and ABC		
10–11	From the MGM release: *The Wizard of Oz*, 1939	© 1939 Loew's Inc. Renewed 1973 Metro-Goldwyn-Mayer Inc.	28	From the MGM release: *The Hollywood Revue of 1929*	©1929 Metro-Goldwyn-Mayer Distributing Corporation. Renewed 1957 Loew's Inc.	36	From the MGM release: *The Hollywood Revue of 1929*	© 1929 Metro-Goldwyn-Mayer Distributing Corporation. Renewed 1957 Loew's Inc.
12–13	From the MGM release: *The Harvey Girls*, 1946	© 1945 Loew's Inc. Renewed 1973 Metro-Goldwyn-Mayer Inc.	30, 31	*The Jazz Singer*, 1927	Copyright © 1927 Warner Bros. Pictures, Inc. Renewed 1955 Warner Bros. Pictures, Inc. All rights reserved. Released through United Artists Corp.	37 (above)	*Happy Days*, 1930	© 1929 Twentieth Century-Fox Film Corporation
14	*Holiday Inn*, 1942	Courtesy Universal Pictures				37 (below), 38	*Show of Shows*, 1929	Copyright © 1929 Warner Bros. Pictures, Inc. Renewed 1956 Associated Artists Productions Corp. All rights reserved. Released through United Artists Television.
15	From the MGM release: *Singin' in the Rain*, 1952	© 1952 Loew's Inc. Renewed 1979 Metro-Goldwyn-Mayer Inc.	32	*The Singing Fool*, 1928	Copyright © 1928 Warner Bros.		

39 (above)	*Paramount on Parade*, 1930	Courtesy Universal Pictures
39 (below)	*King of Jazz*, 1930	Courtesy Universal Pictures
40, 40–41	*Paramount on Parade*, 1930	Courtesy Universal Pictures
42, 43	From the MGM release: *The Broadway Melody*, 1929	© 1929 Metro-Goldwyn-Mayer Distributing Corporation. Renewed 1956 Loew's Inc.
44	*The Gold Diggers of Broadway*, 1929	Copyright © 1929 Warner Bros. Pictures, Inc. Renewed 1957 Warner Bros. Pictures, Inc. All rights reserved. Released through United Artists Television.
45 (above)	*Show Boat*, 1929	Courtesy Universal Pictures
45 (below)	*The Desert Song*, 1929	Copyright © 1943 Warner Bros. Pictures, Inc. Renewed 1971 United Artists Television. All rights reserved.
46, 46–47	*On with the Show*, 1929	Copyright © 1929 Warner Bros. Pictures, Inc. Renewed 1956 P. R. M., Inc. All rights reserved. Released through United Artists Television.
48	*The Vagabond King*, 1930	Courtesy Universal Pictures
49	*Rio Rita*, 1929	© Warner Bros. Inc.
50 (above)	*Just Imagine*, 1930	© 1930 Twentieth Century-Fox Film Corporation
50 (below)	From the MGM release: *Good News*, 1930	© 1930 Metro-Goldwyn-Mayer Distributing Corporation. Renewed 1957 Loew's Inc.
51 (above)	*Delicious*, 1931	© 1931 Twentieth Century-Fox Film Corporation
51 (center)	*Sweetie*, 1929	Courtesy Universal Pictures
51 (below)	*Honey*, 1930	Courtesy Paramount Pictures Corp.
52	*Sunny Side Up*, 1929	© 1929 Twentieth Century-Fox Film Corporation
53 (above)	*The Desert Song* (poster), 1929	Produced by Warner Bros. Inc.
53 (center)	*Sunny Side Up* (poster), 1929	© 1929 Twentieth Century-Fox Film Corporation
53 (below), 54	*The Love Parade*, 1929	Courtesy Universal Pictures
55	*One Hour with You*, 1932	Courtesy Universal Pictures
56	*Monte Carlo*, 1930	Courtesy Universal Pictures
57	*The Smiling Lieutenant*, 1931	Courtesy Universal Pictures
58	From the MGM release: *Hallelujah!*, 1929	© 1929 Metro-Goldwyn-Mayer Distributing Corporation. Renewed 1957 Loew's Inc.
60, 61	*Applause*, 1929	Courtesy Universal Pictures
62	*Love Me Tonight*, 1932	Courtesy Universal Pictures
64	*Footlight Parade*, 1933	Copyright © 1933 Warner Bros. Pictures, Inc. Renewed 1961 United Artists Associated, Inc. All rights reserved.
66, 69	*42nd Street*, 1933	Copyright © 1933 Warner Bros. Pictures, Inc. Renewed 1960 Warner Bros. Pictures, Inc. All rights reserved. Released through United Artists Corp.
70, 71, 72 (above)	*Gold Diggers of 1933*	Copyright © 1933 Warner Bros. Pictures, Inc. Renewed 1960 United Artists Associated, Inc. All rights reserved.
72 (below), 73	*Footlight Parade*, 1933	Copyright © 1933 Warner Bros. Pictures, Inc. Renewed 1961 United Artists Associated, Inc. All rights reserved.
74	*Fashions of 1934*	Copyright © 1934 First National Pictures, Inc. Renewed 1961 United Artists Associated, Inc. All rights reserved.
75, 76, 77	*Dames*, 1934	Copyright © 1934 Warner Bros. Pictures, Inc. Renewed 1961 United Artists Associated, Inc. All rights reserved.
78–79	*Wonder Bar*, 1934	Copyright © 1934 First National Pictures, Inc. Renewed 1961 United Artists Associated, Inc. All rights reserved.
80, 80–81 (above)	*Gold Diggers of 1935*	Copyright © 1935 First National Pictures, Inc. Renewed 1962 United Artists Associated, Inc. All rights reserved.
80–81 (below)	*Gold Diggers of 1937*	Copyright © 1936 Warner Bros. Pictures, Inc. and The Vitaphone Corp. Renewed 1964 United Artists Associated, Inc. All rights reserved.
81	*Flirtation Walk*, 1934	Copyright © 1934 First National Pictures, Inc. Renewed 1961 United Artists Associated, Inc. All rights reserved.
82 (above)	*Broadway Gondolier*, 1935	Copyright © 1935 Warner Bros. Pictures, Inc. Renewed 1962 United Artists Associated, Inc. All rights reserved.
82 (center)	*Hearts Divided*, 1936	Copyright © 1936 Warner Bros. Pictures, Inc. Renewed 1963 United Artists Associated, Inc. All rights reserved.
82 (below)	*Go into Your Dance*, 1935	Copyright © 1935 First National Pictures, Inc. Renewed 1962 United Artists Associated, Inc. All rights reserved.
83	*Ready, Willing and Able*, 1937	Copyright © 1937 Warner Bros. Pictures, Inc. Renewed 1964 United Artists Associated, Inc. All rights reserved.
84, 86, 87	*Flying Down to Rio*, 1933	Courtesy RKO General Pictures
88, 89	*Gay Divorcee*, 1934	Courtesy RKO General Pictures
90, 91	*Roberta*, 1935	© 1935 RKO Radio Pictures, Inc. Renewed 1962 Metro-Goldwyn-Mayer Inc. Successor-in-interest to RKO Radio Pictures, Inc.
92–93, 94, 95 (above)	*Top Hat*, 1935	Courtesy RKO General Pictures
95 (below), 96, 97	*Follow the Fleet*, 1936	Courtesy RKO General Pictures
98, 99	*Swing Time*, 1936	Courtesy RKO General Pictures
100–101	*Shall We Dance*, 1937	Courtesy RKO General Pictures
102	*A Damsel in Distress*, 1937	Courtesy RKO General Pictures
104	*Carefree*, 1938	Courtesy RKO General Pictures
105	*The Story of Vernon and Irene Castle*, 1939	Courtesy RKO General Pictures
108	*Stand Up and Cheer*, 1934	© 1934 Twentieth Century-Fox Film Corporation
109	*George White's Scandals*, 1934	© 1934 Twentieth Century-Fox Film Corporation
110	*George White's 1935 Scandals*	© 1935 Twentieth Century-Fox Film Corporation
111	*Folies Bergère*, 1935	© 1935 Twentieth Century-Fox Film Corporation
112	*You Can't Have Everything*, 1937	© 1937 Twentieth Century-Fox Film Corporation
113 (above)	*On the Avenue*, 1937	© 1937 Twentieth Century-Fox Film Corporation
113 (below)	*One in a Million*, 1936	© 1937 Twentieth Century-Fox Film Corporation
114	*The Littlest Rebel*, 1935	© 1935 Twentieth Century-Fox Film Corporation
115	*Captain January*, 1936	© 1936 Twentieth Century-Fox Film Corporation
116 (left)	*Rose of Washington Square*, 1939	© 1939 Twentieth Century-Fox Film Corporation
116 (right)	*Alexander's Ragtime Band*, 1938	© 1938 Twentieth Century-Fox Film Corporation
116 (below)	*Lillian Russell*, 1940	© 1940 Twentieth Century-Fox Film Corporation
117	*Tin Pan Alley*, 1940	© 1940 Twentieth Century-Fox Film Corporation
118	From the MGM release: *Rosalie*, 1937	© 1937, 1964 Metro-Goldwyn-Mayer Inc.
120	From the MGM release: *Dancing Lady*, 1933	© 1933, 1960 Metro-Goldwyn-Mayer Inc.
121	From the MGM release: *Broadway Melody of 1936*, 1935	© 1935, 1962 Metro-Goldwyn-Mayer Inc.
122	From the MGM release: *Born to Dance*, 1936	© 1936, 1963 Metro-Goldwyn-Mayer Inc.
123	From the MGM release: *Broadway Melody of 1938*, 1937	© 1937, 1964 Metro-Goldwyn-Mayer Inc.
124, 125	From the MGM release: *The Great Ziegfeld*, 1936	© 1936, 1963 Metro-Goldwyn-Mayer Inc.
126–27	From the MGM release: *Rosalie*, 1937	© 1937, 1964 Metro-Goldwyn-Mayer Inc.
126 (below)	From the MGM release: *The Great Waltz*, 1938	© 1938 Loew's Inc. Renewed 1965 Metro-Goldwyn-Mayer Inc.
128–29, 131, 132	From the MGM release: *The Wizard of Oz*, 1939	© 1939 Loew's Inc. Renewed 1966 Metro-Goldwyn-Mayer Inc.
134	From the MGM release: *Maytime*, 1937	© 1937, 1964 Metro-Goldwyn-Mayer Inc.
136	From the MGM release: *The Merry Widow*, 1934	© 1934, 1961 Metro-Goldwyn-Mayer Inc.
137 (above)	From the MGM release: *Naughty Marietta*, 1935	© 1935, 1962 Metro-Goldwyn-Mayer Inc.
137 (below)	From the MGM release: *Rose Marie*, 1936	© 1936, 1963 Metro-Goldwyn-Mayer Inc.
138 (above)	From the MGM release: *Maytime*, 1937	© 1937, 1964 Metro-Goldwyn-Mayer Inc.
138 (below)	From the MGM release: *The Merry Widow*, 1934	© 1934, 1961 Metro-Goldwyn-Mayer Inc.
139	From the MGM release: *The Firefly*, 1937	© 1937, 1964 Metro-Goldwyn-Mayer Inc.
140	From the MGM release: *The Girl of the Golden West*, 1938	© 1938 Loew's Inc. Renewed 1965 Metro-Goldwyn-Mayer Inc.
141	From the MGM release: *Sweethearts*, 1938	© 1938 Loew's Inc. Renewed 1965 Metro-Goldwyn-Mayer Inc.
142 (above)	From the MGM release: *Bitter Sweet*, 1940	© 1940 Loew's Inc. Renewed 1967 Metro-Goldwyn-Mayer Inc.
142 (below)	From the MGM release: *I Married an Angel*, 1942	© 1942 Loew's Inc. Renewed 1969 Metro-Goldwyn-Mayer Inc.
143	From the MGM release: *New Moon*, 1940	© 1940 Loew's Inc. Renewed 1967 Metro-Goldwyn-Mayer Inc.
144 (above)	*Sweethearts* (poster), 1938	Film produced by Metro-Goldwyn-Mayer
144 (below)	*The King Steps Out* (poster), 1936	Film produced by Columbia Pictures
145	*Love Me Forever*, 1935	©1935. Renewed 1963 Columbia Pictures Industries, Inc. Courtesy Columbia Pictures Industries, Inc.
146 (above)	*One Night of Love*, 1934	© 1934. Renewed 1962 Columbia Pictures Industries, Inc. Courtesy Columbia Pictures Industries, Inc.
146 (below)	*One Hundred Men and a Girl*, 1937	Courtesy Universal Pictures
147	*Hitting a New High*, 1937	Courtesy RKO General Pictures
148 (above)	*High, Wide and Handsome*, 1937	Courtesy Universal Pictures
149	*Show Boat*, 1936	Courtesy Universal Pictures
152 (above)	*We're Not Dressing*, 1934	Courtesy Universal Pictures
152 (below)	*Pennies from Heaven*, 1936	© 1936. Renewed 1964 Columbia Pictures Industries, Inc. Courtesy Columbia Pictures Industries, Inc.
153 (above)	*Mississippi*, 1935	Courtesy Universal Pictures
153 (below)	*She Loves Me Not*, 1934	Courtesy Universal Pictures
154 (above left)	*Anything Goes*, 1936	Courtesy Universal Pictures
154 (above right)	*Rhythm on the Range*, 1936	Courtesy Universal Pictures
154 (below)	*The Big Broadcast of 1938*	Courtesy Universal Pictures
155	*Sing You Sinners*, 1938	© 1938 Paramount Pictures Corp. All rights reserved.
156 (above)	*College Swing*, 1938	Courtesy Universal Pictures
156 (below)	*Artists and Models*, 1937	Courtesy Universal Pictures
157	*Collegiate*, 1935	Courtesy Universal Pictures
158	From the MGM release: *Meet Me in St. Louis*, 1944	© 1944 Loew's Inc. Renewed 1971 Metro-Goldwyn-Mayer Inc.
160	From the MGM release: *Girl Crazy*, 1943	© 1943 Loew's Inc. Renewed 1971 Metro-Goldwyn-Mayer Inc.
163	From the MGM release: *Babes in Arms*, 1939	© 1939 Loew's Inc. Renewed 1966 Metro-Goldwyn-Mayer Inc.
164	From the MGM release: *Strike Up the Band*, 1940	© 1940 Loew's Inc. Renewed 1967 Metro-Goldwyn-Mayer Inc.
165	From the MGM release: *Babes on Broadway*, 1941	© 1941 Loew's Inc. Renewed 1968 Metro-Goldwyn-Mayer Inc.
166	From the MGM release: *Girl Crazy*, 1943	© 1943 Loew's Inc. Renewed 1970 Metro-Goldwyn-Mayer Inc.
167	*Girl Crazy* (poster), 1943	Film produced by Metro-Goldwyn-Mayer.
168	From the MGM release: *Lady Be Good*, 1941	© 1941 Loew's Inc. Renewed 1968 Metro-Goldwyn-Mayer Inc.
169	From the MGM release: *Broadway Melody of 1940*	© 1940 Loew's Inc. Renewed 1967 Metro-Goldwyn-Mayer Inc.
170, 171 (left)	From the MGM release: *Ziegfeld Girl*, 1941	© 1941 Loew's Inc. Renewed 1968 Metro-Goldwyn-Mayer Inc.
171 (right), 172	*Down Argentine Way*, 1940	© 1940 Twentieth Century-Fox Film Corporation
172–73 (above)	*Week-End in Havana*, 1941	© 1941 Twentieth Century-Fox Film Corporation
172–73 (below)	*That Night in Rio*, 1941	© 1941 Twentieth Century-Fox Film Corporation
173	*Down Argentine Way*, 1940	© 1940 Twentieth Century-Fox Film Corporation
174	*Springtime in the Rockies*, 1942	© 1942 Twentieth Century-Fox Film Corporation
176 (above)	*Star-Spangled Rhythm*, 1942	Courtesy Universal Pictures
176 (below)	From the MGM release: *Thousands Cheer*, 1943	© 1943 Loew's Inc. Renewed 1970 Metro-Goldwyn-Mayer Inc.
177	*Thank Your Lucky Stars*, 1943	Copyright © 1943 Warner Bros. Pictures, Inc. Renewed 1971 United Artists Television, Inc. All rights reserved.
178 (above)	*The Fleet's In*, 1942	Courtesy Universal Pictures
178 (below)	*You'll Never Get Rich*, 1941	© 1941. Renewed 1969 Columbia Pictures Industries, Inc. Courtesy Columbia Pictures Industries, Inc.
179	From the MGM release: *Anchors Aweigh*, 1945	© 1945 Loew's Inc. Renewed 1972 Metro-Goldwyn-Mayer Inc.
180	*This Is the Army*, 1943	© Warner Bros. Inc. and This Is the Army, Inc.
181	*Tonight and Every Night*, 1945	© 1945. Renewed 1972 Columbia Pictures Industries, Inc. Courtesy Columbia Pictures Industries, Inc.
182	*The Gang's All Here*, 1943	© 1943 Twentieth Century-Fox Film Corporation
183 (above)	*You Were Never Lovelier*, 1942	© 1942. Renewed 1970 Columbia Pictures Industries, Inc. Courtesy Columbia Pictures Industries, Inc.
183 (center)	From the MGM release: *Best Foot Forward*, 1943	© 1943 Loew's Inc. Renewed 1970 Metro-Goldwyn-Mayer Inc.

183 (below) Holiday Inn, 1942 Courtesy Universal Pictures

184 (above) You Were Never Lovelier, 1942 © 1942. Renewed 1970 Columbia Pictures Industries, Inc. Courtesy Columbia Pictures Industries, Inc.

184 (below) From the MGM release: Bathing Beauty, 1944 © 1944 Loew's Inc. Renewed 1971 Metro-Goldwyn-Mayer Inc.

185, 186 From the MGM release: Du Barry Was a Lady, 1943 © 1943 Loew's Inc. Renewed 1970 Metro-Goldwyn-Mayer Inc.

187 Billy Rose's Diamond Horseshoe, 1945 © 1945 Twentieth Century-Fox Film Corporation

188 Pin Up Girl, 1944 © 1944 Twentieth Century-Fox Film Corporation

189 Lady in the Dark, 1944 Courtesy Universal Pictures

190 (above) Hello, Frisco, Hello, 1943 © 1943 Twentieth Century-Fox Film Corporation

190 (center) Sweet Rosie O'Grady, 1943 © 1943 Twentieth Century-Fox Film Corporation

190 (below) Shine On Harvest Moon, 1944 Copyright © 1944 Warner Bros. Pictures, Inc. Renewed 1972 United Artists Corp. All rights reserved.

191 The Dolly Sisters, 1945 © 1945 Twentieth Century-Fox Film Corporation

192 Coney Island, 1943 © 1943 Twentieth Century-Fox Film Corporation

193 (above) Yankee Doodle Dandy, 1942 Copyright © 1943 Warner Bros. Pictures, Inc. Renewed 1970 United Artists Television, Inc. All rights reserved.

193 (below) My Gal Sal, 1942 © 1942 Twentieth Century-Fox Film Corporation

194 From the MGM release: For Me and My Gal, 1942 © 1942 Loew's Inc. Renewed 1969 Metro-Goldwyn-Mayer Inc.

195 From the MGM release: Cabin in the Sky, 1943 © 1943 Loew's Inc. Renewed 1970 Metro-Goldwyn-Mayer Inc.

196, 199 From the MGM release: Meet Me in St. Louis, 1944 © 1944 Loew's Inc. Renewed 1971 Metro-Goldwyn-Mayer Inc.

200, 202 From the MGM release: The Harvey Girls, 1946 © 1945 Loew's Inc. Renewed 1973 Metro-Goldwyn-Mayer Inc.

203 (above) From the MGM release: Easter Parade, 1948 © 1948 Loew's Inc. Renewed 1975 Metro-Goldwyn-Mayer Inc.

203 (center and below) From the MGM release: Good News, 1947 © 1947 Metro-Goldwyn-Mayer Distributing Corporation. Renewed 1974 Loew's Inc.

204 (above) From the MGM release: Summer Holiday, 1948 © 1947 Loew's Inc. Renewed 1974 Metro-Goldwyn-Mayer Inc.

204 (center) From the MGM release: In the Good Old Summertime, 1949 © 1949 Loew's Inc. Renewed 1967 Metro-Goldwyn-Mayer Inc.

204 (below) From the MGM release: Take Me Out to the Ball Game, 1949 © 1949 Loew's Inc. Renewed 1976 Metro-Goldwyn-Mayer Inc.

206 The Shocking Miss Pilgrim, 1947 © 1946 Twentieth Century-Fox Film Corporation

207 (above) Three Little Girls in Blue, 1946 © 1946 Twentieth Century-Fox Film Corporation

207 (below) Mother Wore Tights, 1947 © 1947 Twentieth Century-Fox Film Corporation

208 When My Baby Smiles at Me, 1948 © 1948 Twentieth Century-Fox Film Corporation

209 State Fair, 1945 © 1945 Twentieth Century-Fox Film Corporation

210 Rhapsody in Blue, 1945 Copyright © 1945 Warner Bros. Pictures, Inc. Renewed 1972 United Artists Television, Inc. All rights reserved.

212 Night and Day, 1946 Copyright © 1946 Warner Bros. Pictures, Inc. Renewed 1973 United Artists Television, Inc. All rights reserved.

213 (above left), (below left) From the MGM release: Till the Clouds Roll By, 1946 © 1946 Loew's Inc.

213 (above right), (below right) From the MGM release: Words and Music, 1948 © 1948 Loew's Inc. Renewed 1975 Metro-Goldwyn-Mayer Inc.

214 From the MGM release: Three Little Words, 1950 © 1950 Loew's Inc. Renewed 1977 Metro-Goldwyn-Mayer Inc.

215 The Jolson Story, 1946 © 1946. Renewed 1973 Columbia Pictures Industries, Inc. Courtesy Columbia Pictures Industries, Inc.

216, 218 Cover Girl, 1944 © 1944. Renewed 1972 Columbia Pictures Industries, Inc. Courtesy Columbia Pictures Industries, Inc.

219 Down to Earth, 1947 © 1947. Renewed 1974 Columbia Pictures Industries, Inc. Courtesy Columbia Pictures Industries, Inc.

220 (above) From the MGM release: A Date with Judy, 1948 © 1948 Loew's Inc. Renewed 1975 Metro-Goldwyn-Mayer Inc.

220 (below) From the MGM release: Neptune's Daughter, 1949 © 1949 Loew's Inc. Renewed 1976 Metro-Goldwyn-Mayer Inc.

221 From the MGM release: That Midnight Kiss, 1949 © 1949 Loew's Inc. Renewed 1976 Metro-Goldwyn-Mayer Inc.

222 From the MGM release: The Great Caruso, 1951 © 1951 Loew's Inc. Renewed 1977 Metro-Goldwyn-Mayer Inc.

223 From the MGM release: The Barkleys of Broadway, 1949 © 1949 Loew's Inc. Renewed 1976 Metro-Goldwyn-Mayer Inc.

224, 225, 226, 227 From the MGM release: Ziegfeld Follies, 1946 © 1946 Loew's Inc. Renewed 1973 Metro-Goldwyn-Mayer Inc.

228 (above) From the MGM release: The Pirate, 1948 © 1948 Loew's Inc. Renewed 1975 Metro-Goldwyn-Mayer Inc.

228 (below) From the MGM release: Yolanda and the Thief, 1945 © 1945 Loew's Inc. Renewed 1975 Metro-Goldwyn-Mayer Inc.

229 From the MGM release: The Pirate, 1948 © 1948 Loew's Inc. Renewed 1975 Metro-Goldwyn-Mayer Inc.

230, 231 From the MGM release: On the Town, 1949 © 1949 Loew's Inc. Renewed 1976 Metro-Goldwyn-Mayer Inc.

233 Where Do We Go from Here?, 1945 © 1945 Twentieth Century-Fox Film Corporation

234 From the MGM release: Singin' in the Rain, 1952 © 1952 Loew's Inc. Renewed 1979 Metro-Goldwyn-Mayer Inc.

236, 238, 239, 241 From the MGM release: An American in Paris, 1951 © 1951 Loew's Inc. Renewed 1979 Metro-Goldwyn-Mayer Inc.

242 From the MGM release: Lili, 1953 © 1952 Loew's Inc. Renewed 1980 Metro-Goldwyn-Mayer Inc.

243, 244 From the MGM release: Singin' in the Rain, 1952 © 1952 Loew's Inc. Renewed 1979 Metro-Goldwyn-Mayer Inc.

246 From the MGM release: Seven Brides for Seven Brothers, 1954 © 1954 Loew's Inc.

247, 248 From the MGM release: The Band Wagon, 1953 © 1953 Loew's Inc. Renewed 1981 Metro-Goldwyn-Mayer Inc.

249, 250, 251 Funny Face, 1957 © 1956 Paramount Pictures Corp. All rights reserved.

252 (above) From the MGM release: It's Always Fair Weather, 1955 © 1955 Loew's Inc.

252 (below) From the MGM release: Invitation to the Dance, 1956 © 1956 Loew's Inc.

254 From the MGM release: Les Girls, 1957 © 1957 Loew's Inc. and Sol C. Siegel Productions, Inc.

A poster for Something for the Boys (Fox, 1944).

255, 256 From the MGM release: Gigi, 1958 © 1958 Loew's Inc. and Arthur Freed Productions, Inc.

258 From the MGM release: Summer Stock, 1950 © 1950 Loew's Inc. Renewed 1977 Metro-Goldwyn-Mayer Inc.

260 From the MGM release: The Belle of New York, 1952 © 1952 Loew's Inc. Renewed 1979 Metro-Goldwyn-Mayer Inc.

261 (above) From the MGM release: Royal Wedding, 1951 © 1951 Loew's Inc.

261 (below) From the MGM release: Two Weeks with Love, 1950 © 1950 Loew's Inc. Renewed 1977 Metro-Goldwyn-Mayer Inc.

262 From the MGM release: Small Town Girl, 1953 © 1953 Loew's Inc. Renewed 1981 Metro-Goldwyn-Mayer Inc.

263 From the MGM release: Texas Carnival, 1951 © 1951 Loew's Inc. Renewed 1979 Metro-Goldwyn-Mayer Inc.

264 White Christmas, 1954 © 1954 Paramount Pictures Corp. All rights reserved.

265 (above) There's No Business like Show Business, 1954 © 1954 Twentieth Century-Fox Film Corporation

265 (below) From the MGM release: The Glass Slipper, 1955 © 1955 Loew's Inc.

266 (above left) On Moonlight Bay, 1951 © Warner Bros. Inc.

266 (above right), (below) By the Light of the Silvery Moon, 1953 © Warner Bros. Inc.

267 Calamity Jane, 1953 © Warner Bros. Inc.

268 Red Garters, 1954 © Paramount Pictures Corp. All rights reserved.

268–69 From the MGM release: Jailhouse Rock, 1957 © 1957 Loew's Inc. and Avon Productions, Inc.

270 The King and I, 1956 © 1956 Twentieth Century-Fox Film Corporation

272, 273 (above) From the MGM release: Annie Get Your Gun, 1950 © 1950 Loew's Inc. Renewed 1977 Metro-Goldwyn-Mayer Inc.

273 (below) From the MGM release: Show Boat, 1951 © 1951 Loew's Inc. Renewed 1979 Metro-Goldwyn-Mayer Inc.

275 From the MGM release: Kiss Me, Kate, 1953 © 1953 Loew's Inc. Renewed 1981 Metro-Goldwyn-Mayer Inc.

277 (above) From the MGM release: Kismet, 1955 © 1955 Loew's Inc.

277 (below) From the MGM release: Brigadoon, 1954 © 1954 Loew's Inc.

278, 279 From the MGM release: Silk Stockings, 1957 © 1957 Loew's Inc. and Arthur Freed Productions, Inc.

280 Gentlemen Prefer Blondes, 1953 © 1953 Twentieth Century-Fox Film Corporation

281 (above) Carousel, 1956 © 1956 Twentieth Century-Fox Film Corporation

281 (below) Where's Charley?, 1952 © Warner Bros. Inc.

282–83 The King and I, 1956 © 1956 Twentieth Century-Fox Film Corporation

284, 285 South Pacific, 1958 © 1959 South Pacific Enterprises, Inc. and Twentieth Century-Fox Film Corporation

286 Oklahoma!, 1955 © Rodgers and Hammerstein. By permission.

287, 288 The Pajama Game, 1957 © Warner Bros. Inc.

289 Pal Joey, 1957 © 1958 Columbia Pictures Industries, Inc. Courtesy Columbia Pictures, Inc.

290 Damn Yankees, 1958 © Warner Bros. Inc.

292, 294, 295 A Star Is Born, 1954 © Warner Bros. Inc.

296 (above) The Jazz Singer, 1953 © Warner Bros. Inc.

296 (below) Young at Heart, 1954 © Warner Bros. Inc.

297 (above) Wabash Avenue, 1950 © 1950 Twentieth Century-Fox Film Corporation

297 (below), 298 Daddy Long Legs, 1955 © 1955 Twentieth Century-Fox Film Corporation

299 (above) On the Riviera, 1951 © 1957 Twentieth Century-Fox Film Corporation

299 (below) My Sister Eileen, 1955 © 1955 Columbia Pictures Industries, Inc. Courtesy Columbia Pictures Industries, Inc.

300 (above) From the MGM release: High Society, 1956 © 1956 Loew's Inc., Sol C. Siegel Productions, Inc. and Bing Crosby Productions

300 (below) From the MGM release: The Opposite Sex, 1956 © 1956 Loew's Inc.

302 From the MGM release: The Merry Widow, 1952 © 1952 Loew's Inc.

303 (above) From the MGM release: The Student Prince, 1954 © 1954 Loew's Inc.

303 (below) From the MGM release: Rose Marie, 1954 © 1954 Loew's Inc.

304 From the MGM release: Love Me or Leave Me, 1955 © 1955 Loew's Inc.

306 From the MGM release: Deep in My Heart, 1954 © 1954 Loew's Inc.

307 With a Song in My Heart, 1952 © 1952 Twentieth Century-Fox Film Corporation

308 From the MGM release: I'll Cry Tomorrow, 1955 © 1956 Loew's Inc.

309 From the MGM release: Love Me or Leave Me, 1955 © 1955 Loew's Inc.

310 From the MGM release: Interrupted Melody, 1955 © 1955 Loew's Inc.

311 The Seven Little Foys, 1955 © 1954 Hope Enterprises, Inc.

312 The Eddie Cantor Story, 1953 © Warner Bros. Inc.

313 (above) The Eddy Duchin Story, 1956 © 1956 Columbia Pictures Industries, Inc. Courtesy Columbia Pictures Industries, Inc.

313 (below) The Glenn Miller Story, 1954 Courtesy Universal Pictures

314 My Fair Lady, 1964 Courtesy CBS Theatrical Films

316 The Music Man, 1962 © Warner Bros. Inc.

317 From the MGM release: The Unsinkable Molly Brown, 1964 © 1964 Metro-Goldwyn-Mayer Inc. and Marten Productions, Inc.

319, 320 Gypsy, 1962 © Warner Bros. Inc.

321, 322 From the MGM release: Billy Rose's Jumbo, 1962 © 1962 Metro-Goldwyn-Mayer Inc. and Euterpe, Inc.

323, 324, 325 Funny Girl, 1968 © 1968 Columbia Pictures Industries, Inc. Courtesy Columbia Pictures Industries, Inc.

326–27 Hello, Dolly!, 1969 © 1969 Chenault Productions, Inc. and Twentieth Century-Fox Film Corporation

328 Thoroughly Modern Millie, 1967 Courtesy Universal Pictures

329 Bye Bye Birdie, 1963 © 1963 Columbia Pictures Industries, Inc. Courtesy Columbia Pictures Industries, Inc.

330 (above)	*Sweet Charity*, 1969	Courtesy Universal Pictures
330 (below)	From the MGM release: *Bells Are Ringing*, 1960	© 1960 Metro-Goldwyn-Mayer Inc. and Arthur Freed Productions, Inc.
331	*Flower Drum Song*, 1961	© Courtesy Universal Pictures
332	*How to Succeed in Business Without Really Trying*, 1967	Copyright © 1967 Mirisch Corporation of Delaware. All rights reserved. Released through United Artists Corp.
333	*Finian's Rainbow*, 1968	© Warner Bros. Inc.
334, 335	*West Side Story*, 1961	Copyright © 1961 Beta Productions. All rights reserved. Released through United Artists Corp.
336, 337, 338	*My Fair Lady*, 1964	Courtesy CBS Theatrical Films
339, 340	*Camelot*, 1967	© Warner Bros. Inc.
341	*Oliver!*, 1968	© 1968 Columbia Pictures Industries, Inc. Courtesy Columbia Pictures Industries, Inc.
342, 343	*Mary Poppins*, 1964	© 1964 Walt Disney Productions
344 (above)	*Can-Can*, 1960	© 1960 Suffolk-Cummings Productions, Inc. and Twentieth Century-Fox Film Corporation
344 (below)	*Star!*, 1968	© 1968 Robert Wise Productions and Twentieth Century-Fox Film Corporation
345	*The Sound of Music*, 1965	© 1965 Argyle Enterprises and Twentieth Century-Fox Film Corporation
346 (above)	From the MGM release: *Goodbye, Mr. Chips*, 1969	© 1969 Metro-Goldwyn-Mayer Inc.
346 (below)	*Doctor Dolittle*, 1967	© 1967 Apjac Productions, Inc. and Twentieth Century-Fox Film Corporation
347	*On a Clear Day You Can See Forever*, 1970	© 1969 Paramount Pictures Corp. All rights reserved.
348	*Mame*, 1974	© Warner Bros. Inc.
350	*Fiddler on the Roof*, 1971	Copyright © 1971 Mirisch Productions, Inc. & Cartier Productions, Inc. All rights reserved. Released through United Artists Corp.
352, 353, 354 (above, left and right)	*Cabaret*, 1972	Courtesy Lorimar and ABC
354 (below)	*Grease*, 1978	© MCMLXXVII by Paramount Pictures Corp. All rights reserved.
355	*A Little Night Music*, 1977	Courtesy Sascha-Film Gesellschaft M.B.H. and New World Pictures Inc.
356 (above)	*Hair*, 1979	Copyright © 1979 CIP Film Productions GMBH. All rights reserved. Released through United Artists Corp.
356 (below)	*Jesus Christ, Superstar*, 1973	Courtesy Universal Pictures
357 (above)	*Tom Sawyer*, 1973	Copyright © 1973 United Artists Corp. All rights reserved.
357 (below)	*Lost Horizon*, 1973	© 1973 Columbia Pictures Industries, Inc. Courtesy Columbia Pictures Industries, Inc.
358–59	*Funny Lady*, 1975	© 1975 Columbia Pictures Industries, Inc. Courtesy Columbia Pictures Industries, Inc.
360 (above)	*A Star Is Born*, 1975	© Warner Bros. Inc.
360 (center)	*At Long Last Love*, 1975	© 1975 Twentieth Century-Fox Film Corporation
360 (below)	*Bugsy Malone*, 1976	© 1976 National Film Trustee Co., Ltd. All rights reserved.
361	*New York, New York*, 1977	Copyright © 1977 United Artists Corp. All rights reserved.
362	*The Buddy Holly Story*, 1978	© 1978 Columbia Pictures Industries, Inc. Courtesy Columbia Pictures Industries, Inc.
363	*All That Jazz*, 1979	© 1980 Columbia Pictures Industries and Twentieth Century-Fox Film Corporation
364	*The Rose*, 1979	© 1979 Twentieth Century-Fox Film Corporation
365	*Can't Stop the Music*, 1980	© An Allan Carr Film for EMI Inc.
366 (above)	*The Jazz Singer*, 1980	© EMI Films, Inc.
366 (below)	From the MGM release: *Pennies from Heaven*, 1981	© 1981 Metro-Goldwyn-Mayer Inc.
368	The honeymoon suite in *Top Hat*, 1935	For a film produced by RKO General Pictures
375	*Coney Island*, 1943	© 1943 Twentieth Century-Fox Film Corporation
378	*Something for the Boys* (poster)	For a film produced by Twentieth Century-Fox Film Corporation
381	*Bedknobs and Broomsticks*, 1971	© 1971 Walt Disney Productions
382	*Funny Face*, 1957	© 1956 Paramount Pictures Corp. All rights reserved.
383	From the MGM release: *Pennies from Heaven*, 1981	© 1981 Metro-Goldwyn-Mayer Inc.

SONG & PHOTO CREDITS

SONG CREDITS:

The following song excerpts are used by permission. All rights are reserved and international copyrights secured.

"Anatevka" by Sheldon Harnick and Jerry Bock, © 1964 The Times Square Music Publications Company

"Cabaret" by John Kander and Fred Ebb, © 1966 The Times Square Music Publications Company

"Get Happy" by Harold Arlen and Ted Koehler © 1929 Warner Bros. Inc., Copyright renewed

"Money, Money" by John Kander and Fred Ebb, © 1972 The Times Square Music Publications Company

"Shanghai Lil" by Harry Warren and Al Dubin, © 1933 Warner Bros. Inc., Copyright renewed

"Singin' in the Rain" by Nacio Herb Brown and Arthur Freed, Copyright © 1929, renewed 1957 Metro-Goldwyn-Mayer, Inc. All rights administered and controlled by Robbins Music Corporation

"Song of Paree" by Lorenz Hart and Richard Rodgers (from *Love Me Tonight*), Copyright © 1932 by Famous Music Corporation, Copyright renewed 1959 by Famous Music Corporation

"That's Entertainment" by Howard Dietz and Arthur Schwartz, Copyright © 1953 by Chappell & Co., Inc.

Lyric excerpts from **"Top Hat, White Tie and Tails"** by Irving Berlin (on page 94), © Copyright 1935 Irving Berlin, © Copyright renewed 1962 Irving Berlin. Reprinted by permission of Irving Berlin Music Corp.

"We're Out of the Red" by Lew Brown and Jay Gorney, Copyright © 1934 and 1962 by Movietone Music Corporation, New York; Sam Fox Publishing Company, Inc., Palm Desert, California, Sole Agent

"What a Little Thing like a Wedding Ring Can Do" by Leo Robin and Richard A. Whiting (from *One Hour with You*), Copyright © 1931 and 1932 by Famous Music Corporation, Copyright renewed 1958 and 1959 by Famous Music Corporation

"Who's Complaining" by Ira Gershwin and Jerome Kern, Copyright © 1943 T. B. Harms Company, Copyright renewed. c/o The Welk Music Group, Santa Monica, Calif. 90401

PHOTOGRAPHIC CREDITS:

Ed Clark, *Life* Magazine, © Time, Inc., 1951: 241 (below);

Ralph Crane, *Life* Magazine, © Time, Inc.: 272;

Alfred Eisenstaedt, *Life* Magazine, © Time, Inc.: 231;

Bob Landry, *Life* Magazine, © Time, Inc.: 244 (above).

Special color material researched by Bill O'Connell.

INDEX

Page numbers in boldface indicate references to illustrations.

Director Vincente Minnelli poses with a group of posters of his MGM films.

Bedknobs and Broomsticks *(Disney, 1971). Angela Lansbury as the eccentric English lady named Eglantine Price.*

© *Walt Disney Productions*

Funny Face (Paramount, 1957). In one of the loveliest musical numbers in films, Fred Astaire and Audrey Hepburn dance to "He Loves and She Loves" in the countryside near Paris.

Steve Martin and Bernadette Peters, impersonating Fred and Ginger in Pennies from Heaven *(MGM, 1981).*

384

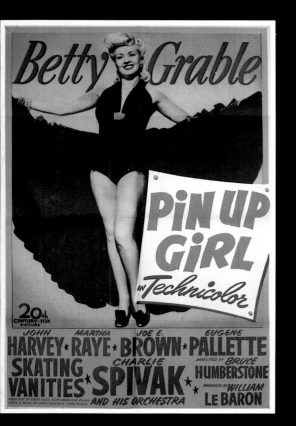